Dangerous Wildlife
IN THE Mid-Atlantic

a guide to safe encounters
at home and in the wild

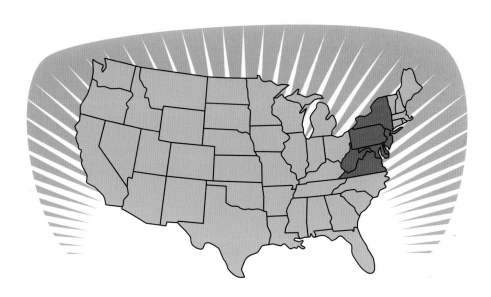

Praise for *Dangerous Wildlife:*
A Guide to Safe Encounters at Home and in the Wild

"I particularly valued the insightful analysis of the real dangers in the marine environment, as opposed to the dangers many people suppose exist. Real understanding promotes a richer world for humans and a safer world for wildlife."

> • Hardy Jones, wildlife film producer,
> co-founder of BlueVoice.org

" ... this compendious guide does much to dispel the feelings of powerlessness and panic often provoked by sensationalized media coverage, of, say, the recent spate of shark attacks along the eastern seaboard."

> • *Publishers Weekly*

Dangerous Wildlife in the Mid-Atlantic

*a guide to
safe encounters
at home and in the wild*

F. LYNNE BACHLEDA

Printed in South Korea
Published by Menasha Ridge Press
Distributed by The Globe Pequot Press
First edition, first printing

Library of Congress Cataloging-in-Publication Data

Bachleda, F. Lynne, 1951–
  Dangerous wildlife in the mid-Atlantic : how to have safe encounters at home and in the wild / by F. Lynne Bachleda.
    p. cm.
  ISBN 0-89732-406-4 (alk. paper)
    I. Dangerous animals--Middle Atlantic States. I. Title.

  QL100 .B32 2001
  591.6'5'0975--dc21

2001054360

Cover photography: Ann and Rob Simpson (Northern Copperhead),
    Ben Cropp Productions/Innterspace Visions (Sand Tiger Shark),
    Rob Curtis/The Early Birder (Virescent Green Metallic Bee)
Text design by Grant M. Tatum
Cover design by Ann Marie Healy

Menasha Ridge Press
P.O. Box 43673
Birmingham, AL 35243
www.menasharidge.com

TABLE OF CONTENTS

ACKNOWLEDGMENTS

THE TEAM AND APPROACH

We conducted extensive research for this volume, and you'll find our most useful sources listed in the back. We aimed for a friendly yet informative style, made every effort at accuracy and detail, and tried to give you a little laugh now and then, too. Determined to provide you with the highest quality information, we turned to our panel of experts. Scientists, physicians, naturalists, and other experts were generous enough to review the text for accuracy and completeness. Our profound gratitude goes to them for their refinement of this work:

Dr. Sean P. Bush, MD, FACEP, is an Associate Professor of Emergency Medicine at the Loma Linda University School of Medicine, where he is also on staff in the ER as an emergency physician and envenomation consultant. He has had a lifelong interest in reptiles and venomous creatures. He has authored over 30 publications on the treatment of bites and stings and has lectured on the local, national, and international level. He is featured in several television documentary productions, including those for National Geographic Explorer and the Discovery Channel. He currently lives in southern California with his wife A'me and a few dozen snakes, lizards, and arachnids.

Richard Carter, Professor of Biology at Valdosta State University, received B.S. and M.S. degrees from the Mississippi State University and a Ph.D from Vanderbilt University. Dr. Carter is a botanist and herbarium curator, and his professional interests include systematic and floristic studies of sedges; the flora of the coastal plain of Georgia; and the identification, distribution, and biology of weeds.

Jonathan Day is a Professor of Medical Entomology at the University of Florida, Institute of Food and Agricultural Sciences, Department of Entomology. He is stationed at the Florida Medical Entomology Laboratory in Vero Beach, where his research focus is the ecology, natural history, and epidemiology of mosquito-borne viruses and their impact on humans, domestic animals, and wildlife.

Tim Krasnansky is a small-animal veterinarian and former medical and technical illustrator living in northern California. He has backpacked, cross-country skied, mountaineered, canoed, mountain-biked, and hunted with his Labrador and Chesapeake Bay retrievers in scattered places throughout the United States, Canada, and Baja. He's only ever been bitten by one dog, his first Chesapeake, Bear, who got him on the butt.

Sharon Mohney is a forester on the George Washington and Jefferson National Forests in Virginia, with 23 years experience in various aspects of forest management, including 11 years managing wildlife programs on ranger districts. She has also overseen programs for timber management, wildfires and prescribed burning, and wilderness recreation.

George Sedberry earned his Ph.D. in Marine Science from the Virginia Institute of Marine Science, College of William and Mary. He is Senior Marine Scientist at the Marine Resources Research Institute of the South Carolina Department of Natural Resources (Charleston), where he has worked since 1980. He conducts research on the biology, conservation, and management of reef fishes and highly migratory oceanic fishes, and on other aspects of marine ecology and oceanography. He is an adjunct professor at the College of Charleston, where he advises graduate students and teaches marine fisheries science.

Many thanks to **BlueVoice.org,** a streaming media website dedicated to raising public awareness about the problems facing the marine environment, especially dolphins and whales.

Many people, then, have collaborated to make the information in this book as reliable as possible, but this volume is no substitute for professional medical advice. Bear in mind, too, that this book looks at diverse forms of life, and life is always unpredictable.

We would also like to profusely thank the many photographers and institutions that helped us to illustrate the various species. They are all individually acknowledged by picture in the Photography and Illustration Credits at the end of this book.

Lastly, the author would like to express her deepest gratitude to managing editor Chris Mohney, for his thorough professionalism, outstanding humor, and sustaining light, and also to publisher Bob Sehlinger, for his bright ideas and abiding friendship.

HOT TIP: HELP IS JUST A PHONE CALL AWAY

Farmers and most gardeners know about the local agricultural agent, and you should, too, even if you never get your hands dirty. Look in the telephone book under your county for a listing something like "agricultural extension service." The person you reach can provide a world of information about the species in your area; the regulatory agencies that can assist you with other important information (for instance, is it legal for you to get rid of wild bees in your house?); your best options (what pesticides to use if you must resort to them); and a host of other free information that can help you get along better in the natural world.

DEDICATION

We will only protect what we love,
and we will only love what we understand.

For the creatures, all of us.

INTRODUCTION

As the title states, this book is about dangerous animals. However, in a significant way, it's also about you. All of us, at one time or another, have been inhibited by fear of the natural world. For example, have you ever foregone a beautiful hike because you're afraid of bears? Do you worry that your playing children might encounter wasps or snakes in the backyard or in the neighborhood woods? Have you ever put off cleaning the attic because you know spiders live there?

Ads for the 1950s horror-science fiction classic *The Fly* warned, "Be afraid! Be very afraid!" Consciously or unconsciously, fear is perhaps one of the reasons you purchased this book: you worry (at least a little bit) about what's out there that might hurt you. Fear derives primarily from a lack of information. Remember being terrified on your first day of school or at the prospect of learning to swim? Most of us were, but once we became informed and understood how things worked, we relaxed and never looked back. Likewise in nature, we humans are often frightened or disturbed by creatures we know little about. Because learning dispels anxiety and fear, our objective in this book is to educate you—to help build a foundation of knowledge that will enable you to enjoy and appreciate the natural world. Grounded in fact and understanding, you'll shed your fear of other creatures, whether you meet them in your basement, your garden, or in the wilderness. You'll learn that, in many ways, encountering wildlife is much like traveling in a foreign country. By increasing perception and appreciation, not only does knowledge make life more interesting, it also makes life safer.

If you picked up this book thinking to add another field guide to your library reference shelf, you won't be disappointed. *Dangerous Wildlife in the Mid-Atlantic* contains a wealth of solid field information, but that's only the tip of the iceberg. It's also loaded with natural history, humor, documented cases of human encounters with wildlife, amazing statistics, and little-known facts that will amaze you (like how a rattlesnake's head can bite even when severed from its body). We've left no stone unturned in providing detailed creature profiles, up-to-date medical information, and just plain practical advice. And though you can use this book like a reference work, we have worked hard to provide you with a fun and compelling cover-to-cover read.

While we won't hammer you relentlessly with science in this text, we do hope to convey a glimpse of the admirable adaptive power we found in the species profiled here. Researching this book proved to be pure pleasure in discovering the variety, vitality, creativity, and downright cunning that animals, ourselves included, have developed in response to millions of years of stimulus and change. Take our word for it: researching *Dangerous Wildlife* has been a love affair with the exquisite plenitude of nature. Also believe us when we tell you that nature is not driven by malice, but by instincts common to us all—an indomitable urge to survive and to carry on with the business of life. In these pages, we will strive to convince you that, armed with the facts in this book, you have very, very little to fear in nature. Unless, of course, you include the human animal, in which case all bets are off. We humans are by far (and always have been) the greatest threat to members of our own species, but that's another book.

As the author, this work became increasingly relevant as I realized that I have personally experienced a stunning litany of the possible dangers included here—several from each chapter, actually—and lived to tell the tales. For example, I discovered a three-foot timber rattlesnake in my yard just before undertaking this book, and I was stung by a wasp inside my publisher's home after talking with him about the aims of our collaboration. So "impressed" was he with my personal encounters, he laughingly implored me not to go to Yellowstone National Park (where grizzlies live) until after I had finished the manuscript.

Although this is not a slender volume, there are comparatively few species that actually possess the potential to harm us. For example, there are approximately 90,000 to 100,000 insects in North America, and we've alerted you to about 50, substantially less than 1%. There are more than 500 reptiles and amphibians; we think you need to know about approximately 20, or 4%. Of course, this book does profile potentially lethal species. But we've also covered the ones that just make us itch, twitch, and swat, like mosquitoes and chiggers; and we also cover creatures such as stinkpot turtles, where it's nice to be aware of their powerful, skunk-like aroma before your child hauls one out of the creek. We talk, of course, about the uncommonly encountered "usual suspects," like bears, rattlesnakes, and sharks, but we don't overlook ubiquitous species like dogs and cats—animals that are much, much more statistically likely to harm you or your children than bears, snakes, or spiders are, no matter where you live.

We have a second agenda and very important task with this volume. Call it mutual respect. Call it coexistence. We hope that after reading this book, you'll appreciate the fact that every snake is not a venomous snake, and for that matter, every venomous snake does not automatically deserve to die. Imminent real danger is one thing; a creature merely going about its business is another. As a wise swamp expert observed while watching a cottonmouth, "If a snake can't live out here, where can he live?" We hope this book will make life safer for you, as well as give you confidence and peace of mind. But we're out to keep the critters alive, too, because in the big picture we need them much more than we need to fear them. With this book, then, we invite you to learn, to live, and to let live.

REPTILES & AMPHIBIANS

DON'T TREAD ON ME

It doesn't take long for a discussion about dangerous critters to get around to snakes. There are other dangerous reptiles and amphibians in the U. S., of course, such as the Gila monster, a venomous lizard in the southwest. Others who are less deadly include a couple of toads that cause skin eruptions or allergic reactions, especially if you have open cuts or sores on your hands; snapping turtles, the largest of which can take off a finger; and a handful of biting (but nonvenomous) salamanders. (Skinks are biters, too, and if your cat eats one it may lose its sense of balance, or even become paralyzed.) By and large, however, when it comes to reptiles and amphibians, the creatures that wreak the most havoc on humans in the mid-Atlantic are venomous snakes. Although the statistical probability of being killed by a snake is less than that of being struck by lightning, it's prudent to understand these formidable predators if they reside where you live or enjoy recreation.

SNAKES

The sight of a snake strikes an emotional chord in most people quite out of proportion with the reptile's potential for causing harm. Unfortunately, ignorance is legion when it comes to snakes, and it's compounded by myth and misinformation. Most snake stories begin with a snake and end with a big rock or a shotgun. And of course, the snake in every story was venomous and launching a direct frontal assault.

Most snakes are harmless, and many snakes, including North America's relatively few venomous species, feed on insects, rats, mice, and other vermin. In the woods and in the neighborhood, snakes are good neighbors, on patrol around the clock helping Orkin keep pests under control. Plus, when's the last time you were kept awake at night by a barking snake?

If you are an avid outdoors person, you might see a snake in the wild twice a year. If you are only an occasional visitor to the great outdoors, you might go an entire lifetime without encountering a snake. No matter where you live, the harmless, nonvenomous species outnumber venomous species by a great margin, so the probability of stumbling onto a venomous snake is very remote. The vast majority of the time, if you do chance upon a venomous snake, you will not be attacked or bitten unless you do something really, really stupid. Finally, even if you are bitten, there's about a 30–50% probability (depending on the species) that the snake will not inject venom. So, you see, there's really no reason to be neurotic about snakes. For confidence and peace of mind, however, it's helpful to know a thing or two about our down-to-earth friends.

HOW PEOPLE ARE BITTEN BY SNAKES

It may amaze you to know that most snakebites, both venomous and nonvenomous, occur as a direct result of trying to handle snakes. Because the method of avoiding being bitten is so obvious in this instance, we won't dwell on it.

Many harmless and most venomous snakes hunt at night. This means they hole up during the day in brush, stacked firewood, lumber piles, and the like, as well as in rock crevices, under rocks, and around streambeds. Bites to the hands, arms, feet, and legs occur when working outdoors clearing brush; moving debris, lumber, or firewood; or putting your hands into rock crevices or under rocks. Hiking off-trail, especially in cane or tall grass, likewise increases the chances of stepping on or near a snake that you don't see.

Other frequently occurring situations leading to snakebite involve trying to kill, remove, or chase away a snake. If you find a snake in your yard, tapping it gently with a long pole or broom handle (while maintaining a safe distance) should suffice to move it along. Even if you positively identify the snake as venomous, you're less at risk by allowing it to move off on its own (or with a little persuasion from your broom) than you are trying to kill it. First, it wouldn't be around in the first place if there wasn't something to eat, and second, assuming the snake occurs naturally in your neck of the woods, there will be more to take the place of the one you kill.

Doctors treat dozens of folks every year who injure themselves trying to kill snakes. Ricocheting pellets, BBs, and buckshot cause more eye injuries than you would believe, and people have also been known to club themselves (and others) with shovels and hack themselves (and others) with axes while flailing away at a snake. Sometimes less-than-cautious individuals capture a snake only to be bitten through the burlap bag or pillowcase they've tossed it in, and, incredibly, a number of people are even bitten by dead snakes (more on this later). It's a dangerous world out there. Make it a little saner by respecting snakes and giving them space.

NONVENOMOUS SNAKES

Nonvenomous snakes are found virtually everywhere, from your backyard to the mountains to the swamp. Examples of nonvenomous biters in the mid-Atlantic include the black racer *(Coluber constrictor),* the corn snake *(Elaphe guttata),* and the northern water snake *(Nerodia sipedon sipedon).* If you are somehow bitten by one, you'll experience very little pain—but figuratively speaking, you'll spend enough adrenaline to set a world record in the high jump. When you calm down, you'll discover a horseshoe pattern of small needle-like pricks where you were chomped. Like any wild animal bite, infection is a possibility (you don't know who that snake's been kissing), so wash the wound well with soap and water and then apply a disinfectant.

If you watch A&E or the Discovery Channel on television, you've probably seen a show or two about big constricting snakes like boas, pythons, and anacondas that dine on just about anything from antelopes to puppies. Well, the good news is that (except as pets) those snakes don't live in the United States. True, we've got a couple of species that are called "boas," but they're not large enough to intimidate a healthy chicken. The largest nonvenomous snake in the United States is the indigo snake, a rare and gentle rat-eating snake found only in Florida, Georgia, Alabama, and Texas.

VENOMOUS OR NONVENOMOUS?

Before we discuss the specific venomous species in your area, let's take a general look at venomous snakes in the U. S. First, there are only four kinds of venomous snakes that you have to worry about: the coral snake, the copperhead, the cottonmouth (also called the water moccasin), and the rattlesnake. Second, the coral snake (not found in the mid-Atlantic area) and the rattlesnake are easily recognizable when mature, though the coral snake is often confused with the nonvenomous scarlet king snake, and the rattlesnake's trademark rattle might sometimes be hidden by leaves, tucked under its body, or broken off. There's also a wide variety of rattlesnake species, some of which do not have "rattlesnake" in their names (sidewinder, massasauga, etc.), and some of these have very inconspicuous rattles even as adults. Copperheads, lacking the telltale rattle of a rattlesnake or the exotic coloration of the coral snake, are more difficult to identify. The most difficult venomous species to ID is the cottonmouth or water moccasin. The cottonmouth, though distinctive enough to the trained eye, bears a certain resemblance to several of the more frequently seen harmless water snakes. Both water snakes and cottonmouths have relatively thick bodies (the cottonmouth being the most stout) with somber coloration and scale patterns. Colors vary somewhat within each species and also appear lighter or darker depending on whether the snake is dry or wet.

The coral snake is a member of the cobra family *(Elapidae)*, while the other venomous snakes found in the U.S. are pit vipers *(Crotalidae)*. Pit vipers, including rattlesnakes, copperheads, and cottonmouths, are so called because of an orifice or "pit" between the eyes and nostrils. Rich with nerve endings and covered by a membrane, the pit helps the snake sense the presence and whereabouts of warm-blooded prey or predators. The pit has been compared to a highly directional dish microphone that can pick up a quarterback's calls from the sidelines. It functions extremely well as a type of radar that enables the snake to "see" its prey or an aggressor solely by heat—not by light, sound, or touch. Elliptical pupils, a swollen-looking head, and undivided sub-caudal (underneath the tail) scales are

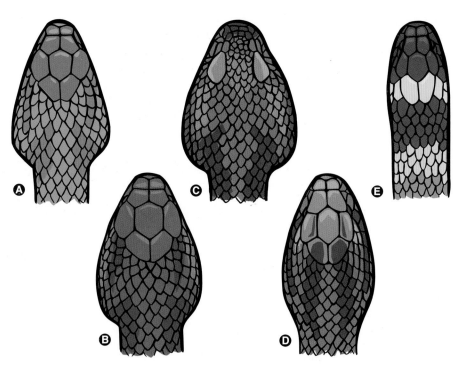

Differing head shapes of venomous snakes: copperhead **(A)**, *cottonmouth* **(B)**, *crotalid rattlesnake* **(C)**, *pygmy rattlesnake* **(D)**, *and coral snake* **(E)**.

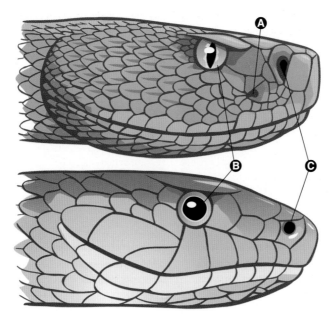

Comparison of pit vipers (top) versus snakes of the cobra family (bottom). Pit vipers have a heat-sensing orifice or "pit" **(A)** *between the eye* **(B)** *and nostril* **(C).**

likewise identifying features of pit vipers.

It is important to note, however, according to the exceptional venomous snake expert Laurence M. Klauber, that some nonvenomous species also have some of these attributes, so it is unsafe to rely solely on these criteria. He maintains that the "only unfailing method is an examination of the snake for hollow or grooved fangs and venom glands, and this will not disclose the degree of danger from its bite." (Klauber, 1997, p. 23) Perhaps you'll agree this is not a job for anyone other than a professional herpetologist. In light of this, your job is to learn as much as you can about the truly dangerous snakes, and, chiefly, to give snakes their due—meaning a wide berth. Blind fear about all snakes, or even about venomous snakes, is not a good line of defense. Knowledge is.

A HARMLESS SNAKE'S DEFENSE

When threatened, many harmless snakes will put on an aggressive display. They may at times overcompensate in these theatrics, for unlike the venomous rattler, for example, they have no real lethal weapon to use. In

A harmless eastern hognose snake (Heterodon platirhinos), often mistaken for a venomous copperhead or rattlesnake.

*The scarlet kingsnake (*Lampropeltis triangulum)*, a harmless snake which resembles the venomous coral snake.*

*This nonvenomous northern banded water snake (*Nerodia sipedon sipedon) *resembles a cottonmouth.*

the mid-Atlantic, the corn snake will sometimes curl up like a rattlesnake. In the southeast, examples of these types of harmless snakes include the pine, corn, hognose, and water snake. In the western U.S., the bull snake and the Sonoran gopher snake will sometimes posture dramatically. Bluffing behavior can include coiling, vibrating the tail (which in leaves can send your heart racing and should stop you in your tracks for assessment), hissing, and lunging. Klauber says it well with his characteristic dry humor: "But it is all bluff; and the difference between being struck by a gopher snake and a rattler is the difference between being hit by two falling objects—a feather in one case, a safe in the other." (Klauber, 1997, p. 22)

"MR. FANGMAN"

All venomous snakes have fangs, whereas nonvenomous snakes do not. Nonvenomous snakes do have, however, lots of small sharp teeth that are quite capable of breaking the skin. A bite from a nonvenomous

snake will look like a series of pinpricks arrayed in a horseshoe pattern. A bite from a venomous snake will leave puncture marks from the fangs. Usually there will be two fang marks, but even venomous snakes miss from time to time, so it's possible to be hit by only one of the fangs. Nonvenomous snakes in the U.S. have a habit of biting and holding on. People who keep nonvenomous species as pets sometimes have to pry the snake's jaws open following a bite in order to remove the snake.

All pit vipers (rattlers, copperheads, cottonmouths) in the U.S. usually strike and release. Sometimes some entanglement such as clothing will make release more difficult, but this is not the behavioral norm. The coral snake, however, tends to hold on after striking, in an effort to secrete more venom into the bite.

The coral snake has relatively short, hollow, fixed fangs in contrast to long hypodermic fangs in the pit vipers. Pit viper fangs rotate forward when striking and fold back against the roof of the mouth when not in use. Coral snakes are small, rarely reaching 2.5 feet in length. Although their venom is potentially lethal, their small mouths make biting humans problematic except for bites to unprotected hands or bare feet.

There is discussion among herpetologists on whether rattlers stab their victims with their fangs or bite them. In the stab, the force of puncture is driven by the forward unfolding of the fangs from the roof of the mouth. In the bite, the force of the action derives from the closing of the jaws. The catch, so to speak, is that venomous snakes also have biting teeth, so sometimes in the confusion of the moment, when snake ID would be extremely useful but is not always rationally considered, it's useful to ascertain fangs versus teeth. If you've got one or two fang marks, it's definitely time to hop in the car (getting someone else to drive if possible) and make an advance call to the hospital to say that you're on your way.

When not in use, a pit viper's fangs lie folded back against the roof of the snake's mouth. Each rests in a sheath of soft, membranous skin. The maxillary bones rotate the fangs forward

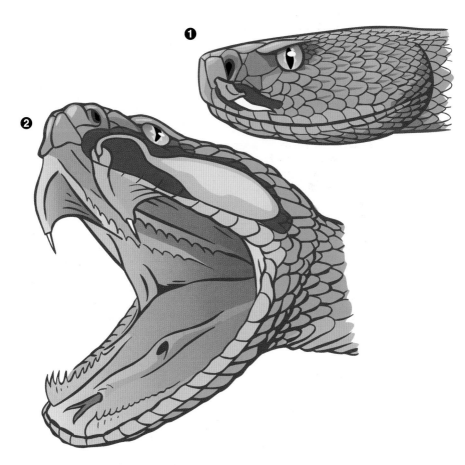

A pit viper's fangs lie folded inside membranous sheaths when not in use **(1)**. *When striking* **(2)**, *maxillary bones rotate the fangs forward and the sheaths fill with venom, which is then injected through the hollow fang into the target.*

when the need to strike arises. As in a fine machine, venom ducts transport venom from glands into the empty sheaths so that venom is forced into the top of each fang and expelled out of the opening near the tip.

Copperheads are small-to-medium-sized snakes with fangs long enough to pierce clothing and footwear. While not to be discounted, they are not as great a threat as are larger rattlers and cottonmouths, who can deliver huge amounts of venom through long fangs. Rattlers are well represented throughout the U.S. but are concentrated in the southwest. Copperheads are mostly found in the east. Cottonmouths and coral snakes have a fairly limited range in the southeast and are only found in Texas in the southwest.

NASTY BABIES

Although mature rattlesnakes are easily recognizable (provided you can see their rattles), immature rattlers can fool you. They are born with a "button" on the end of the tail where their rattle will grow with the periodic shedding of their skin. Young copperheads and cottonmouths are likewise more difficult to identify than adult snakes. Young coral snakes are so tiny that they are rarely seen but display the same banding and coloration as adults. All venomous snakes are born fully equipped with venom and fangs. Often young snakes (harmless and otherwise) will be more pugnacious and ready to defend themselves, so it's wise not to discount a snake just because it's small.

UP FROM THE GRAVE HE AROSE AND BIT POOR LUCY ON THE NOSE

Sometimes people are bitten while handling a dead pit viper. A curious postmortem muscle contraction in the snake can result in a bite to the handler. Although rare, such bites

Distribution of U.S. Snakebites on the Body	
Finger	18.06%
Hand or wrist	12.92%
Arm	9.94%
Upper limb	40.92%
Foot or ankle	35.44%
Leg	22.07%
Lower limb	57.51%
Total limbs	98.43%
Trunk	0.69%
Head	0.88%
Head and Trunk	1.57%
(Klauber, 1997, p. 849)	

have been known to occur even when the head was maimed or severed from the body.

REALLY BAD SPIT

You may be surprised to learn that, like human saliva, the poison of venomous snakes consists mainly of enzymes. When we chew, our saliva initiates the digestive process by helping break down whatever we're eating. The same thing happens when a snake injects venom into its victim. The enzymes in the venom begin digesting the prey even before the victim is swallowed. Snake venom, of course, is more potent than our saliva and works on the snake's prey in ways that are quite different from the role our saliva plays in the human digestive process. Because most venomous snakes strike, inject venom, and release, the prey often runs some distance before it succumbs to the poison and dies. The snake uses its Jacobson's organ—situated within paired cavities of the roof of the mouth (as well as its pit if a pit viper)—to track and find the terminally wounded prey. The famous forked tongue collects data by air sampling for the Jacobson's organ, a chemoreceptor that relays a combination of smell and taste to the snake.

Understanding Venom: Attacking Blood or Nerves

Most snake venom is comprised of both hemorrhagic and neurotoxic elements, though overall there's a wide variety of venom components and mixtures. The hemorrhagic chemicals in snake venom destroy the lining and walls of the blood vessels, destroy red blood corpuscles, and prevent the coagulation of blood. The victim, in other words, bleeds to death from the inside. Neurotoxins in snake venom act on the bulbar and spinal ganglion cells of the central nervous system; they shut down the nervous system, resulting in cardiac arrest and the cessation of respiration. Although snake venom may include some hemorrhagic *and* neurotoxic elements, pit viper bites cause primarily hemorrhagic symptoms, while the bites of coral snakes, cobras, and the like wreak predominantly neurotoxic damage.

To assess the seriousness of a snakebite, you must consider the type of venom, the potency of the venom, the amount of venom injected, and the location of the bite on the body. Drop for drop, the cobra-like, neurotoxic venom of the coral snake is more potent and faster acting than that of the largest rattlesnake. Fortunately, however, the diminutive coral snake can't deliver venom in great quantity, nor does it possess the sophisticated, long-fanged delivery system deployed by the pit vipers. To be killed by a coral snake, you would pretty much have to allow the snake to chew on you. Rattlesnakes, cottonmouths, and larger copperheads, on the other hand, can inject a goodly amount of venom. Their predominantly hemorrhagic venom, however, works more slowly than that of the coral snakes and cobras, and it has decidedly less effect on the nervous system.

Most snakebites are inflicted below the knees or on the hands or forearms. Bites on the upper and lower extremities are less life threatening than bites closer to the heart.

Because most victims have ample opportunity to seek emergency treatment, there are very few fatalities from venomous snakebites. However, surviving the bite is no picnic either. Pit viper bites especially are quite painful and can cause a great deal of long-term tissue damage in the area of the bite.

One such episode happened to a naturalist in 1992 on an eastern diamondback rattler capture-recapture field study. The 112-pound woman sustained three fang punctures on her left hand between her thumb and forefinger. One or two fangs injected venom directly into a vein. Although paramedics arrived within 3 minutes, she became unconscious at the hospital a mere 25 minutes after the bite event. Her heart stopped twice. She spent 16 days in ICU, during which time amputation of her hand was considered. After another 7 days in the hospital, she still required another 14 days of rehabilitation to restore her walking, speech, and cohesive use of language. Six years after the event, which cost more than $162,000 (almost $7,000 for antivenin costs), she still had memory loss, difficulty with minor numerical calculations, severe scarring, and pain.

RISK ASSESSMENT

Although there are a lot of venomous snakes out there, your likelihood of encountering one is fairly remote. If you are walking, hiking, or mountain biking on a marked trail, it's possible, though unlikely, you will encounter a snake. Your chances increase during the spring and fall when snakes make use of the trail's surface to warm themselves, and when the snakes are

Master of disguise: a camouflaged Florida pine snake (Pituphis melanoleucus mugitus).

also more likely to be on the move. In the summer, snakes stay under cover most of the day but may stretch out on the trail in the late afternoon and evening to soak up the residual heat from the surface of the trail. Snakes might make use of a quiet road or driveway for the same purpose.

You are at greatest risk when you leave the trail or road and strike off through the woods. The pit vipers, especially, are masters of camouflage. Sometimes they look like a tree root or blend perfectly with dried grass, brush, or leaves. Off-trail, it's easy to step on or close to an unseen snake. If you are working outdoors, beware of brush piles, downed trees, refuse, woodpiles, and other cool, shady places that snakes occupy to avoid the heat.

You can minimize your risk by staying on a marked trail and keeping a watchful eye. The more open and clear the trail, the easier snakes are to spot. While on the trail, always be vigilant, especially at creek crossings, in rocky areas, and when stepping over fallen trees and branches. Make a habit of stepping onto rocks

and logs, clearing the far side by a foot or more as you proceed.

Although all snakes can and do climb, venomous species in the U.S. are not considered arboreal. This means that you do not have to worry about a venomous snake dropping on you out of a tree while walking. If you are in a boat, it's possible (though highly unlikely) that a venomous snake could drop off of an eye-level (or lower) branch into your boat. The startled reptile's intention, of course, is to evade danger by slipping into the water.

Speaking of water, venomous snakes in the U.S. can bite both in and under water. Even rattlesnakes are good swimmers (the eastern diamondback and the cottonmouth are the undisputed champions), rattlers having negotiated salt water to start new populations on coastal islands.

In the U.S., approximately 7,000 to 8,000 reptile bites are reported annually to the American Association of Poison Control Centers (AAPCC). However, this figure is conservative due to under-reporting. Males are more commonly bitten than females,

This eastern diamondback (Crotalus adamanteus) *hides well on the forest floor.*

Monthly Distribution of Snakebites in the U.S.	
January	7
February	1
March	23
April	83
May	116
June	168
July	252
August	191
September	158
October	65
November	19
December	5
(Klauber, 1997, p. 853)	

with young adults (in the age group 18 to 28 years) receiving 50% of all bites.

Rattlesnakes inflict 66% of all bites by identified venomous snakes in the U.S. Copperheads are responsible for about 24% of venomous snakebites nationwide—though in the southeast, copperheads are responsible for the majority of venomous snakebites. Cottonmouths account for about 10% of venomous

snakebites in the U.S., while fewer than 10 people a year are bitten by coral snakes. Dry bites, in which there is no envenomation, occur in as many as 50% of strikes.

TIMING OF BITES

To no one's surprise, late spring into early fall is when most bites occur. Snakes are prone to hibernation, but you cannot absolutely rule out activity through the winter, since snakebite data indicates a full calendar of bites.

In the U.S., an average of 8 to 15 deaths per year occur as a result of snakebite, almost all from rattlesnake bites (note that lethal bites from non-indigenous species are also included in the data). Cottonmouth and copperhead envenomation causes effects similar to rattlesnake envenomation but is generally less serious. With these, the most common symptoms and signs are limited to local pain and swell-ing. The AAPCC has reported no deaths from cottonmouth or copperhead envenomation since its first annual report in 1983. Overall in the U.S. and Canada, the risk of dying

11

from a venomous snakebite is far less than being killed by lightning, wasps, or bees.

AVOIDANCE AND PRECAUTION

When exploring the outdoors, always tell someone where you are going and when you expect to return. In areas where there are venomous snakes, walk, hike, camp, bike, or work accompanied by at least two companions when possible. If someone is bitten, one person can stay with the victim while the other goes for help. If there are fewer than three people, carry a cell phone. If you come across any snake in the field and don't know positively what it is (or isn't), do not approach it, try to examine it, or photograph it (unless you have a long telephoto or zoom lens). Carry the first aid items discussed below and know how to use them.

ENCOUNTERS

All snakes exhibit a wide range of alertness. A snake on the move will be fully alert, whereas one stretched sunning on a rock or trail may or may not be. A snake's eyes are open all of the time, even when it's sleeping, so you can't judge its wakefulness by observing the eyes. If the snake feels threatened, it will flee or assume a defensive posture. This could be as unremarkable as redirecting its gaze to take you in, or as dramatic as coiling, and if a rattlesnake, shaking its rattle. Often, however, the snake will be quite lethargic. In this case, it will probably not acknowledge your presence. We have seen as many as five dogs walk over a rattlesnake without the snake making the slightest response. Similarly, we have had to prod snakes sunning on the highway to get them off the road before a car made roadkill out of them. Because it takes some experience to gauge a snake's relative alertness, your best bet is to give it a wide berth. In specific terms, pass the snake at a distance at least equal to its body length. If the trail is too narrow to pass the snake at a safe distance, use a long stick to gently prod it off the trail and out of the way. The idea here is to move the snake along without unduly arousing it. Under no circumstances approach closer than one body length of the snake. If a long stick is not available, tossing small pebbles, sand, or twigs at the snake will usually make it move. When roused suddenly, rattlers tend to wake up rather cross, so be gentle for both your sakes.

A snake may be sleeping during the day because it was active at night. With their food sources active at night, snakes are often prowling about in the dark, so (cautiously!) gather that firewood earlier in the day.

THE ETERNAL DILEMMA: WHAT TO WEAR IN RATTLESNAKE COUNTRY?

Because various species of rattlers are distributed throughout the lower 48 U.S., this question is a useful one for everyone who plans to enter potential rattler country.

A rattler can strike from any position with a range roughly equal to half its body length.

What Were They Doing when the Snake Bit?	
Crawling through brush or under a fence	22.5%
Climbing among rocks	18.0%
Walking with inadequate foot or leg coverings	12.0%
Going barefoot in the open	11.0%
Gathering firewood after dark	9.0%
Reaching into hollow logs, heavy grass, or brush; under stones; into holes	5.0%
Snakes encountered in camps	3.5%
Bitten through "snake-proof" footwear	2.0%
Unknown circumstances	17.0%

(Klauber, 1997, p. 963–63)

1. Boots, at least to knee height, will help considerably. These should be constructed of substantial material such as thick, stiff leather or rubber, not of lightweight material such as canvas or nylon. Thickness is the most important feature. Special boots and chaps made of (ostensibly) snake-proof fabric are also available.
2. Trousers worn on the outside, not tucked into boots. The loose cloth will interfere with fang penetration.
3. Shorts, bare feet, sandals, and even nylon athletic shoes provide little to no protection against bites.

Unfortunately, children at play rank high in the statistical lists of those bitten by rattlers. This is likely due in part to the fact that children have no natural or instinctive fear of snakes. What is also unfortunate is that by the time they reach adulthood, most people will likely have a totally disproportionate fear of all snakes that will incapacitate their ability to react with common sense in real encounters.

DO I SMELL CUCUMBERS?

An old myth says it's killer rattlers, not salad, you smell in the wild. Experts, however, maintain that rattlesnakes are almost odorless, and you should certainly not rely on this bit of folklore to warn you about their presence.

FIGHT OR FLIGHT

If you should trigger a coiling response from a rattler lying about in the open, know that the snake is still just as likely to retreat as it is to attack. Most experts with broad field knowledge agree that most rattlers attempt to escape rather than give battle. After all, energy, and perhaps venom, spent on you is that much less to use in the search for supper.

WILL'S STORY

Will's story is a good cautionary tale about venomous bites, no matter where you live. An entomologist, Will was collecting insect specimens along with a friend in southeastern North Carolina. Moving some loose bricks and boards at about 10 a.m., he discovered a very small snake that he initially believed to be a juvenile hognose snake, a harmless species well represented in the Carolinas. Anticipating no danger, Will picked up the snake and was immediately bitten on the third finger of his left hand, near the fingernail. Two small drops of blood appeared at once, and Will experienced immediate and considerable pain. As his hand began to swell, the pain in his finger moderated somewhat.

The snake, which Will dropped, had by this time disappeared. Appropriately concerned and still confused, Will and his friend dismantled the stack of bricks and boards in hope of finding the snake and making a positive identification. After a laborious and lengthy search their persistence paid dividends and the snake was relocated. Close inspection by the two naturalists allowed them to conclude that it was a pygmy rattlesnake about nine inches long.

Because Will was of the opinion that such a tiny snake could not inflict a serious bite, he and his friend continued their collections through the afternoon. His hand and arm continued to swell, however, and around 6 p.m. he decided to consult a doctor. The doctor, who had no experience or special expertise in regard to treating snakebite, tended to agree with Will that the bite couldn't amount to much. He limited his treatment to a thorough cleansing and disinfecting of the wound.

Later, though there were no systemic symptoms, Will had difficulty undressing for bed. His hand and arm were quite painful, but Will was able to sleep fairly well. On awakening in the morning, he felt faint and returned to bed. After a while, he felt better and departed for the field to resume collecting.

The finger by now had turned black, and blood and serum were oozing from the fang punctures. From time to time Will felt faint again. The next morning, almost 48 hours after being bitten, Will joined his friend to resume collecting. That night undressing for bed, Will discovered his left side was swollen, the underside of his arm was black and blue, and a "flabby swelling" had developed under his arm.

The next day, swelling was reduced and the hand was less painful, and blood and serum had stopped oozing from the bite site. Though the finger looked hideous, it gradually improved, and general swelling disappeared on about the eighth day. His finger,

however, was not fully usable for an additional 18 months!

Will's story, relating the symptoms of a bite from one of the tiniest pit vipers, provides a sobering glimpse of the horrors of pit viper envenomation and speaks volumes about the damage a larger crotalid can wreak.

Factors Affecting the Seriousness of a Snake Bite

Many agents interact to make the impact of a bite difficult to predict. They include:

- Age, size, sex, vigor, and health of the victim.
- Victim's susceptibility to protein poisoning, which includes the number of previous bites that might provide partial immunity.
- Emotional condition of the victim. Fear will increase heart rate and thus aid the distribution of venom throughout the body.
- Location of the bite, which is less serious in the extremities or in fatty tissue.
- Nature of the bite, e.g., a direct hit with both fangs fully embedded or a glancing blow or scratch.
- Protection afforded by the clothing—thicker is better.
- Number of bites—two or more are not unheard of.
- Length of hold time for the actual bite.
- Emotional state of the snake. If hurt or violently excited, it is likely to inject more venom.
- Species, age, and size of the snake.
- Condition of the venom glands—were they recently depleted?
- Condition of the fangs—broken, renewed, due for shedding?
- Bacterial microorganisms in the snake's mouth that contribute to infection.
- Nature of first aid treatment.

Frequency of Bite Sign or Symptom Occurence	
Pain	65–95%
Swelling, edema	74%
Weakness	72%
Sweating and/or chills	64%
Numbness, tingling (circumoral, lingual, scalp, feet, etc.)	63%
Pulse rate changes	60%
Faintness, dizziness	57%
Escape of blood into the tissues from ruptured blood vessels (ecchymosis)	51%
Nausea and/or vomiting	48%
Blood pressure changes	46%
Numbness, tingling in the affected part	42%
Decreased blood platelets	42%
Muscle twitches and contractions (fasciculations)	41%
Blisters (vesicles or boli)	40%
Regional lymph adenopathy	40%
Respiratory rate changes	40%
Increased blood clotting time	39%
Decreased hemoglobin	37%
Thirst	34%
Change in body temperature	31%
Local tissue death (necrosis)	27%
Abnormal electrocardiogram	26%
Abnormal amounts of sugar in the urine (glycosuria)	20%
Increased salivation	20%
Bluish discoloration of the skin (cyanosis)	16%
Excess protein in the urine (proteinuria)	16%
Presence of blood in the urine (hematuria)	15%
Unconsciousness	12%
Blurring of vision	12%
Increased blood platelets	4%
Swollen eyelid	2%
Retinal hemorrhage	2%
Convulsions	1%

(Klauber, 1997, p. 849)

SIGNS AND SYMPTOMS OF ENVENOMATION

Fang marks may be present as one or more well-defined punctures or as a series of small lacerations or scratches, or there may not be any noticeable or obvious markings where the bite occurred. The absence of fang marks does not preclude the possibility of a bite (especially if a juvenile snake is involved). However, with adult pit viper envenomation, fang marks are invariably present and are generally seen on close examination. Bleeding may persist from the fang wounds. On the other hand, the presence of fang marks does not always indicate envenomation. Sometimes venom is conserved or is already largely spent on the efforts of a recent hunt.

Venomous snakes do not always inject venom, particularly when they strike in defense or when startled. However, if you are bitten by a venomous snake, you should seek treatment immediately and not wait for the signs and symptoms of envenomation to appear. The specific indications and symptoms that may manifest themselves in a victim who has been envenomated can vary considerably in presence and in severity. The time of development will also vary considerably from case to case. Because almost all venomous snakebites in the U.S. and Canada are inflicted by pit vipers, we limit our list of signs and symptoms to cases of crotalid envenomation (Russell, 1983, p. 281). Not all of these symptoms will necessarily develop, even with severe envenomation.

Neurological symptoms: If the victim is suspected of having been bitten by a coral snake or the Mojave rattlesnake *(Crotalus scutulatus),* the victim may develop neurological symptoms including respiratory obstruction or failure that must be treated as an immediate emergency.

However, some bites from several other species of rattlesnake have also been implicated in resulting respiratory failure.

IF YOU ARE BITTEN

Snakebite Treatment:

Although snakebite first aid is controversial, snakebite treatment is not. In the simplest possible terms, it consists of the following:

- Get the victim to the hospital or treatment center as soon as possible.
- Administer the appropriate antidote (antivenin).

Findlay Russell, a global authority on snakebites, counsels, "If you haven't done anything except get to a hospital, you haven't done anything wrong." (Rubio, 1998, p. 147)

In cases of serious pit viper envenomation, intravenous fluid resuscitation is also important. Of course, proper medical treatment and management of a venomous snakebite is both involved and complex. Fortunately, pertinent considerations and treatment protocols are only a click away on the web (such as at emedicine.com) if your ER doc lacks experience. Antivenin, likewise, is available at most hospitals and even at larger drugstores.

Concerning the Snake:

Make sure that the responsible snake or snakes have been appropriately and safely contained and prevented from inflicting any additional bites. Try to identify (not catch) the offending snake. If you are bitten in the U.S. or Canada and cannot identify the snake, don't worry. More than 99% of all snakebites (excluding bites by non-indigenous species in collections or zoos) are by pit vipers, and the same antivenin is used for treatment regardless of the offending pit viper species (though some bites may require more anti-venin than

others). Coral snake bites, which require a different antivenin, are so rare and the snake so easily identified and differentiated from a pit viper that there's little chance the attending physician will confuse the treatment.

In a characteristic understatement, Dr. Robert E. Arnold acknowledges the impulse for revenge when he writes: "Do not waste time hunting for the snake! Personal reasons may prompt one to find the snake and kill it, but this should be done after the victim is on the way to the hospital. Please do not feel constrained to present the reptile remains to the doctor or hospital for viewing. First, the snake may not be dead and may recover at an inopportune moment. Second, few physicians are able to identify most snakes. Third, it makes no difference what kind of snake it is since only one pit viper antivenin is available." Note, however, that very recently a new kind of antivenin has become available. It's market name is CroFab (*Crotalidae* Polyvalent Immune Fab [Ovine]), and it was approved by the FDA in October 2000 as an effective agent for minimal and moderate crotalid envenomation. It also seems less likely to cause anaphylaxis, an allergic reaction that can prove to be very serious.

Transportation:

Arrange immediately for transportation of the victim to the nearest emergency room or treatment center. Calling 911 is often the best strategy. Although venomous snakebite is a medical emergency, it is not so dire as to warrant a hair-raising dash to the hospital at excessive speeds. Except in a tiny number of cases (where the bite is to the head, neck, or torso), you have time for a sane, controlled drive to the nearest emergency room. If possible, call the ER to let them know you are coming with a snakebite victim.

Wilderness Situations:

The objective is to get to a hospital and antivenin as quickly as possible. Generally speaking, you want to be very still after being bitten because activity accelerates the spread of the venom. In a remote area, however, obtaining treatment expeditiously is more important than being still, so you'll want to set off toward help, adverse effects of movement notwithstanding.

When walking to find help, head for the closest road, house, phone, or site of known human habitation. If alternative routes are available, choose the one that requires the least aerobic exertion, even if it is a little longer. If you are in the wilderness, do not compound your problems by leaving the trail and getting lost. Continue on the trail in the direction most likely to lead to help. Depart from the trail only if a road or house comes into view and you are certain you can reach it.

You may have some very tough decisions to make. What if you encounter a person who is willing to assist? Do you send them ahead to find help while you remain still, or do you continue plugging along? Every such decision must be made in the context of which alternative will get you to professional medical help soonest.

Wilderness Evacuations:

There are very few endeavors as strenuous as carrying a person over a trail or cross-country. The safe evacuation of a nonambulatory person in the wilderness requires at least six and preferably eight or more persons. When fewer than six able people are present, it is almost always more prudent to go for help than to attempt evacuation.

THE GREAT SNAKEBITE FIRST AID CONTROVERSY

You should know that the preferred first aid for snakebite has changed a number of times during the past several decades and continues to be hotly debated. Gone are the days of making "X" incisions over the fang marks, applying tourniquets, sucking venom from the wound with your mouth, packing the bitten limb in ice, or plying the victim with whiskey.

First aid today, defined as measures taken prior to the victim receiving professional medical attention, is complicated by the terrible potential of pit viper venom to destroy tissue and disfigure limbs. Sometimes there are very real trade-offs where a life is saved only at the expense of a limb. Much of the debate centers around the advisability of restricting the circulation of pit viper venom through the use of constricting bands between the bite site and the heart. Restricting the venom can preclude or delay systemic toxic effects but can also contribute to increased tissue destruction at the bite site and on the affected limb. The following summation of the debate is from Herpmed's Snakebite Emergency web page. It recommends the use of containment bandages for pit viper bites.

"This website suggests the use of containment or sequestration of injected venom at or near the bite site using broad (three inch to six inch wide) compression bandaging such as a crepe or Ace-type elastic bandage. This protocol is also known as "pressure/immobilization." This is the standard worldwide accepted first aid treatment for bites by elapid snakes such as cobras, coral snakes, and many Australian species. This method has delayed the onset of serious snakebite symptoms for as long as 24 hours in Australia, where victims of deadly bites were far from

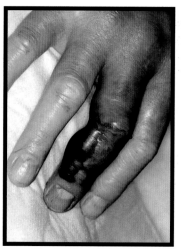

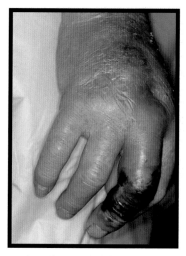

Six hours after rattlesnake bite

13 days after rattlesnake bite

medical assistance. The method remains controversial in the U.S. for pit viper envenomations.

"The use of containment/sequestration for certain types of pit viper bite is felt by some experts to increase the risk of disfiguring local tissue, which may subsequently necessitate skin grafts, extensive repair, and prolonged treatment once the acute, life-threatening phase of the event has passed. Other experts recommend containment/sequestration because they believe that the spread of venom to vital organs can be life-threatening, and that you have no way of knowing how life-threatening a snakebite is in the first moments of the event. Therefore, it is essential to recognize that there is a trade-off: containment as a life-saving measure at the risk of local tissue damage that, while not necessarily life-threatening, could be disfiguring, painful, and/or which could require extensive follow-up treatment. We therefore urge readers who decide to use containment/sequestration on **any** type of snakebite to do so as a life or death decision and to make this decision in recognition of the above information.

"In addition, some U.S. crotalid bites, particularly from large species, result in widespread damage to limbs even when bites are to digits and hands or feet. Thus the wide-area, low-pressure wraps can prevent the spread of venom [as well as] more widespread damage. Again, some experts feel that this increases the intensity of more localized damage. Although snakebite mortality without these dressings may be low, we [are aware] of many unnecessary and tragic deaths as well as widespread disfigurement without their use, and in general advocate their use if properly applied."

It should be emphasized that the effectiveness of low-pressure wraps is still controversial among experts. Also contested are the use and efficacy of negative pressure devices, called "extractors," that are attached like a suction cup over one or more fang marks to extract venom.

Concerning the Victim: Universally approved, noncontroversial first aid includes the following:
- Clean and disinfect the wound.
- Keep the victim still.

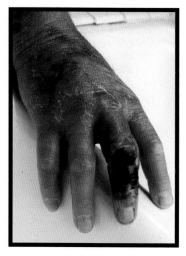

19 days after rattlesnake bite

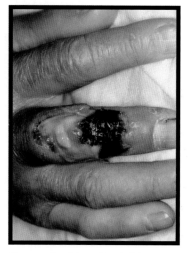

Seven weeks after rattlesnake bite

- Remove rings, bracelets, watches, jewelry, boots, shoes, and tight clothing on the affected limb in anticipation of swelling.
- With a pen, mark the border of advancing swelling every 15 minutes.
- Maintain the bitten limb in a gravity neutral position (i.e., exactly at heart level).
- Calm and reassure the victim.

WHAT NOT TO DO IF BITTEN:

- Do not eat or drink anything unless directed or approved by medical sources.
- Do not engage in strenuous physical activity.
- Do not apply oral (mouth) suction to bite.
- Do not cut into or incise bite marks with a blade.
- Do not drink any alcohol or use any medication.
- Do not apply either hot or cold packs.
- Do not apply a tourniquet or use sticks or other hard objects for splints.

- Do not use a stun gun or electric shock of any kind.
- Do not give antivenin in the field because of the risk of severe allergic complications.

WHAT TO DO IF BITTEN:

Constrictive Bandaging: Review the discussion above regarding the controversial nature of constrictive (pressure/immobilization) bandaging for pit viper bites. If you elect to use this application, here's what to do.

1. Keep the victim calm and reassured. Allow him or her to lie flat and avoid moving. If possible, allow the bitten limb to rest at a level equal to or slightly lower than the victim's heart.
2. Allow bite to bleed freely for 15 to 30 seconds.
3. Cleanse and rapidly disinfect the area with Betadine (assuming the victim is not allergic to iodine or shellfish).
4. Immediately wrap a large constricting band snugly about the bitten limb at a level just above the bite site, i.e., between the bite site and the heart. Ace

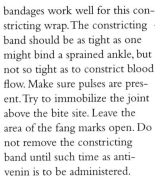

bandages work well for this constricting wrap. The constricting band should be as tight as one might bind a sprained ankle, but not so tight as to constrict blood flow. Make sure pulses are present. Try to immobilize the joint above the bite site. Leave the area of the fang marks open. Do not remove the constricting band until such time as antivenin is to be administered.

5. Apply hard, direct pressure over the bite using a 4x4 gauze pad folded in half twice. Tape in place with adhesive tape or bind with a bandana or other clothing. Soak gauze pad in a Betadine solution if available and if the victim is not allergic to iodine or shellfish.

6. Apply a second constricting band (as described in step 4 above) below the bite. Make sure pulses are present.

7. If possible, try to keep the bitten extremity at heart level or in a gravity-neutral position. Holding it above heart level speeds the circulation of venom through the body while holding the extremity below heart level can increase swelling.

8. Bites to face, torso, or buttocks are more problematic. Disinfect the bite site and apply a pressure dressing with gauze pads and tape.

9. Observe the victim closely for signs and symptoms of envenomation. These usually manifest between 15 minutes and two hours after the bite occurred. If **none** of the signs or symptoms have been noted after two hours, there is a possibility that the victim received a dry bite (no venom injected). Remove the constricting band, watching carefully for any changes in the victim's status. If any changes occur, assume the patient has been envenomed. If signs and symptoms still fail to manifest, continue close observation of the victim for an additional 12 to 24 hours.

The primary and essential treatment for venomous snakebite is the administration of the appropriate antivenin by a trained physician. All of the foregoing first aid procedures are intended to minimize the effects of envenomation until professional medical treatment can be obtained.

★ **Remember,** Ace bandages or other wide bandaging must **not** be wrapped so tight as to cut off systemic venous or arterial circulation. Properly applied, such bandages will **not** compromise the systemic circulation.

What To Tell Them at the Hospital:

Because venomous snakebite is rare, it's possible that the attending physician knows little or nothing about snakebite management. Our recommendation is to directly question the physician concerning his experience with snakebite. You can also tactfully do the following:

- Ask staff to contact Poison Control immediately.
- Locate nearest antivenin resource (for U.S. and Canadian species: Wyeth Laboratories, (610) 688-4400).
- Ask staff to use physician consultants available through Poison Control (www.aapcc.org).

Centers with special experience in managing rattlesnake envenomations:
- Arizona Poison Control (602) 626-6016
- Rocky Mountain Poison Control (800) 726-3737
- San Diego Regional Poison Control (619) 543-6000

The Antivenom Index, published by the American Zoo and Aquarium Association and the American Association

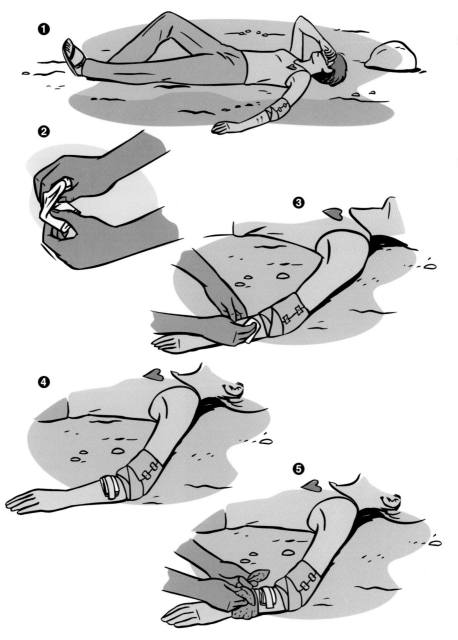

Snakebite First Aid: **(1)** *Victim lies flat and avoids moving. Cleanse and disinfect wound. Allow wound to bleed freely for 15–30 seconds; immediately wrap a constricting bandage above bite site between the bite and heart, making sure NOT to cut off the flow of blood.* **(2)** *Fold a 4x4" gauze pad in half twice; soak pad with disinfecting solution.* **(3)** *Using the gauze pad, apply hard, direct pressure over the bite.* **(4)** *Tape pad in place with adhesive tape or another bandage.* **(5)** *Apply a second constricting bandage below the bite, making sure pulses are present.*

of Poison Control Centers, lists the locations, amounts, and various types of antivenin stores. Antivenin *(Crotalidae)* Polyvalent, Wyeth has for some time been the only commercially available antivenin in the U.S. for pit viper envenomation. CroFab, a new antivenin reputedly more specific to U.S. pit vipers and less likely to cause an allergic reaction, appeared on the market in October 2000.

Rattlesnakes

CAPABILITIES

A rattler can strike from any position with a range roughly equal to half its body length. Body length is difficult to ascertain in a coiled specimen, so err on the generous side. Contrary to popular assumptions, the snake does not have to be coiled to strike, nor will it necessarily shake its rattle. A highly agitated rattlesnake may continue its trademark rattle for as long as three hours. A rattlesnake strike is blindingly quick—less than one second—so don't count on evading it, particularly when the rattler sees you first. When it bites, it may or may not inject venom. Venom is never completely depleted, so do use high caution even after the initial strike. The larger the snake, the longer the fangs—though even relatively small pit vipers can easily pierce clothing and most footwear. Their top crawling speed is less than three miles per hour (slower than a moderate human walking pace). They will not "chase" you, but even if they did they would not "catch" you.

PERSONALITY

Though potentially deadly, all rattlesnakes are retiring and skittish. Aggression toward humans and animals too large to eat is rare unless the snake is startled, stepped on, or otherwise threatened. As a cold-blooded animal, the ambient air temperature affects the snake's general level of alertness and activity. The snake will alternatively use sun, shade, and water to attain an optimal internal body temperature of 89 to 90° Fahrenheit. This is, however, not necessarily what the air temperature is. One or more times a year the snake will shed its skin. When this occurs, the protective lenses of the eyes become opaque, thus making the snake essentially blind for a period. The rattler will be much more irritable and aggressive during the time its eyesight is compromised, but it is thought that snakes are even more prone to hiding during this vulnerable stage. As it is with all venomous snakes, most bites occur during attempts at handling, capturing, or killing the snake.

Timber/canebrake rattlesnakes (Crotalus horridus) *at home.*

WHERE THEY ARE

Rattlesnakes are very adaptable, so they live just about everywhere. Their natural habitat varies from sea level swamp to rocky or wooded terrain. They can be found in river bottoms, on mountaintops up to 10,000 feet (11,000 in California), in caves, rock outcroppings and overhangs, hammocks, wooded hillsides, and grass or cane thickets. If human encroachment impacts their habitat, they may stick around instead of relocating. Thus, it is not unusual to find rattlesnakes on farms or even around subdivisions, especially new ones. Mountainous rattlers are more apt to be active before and after thunderstorms. Rattlers have been know to survive 4° Fahrenheit weather for a brief interval, and are known to endure several days of 37° weather with no ill effects.

A Day In the Life of Mr. or Ms. Rattler

A rattler's level of activity is determined by the temperature and its need for food and water. A fair weather kind of creature, it will be up and around during the temperate days of the spring and fall. During the heat of summer it holes up someplace cool during the day and goes shopping at night. How often it eats depends on the amount of activity, factoring in the trying demands of the breeding season. Mostly, however, a rattler's a couch potato, laying low and doing as little as possible. Where a rattler hangs out depends on the temperature. If it's cool, the rattler might be on the rock; if it's hot, underneath the rock. When it comes to eating, sometimes a rattler goes hunting, and sometimes it waits for home delivery.

If You Hear a Rattlesnake's "Buzzing" Warning

Freeze! Quietly assess the terrain while standing still. If the rattler does not retreat after several unnerving minutes, make sure you can safely back up (without perhaps stepping on another rattlesnake) and then slowly step back, allowing the rattler the opportunity to retreat to safety for both your sakes.

TIMBER/ CANEBRAKE RATTLESNAKE
Crotalus horridus

• DANGER

Timber and canebrake rattlesnakes are potentially lethal, but the toxicity of venom varies.

• ABUNDANCE & RANGE

Timber rattlers are present throughout the region, with the exceptions of eastern Virginia and Maryland; Delaware; and western Pennsylvania. A threatened species in some states, with declines due to massive loss of habitat, the timber rattler is protected in most northeastern states.

• SIZE

These snakes mature at a fat 3 to 4 feet, but they can reach 5 to 6 feet.

• DESCRIPTION

The northern variety of the timber rattler is washed-out yellow, brown, gray, or black in color with dark black blotches which form a cross-band or chevron pattern on the body. The head is broad, flat, and triangular in shape, with small orifices or "pits" between the eyes and snout, giving rise to the term "pit viper." The southern variety, known until recently as the canebrake rattler, is brownish, faded yellow, or pinkish gray with similar dark banding blotches. A dark stripe behind the eyes and a tan or reddish-brown stripe running along the spine generally distinguish the southern variety. Both forms have a velvety black tail and a rattle. Timber rattlesnakes are among the most naturally camouflaged of all rattlesnakes and can make themselves almost invisible on the forest floor.

• SIMILAR SPECIES
Massasaugas have nine plates on their head crown, versus the numerous small scales of the timber rattler.

• DIET
These snakes eat mostly rodents, including rats, squirrels, and chipmunks, as well as rabbits. Some devour amphibians, lizards, and small birds.

• REPRODUCTION
They mate in spring and autumn and give birth every other year in late August to early September.

• HABITAT
These rattlers prefer wooded hills, meadows, grasslands, and prairies. Den sites are in rock outcroppings and talus (rock debris) slopes. Elevation range is sea level to 6,600 feet.

• TRAITS
Relatively mild-mannered, they likely prefer retreat to combat. Despite a harsh rattle when disturbed, this snake will generally glide away, sounding its warning in retreat. If cornered, expect it to fight fiercely.

EASTERN MASSASAUGA
Sistrurus catenatus catenatus

• DANGER
Potentially lethal, but the massasauga's short fangs and relatively low venom capacity make this very unlikely.

• SIZE
Mature snakes range from 18 to 39.5 inches, but most do not exceed 30 inches.

• ABUNDANCE & RANGE
Massasaugas inhabit northwestern Pennsylvania and isolated pockets in central New York.

• DESCRIPTION
In the eastern subspecies, this snake has a brownish to dark gray body with large near-round black spots extending down the back. Overall body color can approach black without close inspection. The belly is primarily black with a few light markings.

• SIMILAR SPECIES
Timber rattlers have black-tipped tails.

• DIET

Mice and other small vertebrates, such as lizards, frogs, birds, and snakes.

• REPRODUCTION

Breeding in April to May yields live-born young from July to September. Litters contain 2 to 19 juveniles, each 6 to 9 inches in length.

• HABITAT

Bogs, swamps, marshlands, and flood plains in the mid-Atlantic region are the more common habitats, but these snakes can also be found in dry woodlands.

• TRAITS

Typically mild-mannered, these snakes may require considerable provocation before they even start to rattle. Also known as the "swamp rattler" or "black snapper," the name "massasauga" is Chippewa for "great river mouth," referring to the wetland country this snake inhabits at the mouths of rivers. They tend to be active at twilight or at night during hot summer days.

The "Moccasin" Family

Copperheads, which are sometimes called "highland moccasins," and cottonmouths, sometimes referred to as "water moccasins," are of the genus *Agkistrodon,* another member of the *Viperidae.* These snakes were the likely progenitors of the other crotalids on the North American continent, and they share the same facial pits as their venomous descendants, the rattlers. Copperheads and cottonmouths also both vibrate their tails in a lively fashion, giving the false impression that they are rattlesnakes, especially if they are stirring dry leaves. Of course, only rattlesnakes have rattles on their tails.

WHAT'S IN A NAME?

Both the copperhead and cottonmouth (whose mouth interior is white and on display when the animal is threatened) are aptly and graphically named. It is, therefore, probably useful and more accurate to refer to them by these names, rather than "moccasins," to help aid identification. Technically, though, most snakes have white linings in their mouths—cottonmouths just show it off more. Also, nonvenomous water snakes are often fatally lumped together with the dangerous and lethal cottonmouth under the water moccasin umbrella.

COPPERHEAD

SUBSPECIES:

Northern copperhead
Agkistrodon contortrix mokasen
Southern copperhead
Agkistrodon contortrix contortrix

• DANGER

Copperheads are potentially lethal, especially to a small child, but their bite is highly unlikely to produce death due to several factors. These

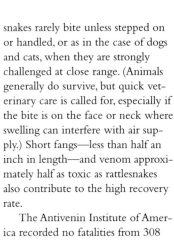

snakes rarely bite unless stepped on or handled, or as in the case of dogs and cats, when they are strongly challenged at close range. (Animals generally do survive, but quick veterinary care is called for, especially if the bite is on the face or neck where swelling can interfere with air supply.) Short fangs—less than half an inch in length—and venom approximately half as toxic as rattlesnakes also contribute to the high recovery rate.

The Antivenin Institute of America recorded no fatalities from 308 copperhead bites over a ten-year period, with a variety of first aid responses.

• ABUNDANCE & RANGE

Two subspecies of copperheads dwell in the mid-Atlantic region. The **northern copperhead,** also called "chunkhead," "pilot," or "adder," is found throughout the seven-state area, except for New Jersey and northern Delaware across into the northern peninsula of Maryland. This territory has no copperheads of either subspecies. The **southern copperhead** overlaps the northern variety in eastern Virginia and in southern Maryland and Delaware.

• SIZE

Mature snakes can range from 22 to 53 inches, but most adults measure 24 to 36 inches. Juveniles are 7 to 10 inches.

• DESCRIPTION

All copperheads have coppery to rusty-colored heads. The **southern copperhead** has a pinkish or pale beige ground color marked by a darker, slender-waisted hourglass pattern formed by side markings that narrow across the back. The **northern copperhead** has a coppery-red head with the same hourglass pattern, accompanied by small dark spots between the crossbands, and dark, rounded spots at the sides of the belly.

• SIMILAR SPECIES

Great numbers of snakes are killed in the belief that they are copperheads. Copperheads, as pit vipers, have facial pits. Milk snakes have wide (not narrow) markings on the center of their backs. Hognose snakes have turned-up snouts, raised foreheads, and dark brown, round-pupiled eyes, and they hiss and flatten their necks and heads when threatened. Water snakes are seldom far from water, and if threatened, they retreat to it. Fox snakes also have a coppery-colored head, but their dorsal (back) blotches are widest, not narrowest, over the spine. Corn snakes are also frequently mistaken for copperheads.

• DIET

Copperheads feed on seasonally available prey, including mice, frogs, insects, lizards, smaller snakes, birds, and the gleanings of small mammal nests.

• REPRODUCTION

Mating season is from spring to fall with a peak in April and May. Young are born in August to early October, and they have a yellowish or greenish tail tip.

• HABITAT

Northern copperheads prefer adjacency to woodlands and creeks, often occupying suburban neighborhoods. In summer, you may find this snake foraging in open clearings, swamp edges, rocky slopes, and humans' debris (discarded sheets of plywood, roofing metal, or piles of sawdust). **Southern copperheads** dwell in shady areas where leaves, branches, and logs afford excellent camouflage for their ambush hunting techniques. With heavy ground cover to support numerous forest-floor prey, as many as six or seven copperheads can share a single acre.

•TRAITS

Supremely adept at camouflage, copperheads are often accidentally stepped on, which causes a quick reactive strike. Because these animals are essentially nonaggressive, if you recognize them ahead of time, you're likely to experience nothing more than shock at how closely they can blend into their surroundings. Copperheads tend to bask during the day, and as the days grow warmer, the snakes become more nocturnal. Energy requirements are low, so that many eat only once every three weeks, even during the active season from March to October. Loss of habitat has produced the frequent intrusion of copperheads in suburban or previously inhabited areas, where the snake adapts well. Fortunately, its retiring nature and less toxic venom have minimized the number of deeply unfortunate encounters with humans.

EASTERN COTTONMOUTH
Agkistrodon piscivorus piscivorus

• DANGER

Cottonmouths are potentially lethal, but the mortality rate in the U.S. is less than one person per year. Venom is less toxic than most rattlesnakes, but bites can result in serious tissue death.

• ABUNDANCE & RANGE

Mid-Atlantic cottonmouths are found only in the coastal lowlands of southeastern Virginia.

• SIZE

These snakes range from 30 to 48 inches at maturity, but the record adult length is 74 inches. Juveniles are 7 to 13 inches.

• DESCRIPTION

This is a heavy-bodied, dark-colored water snake whose head is noticeably wider than the neck. Intergrades, or specimens that show the genetic evolution between species or subspecies, are common throughout the range. Bodies of older individuals may be almost black or dark gray and without markings, but younger specimens have olive, brown, or black ground color. Sometimes, cottonmouths may be without pattern, or they may have dark crossbands with serrated edges. The white "cottonmouth" is visible as the snake opens its jaws in a gaping defensive posture that does not necessarily imply imminent aggression. A wide berth, however, should always be given water snakes within cottonmouth territory.

• SIMILAR SPECIES

Large water snakes are often mistaken for cottonmouths, but these harmless varieties lack the pit viper's trademark facial pits, and they also have round pupils. Behavior is another indicator. Water snakes will take to the water when disturbed, where they will swim low in the water with their posterior half below the waterline. Cottonmouths may retreat into water, where they swim with a head held high, leading a buoyant body; but they are more likely to hold their ground, gape open their mouths in a passive defense, coil, and twitch their tails when threatened. Unlike other water snakes, cottonmouths almost never bask in tree limbs.

• DIET

Frogs and fish are a staple food, but cottonmouths will eat any small mammal it can swallow, which can include adult swamp rabbits. Insects, especially cicadas, and smaller cottonmouths, sizeable water snakes, and young alligators form part of the diet. Inclusion of carrion in their diet sometimes entices cottonmouths to dead or struggling fish.

• REPRODUCTION

Cottonmouths mate in the spring and fall to give birth in August to September. Young cottonmouths are strongly patterned with yellowish tail tips.

• HABITAT

Eastern cottonmouths prefer brackish or fresh still-water environments with heavy vegetation and few humans.

• TRAITS

In part because larger specimens will eat smaller ones, cottonmouths do not nest. Therefore, the folktale about water skiers falling into a nest and being bitten to death is not true. This misconception is based on the fact that harmless water snakes will sometimes congregate together in drying creek beds. Cottonmouths tend to flee disturbances in the water, not attack the source. On land, they are more prone to hold their ground than retreat. This is more true for larger specimens. They do bite underwater, but only for prey, not for defense. Since they are not true aquatic animals, underwater biting is rare. They are more likely to take fish by cornering them in shallow water, and are frequently found foraging along shorelines and banks. They bask on floating vegetation.

THE MOST IMPORTANT THINGS TO KNOW ABOUT VENOMOUS SNAKES

In the general populace, fear of venomous snakes far outstrips understanding or even appreciation of their place in the natural order. Though potentially lethal when trespassed upon, they mind their own business and still are often deprived of habitat and respect, not to mention compassion. The subject of many myths, venomous snakes in particular are worthy of our study and contemplation—for our sake, as well as theirs.

Laurence M. Klauber wrote eloquently of the rattlesnake, but his words have a broader application to all venomous snakes:

Of all these myths, that which has most deeply affected human impressions and attitudes toward rattlesnakes is the one that pictures these snakes as malignant, vindictive, and crafty, with an especial hatred of mankind. Recently a radio commentator called rattlesnakes the "symbol of pure evil."

But a rattlesnake is only a primitive creature with rudimentary perceptions and reactions. Dangerous it surely is, and I hold no brief for its survival except in remote areas where its capacity to destroy harmful rodents may be exercised without danger to man or his domestic animals. But that the rattlesnake bears an especial enmity toward man is mythical. It seeks only to defend itself from injury by intruders of superior size, of which man is one. It could not, through the ages, have developed any especial enmity for man, since the first human being any rattlesnake may encounter is the usually the last. (Klauber, 1997, p. 1291)

TURTLES

BROAD-BASED APPEAL

Turtles embrace "a philosophy of meditation and passive resistance," mused esteemed biologist Archie Carr in his enduring 1952 *Handbook of Turtles*. "The magnetism of turtle personality stems more from good-humored quaintness and elfin drollery than from intellectuality," Carr added with nonscientific yet accurate affection.

BITING BACK

Indeed, many of us do find these 200-million-year-old reptiles of the *Testudines* order irresistible, and most turtles are harmless and charming. Their appeal figures prominently in the great Hindu and Native American creation mythologies, and they have been esteemed in Greece and China for millennia. A few species, however, would make University of Tennessee Lady Vols basketball Coach Pat Summitt proud. Pat preaches "Defense! Defense! Defense!," a strategy that some of the biting and "stink bombing" turtles have mastered.

Turtles have no teeth, but they do have beaks with hard, sharp edges for cutting food. Some are capable of surprising neck extensions, and even more surprising, lightning-quick striking speed. Put all this under one shell, and you have the legendary snapping turtles known for their irascibility and aggressively defensive responses.

Snapping turtles are among the largest of the freshwater turtles, with lengths up to 26 inches for the alligator snapper species (found in the southeastern and south central U.S.) and 18.5 inches for the common snapping turtle found in the eastern

two-thirds of the country. These species sport an imposing, truly prehistoric-looking head and commanding jaws. The snapping turtle likes to rest in warm shallows and often burrows in the mud, leaving only its nostrils and eyes exposed, poised to "snap" up some prey. The snappers are highly aquatic, and they rarely bask.

In the more northern reaches, the turtles do hibernate, but there are reports of common snappers moving under the ice in the middle of New England winters. For this reason, you should not automatically assume that snappers are dormant in the chillier months.

Sensing Trouble

Turtles avoid danger by sensing vibration, relying more on this touch sensitivity than they do on their other senses. Snapping turtles will try to depart the scene if threatened, so the danger to swimmers, boaters, and people who are fishing is minimal. Snappers will, however, try to steal fishing bait or caught fish hung on stringers. In this case, it's best to cut the line rather than tangle with the snapper's "business end." Waders, especially children who might like to creep along any permanent freshwater or even brackish shores, would do well to be wearing shoes as a general practice to avoid cans and glass, if nothing else. Generally, though, if accidentally stepped on in the water, snappers will behave rather well and just pull in their heads. They rarely if ever bite people underwater.

No Teasing or Squeezing

Snapping turtles on land, however, are definitely reptiles to be respected. Most harmful encounters are initiated by people who try to tease or capture a snapping turtle. When a serious bite is inflicted, it is hard to

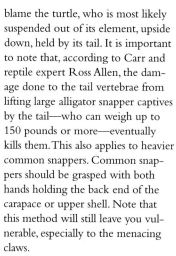

blame the turtle, who is most likely suspended out of its element, upside down, held by its tail. It is important to note that, according to Carr and reptile expert Ross Allen, the damage done to the tail vertebrae from lifting large alligator snapper captives by the tail—who can weigh up to 150 pounds or more—eventually kills them. This also applies to heavier common snappers. Common snappers should be grasped with both hands holding the back end of the carapace or upper shell. Note that this method will still leave you vulnerable, especially to the menacing claws.

For smaller specimens, carry the animal by the base of the tail with the plastron, or underside, toward your body.

ATTITUDE

Legends of amputated feet are exaggerated, but snapping turtles are quick, agile, powerful, and not to be messed with. The Georgia Wildlife Federation offers this caution: "If the common snapping turtle is pestered while on land, it will repeatedly try to bite. . . . Even a small snapper can inflict a painful wound with its hooked beak. If handled, which is definitely not recommended, be very careful . . . Because a well-placed bite from the common snapping turtle can sever a few fingers at one time."

Common snappers have a reputation for tenacity, as well as ferocity. Artist David Carroll, who beached one to draw it, recalled that "a snapping turtle cornered on land, or in shallow water with no escape route, will keep turning in a tight circle to face any challenger, with neck and legs set for a strike and jaws slightly apart. These creatures will not back down."

Although these instances may be somewhat exaggerated, plenty of caution usually prudent when wildlife is involved. Here's another story in which it seems that turtle revenge was even in play, according to Jonathan's episode on the Saco River in New Hampshire:

In most places, the water was not very deep but it was quite clear. As we were coasting downstream, someone spotted a turtle moving along the bottom. I had always been interested in turtles as a kid—I remember that my parents often would stop the car when we saw one on the side of the road so that I could look at it and then move it away from the road. But I had never seen a turtle this size! This was a BIG turtle. All of a sudden I had the urge to investigate it more closely. Without giving it much thought, I jumped over, reached under the water, grabbed the turtle from behind and picked it up.

It turned out to be a snapping turtle, not the typical box turtle that I was used to. The shell was about 15 or 18 inches across and about 20 or 25 inches long. It had rather dangerous-looking claws (actually, let me just say dangerous, forget the "looking" part) and a long, rough tail. It apparently did not share my enthusiasm and seemed most interested in getting away. I showed it off for a few pictures, but just after the pictures were taken, the turtle figured out how to reach my hands with its back claws. I quickly dropped it back into the water and turned to climb into my canoe. I didn't actually see it happen, but others told me that the turtle turned and tried to bite me as I climbed back into my canoe.

Should you be bitten by a turtle, use common sense by cleaning the wound, applying antiseptic, and seeking medical attention. Snapping turtles eat carrion, among other things, so the risk of infection from a bite is a real one.

Your Nose Knows

Although all turtles can bite, the musk and mud turtle family, ranging in size up to about six inches in length, relies primarily on a completely different strategy. Two pairs of musk glands, located just under the turtles' carapace, can release an olfactory secretion that earns these turtles nicknames such as "stinkpot," and "stinking jim." Similar to a skunk's release, this defensive mechanism is not dangerous, just powerfully unpleasant (though not as intense as skunk stink). So strong is this reflexive maneuver that young turtles who have not yet even hatched are capable of firing their salvo for those who venture to rob a nest of eggs. These bottom crawlers rarely leave the water except during heavy rain and to nest. Sometimes musk and mud turtles are mistaken for juvenile snappers, but snappers have long tails with a jagged, saw-toothed pattern on the top. Musk and mud turtles, by comparison, have short tails.

Mood Swings

Who among turtles is likely to avenge being handled or disturbed? Carr observed that the turtles with the more inadequate shells for defense—those that are softer or smaller and prevent a full retreat or protection—are "generally the most irascible." This rule of shell, however, cannot be slavishly followed, for although generalizations among species can be applied, many writers have commented that individual turtles may, in a word, be "moody," so that even the "confirmedly meek and pacific box turtle may have periods of aggressive, ill temper."

Gastronomic Alert!

Snapping turtles often end up in soups and stews, but do not eat box turtles! Box turtles include poisonous mushrooms in their diet that have, according to the National Audubon Society, "killed many a human who has eaten their flesh." In addition, many turtles are protected by state laws—in Georgia, 13 species of turtle are protected (including alligator snappers and box turtles).

Turtle Safety Precautions

- Wear shoes when wading.
- Do not engage snapping turtles or mud and musk turtles—or risk the danger of bites, claw-marks, or odor release. Snapping turtles, especially, are most prone to attack when handled or cornered on land.
- If you are bitten or scratched, wash the wound with disinfectant and seek medical attention.
- If a snapping turtle takes your bait or lure, it's best to cut the line rather than "tango" with the turtle.
- If you must carry a snapping turtle, carry small animals by the base of the tail with the plastron (underside) facing but well away from your leg. For common snappers, grasp them by the back of the carapace with both hands. Carrying larger specimens by the tail will eventually kill them.

COMMON SNAPPING TURTLE

Chelydra serpentina serpentina

• DANGER
The snapper has an extremely powerful bite and is much more prone to bite on land, where it is known for repeated attacks with elevated hindquarters that launch a forward lunge. Any bite, no matter how small, should be washed with disinfectant and dressed appropriately. Because snappers eat carrion (among other things) and thereby carry bacteria, seek professional medical assistance. Formidable claws may also make deep scratches.

• ABUNDANCE & RANGE
Common throughout the mid-Atlantic region, as well as in the eastern two-thirds of the U.S.

• SIZE
These turtles can range in size from 8 to 18.5 inches, but generally mature to 15 inches. Average weight is 10 to 35 pounds, but a record wild catch weighed 75 pounds.

• DESCRIPTION
A massive primordial head with powerful hooked jaws and a long tail (equal in length to the carapace) with "sawtooth" ridges dominate the appearance. Long neck with brown to yellow skin enables an impressive reach to bite. The carapace (upper shell) is oval, and tan to dark brown or almost black.

• SIMILAR SPECIES
None, since no other species in the mid-Atlantic has the snapper's distinctive, long, saw-toothed tail.

• DIET
Snapping turtles feed on snails, vegetation, frogs, toads, young waterfowl, smaller turtles, fish, mussels, crayfish, snakes, and carrion.

• REPRODUCTION
The snapping turtle emerges from its winter retreat and mates from April to November, with peak egg-laying activity in June. Females are not known for maternal protection of nests.

• HABITAT
Though they are sometimes found in brackish environments, these turtles prefer fresh water with muddy bottoms and plentiful vegetation, including shallow ponds, streams, canals, and the edge of lakes or rivers.

• TRAITS
Notoriously cranky, especially on land, the snapper is active day and night. It is a highly aquatic animal and an excellent swimmer that prefers to spend its time resting in warm shallows, buried in the mud with nostrils and eyes exposed. When disturbed in the water, it will likely try to swim away quietly rather than retaliate as it does with relentless vigor on land. While it generally hibernates from November to April in a muskrat lodge, under a mud bank overhang, or under vegetative debris, it may also be active during the colder months.

Musk and Mud Turtles

Capture a musk or mud turtle, or more probably have it appear at the end of your fishing line, and you'll likely know it. These approximately 10 species of the *Kinosternidae* family share glandular openings on each side of the body that discharge a musky secretion when the animal is threatened. Hence the nicknames "stinkpots" and "stinking-jims." Some of these turtles are aggressively defensive, too, relying on long necks and sharp beaks to express their discontent if the stink doesn't do the job.

The musk and mud family members are distinguished by small (two to five inch) carapaces, or upper shells, that are oval and smooth. (The relatively innocent razorback can reach almost 6 inches.) To delineate further among the species and subspecies, you would have to examine the plastron (lower shell) to determine its size, number of hinges, and shape of scutes (hard scales). Musk varieties have a smaller plastron, a single hinge, and squarish versus triangular pectoral scutes.

STINKPOT TURTLE
Sternotherus odoratus

• DANGER
Males, especially, are aggressive biters if handled. Long neck enables biting reach as far as the turtle's back limbs. When disturbed, this one secretes a foul-smelling, yellowish solution from two glands under the border of the carapace.

• ABUNDANCE & RANGE
Stinkpots are commonly found throughout the mid-Atlantic, with the exceptions of the southern edge of the Maryland peninsula; northern and western Pennsylvania; and northern West Virginia.

• SIZE
3 to 5.25 or more inches.

• DESCRIPTION
A smooth, highly domed, olive-brown to dark-gray carapace sometimes covered with algae has three keels (ridges down the back). On these turtles, you'll find two light stripes on the head and barbels (soft fleshy projections) on the chin and throat.

• SIMILAR SPECIES
The stinkpot resembles other musk and mud turtles, all of whom may

release a foul substance. They are most often mistaken for baby or young snapping turtles, who have long tails with sawtooth projections along the top ridge.

• DIET
These turtles feed on fish, mussels, crayfish, vegetation, carrion, and organic material found on freshwater bottoms.

• REPRODUCTION
After mating underwater, the female nests from February to June, depending on the local climate (range includes Florida to New England). Eggs hatch 9 to 12 weeks later.

• HABITAT
Stinkpots like fresh water, especially muddy-bottomed slow streams, rivers, and ponds, and prefer shallow areas for basking.

• TRAITS
These strongly aquatic creatures are often seen slowly patrolling water bottoms in search of food. They rarely leave the water, but do bask in trees because their smaller size and agile legs make climbing easier than for other species—they've been observed as high as six feet above the water reclining on a tree branch. If a turtle drops into your canoe, it is likely one of these musks or another in the musk family who was sleeping and lost its balance upon waking up to your arrival. In this instance, try to use your paddle to gently scoop or coax the animal back into the water. Aggressive behavior on your part will only give rise to more of the same from the turtle.

EASTERN MUD TURTLE
Kinosternon subrubrum subrubrum

• DANGER
The mud turtle may bite if threatened and can release a strong defensive musk secretion.

• ABUNDANCE & RANGE
Common in their range, eastern mud turtles are found in the eastern half of Virginia, Maryland, Delaware, and New Jersey.

• SIZE
Mud turtles range from 2.75 inches to 4.5+ inches.

• DESCRIPTION
The mud turtle's smooth, patternless carapace is olive to dark brown, (almost black), and its plastron is yellowish brown. Head may be spotted, streaked with yellow, or mottled.

• SIMILAR SPECIES
Striped mud and yellow mud turtles are comparable.

• DIET
Mud turtles feed on snails and insects.

• REPRODUCTION
After breeding in mid-March to May, eggs are typically laid in June in

sandy, loamy soil such as that found in alligator nests or beaver or muskrat lodges.

• HABITAT

Mud turtles prefer fresh or brackish water that is slow-moving, where they can prowl about on soft bottoms heavy with vegetation.

• TRAITS

A mud turtle's nature varies unpredictably between mild and nasty. Though aquatic, this turtle will traverse overland in search of new water sources if its present habitat dries up. It is generally active from April to October and is often found near muskrat lodges.

TOADS AND FROGS

AMPHIBIAN ASSISTANCE

Shout it from the highest toadstool: "Warts and all—especially if you don't want even more insects—you gotta love toads and frogs." These amphibian changelings of the *Anura* order are critical in helping to manage the perpetually thriving insect population—and then there's that great singing voice. With a few minor exceptions, toads and frogs are generally not harmful to humans. Dogs and cats, however, sometimes have lethal run-ins.

WARTS?

Yes and no. Yes, the surface of a toad's skin is described as "warty," but no, you can't catch warts from handling them. Warts have viral causes, and although a toad's rough body texture looks like it might be dangerous, the worst that can happen if you handle them or their smoother-skinned cousin the frog is an allergic reaction with runny eyes and nose. But if you try to eat them . . .

THEY LEAVE A REALLY BAD TASTE IN YOUR MOUTH

Toads have an enlarged pair of parotid glands situated on various locations (depending on the species) on their cranial crests. These glands secrete a poison, viscous and white, which is released into the mouths of predators. An inflamed mouth and throat, nausea, irregular heartbeat, and in some cases, death, discourage or prevent a second helping of toad. Some frogs have a similar secretion which serves the same function.

DOGGIE DOWNERS AND KITTY KILLERS

Dogs, and less frequently cats, seem to have a hard time resisting this easy prey. According to the *Journal of Venomous Animals and Toxins*, "dogs can be intoxicated biting or ingesting the toad that secretes the poison in the oral mucous of the predator. The effects of the toad venom are, mainly, cardiotoxic in nature resembling, the digitalic intoxication. In 1935, a child died in Hawaii after having ingested a toad hunted by its father in a sugar cane field. . . . chemical composition of the toad venom is very complex and varied among the species belonging to this genus. . . . The effects of the poison almost appear immediately after the accident."

An eastern american toad (Bufo a. americanus) *sounding the call of the wild. Note the poison-secreting parotid glands (the large lumps behind the eyes).*

The Colorado river toad *(Bufo alvarius),* found in extreme southern California to extreme southwest New Mexico, and the marine or "giant" toad *(Bufo marinus),* found in extreme south Texas and introduced into south Florida, are the most toxic.

Symptoms of Dangerous Toad and Pet Encounters

The degree of symptoms depends upon the amount of toxin absorbed. Basic symptoms are:

- Immediate and heavy drooling that can sometimes be foamy.
- Head shaking as though the dog or cat is trying to rid itself of a sensation.
- Crying.
- With moderate toxin ingestion, uncoordinated movement and staggering will be evident.
- In more severe situations, the animal cannot walk or stand.
- In the most extreme cases, convulsions and death can occur.

Other conditions may trigger similar symptoms, so try to ascertain whether the dog or cat has ingested a toad. A history of the pet's playing with a toad is helpful information.

Pet First Aid

1. If you know or strongly suspect that your dog or cat has been poisoned by a toad, immediately flush out its mouth with water. Rinse the animal's mouth for approximately five minutes. The use of a garden hose for continuous flow is advisable, provided you are careful not to choke or drown the animal. Extreme care should be taken that the animal does not swallow the rinse water.
2. At present, no medicines commonly found in the home are considered of any value in first aid treatment of this condition.

It is important to obtain the services of your veterinarian to give specific antidotes by injection as soon as possible, especially when there is any doubt about how severely poisoned your pet may be. Remember, too, that the smaller the dog or cat, the greater the possibility of serious toxicity. Since many toad poisonings occur in the evening or nighttime hours, call your nearest animal emergency clinic for assistance.

NO KISSING, NO KIDDING

It's true that toads and frogs do secrete fluids from their skins, and some people are allergic to these secretions. Some allergic reactions occur after skin contact, but most are brought on by mucous membrane contact. Therefore, after handling toads or frogs, it's wise not to touch your mouth, nose, or eyes until after you have washed your hands with soap.

POISON PROTECTION?

Probably because it undergoes a radical transformation, beginning life as a water-bound tadpole that drops its tail, grows legs, and then lives on land, the toad figures heavily in fairly tale and legend. One such legend is the "toadstone." This is "a stone or similar object held to have formed in the head or body of a toad often worn as a charm or an antidote to poison."

Don't bet on it.

Toad and Frog Safety Precautions

1. It is unlikely that you or your children will have adverse reactions from handling toads and frogs. However, handling generally produces stress in the animals and will likely cause them to release secretions to which you may be allergic.

2. If you do handle frogs or toads, wash your hands thoroughly before touching your nose, eyes, or mouth (and certainly before eating). This applies even if you do not think that the animal has discharged any fluid.

3. If you suspect your dog or cat has bitten or eaten a toad or a frog, rinse its mouth with water as above and rush the animal to the vet. Death can occur within 30 to 60 minutes after ingestion.

About the Listed Species: Species described below are listed both for their great abundance and/or noted toxicity, but the handling/washing caution applies to all toads and a few frogs.

AMERICAN TOAD

Bufo americanus

• DANGER

Skin secretions are irritating to mucous membranes and may prove fatal to dogs and cats, especially if the animal is ingested. Even if you think no secretions have been released, after handling an American toad, refrain from touching your eyes, nose, or mouth until you wash your hands well with soap.

• ABUNDANCE & RANGE

Abundant throughout the rest of the mid-Atlantic, the American toad is not found in northern Maryland and Delaware, nor in southern New Jersey.

• SIZE

These toads are 2 to 3 inches with a recorded maximum of more than 4.25 inches.

• DESCRIPTION

They are olive, brown, or brick red with assorted patterning in lighter colors, but may also appear almost as plain brown. Belly is usually spotted, and a light stripe may run down the middle of the back. Parotid glands do not touch the prominent cranial crest.

• SIMILAR SPECIES

American toads resemble the Fowler's toad, but the Americans have many dark markings on their chests. Woodhouse toads can also resemble the Americans, but they have plain undersides with numerous warts of similar size.

• DIET

American toads are hearty eaters, especially of insects and some other invertebrates.

• REPRODUCTION

They breed in shallow bodies of water (ditches, shallow streams, temporary pools of standing water) from March to July, leaving egg strings attached to vegetation.

• HABITAT

The American toad makes its home wherever abundant insects and moisture can be found, including domestic sites such as suburban yards, around water spigots next to houses, and in wilderness areas, including mountainous forests.

• TRAITS

This toad is generally (but not exclusively) nocturnal. It does not bite or attack, avoids contact, and is "passively aggressive" only through release of skin secretion.

EASTERN SPADEFOOT TOAD

Scaphiopus holbrookii

• DANGER

Nonlethal allergic reactions are common in humans after handling. Symptoms may include watering eyes (if you rub your eyes after handling), substantial amounts of nasal mucous discharge, and extremely powerful sneezing.

• ABUNDANCE & RANGE

The spadefoot is found throughout the mid-Atlantic, with the exceptions of western Pennsylvania, West Virginia, and along Virginia's south-central border.

• SIZE

This toad ranges from 1.75 inches to 3.25 inches.

• DESCRIPTION

Spadefoots are named for their black or dark "spades"—horny, sharp-edged extensions on each hind foot that enable the animals to burrow down vertically into loose or sandy soil. Not true toads, they lack parotid glands and are relatively smooth skinned. The eastern species has two light-colored, somewhat irregular lines that begin at the eyes and run down the back. Body color varies from olive through brown to black. Underbelly is white or gray.

• SIMILAR SPECIES

The eastern is the only spadefoot east of the Mississippi River.

• DIET

Spadefoot toads eat insects.

• REPRODUCTION

Spadefoots generally breed from March to September, and eggs appear after heavy rains, especially in temporary pools where they are attached to vegetation. Spadefoot reproduction is sometimes referred to as "explosive" because the eggs hatch within 2 days.

• HABITAT

These toads prefer loose, sandy, or gravelly soil in brushy, forested, or cultivated land where they can use their trademark "spadefoot" tool to burrow.

• TRAITS

Spadefoots are generally reclusive, remaining underground for weeks or months until a damp or rainy night summons them out to the mouths of their burrows. Their underground dwellings provide them a secure base from which to escape inhospitable weather and events, such as brushfires.

FOWLER'S/ WOODHOUSE TOAD

Bufo woodhousii fowleri

• DANGER
Humans may experience a nonlethal allergic reaction after handling that may manifest as runny eyes and nose (if you rub eyes or nose after handling). Skin secretions are an allergic agent.

• ABUNDANCE & RANGE
This toad—a subspecies of the woodhouse species—is found throughout the mid-Atlantic region, with the exception of northern Pennsylvania.

• SIZE
They range in size from 2.5 to 5 inches.

• DESCRIPTION
Gray-yellowish-brown, with a brown-spotted back, this toad's parotid glands touch the cranial bulge. Belly is usually yellowish-white but sometimes has a darkened breast spot.

• SIMILAR SPECIES
The American toad has numerous dark marks on its breast.

• DIET
They feed on insects.

• REPRODUCTION
They reproduce from March to August.

• HABITAT
This toad prefers sandy soils near water sources, such as ditches, marshes, and rain pools.

• TRAITS
Usually appears at night and is often the toad found under lights where it can easily feast on insects. Voice has been described as "like the bleat of a sheep with a cold" (Behler, 1998, p. 398).

SALAMANDERS

SOFT BODIES OF THE NIGHT

In the great crawling forward of evolution, salamanders made the transition to land locomotion and air breathing, but never completely abandoned the moisture factor they still require. By body shape alone, they sometimes resemble lizards, but lizards have scaly skin, claws, and external ear openings. Salamanders, who often sport a "fringe" of gills near the head that resembles a feather boa, can also look like eels.

Salamanders are secretive, private, nocturnal creatures who are quite content to mind their own business, often hiding under rocks and in moist leaf litter. Out of sight during the day, they are hardly more visible at night. All of them would rather beat a retreat, so there is no need to worry about accidentally stepping on one. Only a small number are poisonous or aggressive, but a few species have some defensive tools that make them wise to avoid. The most frequent point of contact with humans comes when people hook a salamander while fishing.

NO BEAUTY QUEEN OR KING

The eastern hellbenders, who can grow to a whopping record 29+ inches, are widely perceived as venomous, and many fishermen sacrifice gear rather than unhook them. This bit of folklore may stem from the fact that hellbenders are not going to win any beauty pageants, even among salamanders. In truth, though, they are completely harmless, so the sensible and humane thing to do is to unhook and release them. This may prove somewhat difficult because hellbenders are exceedingly slimy.

BITING BACK

A handful of salamanders are biters. You should always take antiseptic measures with any bite, and although these wounds might hurt, salamanders will not harm you unless you get an infection. Salamanders often live under rocks in or near streams, so you can expect their mouths might carry some bacteria (although not as much as ours).

"STUCK ON YOU"

A couple of other species can secrete a sticky substance that is sometimes irritating to skin or nearly impossible to get off your hands. Like superglue, the stuff just has to wear off.

TWO-TOED AMPHIUMA

Amphiuma means

• DANGER

These salamanders are nonvenomous, but they are fierce biters.

• ABUNDANCE & RANGE

In the mid-Atlantic region, they are found only in the southeastern corner of Virginia.

• SIZE

They range in size from 14.5 to 45+ inches, but mature size is more commonly 30 inches.

• DESCRIPTION

These salamanders are eel-like and gray or grayish brown with two pairs of very small, feeble legs, each with two toes.

• SIMILAR SPECIES

They resemble nothing else in the region.

• DIET

They feed on crayfish, worms, insects, mollusks, frogs, fish, and small snakes.

• REPRODUCTION

They lay eggs from June to July. The female lays coiled around the 200 or so eggs during the five-month incubation period. Born with gills that soon disappear, hatchlings are about 2 inches long.

• HABITAT

Drainage ditches and the shallows of swamps, bayous, rice fields, streams, ponds, and the like.

• TRAITS

Nocturnal and nasty-tempered, two-toed amphiumas are carnivorous. If the weather is wet enough, they may leave the water temporarily to move overland. The amphiuma establishes lairs in mud or bottom debris where it burrows with only its head protruding so as to capture food. The one- and three-toed varieties seem not to have the bad reputation of biting as does the two-toed species.

SLIMY SALAMANDER
Plethodon glutinosus

SUBSPECIES:

Atlantic coast slimy salamander
Plethodon chlorobryonis
White-spotted slimy salamander
Plethodon cylindraceus
Northern slimy salamander
Plethodon glutinosus

• DANGER

This salamander is non-threatening, but its skin glands secrete a gluey substance that is so adhesive it generally has to just wear off.

• ABUNDANCE & RANGE

The Atlantic coast subspecies is found in southeastern Virginia; the white-spotted subspecies is found in the remainder of Virginia; and the northern subspecies is found in the rest of the mid-Atlantic, with the exception of Maryland and southern Delaware.

• SIZE

4.5 to 8+ inches.

• DESCRIPTION

The slimy salamander is shiny black with large light spots (yellow, gray, or white) on the sides and scattered flecks of similar color on the head. Dorsum (upper surface) is generally black. The species is actually comprised of 13 genetically distinct subspecies (the three mid-Atlantic subspecies are named above) that are virtually undistinguishable except to the well-trained eye.

• SIMILAR SPECIES

The placement of spots distinguishes this salamander from the few other similar dark-colored salamanders in the mid-Atlantic region.

• DIET

It feeds on invertebrates of the forest floor such as worms, snails, and slugs.

• REPRODUCTION

Females guard nests of eggs laid in underground retreats. Larvae hatch in late summer.

• HABITAT

This salamander is found in woodland forests to 5,500 feet, cave entrances, moist ravines or hillsides, and wooded flood plains.

• TRAITS

Shy and reclusive, the slimy salamander is nocturnal and active year-round in the warmer climates, and it hunts for prey on the forest floor after rain.

INSECTS & ARACHNIDS

MORE BUZZ THAN BITE

This is the deadliest chapter. If you are going to have a fatal or life-threatening encounter with another (non-human) creature, it will likely be with an insect or an arachnid, or the disease organisms they carry. Some of this probability derives from the sheer number of these creatures. In the U.S., there are approximately 91,000 described species of insects, plus at least 71,000 undescribed species. What does this mean in terms of insect proximity? "A whole lotta crawlin,' creepin,' and flyin' on." Soil samples in North Carolina five inches deep yielded an estimated 124 million animals per acre. Similar studies in Pennsylvania produced an estimated 425 million animals per acre. If you walk through a grassy field, you will likely be sharing the great outdoors with literally thousands of arachnids, mostly spiders, which, we hasten to add, almost definitely will not harm you.

Before the idea of these creepy crawlies overwhelms you, keep in mind several things. The vast majority of these creatures are not only beneficial to life on earth—they are absolutely essential to it. Imagine a planet without "sanitary engineer" insects to break down the bodies of all the dead or to process fecal matter back into the food chain. A world without the pollination of fruits, vegetables, nuts, and flowers would be a barren wasteland indeed. As the bee said to the plant, "Honey, you need me. Without me you'd lose your bloomers." And without spiders and other predatory insects, you would have to rely more on pesticides to keep other insects in their place—hardly a healthy solution in the long run.

The primary thing to remember is that only a tiny handful of these insects and arachnids are dangerous to humans. Estimates say that in the U.S., about 50 to 100 people die each year from insect stings and arachnid bites (at least three to four times more than from snakebites). The great bulk of major episodes involve cases of anaphylactic shock—an allergic reaction to a sting that is immediately treatable *if* you know you are at risk, and some 1 to 2 million Americans are. True, there are some very dangerous illnesses carried by insects, and we will examine these. Spider and tick bites and scorpion stings are nothing to disregard either. By and large nationwide, however, if you minimize your exposure to bees, wasps, fire ants, ticks, mosquitoes, a very few spiders, and scorpions, your chances of a dangerous encounter are very, very small.

WHAT ARE INSECTS AND ARACHNIDS?

Creatures from the *Insecta* and *Arachnida* classes are all arthropods, meaning they belong to the phylum of creatures that have jointed legs and a hard exoskeleton that protects their organs and gives their bodies shape. Despite their myriad appearances, adult insects have three pairs of jointed legs and three body parts (head, thorax, and abdomen). On insect heads you'll find their eyes (often of the compound type), a pair of antennae, and mouth parts. The thorax has three segments, each with its own pair of legs. Wings, if present, will be found on segments two or three. The abdomen, which does not usually have appendages, has a hind tip called the terminalia. This is where the insect has its egg-laying, mating, or defensive equipment. The venomous stingers of wasps and bees, for example, are found here. Other insect groups include mosquitoes, black flies, biting midges, and lice.

Arachnids, on the other hand, have four pairs of legs, no antennae, and only two body sections because (with a few exceptions) their head and thorax are joined into one form called the cephalothorax. Arachnids include spiders, scorpions, ticks, and mites.

To the average person, if a creature crawls on more than four legs, it's an insect. But as we mentioned earlier, insects are just one of the major types of arthropods; arachnids are the other. Arachnids include spiders, ticks, mites, and scorpions, but often when people speak of arachnids, they are generally referring to spiders, including tarantulas. Spiders are the

largest group of arachnids, so it is fitting that the Greek word for spider, "arachne," gives the gang its name. Arachne was a young girl who bested the goddess Athena in a weaving contest. After Athena tore the winning work into pieces, Arachne hanged herself in despair. Athena loosed the rope and saved her life, but the rope was changed into a cobweb and Arachne became a spider.

Like snakes, spiders sometimes generate fear (in this case, arachnophobia) in people, a fear which is quite real, but is, as you will see, disproportionate

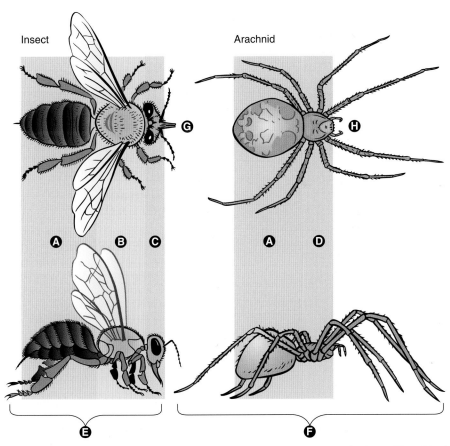

Both insects and arachnids have an abdomen **(A)**. *Insects have two more segments: the thorax* **(B)** *and head* **(C)**, *whereas in arachnids the two are fused into the cephalothorax* **(D)**. *The most visible difference is that insects have six legs* **(E)** *while arachnids have eight legs* **(F)**. *Lastly, insects have two antennae and two compound eyes* **(G)**, *while arachnids have two chelicerae and (usually) eight simple eyes* **(H)**.

to the dangers involved. Only one kind of spider in the mid-Atlantic can cause you serious harm. If you shudder at spiders, though, you are not alone. Remember, for the little miss in the Mother Goose rhyme, "all it took was just one look."

Little Miss Muffet,
sat on a tuffet,
Eating her curds and whey;
Along came a spider,
who sat down beside her
And frightened Miss Muffet away.

BEES AND WASPS

In the scientific world, these creatures are grouped in the order *Hymenoptera*. The name refers to their "membrane wings" because all of these insects have two pairs of clear, window-like wings, and the females have an abdomen that ends in an egg-laying organ and/or a stinger. Ants are also in this group because at a certain stage of life they do have wings, at which point they are often mistaken for termites. Many ants have stingers, too, and we'll talk about the most potent species later in this chapter. Some of these creatures can give you a serious problem, but generally only if you are prone to anaphylactic shock (see more below on this medical emergency condition) or if you provoke multiple stings. If that happens, then pardon us, but they have the wings, and you need the prayer.

OH SO SOCIAL AND SOLITARY

There is another useful way to think about *Hymenoptera*: Are they social or solitary spirits? This point fascinates scientists because the *Hymenoptera* fill the spectrum. Honeybees, famous for their organized social structure, are at one extreme. At this end of the scale, you'll also find the bumblebees and the true wasps, who include hornets and yellow jackets in their family. These insects are considered to be "eusocial," meaning truly social.

Eusocial insects exhibit both cooperation in division of labor and reproduction expressed within overlapping generations. For example, in honeybees there is a sharp division between the sterile caste of female soldiers and workers and the reproductive caste comprised of the queen and her male drones. In executing her duties, a soldier will defend the nest by spraying, stinging, or biting intruders, and a worker will enhance the nest, care for the eggs, larvae, pupae, and queen, and forage for food. Male drones live only long enough to fertilize the potential millions of eggs laid by the queen. This famous social structure has an extra dimension to it: the ultimate self-sacrifice of life the soldiers make to defend the nest or colony so that the gene pool survives. Some people have called this cooperative behavior "biological altruism." What this means is that eusocial insects have absolutely no qualms about attacking you in defense of their nest, even if it means certain death for them. They also have powerful venom to achieve their purposes.

But not all *Hymenoptera* are eusocial. At the other end of the spectrum are the solitary species such as carpenter bees (the big ones that bore holes in your garage roof supports); sweat bees (the small ones that sting you mildly when you are working to repair the garage roof); and the mud or dirt daubers of the digger wasp family (the mysterious ones you wonder about that have built those mud tubes on your garage walls). It's a little confusing, we know. It would be simpler if all "bees" and "wasps" were eusocial and that was that, but nature just won't cooperate that way. Think of it as a big family where some of the brothers and sisters are nurses and some are writers. Their daily lives and contributions are quite different, but the individuals are closely related, and they may even resemble each other physically.

The reason all of this matters is that in contrast to the eusocial insects who have the powerful stinging venom, the sting of the solitary bees and wasps is usually a much less powerful and less painful sting. Scientists disagree on this distinction however, perhaps because pain is a very relative experience. To avoid all pain, you want to studiously avoid all the species described in this section.

WHAT ARE WE TALKING ABOUT HERE?

We'll describe the individual eusocial and solitary *Hymenoptera* you're likely to encounter in the species profiles later in this chapter, but in the main when we talk about "bees" (including hornets and yellow jackets) here, we'll be generally addressing the powerful eusocial species whose stings you especially want to avoid. We will specify when we are talking exclusively about honeybees or bumblebees or yellow jackets, for example, but when we just say "bee" or "bees" you can apply that to mean eusocial insects in general.

HOW BEES STING

Soldier bees, all female, will sting you in defense of the nest with their modified ovipositors (egg-laying apparatus) located on the end of the abdomen. In honeybees, that sting is barbed in such a way that once it penetrates, say, the skin of a human, the bee cannot extract it. The honeybee soldier must pull away, leaving her sting and venom sac in you (along with some of her internal organs). With much of her abdomen then ripped away, she is destined to die. Meanwhile, her stinger continues to inject venom into you, the presumed attacker, even after the soldier has retreated. No matter whether the bee has left her stinger in you or not, something even more powerful has happened. She has also sent a chemical telegram to her cohorts that says, "Come and sting the daylights out of this aggressor right now, and here's a map of how to reach him!"

HOW SOME BEES COMMUNICATE: DANCING, SMELLING, AND BELLY-RUBBING

Communication among the eusocial insects involves a complex and powerful network of behaviors and adaptations differently applied to various situations. To give you an example of the forces at work, let's look at food-gathering communication. Once again, the honeybees have elevated this exceptional and mysterious connective ability literally to an art form: they dance. The round or circle dance indicates nectar and pollen supplies within 80 feet. Other honeybees read the dance by sensing air vibrations and touching the dancer's antennae. In the even more remarkable waggle dance, the dancer indicates food sources more than 320 feet away from the nest by dancing a figure-8 shape that indicates distance and direction relative to the position of the sun. In the vibration dance, a worker vibrates its belly while in contact with other honeybees. In this way, honeybees are rallied to the waggle dance to increase food foraging.

Other bees have their own specialized means of transmitting messages. For example, a second and extremely powerful communication channel for bees is the distribution of pheromones, species-specific chemicals released to stimulate a specific behavioral or physiological response. These pheromones are invisible and linger in the air long enough to get the job done. So, for example, when a bee is injured, she releases pheromones to summon the troops to pick up the fight. Because of the tightly woven social structure within the hive, you can be sure that more soldiers will respond to her call—even if it means their deaths, too, in defense of the nest.

A honeybee stinger is barbed, and the bee cannot extract the stinger once it is used **(1)**. *After a soldier bee has retreated, the stinger, venom sac, and some internal organs remain behind* **(2)**. *The stinger continues pumping venom and sending out a chemical alarm to other bees; the bee that left its stinger eventually dies.*

What to Do if You Are Stung by a Bee

If you only have one or just a few insects on you, try to remain calm and brush them from your skin promptly with deliberate movements to prevent additional stings. Then, quietly and immediately leave the area.

Next, look for a stinger that resembles a small wood splinter still embedded at the point of attack. If you see one, you were stung once by a honeybee.

- Remove the stinger by scraping it away with a fingernail, a knife, a credit card, etc. If you do this within 30 seconds, you will reduce the impact of the sting. Even a few seconds either way can make a big difference. Contrary to conventional advice, it has been shown that grasping the stinger does not increase the venom dose.
- Proceed as below.

Other bees and wasps do not leave their stingers. If no stinger is present, do the following:

- Wash the wound with soap and water and apply an antiseptic.
- Apply a cold compress. Ice should help reduce the swelling, though it should not be applied directly to skin.
- Elevate the affected arm or leg and apply ice or a cold compress to reduce swelling and pain.
- Pain may be reduced by the application of a paste (poultice) of meat tenderizer and water.
- Use topical steroid ointments or oral antihistamines to relieve itching.
- For stings in the mouth or throat, suck on ice and seek medical attention right away.
- If blisters form, gently clean them with soap and water to prevent secondary infections; do not break blisters.
- See your doctor if swelling progresses or if the sting site seems infected.

HIVE JIVE: WHEN ARE THEY JUMPIN'?

In their near-perfect progression toward survival, bees have predictable cycles of activity based on the time of year. Typically, the queen spends the winter in the hive with a small staff of workers, and they begin expanding the existing colony or building a new one in the spring. In spring, swarms may be observed as the colony searches for a new location to live as new queens and young workers take flight from old crowded hives with younger workers in search of the right spot. As the queen tires, the swarm lands on something, such as a tree branch, where the colony can stay huddled together, protecting her while a few scout bees continue the search. Because a swarm is in essence a group of homeless bees, they are less protective than they might be about the hive, so they are not as likely to sting because they do not feel as defensive. Remember, though, that protection of the queen is always an issue. As for making the bees leave, it is best to let them stay put. They will probably move on to a more out-of-the-way place to secure a nest in a day or two.

Once the new location is selected, nest building and egg laying begins. The queen's body may hold millions of eggs, and she will likely lay most of these in her lifetime. These eggs will be fertilized by the male drones while the female workers and soldiers attend to nest building, caring for the hive and its young, and food production. Drones are most numerous during the summer, but as food becomes scarce toward the fall, the workers kill them by stinging and remove them from the hive. Fall is another season when swarming may occur because the hive becomes too large. Winter activity in the hive depends on the food supply. On warmer winter days, workers may leave the hive in search of early blooming flowers.

The bottom line on the bee calendar is this: Do not assume that you cannot be stung in the winter. It is true that your risk is diminished compared to summer's frequent activity, but you can be stung at any time of year.

Experienced beekeepers have also noted that bees are in better moods on bright, sunny days. Like us, they seem to be more moody and irritable on rainy, cooler days.

Bees settle down into the hive at night after a hard day's work, but they can certainly be disturbed after dark; so if you know of a nest, treat it with respect at all times.

"WHERE THE BEES ARE . . ."

Our bee friends can be found in many types of habitats: beneath stones and wood; in the ground; near water; in living wood and rotting wood; and, of course, near flowering plants and at picnics, especially if soft drinks, sweets, or beer are on the menu. Picture a bear gouging for honey with its paw stuck in an old log or in the hollow of a tree—that's what you *don't* want to do. Nor do you want to walk barefoot in blooming clover, as appealing as that sounds.

A rule of thumb is that the activity of the hive is a private affair, so be prepared to be surprised.

These insects require and are adept at seeking shelter, so they may want to "freeload" on you—setting up their residence in your garage, for example. Wasp and hornet nests suspended from house eaves and from tree branches are obvious places to avoid. Should you locate one around your house, call your county agricultural extension agent for advice on how to remove it. Several sprays are commercially available to kill the insects, but should you decide to eliminate them yourself, use extreme caution. Many people have incurred multiple stings by provoking the anger of the whole hive. Likewise, children anger them by throwing rocks at hives.

HOW DO BEES FLY?

Honeybees "make a beeline." Other eusocial and solitary bees and wasps tend to exhibit loopy flight patterns.

WHY THEY STING YOU

Bees and their close kin—we'll talk about ants shortly—are not aggressive by nature. While this may be hard to believe if you've been stung, try to remember what you were doing that triggered the insects' defensive response.

For example, Geneva tells this story: "It was midday, probably in late July or August. It was really hot outside, but rain was coming in and I wanted to get the grass cut that day. I cranked up the mower. It was not exactly a whisper-jet model, but none of them are. I'd been mowing my yard for about an hour, so I was pretty sweaty. All of a sudden, yellow jackets were flying all around me and stinging me like fire! Where had they come from? I had no idea! I started trying to swat them off me, and just by instinct I ran from where I was being stung. I think I even took off my clothes right there in the neighborhood to get them off me!"

What happened? Geneva had unwittingly called out the cavalry. To the yellow jackets, whose nest was underground, the lawnmower sounded like the equivalent of a "chopper" squadron suddenly appearing right over your house— ready to open fire, for all you know. In short, it angered the insects mightily. Their pheromone alarm was set off, and of course Geneva's sweat didn't calm the defenders down, nor did the fact that she started swatting at them. (Not swatting while being stung takes a supreme amount of will, we might add.) The time of day and year played a part, too. Already very active, the yellow jackets were certain to respond at midday. Because it was later in the summer, the yellow jackets were naturally more aggressive.

In another case, again in late summer, a car pulled into a gravel driveway next to a yellow jacket nest only five feet away. A young Bible salesman stepped out, inadvertently of course, where yellow jackets had their nest in the ground. Whether it was the engine sound, his footfall, or a combination of these factors, the yellow jackets set out after him. He started running and was picked up down the street by the car driver, but he suffered multiple stings before he could escape.

In both cases, while the insects seemed like the aggressors, in fact they were only protecting the thing they care most about in life: their extended and extensive family.

More Stinging Stories

Yellow jackets are especially menacing because they often build their paper nests underground, and it's common to invoke their wrath without any foreknowledge. Hornets, on the other hand, are wasps that build their nests, also of paper, above ground where you can generally see them. Nevertheless, the story below indicates how easy it is to get into trouble with them, and one way you might get out of it.

Juanita has been an outdoorswoman her whole life. She grew up in the panhandle of Florida in the 1940s and 1950s when it teemed with wildlife, uncrowded by the people who are now discovering its wondrous beauty. Her daddy took her on his fishing expeditions where he would gently prod the snakes resting in the trees with his boat paddle "just to see which way they'd fall—in the boat or out of it." Juanita dryly adds, "I developed a strong prayer life early on." When Juanita was teaching paddling, she cautioned people that there are two primary dangers on the river: the white-water rapids and the

Wasps and hornets have a variety of homes: hornets create large enclosed nests **(A)**, *paper wasps create multicelled structures* **(B)**, *mud daubers make nests of parallel mud tubes* **(C)**, *and yellow jackets have their nests underground or in tree stumps* **(D)**.

hornet nests in the overhanging tree branches. She tells this story:

"I had a young woman in the front of my canoe who was just learning to paddle. We had eddied out on the Hiwassee River for a breather, and even though I had given this group of students my standard warnings, she reached up to grip a tree branch without looking to see that it housed a hornet's nest. I saw what was about to happen, but before I could stop her she had inadvertently rattled their nest by grasping the branch. Out they came! Right on time and mad as you-know-what. I yelled to her, "Dive in the water and swim away now! I'll pick you up in the canoe. Do it!" The novice took the advice and plunged in the river. Staying above water in the canoe, Juanita sustained a few stings, but she saved the girl from that pain because the hornets can't dive into the water to sting.

One lesson of this story is that if it is an option to submerge yourself safely in water and swim away from the scene of the attack, by all means do so. When you come up for air, do so briefly and re-submerge as soon as possible so the insects won't be able to sting your face and neck. Try to swim at least five yards away if you can, more if possible, to slip away from their defensive anger.

WHO'S GOT THE WORST TEMPER?

The cliche "mad as a hornet" tops the list, but not all hornets are equally defensive. Yellow jackets are probably tied with them for first place. Other paper wasps are probably somewhat more tolerant of the kinds of minor disturbances created by people than are hornets or yellow jackets. When it comes to bees, it depends on the strain. So really, it makes the best sense to treat all these insects with equal respect.

How Much Does a Sting Hurt?

Spider wasp (western U.S.)	4	Harvester ant	3
Paper wasp	0–3	Baldfaced hornet	2
Hornet	2	Yellow jacket	2
Imported fire ant	2	Honeybee	2
Bumblebee	2	Velvet ant	1–2
Sweat bee★	0–1		

0   No pain. The result of encounters with insects whose stingers are too small or weak to penetrate human skin.

1   Pain so slight as to constitute no real deterrent. Sting is perceived, but most people do not say it "hurts."

2   Painful. The "great mass of painful stings."

3   Sharply and seriously painful. Differentiated from level 2 pain by the production of, apart from any surprise or fear, loud cries, groans, and/or long preoccupation with the pain.

4   Traumatically painful. Often medically serious events with strong physical reactions and long-lasting pain.

★   The sweat bee was not part of this survey, but is included here because it is frequently encountered.

The relative pain scale above was adapted from "A Pain Scale for Bee, Wasp, and Ant Stings," a scientific paper by Christopher K. Starr, ("A Simple Pain Scale for Field Comparison of Hymenopteran Stings," Journal of Entomological Science, vol. 20, no.2:225-31, published by the Georgia Entomological Society.)

Africanized Honeybees: Are They "Killers"?

This species deserves special attention in the personality profiles department primarily because it has gotten so much attention in the media, some of it a scary exaggeration. African honeybees were imported to Brazil in 1956 to enhance honey production in the tropics. Some of these bees escaped into the wild and have gradually moved towards North America. These so-called "killer bees" really are more aggressive than the typical European honeybees widely kept for honey production.

How did the African bees develop their contentious style? The squarely scientific *American Insects: A Handbook of the Insects of America North of Mexico* (Second Edition) by Ross H. Arnett, Jr. explains the collaborative origin of the African bee's legendary aggression:

. . . the so-called African Bee needs explanation. In Africa there is an interesting triumvirate: a bird, the honey bee, and man. The bird is the honeyguide, a robin-sized relative of the woodpeckers. It is a cuckoo-type bird that parasitizes the nests of other birds, but it also has an appetite for beeswax. When these birds find a wild beehive, they fly to the nearest native village and set up such a racket that the villagers realize that they are being directed to a honey store. They follow the bird, smoke out the bees, and gather the honey. The birds then receive a generous supply of wax for their efforts. This kind of cooperation has been going on for thousands of years; no one knows how long, but long enough for the bees to have developed a great "hatred" for man, "hate" being expressed in the form of a genetic change, through selection, that makes them unusually aggressive (for bees) if their hive is approached. (Arnett, 2000, p. 610)

As the African and European honeybees have interbred, the African's temperament seems to have been moderated, while the disease resistance, work ethic, and high honey output of the Africanized strain remains intact in the hybrid. The honey in your house now might well be the product of these two intermingling. The Africanized bee defends its nest, to be sure, but the notion of a moving swarm hovering over the landscape, just looking for a cow or a child to sting to death is a gross exaggeration. Of course, if you are allergic to bee stings, or if you tie or pen your dogs near a known nest, the danger is much greater. It is also worth noting, however, that the venom of this hybrid strain is no stronger than that of the average domestic honeybee.

The "bravo bees," as some beekeepers call them, are found in Texas and the southwest. Their "killer bee" name is an exaggeration that makes for good press. The fact is, it isn't the type of sting you receive that determines the severity. It's the number of stings you receive, where they are located on your body, and especially your own immunological reaction.

ANAPHYLACTIC SHOCK: A LIFE AND DEATH SITUATION

The majority of insect bite or sting cases that result in fatal or major medical episodes are cases involving anaphylactic shock. This is a form of allergic reaction.

Allergic reactions to stings range from mild to severe. When the reaction is massive and immediate it is called "anaphylaxis," which is a life-threatening situation. These reactions result from the body's release of antibodies to combat the sting venom. Severe allergic reactions occur when the body overproduces these antibodies, and some medical authorities hold that subsequent stings tend to produce increasingly more severe allergic reactions in

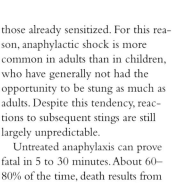

those already sensitized. For this reason, anaphylactic shock is more common in adults than in children, who have generally not had the opportunity to be stung as much as adults. Despite this tendency, reactions to subsequent stings are still largely unpredictable.

Untreated anaphylaxis can prove fatal in 5 to 30 minutes. About 60–80% of the time, death results from an inability to breathe due to swollen airways that prevent air flow to the lungs. Other deaths are triggered when blood vessels dilate or expand so much that blood flow to vital organs is reduced to fatal levels.

Severity of the sting can depend on the location. Wounds on the neck can affect breathing, and swallowing a yellow jacket, for example (who craves the sugar in your soft drinks) can result in a sting inside your throat that can cause strangulation. (For a close call of this type of episode, see "Sweet Sugar" below.)

According to the National Jewish Medical and Research Center's "Lung Line," if you are at the extreme end of the insect venom sensitivity scale, any insect bite or sting can trigger an allergic reaction that may result in anaphylactic shock. This includes the less powerful sting of solitary insects such as sweat bees.

Symptoms of Anaphylactic Shock

After an insect sting, watch for these conditions:

- Soreness and swelling not only at the sight of the sting, but also on other parts of the body.
- Fever and/or chills.
- Joint or muscle pain.
- Sneezing, coughing, or wheezing.
- Shortness of breath.
- Tightness and swelling in the throat.

- Tightness in the chest.
- Severe itching, burning, rash, or hives on the skin beyond the sting area.
- Swelling of face, tongue, mouth, or lymph glands.
- Blue skin color around lips, mouth, and fingernails.
- Dizziness or light-headedness.
- Stomach cramps, nausea, and vomiting.
- Unconsciousness.

Anaphylactic shock is a severe medical emergency, and must be treated immediately with epenephrine, a form of adrenaline. This drug works by opening up airways, causing blood vessels to constrict, and forcing the heart to beat with more vigor.

You can get a "bee sting kit" with antihistamine tablets, alcohol swabs, and a pre-loaded syringe with epinephrine by prescription from your doctor, that is to say, *in advance of the medical emergency*. Do not expect to drive to the drugstore and purchase one at the point of need. The cost of a kit runs about $40 to $45.

Learn how to self-administer the epinephrine according to your doctor's instructions, and replace the device before the clearly labeled expiration date. The shelf life of a kit is about a year, but the fine print in the kit will tell you that if the epinephrine has turned an amber color, it's time to replace it.

Remember that injectable epinephrine is rescue medication only, and you must still have someone take you to an emergency room immediately if you are stung. Additional medical treatment may be necessary. Those with severe allergies may want to consider wearing a special bracelet or necklace that identifies the wearer as having severe allergies to insect stings and bites and which supplies other important medical information.

The Buzz Is: Take the Bee Sting Kit with You!

You are at risk for anaphylactic shock if you have increasingly more pronounced reaction to insect stings over time. If this is the case, get an insect sting kit and make it second nature to have it readily available. This especially applies if you regularly walk, hike, horseback ride, bike, or camp where epinephrine is more than five minutes away—which means just about everywhere except the hospital. Insect sting kits come with a belt clip to make them easier to take along.

The recommended storage temperature for epinephrine is 59–86° Fahrenheit, so keeping one in the glove compartment of your car is not a good solution, especially in the summer when your risk of stings is highest. If you have one handy, it may really prove worth the hassle one day, so put one in your pack, or on your saddle or bike, if not on your belt.

Long-Term Prevention of Anaphylactic Shock

If you have a severe allergy to insect venom and are concerned because you spend a great deal of time outdoors, consider receiving insect venom immunotherapy, a highly effective vaccination program that actually prevents future allergic sting reactions in 97% of treated patients. During immunotherapy, the allergist administers gradually stronger doses of venom extract every few weeks over a period of three to five years. This helps the patient's immune system to become more and more resistant to future insect stings. Your allergist can provide you with the proper tests and screening for this type of treatment.

TO "BEE" STUNG OR NOT TO "BEE" STUNG

There are several things you can do to reduce your risk of being stung by all types of bees and wasps:

- Do wear white or light-colored clothing with a smooth finish. Hunters, for example, should opt for lighter-colored camouflage.
- Do wear closed-toe shoes outdoors and avoid going barefoot.
- Do avoid loose-fitting garments that can trap insects between material and skin.
- Do check your property regularly for bee and wasp colonies. Honeybees, for example (especially Africanized honeybees that are now found in Texas and in parts of the southwest) nest in a wide variety of places. Check animal burrows, water meter boxes, loose building siding, overturned flowerpots, trees, and shrubs.
- Do keep pets and children indoors when using weed trimmers, hedge clippers, tractor power mowers, chain saws, etc. Attacks frequently occur when a person is mowing the lawn or pruning shrubs and inadvertently strikes a nest that may be above ground (bees, wasps, and hornets) or below ground (yellow jackets).
- Do avoid excessive motion when near a colony. Bees are much more likely to respond to an object in motion than a stationary one.
- Do not wear leather, which is reportedly particularly irritating to bees, wasps, hornets, and yellow jackets.
- Do not wear brightly colored, dark, rough, or wooly material.
- Do not wear perfumes, lotions (including sunscreen), hair sprays, and other odorous substances.

- Do not pen, tie, or tether animals near beehives or nests.
- Do not leave sweet foods or beverages (including diet or sugar-free drinks) in exposed areas as the sugary content will attract stinging insects. (See the "Sweet Sugar" story below.) Avoid garbage collection areas for this same reason. Such insects make no distinction for "diet" drinks.

"Sweet Sugar"

When you think about it, it's obvious that eusocial and solitary bees and wasps have a sweet tooth—they're nectar-bound. Here's an account from insecticide manufacturer RESCUE®'s website "Yellow Jacket Horror Stories" contest that will make you think twice as you slurp your own sugary concoction in the summer.

I was recently stung [by a yellow jacket in August] in the back of the mouth after picking up my soda can. I will never forget this experience and hope no one else ever has to go through it either. I was very worried about hearing cases of allergic reactions and what could happen to me. I tried to immediately spit the unknown substance out, but it was too late. The bugger had already stung me. Immediately, there was a rush of stinging in my mouth. I tried to use cold water to dilute the poisonous potion, but it was too late. I was surprised that there was nothing I could do. I thought to myself, 'Boy, what a stupid thing to do, leave a can of Coke and then come back 15 minutes later to get stung.'

A few years earlier, my boy Robby had been stung by a bee on the lower lip, and it swelled up quickly. We had to rush him to Doctors on Duty because he had an allergic reaction. I thought that this could have been my turn, but I was lucky. The back of my throat became sore immediately. It became very hard to swallow, like a sore throat can be when you have a bad cold.

I tried cold ice water on the back of my throat, tipping my head back, but it only felt good when I left it there, and the pain came back when I swallowed the water. I tried to take Advil, 4 tablets, 1,000 mgs, and started to feel a little better, but still was very uncomfortable when I swallowed. A couple of hours later, still no relief. I thought at this time I was through the allergic stage, and only had to put up with the pain when I swallowed. It was about 9:30 p.m., so I decided to go to bed early. The pain was still present, and I was restless and couldn't fall off to sleep because I was worried that I would swell up more and lose my breathing. I arose from the bed an hour later and found some Benadryl Elixir, and immediately took three teaspoons full and then sat up a few minutes with my family. I went back to bed around 11 p.m., but I still was feeling the wrath of the yellow jacket sting. I finally fell asleep 30 minutes later, but tossed and turned all night, waking up every hour or so.

The next morning, about 5 a.m., I still was swollen, and could not swallow without pain. I was surprised that the pain did not go away overnight. I took 3 more Advils and grabbed a cup of coffee and headed out to work. I was thinking about staying home, but I knew I had to go to work and follow up on a hot job. I tried to eat a piece of fruit, a pear, and my throat felt good when the cool fruit touched it. By noon, the swelling had subsided, and I was getting back to normal. I will never forget this ordeal and hope no one experiences what I went through.

I would like to recommend to everyone out there who knows that there are yellow jackets hovering around, please do not allow yourself or your friends to drink soda pop out of a can!!!!!

Have them put it in a glass or keep their thumb over the can's opening when they are not drinking. Please be aware of what I went through and protect yourself as well as your loved ones.

Don't Sweat It

Here's another way to avoid stings: Bees also get agitated by perspiration odor. This seems to support the thinking of long-time, expert beekeeper, L.L. Lanier of Wewahitchka, Florida, who told us that bees can tell when you are afraid because you emit an odor of fear that they can detect. It signals to them that an aggressive confrontation is about to begin, so they sting you in advance of the expected attack. While we have not found scientific reporting *per se* to support this theory, it certainly does follow with what we know about pheromones and insects: they use invisible chemical signals to communicate for food gathering, mating, and defense.

A note about sweat bees: Although there are 502 species of *Halicitidae* in the U.S., only about 12 of these are attracted to human sweat. These sweat bees will sting if they are pressed by clothing or trapped in the bend of an arm or a leg, but their sting is not usually very painful and triggers only minor reactions in normally sensitive individuals. However, in extremely sensitive individuals, the sweat bee sting can trigger anaphylactic shock.

Don't Swat It

Bottom line: Keep your cool around bees, wasps, yellow jackets, and the like. They can detect motion much faster than we can and will most likely read it as an aggressive gesture. When they are simply "buzzing" around you (not stinging), resist the temptation to swat at them. The best defense is to remain motionless or walk away slowly. If just one or a few start to sting you, protect your face with your hands while you walk away, because these insects prefer to sting you here if they can. If necessary and possible, lie still with your face down on the ground.

Lunch on the Deck on a Late Summer Day

It's September and you know that cold weather will come before too long. The desire to have lunch on the unscreened deck is irresistible. You make a sandwich and head out with a cold drink. In about 60 seconds, the bees or wasps have arrived to share in your midday repast. This is the perfect situation to exercise your good judgment. You can:

- Ignore them, which means no swatting, sweating, cursing, or panic. You should, of course, take care not to accidentally ingest one of those flying friends.
- Just give it up and go back inside. This is the option to take if you or your guests cannot resist swatting at them.
- Get the insecticide spray and go to work. This is not really a good option because you are outside in their world offering the natural attraction of food. In most cases, even if you kill some *Hymenopterans* with spray, others will be right along behind them.

Danger in Numbers: Make a Run for It!

Humans have used swarms of bees positively and negatively throughout history. As far back as Exodus, which talks about sending hornets to drive out Hivites, Canaanites, and Hittites, people have used bees' proclivity to sting humans and animals ferociously, painfully, and when anatomically possible, repeatedly. Hives were often kept behind the fortified wall of medieval cities and hurled from walls onto the invading enemy, a technique that helped King Henry I of France rout the Duke of Lorraine when his panicked, stung horses led an ignominious and rapid retreat.

If you happen to engage the wrath of a swarm of bees, yellow jackets, or hornets, run as far and fast as you can

away from the hive, nest, or whatever the insects were protecting. Do not flail or swing your arms, as this may further annoy them.

You can expect to be chased, but not far. Estimates range from 25 to 100 yards for species except the Africanized honeybee, or so-called "killer" bee, who will likely chase you farther than other species. Just keep running. The worst-case reports are of Africanized bees chasing folks for a quarter mile, but we can only pray that this is folktale tall-telling. It is a known fact, however that these bees, found largely in the southwest and Texas, will flat come after you and don't want to quit the race. Now there's yet another reason to wear comfortable shoes!

Get to shelter or the closest house or car as quickly as possible. Don't worry if a few bees become trapped in your home. If several bees follow you into your car, drive about a quarter of a mile, lower the windows, and let the bees out of the car.

If for some reason you cannot run, you can follow Juanita's course of action. One fall day she was out with a friend who was using a metal detector to search for lost treasures in an old mountain town. Juanita said, "You get in the wrong place at the wrong time. I must have disturbed a yellow jacket nest somehow, because they were swarming all around us—me mostly, so it wasn't the metal detector or anything like that. I had on a long-sleeved shirt, fortunately. I was trying to shrink my body inside that shirt with only indifferent success. As the yellow jackets started to sting my hands, I started to talk to myself out loud, 'Just be quiet. Resist the urge to start screaming and running.' I started walking deliberately away and when I reached a distance of about 20 to 30 feet away they had stopped stinging me. Maybe it was or wasn't the right thing to do, but my childhood training had ingrained in me the need not to run in a situation like that. I ended up with about 15 stings on one hand and about 20 on the other. I didn't swell too badly, though, because I was able to play the piano in church that night."

If you aren't physically able to run in a multiple sting situation, immediately start walking away from the site of attack. Eventually you will reach safety.

MULTIPLE STINGS

Juanita was extremely lucky because she was not sensitive to insect venom. According to poison control center experts, multiple stings—say 30 to 40—will likely cause a severe reaction even in an unsensitized individual, not to mention go a long, long way toward making you extremely sensitive to stings in the future. Body weight plays a factor here, too, so that the reactions of a slender child to multiple stings may well be more extreme than those of a relatively sting-free adult.

Symptoms from such multiple stings can include:

- Chills.
- Fever.
- Vomiting.
- Pulmonary edema (swelling).
- Breathing difficulty.
- Drop in blood pressure.
- Collapse.

Multiple stings, especially ones that trigger these symptoms, should be attended to by a medical professional or medical emergency response team as soon as possible.

GOOD RIDDANCE

There are many products on the market to help you wipe out individual bees and wasps and their nests, be they in the ground, in the trees, under the eaves, or in your wood. Before you tackle a major eradication project—and some folks might think a small, single nest is just such a case—you might want to contact your county agricultural extension agent or a pest control expert for advice. You might find out some surprising things. Charles did.

Charles and Ann live in a wonderful contemporary house in Birmingham. One day they discovered that a colony of wild honeybees had decided to take up residence *inside the house*. When Charles wisely called a pesticide company to take care of the problem, he learned that wild bees are legally protected in Alabama. This is because honeybees are a vital link to U.S. agriculture. Each year, pollination by honeybees adds at least $10 billion to the value of more than 90 crops. They also produce about $150 million worth of honey each year.

- There may be restrictions on what you can and cannot do regarding bees. First, call your county agricultural extension office to ask for help.
- Do not presume that every nest or bee you may find on your property is a terrible threat and therefore must be destroyed. Apart from the economic value of honeybees, most *Hymenopterae* are a critical link in the ecosystem, and many beekeepers in the south will tell you that bee populations are down with negative consequences for our trees, fruits, flowers, and vegetables. If you and your family are not dangerously allergic and the location of the colony poses no real threat or inconvenience, let it be.
- If you determine that the colony must go, it's a good idea to get professional help rather than remove bees yourself.

Getting Rid of Yellow Jacket Nests

Anyone who has angered yellow jackets in a suburban neighborhood will tell you that wasps and people in proximity definitely do not mix. The National Audubon Society's excellent *Field Guide to Insects and Spiders* recommends a seemingly low-risk method of ridding your yard of underground yellow jacket nests. At night, place a transparent bowl over the nest opening. Make sure it is set firmly into the ground. When daylight comes, the adults will be confused and unable to escape and seek food. They will not dig a new escape hole and will soon starve to death. Use caution with this method, for yellow jackets will often have a "back door" escape route already in place. If this is the case, you must treat that exit in the same way. Locate these nest openings only by careful observation at the greatest possible distance. While this method seems regrettably cruel (and is untried by the author), it is an alternative to highly effective chemical treatments and may avert a highly painful and even dangerous event.

If you destroy a yellow jacket nest, it is unlikely that a new colony will take up residence that season. In subsequent years, odds are even that yellow jackets will inhabit the former nest or take up residence elsewhere in your yard or neighborhood.

Bees

BUMBLEBEE
Bombus spp.

• DANGER

The bumblebee's sting is potentially lethal for those highly allergic and prone to anaphylactic shock. Other reactions vary according to number of stings, location of stings, ratio of venom to body weight, and individual sensitivity.

• ABUNDANCE & RANGE

Bumblebees are very common throughout the eastern U.S.

• SIZE

0.4 to 0.8 inch.

• DESCRIPTION

Their hairy bodies are bright yellow and black.

• HABITAT

They nest in ready-made hollows such as deserted mouse nests.

• COMMENTS

Bumblebees are extremely important in pollination. Red clover is a prime example, depending on bumblebees for its propagation.

DIGGER BEE
Anthophora spp.

• DANGER

The digger bee's sting is potentially lethal for those highly allergic and prone to anaphylactic shock. Other reactions vary according to number of stings, location of stings, ratio of venom to body weight, and individual sensitivity.

• ABUNDANCE & RANGE

Digger bees are found throughout most of North America.

• SIZE

0.3 to 0.5 inch.

• DESCRIPTION

Clear wings with smoky tips attached to black body and legs. Short, dense yellowish hairs on head, thorax, and first abdominal section.

• HABITAT

They are found in gardens and fields.

• COMMENTS

The digger bee has both social and solitary traits. They often nest together in large groups, but the individual nest is constructed of mud in clay or sand and designed to hold one egg and a mixture of honey and pollen.

HONEYBEE
Apis mellifera

• DANGER
The honeybee's sting is potentially lethal for those highly allergic and prone to anaphylactic shock. Other reactions vary according to number of stings, location of stings, ratio of venom to body weight, and individual sensitivity.

• ABUNDANCE & RANGE
Honeybees are common throughout the U.S.

• SIZE
0.5 to 0.75 inch.

• DESCRIPTION
Honeybees are mostly reddish brown and black with paler rings on the abdomen that are usually yellow-orange. Their wings are translucent, and their heads, legs, and antennae are nearly black.

• HABITAT
Hives are found in hollow trees and in beekeepers' freestanding wooden apiaries. Workers seek flower nectar in meadows, woods, and gardens.

• COMMENTS
Imported to North America in the 1600s by European settlers, honeybees are used to pollinate crops as well as produce honey.

• DANGER
The sweat bee's sting is potentially dangerous for those especially allergic and prone to anaphylactic shock.

SWEAT BEE
Halictus spp.

Other reactions vary according to number of stings, location of stings, ratio of venom to body weight, and individual sensitivity. All other factors being equal, the sting of a sweat bee is likely the weakest of all bees and wasps.

• ABUNDANCE & RANGE
Sweat bees are found throughout the U.S.

• SIZE
Very small, from 0.25 to 0.5 inch.

• DESCRIPTION
Sweat bees are black or brownish, some with greenish or bluish metallic appearance.

• HABITAT
Nests are burrows in clay, in sand banks along streams, and along roadways or railroad embankments.

• COMMENTS

Although there are 502 species of *Halictidae* in the U.S., only about 12 of these are attracted to human sweat. These sweat bees will sting if they are pressed by clothing or trapped in the bend of an arm or a leg, but their sting is not usually very painful and triggers only minor reactions in normally sensitive individuals. However, in extremely sensitive individuals, the sweat bee sting can trigger anaphylactic shock.

VIRESCENT GREEN METALLIC BEE

Agapostemon virescens

• DANGER

This bee's sting is potentially lethal for those highly allergic and prone to anaphylactic shock. Other reactions vary according to number of stings, location of stings, ratio of venom to body weight, and individual sensitivity.

• ABUNDANCE & RANGE

This bee is found from Maine south to Florida and west to Texas, and in the northwestern U.S.

• SIZE

0.3 to 0.5 inch.

• DESCRIPTION

Metallic green thorax and black antennae and legs. Males have yellow hair on their abdomen; females have white. The wings are a dusky brown.

• HABITAT

Gardens and fields with sandy soil.

• COMMENTS

These sociable bees construct an underground colony that has a single entrance guarded by a single bee that places its head level to the earth to plug the entrance. Bees returning to the colony with nectar have the "right-of-way" over bees exiting the hive.

True (Vespid) Wasps

BALDFACED HORNET

Vespula maculata

• DANGER

This hornet's sting is potentially lethal for those highly allergic and prone to anaphylactic shock. Other reactions vary according to number of stings, location of stings, ratio of venom to body weight, and individual sensitivity.

• ABUNDANCE & RANGE
The baldfaced hornet is found throughout the continental U.S.

• SIZE
0.5 to 0.75 inch.

• DESCRIPTION
This hornet's body is patterned with black and white.

• HABITAT
Baldfaced hornets nest in woodlands edges, suburban yards, and meadows.

• COMMENTS
These hornets are very commonly found on flowers. In spring, the female chews wood to craft a small, pendant nest of gray pulp; nests can eventually grow to the size of a basketball. The nest is usually suspended high in trees, but it may also be near the ground and is always in the open. The doorway to the nest is at the bottom. Adults are extremely protective of the nest and will sting repeatedly in defense of it.

EUROPEAN HORNET
Vespa crabro

• DANGER
The European hornet's sting is potentially lethal for those highly allergic and prone to anaphylactic shock. Other reactions vary according to number of stings, location of stings, ratio of venom to body weight, and individual sensitivity.

• ABUNDANCE & RANGE
These hornets are found throughout the eastern U.S. (except Florida), but they are more common at the western borders of the region.

• SIZE
0.75 to 1+ inches.

• DESCRIPTION
The body is reddish brown with a bright yellow abdomen with dark crossbands. There is sometimes a yellow stripe on the head and thorax.

• HABITAT
They are found in woodlands and urban areas.

• COMMENTS
Also called giant hornets, they will defend the nest, but otherwise they avoid confrontations.

PAPER WASP

Polistes spp.

• DANGER

Paper wasps' stings are potentially lethal for those highly allergic and prone to anaphylactic shock. Other reactions vary according to number of stings, location of stings, ratio of venom to body weight, and individual sensitivity.

• ABUNDANCE & RANGE

They are common throughout the U.S.

• SIZE

0.5 to 1 inch.

• DESCRIPTION

These long-legged wasps are brown-reddish brown to black. They have yellow rings on the abdomen, but fewer yellow markings than yellow jackets or hornets.

• HABITAT

They nest near buildings, in meadows and fields, and in gardens on flowers.

• COMMENTS

Not as easily riled as yellow jackets and hornets, the paper wasp nevertheless has a painful sting. Paper nests lack outer paper coverings and have only one comb attached to a support.

POTTER WASP

Eumenes fraternus

• DANGER

The potter wasp's sting is potentially lethal for those highly allergic and prone to anaphylactic shock. Other reactions vary according to number of stings, location of stings, ratio of venom to body weight, and individual sensitivity.

• ABUNDANCE & RANGE

They are found from the Atlantic seaboard west to Texas.

• SIZE

0.6 to 0.75 inch.

• DESCRIPTION

The potter wasp is primarily black with yellow on the face, across the front, and on the rear thorax; it also has a yellow dot on the pedicel (basal stalk of the abdomen) and abdomen; and a yellow ring-tipped abdomen. Smoky, dark-colored wings have a spot, known as a stigma.

• HABITAT

Potter wasps are found at the edges of forests an in meadows with shrub undergrowth.

• COMMENTS

The female constructs a spherical chamber of mud that is impervious to rain. Each sealed chamber contains an anesthetized caterpillar or sawfly larva to feed to the individual wasp larva.

• COMMENTS

These wasps sting viciously if their nests are disturbed. The nests are made of wood pulp and saliva and are often seen hanging in the spring from roof eaves or under shrubbery close to the ground.

SANDHILLS HORNET
Vespula arenaria

• DANGER

The sandhills hornet's sting is potentially lethal for those highly allergic and prone to anaphylactic shock. Other reactions vary according to number of stings, location of stings, ratio of venom to body weight, and individual sensitivity.

• ABUNDANCE & RANGE

This insect is found across the northern U.S.

• SIZE

0.6 to 0.75 inch.

• DESCRIPTION

Patches of bright yellow on the sides of head, thorax, legs, and on each abdominal segment stand out against the black body. The wings are dusky brown-black.

• HABITAT

True to their name, they are found in sandy areas.

YELLOW JACKET
Vespula **spp.**

• DANGER

The yellow jacket's sting is potentially lethal for those highly allergic and prone to anaphylactic shock. Other reactions vary according to number of stings, location of stings, ratio of venom to body weight, and individual sensitivity.

• ABUNDANCE & RANGE

They are found throughout the U.S.

• SIZE

0.5 to 0.75 inch.

• DESCRIPTION

The body is yellow and black or black and white.

• HABITAT

Yellow jackets are found in woodlands edges, suburban yards, and golf courses. Nests are underground or at ground level in stumps and logs.

• COMMENTS

They often appear at picnics in search of food (sweets, meat, and other substances), but do not generally sting at picnics unless accidentally contacted on food. Highly protective of their nests, yellow jackets will sting repeatedly with only slight provocation. Because nests are underground, people most often disturb them with no advance warning.

Sphecid Wasps

BLACK-AND-YELLOW MUD DAUBER

Sceliphron caementarium

• DANGER

The mud dauber's sting is potentially lethal for those highly allergic and prone to anaphylactic shock. Other reactions vary according to number of stings, location of stings, ratio of venom to body weight, and individual sensitivity.

• ABUNDANCE & RANGE

The mud dauber is common throughout the U.S.

• SIZE

1 to 1.25 inches.

• DESCRIPTION

The body is non-metallic black with yellow markings.

• HABITAT

Nests of parallel earthen tubes are found in a variety of sheltered areas such as meadows under rocks, cliffs under rock overhangs, and in human habitation areas such as under overhanging roofs, outbuildings, sheds, and on the sides of old cars.

• COMMENTS

Mud daubers can sting painfully. Females can be found at edges of ponds or pools collecting mud to be shaped by their mandibles into balls to form linked tubular cells. Inside these cells, the female stuffs a paralyzed spider and an egg that will hatch into a larvae. After feeding on the spider, the young mud dauber will then dig its way out of the closed tube.

CICADA KILLER

Sphecius speciosus

• DANGER

The cicada killer's sting is potentially lethal for those highly allergic and prone to anaphylactic shock. Other reactions vary according to number of stings, location of stings, ratio of venom to body weight, and individual sensitivity.

• ABUNDANCE & RANGE
Cicada killers are common in the U.S. east of the Rocky Mountains.

• SIZE
1.25 to 2 inches.

• DESCRIPTION
Their black or rust-colored bodies have yellow bands on the thorax and upper abdomen. Legs are yellowish-brown.

• HABITAT
They are found in forests and urban areas, including city parks where they burrow along roadsides, under sidewalks, in lawns, and along embankments.

• COMMENTS
The cicada killer reportedly has one of the most severe insect stings. A large and strong flier, it captures cicadas, often in flight, and paralyzes them for deposit in an underground nest where the cicada killer larvae feed on the cicada. The young cicada killer emerges in mid to late summer.

COMMON/EASTERN SAND WASP
Bembix americana spinolae

• DANGER
The common sand wasp's sting is potentially lethal for those highly allergic and prone to anaphylactic shock. Other reactions vary according to number of stings, location of stings, ratio of venom to body weight, and individual sensitivity.

• ABUNDANCE & RANGE
This wasp is found throughout the U.S.

• SIZE
0.5 to 0.75 inch.

• DESCRIPTION
Their stout bodies have yellowish green and black markings on head, thorax, and abdomen.

• HABITAT
They are found in soft-soil areas such as sandy meadows, along lakes, and on beaches.

• COMMENTS
They maintain their nests from year to year but are not social in the usual sense. They will, however, fly *en masse* against intruders. Readily adaptable to humans, they are not deeply

aggressive. They may congregate on branches of trees and shrubs where they appear to be sleeping. They burrow into soft soils to lay eggs.

FLORIDA HUNTING WASP

Palmodes dimidiatus

• DANGER

This wasp's sting is potentially lethal for those highly allergic and prone to anaphylactic shock. Other reactions vary according to number of stings, location of stings, ratio of venom to body weight, and individual sensitivity.

• ABUNDANCE & RANGE

The Florida hunting wasp is found throughout the U.S. except in the northwest.

• SIZE

0.75 inch.

• DESCRIPTION

Its head, thorax, legs, and lower abdomen are blue-black, as are wings. Upper abdomen is brownish red.

• HABITAT

It is found in open areas such as fields and meadows as well as woods.

• COMMENTS

The Florida hunting wasp can sting painfully.

GREAT GOLDEN DIGGER WASP

Sphex ichneumoneus

• DANGER

The great golden digger wasp has a potentially lethal sting for those highly allergic and prone to anaphylactic shock. Other reactions vary according to number of stings, location of stings, ratio of venom to body weight, and individual sensitivity.

• ABUNDANCE & RANGE

This wasp is found throughout the U.S.

• SIZE

0.75 to 1 inch.

• DESCRIPTION

Its body is black, with part of the abdomen and legs reddish with golden pile. Wings are smoky yellow.

• HABITAT

It nests in hard-packed soil or sand along meadows, especially open areas with little vegetation, including inside the floors of old abandoned buildings.

• COMMENTS

Females dig vertical burrows that radiate from a central entryway. These tunnels are sometimes found between the stones of a garden terrace.

STEEL-BLUE CRICKET HUNTER

Chlorion aerarium

• DANGER

The steel-blue cricket hunter's sting is potentially lethal for those highly allergic and prone to anaphylactic shock. Other reactions vary according to number of stings, location of stings, ratio of venom to body weight, and individual sensitivity.

• ABUNDANCE & RANGE

They are found throughout the U.S.

• SIZE

0.5 to 0.75 inch.

• DESCRIPTION

The body and wings are a dark "steel-colored blue" with black antennae and legs.

• HABITAT

They nest in meadows near sandy areas.

• COMMENTS

The female digs a burrow in sandy soil to deposit a single egg attached to prey that will serve as food for the hatching larva.

THREAD-WAISTED WASP

Ammophila **spp.**

• DANGER

The thread-waisted wasp's sting is potentially lethal for those highly allergic and prone to anaphylactic shock. Other reactions vary according to number of stings, location of stings, ratio of venom to body weight, and individual sensitivity.

• ABUNDANCE & RANGE

These wasps are found throughout the U.S.

• SIZE

0.5 to 2+ inches.

• DESCRIPTION

The abdomen is orange-red and head and legs are gray-black. Longer hind legs distinguish this species.

• HABITAT

They nest in open areas such as meadows, on the ground, or on clusters of flowers.

• COMMENTS

These are also called digger wasps. Females use "tools" such as pebbles to tamp soil, a behavior that has attracted much interest from scientists. Some species have more than one nest at a time. They can sting painfully.

ANTS

If you agitate them enough, most ants are capable of bites and/or stings. The fire ant *(Solenopsis geminata)* deserves special mention for its speedy aggression, notorious stings, and relentless geographical advance.

At present, the fire ant is confined to the southern parts of the U.S. and along the Pacific coast, so folks in the mid-Atlantic region can cross this one off their worry list for the time being. The ants profiled here have distinguished themselves for their proclivity to bite or their powerful sting.

BLACK CARPENTER ANT
Camponotus pennsylvanicus

• DANGER
The black carpenter ant's bite is painful, but it doesn't sting.

• ABUNDANCE & RANGE
This ant is common throughout the eastern U.S.

• SIZE
0.25 to 0.5 inch.

• DESCRIPTION
Its body is black, and its enlarged abdomen has long yellow-gray hair.

• HABITAT
It nests in dead wood, including houses, poles, dead tree trunks, and logs.

• COMMENTS
This ant is a pest for buildings, but usually only in old wood where it can cause substantial damage.

COMMON EASTERN VELVET ANT/ "COW KILLER"
Dasymutilla occidentalis

• DANGER
The sting of the "cow killer" is potentially lethal for those highly allergic and prone to anaphylactic shock. Other reactions vary according to number of stings, location of stings, ratio of venom to body weight, and individual sensitivity.

• ABUNDANCE & RANGE
It is found in the eastern U.S. and is common throughout the southeast,

becoming more rare in the northern latitudes.

• SIZE

0.5 to 1 inch.

• DESCRIPTION

Its body is covered with long hairlike bristles (setae) of white, orange, red, or black that form patterns.

• HABITAT

This insect is found in meadows, woodland edges, clover fields, and near flowers.

• COMMENTS

Eggs are laid in bumblebee nests, and larvae emerge to feed on bee larvae. This is sometimes also called the "red velvet cow killer," but the red velvet ant is actually another related species found in the southwest U.S. Neither are true ants—they are actually wasps. Resembling ants in appearance and in movement (plus name), they are included here for easier identification. The sting of workers is reported to be so severe it could "kill a cow." This species is also noted for its speed and ferocity.

LINED ACROBATIC ANT
Cremastogaster lineolata

• DANGER

This ant may bite when disturbed.

• ABUNDANCE & RANGE

It is found throughout the eastern U.S.

• SIZE

0.1 inch.

• DESCRIPTION

It is black to light brown with a distinctive heart-shaped abdomen.

• HABITAT

This ant is found in exposed earth; under stones, logs, and stumps; and in the woodwork of houses and outbuildings.

• COMMENTS

Although these ants do not feed on wood, their colony enlargement can damage structures. They have a symbiotic relationship with aphids, trading protection of aphids for honeydew. Not only can they bite when disturbed, they can also emit foul odors.

LICE

A LOUSY RELATIONSHIP

As May R. Berenbaum notes in her fine book, *Bugs in the System: Insects and Their Impact on Human Affairs,* "life for us humans has probably been lousy ever since we first appeared on the planet." We even have evidence from Egyptian tombs that lice were mummified along with the humans they inhabited, but the relationship almost certainly predates that era. There are two kinds of lice: the biters and the suckers. It's those "little suckers" that find us humans so attractive. In fact, we are host to three types of lice, a rare distinction among mammals.

HANGING BY HAIRS AND THREADS

The least harmful (but still irritating) louse lives in pubic hair (but sometimes also in beards, mustaches, and eyebrows), where it can hang on to a single hair for virtually its whole life by its relatively substantial claws. Hence the nickname "crabs." These lice *(Phthirus pubis)* are spread during intimate contact, but can survive for a short time off the host, which gives rise to the speculation about the long jump event in the "crab Olympics." Berenbaum gives a smiling nod to nastier bathrooms in this outlandish graffito:

Don't bother to stretch
Or stand on the seat.
The crabs in this place
Can jump thirty feet.

Symptoms of Pubic Lice

- Pubic itching (sometimes in public!)
- Visual evidence of lice or nits on pubic hair.

Treatment of Pubic Lice

- Apply permethrin 1% cream rinse (available without prescription) to affected areas and washed off after 10 minutes;
- or apply lindane 1% shampoo (prescription needed for this generic name, more commonly known as "Kwell") for four minutes to the affected area and then thoroughly wash off. This regimen is not recommended for pregnant or lactating women or for children age two or younger;
- or apply pyrethrins with piperonyl butoxide to the affected area and wash off after 10 minutes.

The lindane regimen is the least expensive therapy. Toxicity from lindane has not been reported when treatment was limited to the recommended four-minute period, but use care and follow the directions closely. Permethrin has less potential for toxicity than lindane.

Other Treatment Considerations and Follow-Ups Talk to your pharmacists about other treatment options, and take note about what remedies should not be applied to the eyes. Eyelashes should be treated by applying ophthalmic ointment to the eyelid margins twice a day for 10 days.

Bedding and clothing should be decontaminated (either machine-washed or machine-dried using the heat cycle or dry-cleaned) or removed from body contact for at least 72 hours. Fumigation of living areas is not necessary.

If symptoms persist after one week, re-treatment may be necessary if lice are found or if eggs are observed at the hair-skin junction. Patients who do not respond to one of the recommended regimens should be retreated with an alternative regimen.

Sex partners within the preceding month should be treated.

WHAT ARE HEAD LICE?

They are insects found on the heads of people. Having head lice is very common, and as many as 6 to 12 million people worldwide get head lice each year.

Nit-Picking for Head Lice

Head lice *(Pediculus humanus capitis)*, whose eggs are called "nits," mature in about three weeks, and tend to infect children, especially those with long hair. With a maximum length of 0.25 inch, head lice are visible to the human eye, but they are often camouflaged by the fact that they are the color of the hair they inhabit. Infestations can spread rapidly among children in school, but treatment with insecticidal soap and a fine-tooth comb for "nit-picking" usually does the trick.

Who Is at Risk For Getting Head Lice?

Anyone who comes in close contact with someone who already has head lice, contaminated clothing, and other belongings may be at risk. Preschool and elementary-age children ages 3 to 10 and their families are infested most often. Girls get head lice more often than boys, and women more than men. In the U.S., African-Americans rarely get head lice.

What Do Head Lice Look Like?

Nits (the eggs) are hard to see and are often confused for dandruff or hair spray droplets. Nits are found firmly attached to the hair shaft, and they are oval and usually yellow to white for the first 24 hours after being laid, after which they darken to brown. They take about one week to hatch into a nymph that looks like an adult head louse, but smaller. Nymphs mature into adults about seven days after hatching. To live, the nymph must feed on blood. The adult louse is about the size of a sesame seed, has six legs, and is tan to grayish-white. In persons with dark hair, the adult louse will look darker. Adult lice can live up to 30 days on a person's head. If the louse falls off a person, it dies within two days.

Where Are Head Lice Most Commonly Found?

On the scalp behind the ears and near the neckline at the back of the neck. Head lice hold on to hair with hook-like claws found at the end of each of their six legs, and they are rarely found on the body, eyelashes, or eyebrows.

What Are the Signs and Symptoms of Head Lice Infestation?

- Tickling feeling of something moving in the hair.
- Itching, caused by an allergic reaction to the bites.
- Irritability.
- Sores on the head caused by scratching that can sometimes become infected.

How Did My Child Get Head Lice?

By contact with an already infested person through:
- Play at school and at home (slumber parties, sports activities, at camp, on a playground).
- Wearing infested clothing, such as hats, scarves, coats, sports uniforms, or hair ribbons.
- Using infested combs, brushes, or towels.
- Lying on a bed, couch, pillow, carpet, or stuffed animal that has recently been in contact with an infested person.

How is a Head Lice Infestation Diagnosed?

Look closely through the hair and scalp for nits, nymphs, or adults. Finding a nymph or adult may be difficult; there are usually few of them

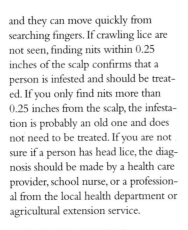

and they can move quickly from searching fingers. If crawling lice are not seen, finding nits within 0.25 inches of the scalp confirms that a person is infested and should be treated. If you only find nits more than 0.25 inches from the scalp, the infestation is probably an old one and does not need to be treated. If you are not sure if a person has head lice, the diagnosis should be made by a health care provider, school nurse, or a professional from the local health department or agricultural extension service.

THE DARK DANGER OF BODY LICE

By far, the most potentially dangerous lice are body lice *(Pediculus humanus)*, parasitic insects that live on the body and in the clothing or bedding of infested humans (causing a condition called pediculosis). Infestation is common, found worldwide, and affects people of all races. *Pediculus* can survive in clothing apart from a human host, where they can multiply with astonishing fecundity. One account reported over 10,000 lice and 10,000 nits in a single shirt. Body lice infestations spread rapidly under crowded conditions where hygiene is poor and there is frequent contact among people.

Body lice can produce intense itching, with swelling and skin damage at the site of the bite. This can also bring about a discoloration of the skin in heavy infestations known as "vagabond's disease." In the U. S., body lice are usually found only in homeless, transient populations who don't have access to changes of clothes or frequent baths. Infestation is unlikely in anyone who bathes regularly.

Can Body Lice Transmit Disease?

Yes. The real danger of body lice is as a carrier of typhus, which can be lethal. Here's how a transmission

might occur: Jim has typhus. When a louse feeds on him, the infectious typhus organism *Rickettsiae* kills the louse, but before it dies the louse passes on thousands of pathogens through its feces. The feces dry quickly in the air and easily gain entrance to the human body through our moist eyes, nose, or mouth membranes. In another scenario, John, who is not initially infected, can get typhus if he crushes infected lice while scratching them. Then the fecal-carried infection enters John at the point of the bite on his body.

Typhus epidemics often strike where people are forced to live together in crowded, dirty conditions, such as in jail, in refugee camps, or in the military prior to World War II. Historically, typhus has killed many thousands of people worldwide. Although it is a very negligible threat for ordinary folks in North America, the World Health Organization reports it is still endemic in the highlands and cold areas of Africa, Asia, and Central and South America. The onset is often characterized by the sudden appearance of headaches, chills, prostration, high fever, coughing, and severe muscular pain. A macular eruption (dark spot on the skin) appears on the fifth to sixth day, initially on the upper trunk, which then spreads to the entire body excepting, usually, the face, palms and soles of the feet. Although typhus is now treatable with a single dose of 200 mg of doxycycline, the disease proves fatal for up to 20% of those infected. It is not possible to contract typhus from either head or pubic lice.

Where Are Body Lice Found?

Body lice are found on the body and on clothing or bedding used by infested people; lice eggs are laid in the seams of clothing or on bedding. Occasionally, eggs are attached to body hair. Lice found on the hair and head are not body lice; they are head lice.

What Are the Signs And Symptoms of Body Lice?

- Itching and rash, your body's allergic reaction to the lice, are common.
- Long-term body lice infestations may lead to thickening and discoloration of the skin, particularly around the waist, groin, and upper thighs. Sores on the body may be caused by scratching. These sores can sometimes become infected with bacteria or fungi.

How Are Body Lice Spread?

- Directly through contact with a person who has body lice.
- Indirectly through shared clothing, beds, bed linens, or towels.

What Do Body Lice Look Like?

There are three forms of body lice: the egg (sometimes called a nit), the nymph, and the adult. Nits are generally easy to see in the seams of clothing, particularly around the waistline and under armpits. They are about the size of a small ant. Nits may also be attached to body hair. They are oval and usually yellow to white for 24 hours after being laid (after which they darken to brown) and may take 30 days to hatch. The egg hatches into a baby louse called a nymph. It looks like an adult body louse but is smaller. Nymphs mature into adults about seven days after hatching. To live, the nymph must feed on blood. The adult body louse is about the size of a sesame seed, has six legs, and is tan to grayish-white. Adult lice need to feed on blood to live, and if the louse falls off a person, it dies within 10 days.

How Is a Body Lice Infestation Diagnosed?

To locate lice, look closely in the seams of clothing and on the body for eggs and for crawling lice. Diagnosis should be made by a health care provider if you are unsure about infestation.

How Are Body Lice Treated?

Give the infested person a clean change of clothes and a shower, and launder all worn clothing, bed linens, and towels. When laundering items, use the hot cycle (130°F) of the washing machine. Set the dryer to the hot cycle to dry items. Additionally, a 1% permethrin or pyrethrin lice shampoo (also called pediculicide) can be purchased at a drugstore without a prescription and then applied to the body. Medication should be applied exactly as directed on the bottle or by your physician.

Head Louse
Pediculus humanus capitis

- **DANGER**
Head lice cause itching.

- **ABUNDANCE & RANGE**
They are found worldwide.

- **SIZE**
0.1 inch.

- **DESCRIPTION**
They have flat, oval, or somewhat elongated gray bodies.

- **HABITAT**
They nest in human hair, especially behind the ears or on the neck.

- **COMMENTS**
They are transmitted by combs, brushes, hats, and headrests.

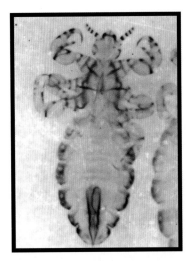

HUMAN BODY LOUSE
Pediculus humanus humanus

- **DANGER**
The body louse can transmit typhus.

- **ABUNDANCE & RANGE**
It is found worldwide.

- **SIZE**
0.1 inch.

- **DESCRIPTION**
Body lice have flat, oval, or some-what elongated gray bodies.

- **HABITAT**
They are found on human bodies, especially in clothing, where they then return to the body to feed on blood.

- **COMMENTS**
The body louse is also known as a "cootie."

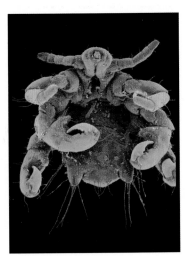

PUBIC LOUSE
Phthirus pubis

- **DANGER**
Pubic lice cause itching.

- **ABUNDANCE & RANGE**
They are found worldwide.

- **SIZE**
0.1 inch.

- **DESCRIPTION**
They have flat, oval, or somewhat elongated gray bodies.

- **HABITAT**
They live on human bodies in pubic hair, armpit hair, beards, and eyebrows.

- **COMMENTS**
The pubic louse is also known as a "crab louse." It is transmitted only by human-to-human contact because the louse does not leave these body regions.

FLEAS

"FLEA BITE US"

Fleas are unique in the insect world—so unique, in fact, that entomologists are uncertain who their closest insect relatives are. With more than 2,000 species of fleas worldwide, every country has at least one species that finds human blood to be a fine, fine thing on which to feast. Fleas bite skin with piercing-and-sucking mouth parts, similar to those of mosquitoes, that go on to penetrate blood vessels. Then fleas literally use the pumps in their heads to draw our blood into their bodies. In exchange, they give us their saliva, which is what triggers the intense itching associated with flea bites. Their flattened, thin bodies, housed in exceptionally strong exoskeletons, make navigation among hairs easier, and just when you think you might nail the suckers, they jump! The jumping varieties can spring about 12 inches in one hop, which when you consider their size, is a rather impressive feat. They accomplish this by using their muscular hind legs, but also by resilin, an elastic protein in their thorax. Similar to rubber, this protein can store and release energy when required.

Fleas aren't very picky. Humans share their fleas with other animals and vice versa. The cat flea will feed on cats, on us, and on dogs. "Our" fleas *(Pulex irritans)* will also nosh on cats, dogs, skunks, coyotes, pigs, rats, spiny anteaters, ducks, owls, and who knows whom else? The Oriental rat flea finds rodents to its liking, but it also enjoys people in literally plague-size proportions.

THE PLAGUE: IT'S NOT JUST FOR THE MIDDLE AGES ANYMORE

It's hard to imagine a pandemic of plague sweeping over regions and affecting great numbers, but from our first historical account, it's likely that over 200,000 people died in Constantinople in four months in 541 A.D. In the wake of that first sweep, some estimates place the death rate at 50% of the entire population of southern Europe. Plague reappeared in 10- to 24-year cycles for the next two centuries, and then another big wave swept through Europe in 1348, wherein approximately one out of every three people bit the "black death" dust. Another massive scourge in London in 1664–1665 rendered about 7,000 fatalities *per week*. In a misguided attempt to clean the city, the Lord Mayor at the time ordered the death of all cats and dogs. That was a drastic mistake, for the cats and dogs had preyed on the city's rodent population.

Yersinia pestis is at its source a bacterial disease of rodents. When fleas feed on an infected rat, for example, they suck in bacteria with blood. The bacteria multiply with ferocious speed in the stomachs of the fleas, so much so that the flea is unable to ingest more blood. As it keeps on attempting to feed, it regurgitates the bacteria into the host at the site of the bite. Even when infected, many rodents do not exhibit disease symptoms, but other small wild mammals die rapidly and in great misery. When this bacterial disease infects wild animals, it is called sylvatic plague. When it infects humans through the bite of fleas infected with the plague bacteria, it takes the form of septicemic plague, pneumonic plague, or bubonic plague.

Septicemic plague takes such a rapid course, overwhelming the liver and spleen, that death often occurs in one day—usually before the infected person even has a chance to pass on the disease. Trappers who might unknowingly skin plague-infected animals should use extra caution not to cut themselves with their skinning knives, as flea bites, as well as accidental breaks in the skin, initiate this almost certainly deadly infection.

Pneumonic plague is not carried by the flea vector, but travels airborne in sputum. That is, you must breathe in the bacteria spewed by the bloody cough of someone who has the infection, which almost no one does in the U.S. In sickened individuals, body temperature falls, and the infection in the lungs produces bloody sputum after a two to three day incubation period. Fatalities are near 100% if infected persons are not treated, but your chance of contracting pneumonic plague in the U.S. is even slimmer than getting septicemic plague, in which you would need to handle an infected wild animal, be bitten by its infected flea, or have that animal's fluids enter your body directly. These scenarios make the risk of contracting these forms of plague minuscule in this country, unless you have some pretty exotic habits.

Unfortunately, your chances of contracting bubonic plague in the U.S. are slightly better. The Center for Disease Control (CDC) reports that the last urban plague epidemic occurred in Los Angeles in 1924–1925. Since then, human plague in the U.S. has occurred as mostly scattered cases in rural areas (an average of 10 to 15 persons each year). Globally however, the World Health Organization reports 1,000 to 3,000 cases of plague every year, and as recently as 1996 "Plague" was the *Newsweek* cover

story, in part because it also exists in Africa, India, Asia, and South America.

According to the CDC, in North America, plague is found in certain animals and their fleas from the Pacific Coast to the Great Plains and from southwestern Canada to Mexico. Most human cases in the U.S. occur in:

- Northern New Mexico, northern Arizona, and southern Colorado
- California, southern Oregon, and far western Nevada

Bubonic plague takes its name from the development of a "bubo," the inflammatory, necrotic, and hemorrhagic swelling of a lymph gland, especially around the groin, that is a reaction to the bacillus invasion. The bacterial spread occurs along the lymphatic channels, and potentially seeds every organ, including the lungs, liver, spleen, kidneys, and, rarely, the meninges (membranes enveloping the brain and spinal cord). The nursery rhyme vividly recounts the scene that has claimed an estimated 200 million human lives in the course of recorded history:

Ring around the rosey
   (the bubo)*,*
Pocketful of posies
   (a Middle Ages means of
   "warding off" the disease)
Ashes, ashes,
We all fall down!
   (bite the dust, as we say)

A person usually becomes ill with bubonic plague two to six days after being infected. When bubonic plague is left untreated, plague bacteria invade the bloodstream. When plague bacteria multiply in the bloodstream, they spread rapidly throughout the body and cause the severe and often fatal condition.

Breakthroughs in Transmission Theories

After germ theory emerged in the nineteenth century, the notion of miasma, or poisonous air as the genesis of plague, gave way to theories about bacterial infection origins. Two Hong Kong scientists working independently, Shibasaburo Kitasato and Alexandre E.J. Yersin, identified the bacterium in 1894. In 1903, the wealthy English flea collector (strange, but true) Charles Rothschild described the then unknown Oriental rat flea *(Xenopsylla cheopis)* as the chief vector of the plague. This was confirmed in 1905.

Plague Vectors

The plague organism can be transmitted to a human via the bite of a vector, or transmitter. Although infected rodents and their infected fleas are the primary vectors worldwide, other species that can serve as hosts include domestic cats, dogs, squirrels, chipmunks, marmots, deer mice, rabbits, hares, rock squirrels, camels, and sheep.

Close contact with any potentially infected host or rural environment should raise suspicion for the plague. Prairie dogs are the most common transmitters in rural areas. Historically, the rat has been thought to be the main plague host; however, currently in the U.S., the ground and rock squirrel are the most common hosts. In recent years, the domestic cat has emerged as a prominent host that transmits the plague to veterinarians.

Risk of Plague in the Mid-Atlantic U.S.

An average of 18 cases per year have been reported in the entire U.S. over the last few decades. Your chances of contracting plague in the mid-Atlantic are virtually nonexistent, but if you do travel to New Mexico, Arizona, Colorado, Utah, and California, be suspicious of flea bites because one of the largest animal concentrations of the plague worldwide exists in these states. Plague can be acquired at any time during the year. Since 1926, only one case of imported plague has been reported in the U.S. That is to say, our cases are domestic in origin. More than half of the plague cases occur in males, and about half of the cases occur in persons under the age of 20.

Plague Symptoms

- Fever.
- Chills.
- Muscular pain.
- Sore throat.
- Headache.
- Weakness.
- Malaise.
- Enlarged, painful, swollen lymph node.
- Abdominal pain, nausea, vomiting (bloody at times).
- Constipation, diarrhea, and black or tarry stools.
- Gastrointestinal complaints (may precede a bubo).
- Cough, which may produce bloody sputum.
- Shortness of breath.
- Stiff neck (if meningitic infiltration by the plague bacillus has occurred).

Plague Mortality Rates

Plague is certainly not the automatic, dreadful death sentence it was in centuries past. A patient diagnosed with suspected plague should be hospitalized and medically isolated. Laboratory tests should be done, including blood cultures for plague bacteria and microscopic examination of lymph gland, blood, and sputum samples. Antibiotic treatment should begin as soon as possible after laboratory specimens are taken.

- Bubonic plague has a 1–15% mortality rate in treated cases and a 40–60% mortality rate in untreated cases.
- Septicemic plague (primary or secondary) has a 40% mortality rate in treated cases and a 100% mortality rate in untreated cases.
- Pneumonic plague (primary or secondary) has a 100% mortality rate if not treated within the first 24 hours of infection.

The Plague of the Future

"The specter of pandemic, however, remains," writes Berenbaum in *Bugs in the System*. "Bubonic plague is far from an historical curiosity, even in the U.S. Almost 300 cases were diagnosed between 1956 and 1987, half of these in New Mexico, where plague is widely established in populations of feral rodents. Bacteria of all description have been known to develop resistance to antibiotics; if multiple resistant strains of *Y. pestis* were to develop, mortality rates would undoubtedly rise again, although never to the levels of previous centuries, during which neither the causative agent nor its insect collaborator were known." (Berenbaum, 1995, p. 219)

As Dr. Demetres Velendzas writes on emedicine.com: "Unlike smallpox, the plague will never be eradicated. It lives in millions of animals and on billions of fleas that reside on them. It is a disease of the desert, the steppes, the mountains, and the forest."

HUMAN FLEA
Pulex irritans

• DANGER
The flea is potentially lethal as it can transmit forms of plague.

• ABUNDANCE & RANGE
It is found worldwide.

• SIZE
0.1 inch.

• DESCRIPTION
This flea's pale to dark brown flattened body has a hard, shiny armor.

• HABITAT
It is found in dense hair and clothing. Larvae are found under rugs and in lint/hair/organic matter, such as that found in vacuum cleaner bags.

• COMMENTS
In addition to humans, adults also feed on the blood of pigs, rodents, canines, felines, mules, and deer.

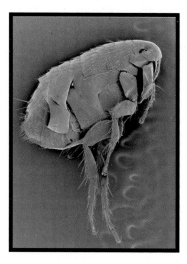

ORIENTAL RAT FLEA
Xenopsylla cheopis

• DANGER
The oriental rat flea is potentially lethal as it can transmit bubonic plague.

• ABUNDANCE & RANGE
It is found worldwide.

• SIZE
0.1 inch.

• DESCRIPTION
Its pale to reddish dark brown flattened body has a hard, shiny armor.

• HABITAT
The Oriental rat flea is common in rodent nests, especially those of rats, and it is often found at waterfronts along coastal areas.

• COMMENTS
This flea likely originated in Egypt's Nile Valley (*"cheopis"* is from Cheops, second king of the Fourth Egyptian Dynasty, builder of the Great Pyramid at Giza) from where it spread worldwide via rats aboard ships.

MOSQUITOES

THE INSECT YOU LOVE TO HATE

You've nestled down in a hammock to read, raised your glass to toast the campfire circle, bedded down in the bag to sleep, or crouched in the garden to weed, and then you hear that high, horrible buzzing beside your ear. Damn! The mosquitoes are here!

They are more than an annoyance and more than an itch you want to scratch or smack. Mosquitoes mainline potentially deadly diseases: malaria, yellow fever, dengue, and encephalitis. About the best thing we can say for mosquitoes is that they are a major food source for birds, fish, and bats.

"PULL OUT, BETTY! YOU'VE HIT AN ARTERY!"

Many of us can remember Gary Larson's wonderful *Far Side* cartoon depicting a mosquito who had tapped into a human "gusher" and was about to explode. In fact, female mosquitoes (it's only the females who feed on blood—the males swill only nectar) do "drill" for the blood they use to form eggs. They accomplish this with their probiscus that first "thumps" us, searching for a suitable place to drill. Next, a flexible, knifelike extension, the stylate, pierces the skin and probes under it in several directions in search of a capillary. The mosquito's saliva has an anti-clotting protein to induce the blood flow. When our bodies produce histamine to combat this agent, swelling and itching starts.

HOW MOSQUITOES TARGET US

The head of a mosquito, it has been said, "bristles with more antennae and sensors than a modern warship." Mosquito eyes can detect motion, as well as assess color and contrast. The head is also equipped with carbon dioxide detectors, which is what we exhale. Heat (from our bodies) and lactic acid (from our skin) can also be detected with the insect's head gear. So with all these sensors, when we wear perfumes and colognes or use fragrant shampoos, soaps, and hair sprays, we beam a strong signal to the girls saying, "Eat me!"

WHEN AND WHERE THEY ARE

Short answer: everywhere, almost all the time. From tropical jungles to arctic tundra; from 4,000 feet below sea level in African gold mines to 14,000 feet above sea level in Kashmir; and in all the places in between

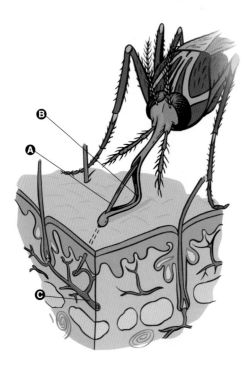

A mosquito feeds by piercing skin with its sharp, hollow stylate (A), part of the probiscus contained within a sliding sheath called the labium (B). The stylate pokes around until it finds a suitable blood capillary (C) to suck blood from.

you'll find one of the 3,200 global species. Not all of these feed on blood, which is a very good thing. If there were more of them that fed on us, we could have even more deadly diseases. More people, certainly, are bitten during the warmer months, but the calendar for bites can be surprisingly long depending on where you live. People in Miami, of course, will be swatting more months of the year than those in Maine.

Dusk seems to be the preferred time of day for our tiny vampire-like friends, but in marshy areas especially, the sucking never stops.

VECTORS OF DEATH

As carriers of disease, or vectors, mosquitoes are the global champs. Of all the insects, mosquitoes are probably the most harmful to humans because of what they transmit. Malaria alone kills at least two million people per year worldwide. Mosquitoes also carry diseases that are serious threats to dogs, horses, and birds.

Don't think that the deadly diseases mosquitoes transmit are restricted to far-off tropical lands. The U.S. has cases of malaria, six types of encephalitis, and dengue fever each year—all of them mosquito-borne. The 1999 cases of west Nile virus in New York added a new disease to the list.

The mosquito problem is perpetual. For example, *Aedes aegypti,* a species likely brought by the slave ships from Africa, carried yellow fever with it. Yellow fever was a formidable scourge in the U.S. It wasted coastal populations and then traveled further inland to cities like Memphis and Philadelphia, where one outbreak killed 5,000 people—about 10% of Philly's population. Many such U.S. cities struggled more than once with the "yellow death," with at least 135 outbreaks from 1668–1893 of "yellow jack," as it was also called in reference to the yellow quarantine flag. Al-though yellow

Confirmed Cases of Encephalitis in the Mid-Atlantic U.S. 1964–1997				
	EEE*	LAC	SLE	TOTAL
Delaware	0	0	1	1
Maryland	0	1	9	10
New Jersey	0	3	131	136
New York	0	51	9	60
Pennsylvania	0	7	36	43
Virginia	0	10	7	17
West Virginia	0	288	12	300
MID-ATLANTIC	**0**	**360**	**205**	**567**

* Confirmed and probable. Source: Centers for Disease Control

fever is not a present danger in the U.S., other arboviruses (viruses borne by arthropods) are very much a current health concern.

Encephalitis

Encephalitis is an inflammation of the brain. Arboviral encephalitides have a global distribution, but there are six main virus agents of encephalitis in the U.S. Those strains that are harmful to humans and domestic animals are: eastern equine encephalitis (EEE), western equine encephalitis (WEE), Venezuelean equine encephalitis (VEE), St. Louis encephalitis (SLE), west Nile virus (WV), and LaCrosse (LAC) encephalitis, all of which are transmitted by mosquitoes. Most cases of arboviral encephalitis occur from June through September, when arthropods are most active. In milder (i.e., warmer) parts of the country where arthropods are active late into the year, cases can occur into the winter months.

To put these statistics in perspective, an average of fewer than 18 people per year in the mid-Atlantic get encepahlitis of any kind.

The majority of human infections may lack overt symptoms, or they may result in a nonspecific flu-like syndrome. Onset may be insidious or sudden with fever, headache, myalgias, malaise, and occasionally prostration. Infection may, however, lead to encephalitis, with a fatal outcome or permanent neurologic aftereffects. Fortunately, only a small proportion of infected persons progress to fullblown encephalitis.

Because the arboviral encephalitides are viral diseases, antibiotics are not effective for treatment and no effective antiviral drugs have yet been discovered. There are no commercially available human vaccines for these U.S. diseases. Treatment is supportive, meaning it attempts to deal with problems such as swelling of the brain, loss of the automatic breathing activity of the brain, and other treatable complications like bacterial pneumonia.

WEST NILE VIRUS

West Nile (WN) virus was first isolated in the West Nile District of Uganda in 1937. The virus became recognized as a cause of severe human meningoencephalitis (inflammation of the spinal cord and brain) in elderly patients during an outbreak in Israel in 1957. WN is closely related to St. Louis encephalitis virus found in the U.S. Equine disease was first noted in Egypt and France in the early 1960s. Recent outbreaks of WN virus encephalitis in humans have occurred in Algeria in 1994, Romania in 1996–1997, the Czech Republic in 1997, the Democratic Republic of the Congo in

1998, Russia in 1999, and Israel in 2000. WN's first appearance in the Western Hemisphere was in the U.S. in 1999. It is not known from where the U.S. virus originated, but it is most closely related genetically to strains found in the Middle East.

In 1999, 62 cases of severe disease in humans, including 7 deaths, occurred in the New York area. One of the species of mosquitoes found to carry West Nile virus is the *Culex* species which survives through the winter, or "overwinter," in the adult stage. That the virus survived along with the mosquitoes was documented by the widespread transmission the summer of 2000. Cumulative maps from the CDC depicting the virus in humans, horses, wild birds, sentinel chickens, and mosquitoes reflect a concentration in New Jersey, New York, and Connecticut in 1999 that spread along the eastern seaboard from New Hampshire to North Carolina in 2000. In 2001, the disease expanded from New Hampshire to Florida and west to Illinois, Wisconsin, and Louisiana. While this sounds frightening, it is very important to know that as of September 10, 2001, only six human cases have been verified in 2001 (New Jersey, one; Georgia, one; and Florida, four).

When is West Nile Virus Most Common and How is it Transmitted?

In the U.S., West Nile encephalitis cases occur primarily in the late summer or early fall.

People get West Nile encephalitis through the bite of mosquitoes infected with West Nile virus after the mosquitoes have fed on infected birds. Infected mosquitoes can then transmit West Nile virus to humans and animals while biting to take blood. Even if you live in an area where birds or mosquitoes with West Nile virus have been reported and a mosquito bites you, you are not likely to get sick. This

is because even in areas where mosquitoes do carry the virus, less than 1% of mosquitoes are infected. Even if the mosquito is infected, less than 1% of people who get bitten and become infected will get severely ill. Most West Nile–infected humans have no symptoms, which means that the chances you will become severely ill from any one mosquito bite are extremely small. West Nile encephalitis is not transmitted person-to-person. There is no documented evidence that a pregnancy is at risk due to infection with West Nile virus. As yet, no vaccine for WN virus exists, but several companies are working on it. The CDC monitors the disease very closely and frequently updates the data on the USGS web pages under the Center for Integration of Natural Disaster Information (CINDI) at cindi.usgs.gov.

West Nile Virus & Animals

Although the vast majority of infections have been identified in birds, through September 10, 2001, the CDC has received reports of WN virus infection in horses, cats, bats, chipmunks, skunks, squirrels, domestic rabbits, and raccoons. There is no evidence that a person can get the virus from handling live or dead infected birds, but it's always a good idea to avoid bare-handed contact when handling any dead animals. Use gloves or double plastic bags to place the carcass in a garbage can. There is no documented evidence of person-to-person or animal-to-person transmission of West Nile virus. Basic veterinary infection control precautions should be followed when caring for a horse suspected to have this or any viral infection.

Who is at Risk for West Nile Virus?

Residents of areas where virus activity has been identified are at risk of getting West Nile encephalitis, and people over 50 years of age have the highest risk of severe disease.

Symptoms of West Nile Encephalitis

Most infections are mild, and symptoms include:

- Fever.
- Headache.
- Body aches.
- Occasional skin rash and swollen lymph glands.

More severe infection may be marked by:

- Headache.
- High fever.
- Neck stiffness.
- Stupor.
- Disorientation.
- Coma.
- Tremors.
- Convulsions.
- Muscle weakness.
- Paralysis.
- Rarely, death.

Contact your health care provider if you have concerns about your health vis-à-vis West Nile virus. Especially if you live in an area where WN virus has been reported, or if you or your family members develop symptoms such as high fever, confusion, muscle weakness, and severe headaches, see your doctor immediately. Your physician will first take a medical history to assess your risk for WN virus. If you are determined to be at high risk and have symptoms of West Nile encephalitis, your provider will draw a blood sample and send it to a commercial or public health laboratory for confirmation.

Cautionary Notes for Duck and Other Wild Game Hunters

Because of their outdoor exposure, game hunters may be at risk if they become bitten by mosquitoes in areas with West Nile virus activity. The extent to which WN virus may be present in wild game is unknown. Hunters should follow the usual precautions when handling wild animals. If they anticipate being exposed to mosquitoes, they should apply insect repellents to clothing and skin, according to label instructions, to prevent mosquito bites.

Mosquitoes transmit arboviral encephalitis among several different hosts, including humans.

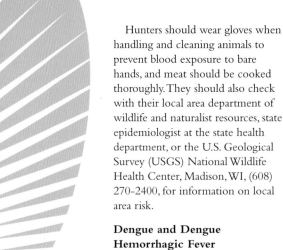

Hunters should wear gloves when handling and cleaning animals to prevent blood exposure to bare hands, and meat should be cooked thoroughly. They should also check with their local area department of wildlife and naturalist resources, state epidemiologist at the state health department, or the U.S. Geological Survey (USGS) National Wildlife Health Center, Madison, WI, (608) 270-2400, for information on local area risk.

Dengue and Dengue Hemorrhagic Fever

Dengue is a mosquito-borne infection which in recent years has become a major international public health concern. As of 1997, dengue is the most important mosquito-borne viral disease affecting humans. Its global distribution is comparable to that of malaria, and an estimated 2.5 billion people live in areas at risk for epidemic transmission. Each year, tens of millions of cases of dengue fever occur, and depending on the year, up to hundreds of thousands of cases of Dengue Hemorrhagic Fever (DHF). The case-fatality rate of DHF in most countries is about 5%; most fatal cases are among children and young adults.

Dengue fever is a severe, flu-like illness that affects infants, young children, and adults, but rarely causes death. The clinical features of dengue fever vary according to the age of the patient. Infants and young children may have a nonspecific fever with rash. Older children and adults may have either a mild fever or the classical incapacitating disease with abrupt onset and high fever, severe headache, pain behind the eyes, muscle and joint pains, and rash. Dengue hemorrhagic fever is a potentially deadly complication that is characterized by high fever, hemorrhagic phenomena, often with enlargement of the liver, and in severe cases, circulatory failure.

The illness commonly begins with a sudden rise in temperature accompanied by facial flush and other nonspecific constitutional symptoms of dengue fever. The fever usually continues for two to seven days, and can be high enough to trigger convulsions and hemorrhagic phenomena. In moderate DHF cases, all signs and symptoms abate after the fever subsides. In severe cases, the patient's condition may suddenly deteriorate after a few days of fever. The temperature drops, is followed by signs of circulatory failure, and the patient may rapidly go into a critical state of shock and die within 12 to 24 hours, *or* quickly recover following appropriate volume replacement therapy.

There is a small but significant risk for dengue outbreaks in the continental U.S. Two competent mosquito vectors are present *(Aedes aegypti* and *Aedes albopictus),* and under certain circumstances, each could transmit dengue viruses. This type of transmission has been detected three times in the last 16 years in south Texas (1980, 1986, and 1995). Moreover, numerous viruses are introduced annually by travelers returning from tropical areas where dengue viruses are endemic. From 1977 to 1994, a total of 2,248 suspected cases of imported dengue were reported in the U.S., and 481 cases (21%) were confirmed as dengue. Many more cases probably go unreported each year because surveillance in the U.S. is passive and relies on physicians to recognize the disease, inquire about the patient's travel history, obtain proper diagnostic samples, and report the case. These data suggest that southern Texas and the southeastern U.S., where *Aedes aegypti* is found, are at risk for dengue transmission and sporadic outbreaks. However, this mosquito is not found in the mid-Atlantic region.

Mosquitoes generally acquire dengue while feeding on the blood of an infected person. Once infected, a mosquito is capable of transmitting the virus to susceptible individuals for the rest of its life during probing and blood feeding. Infected female mosquitoes may also transmit the virus to the next generation of mosquitoes via their eggs. The virus circulates in the blood of infected humans for two to seven days, or approximately the same time as they have fever. *Aedes* mosquitoes may acquire the virus when they feed on an individual at this time.

There is no specific treatment for dengue fever, but careful clinical management by experienced physicians and nurses frequently saves the lives of DHF patients. With appropriate intensive supportive therapy, mortality may be reduced to less than 1%.

Vaccine development for dengue and DHF is difficult because any of four different viruses may cause disease, and because protection against only one or two dengue viruses could actually increase the risk of more serious disease. Nonetheless, progress is gradually being made in the development of vaccines that may protect against all four dengue viruses. Such products could be commercially available within several years.

At present, the only method of controlling or preventing dengue and DHF is to combat the vector mosquitoes. In Asia and the Americas, *Aedes aegypti* breeds primarily in man-made containers like earthenware jars, metal drums, and concrete cisterns used for domestic water storage, as well as discarded plastic food containers, used automobile tires, and other items that collect rainwater. In recent years, *Aedes albopictus,* a secondary dengue vector in Asia, has become established in the U.S.. The rapid geographic spread of this species has been largely attributed to the international trade in used tires.

Malaria

In the 1880s and before, malaria was prevalent in the U.S. along the Atlantic seaboard throughout the lower southeastern states, and it also widely blanketed the mid-U.S. from Canada down to Mexico. Through eradication efforts, by 1912 the disease prevalence had largely retreated from the midwest, but held firm in east Texas; Arkansas; Mississippi; Louisiana; parts of Georgia, Tennessee, and Kentucky; throughout Florida and up the Atlantic seaboard. While nowhere near the levels reported in the U.S. through the 1940s, malaria transmission still occurs sporadically in this country due to the persistence of mosquitoes capable of transmitting the parasite. Each year there are over 1,000 cases of imported malaria reported in the U.S.

The CDC received reports of 1,275 cases of malaria in persons in the U.S. and its territories who had onset of symptoms during 1993, a 40 percent increase over the 910 malaria cases reported for 1992. Through 1993, almost all cases of malaria diagnosed in the U.S. were imported from regions of the world where malaria transmission was known to occur. Malaria is reported frequently in U.S. travelers and military or other personnel deployed in endemic areas. Each year, a few congenital infections and infections resulting from exposure to infected blood and blood products have been acquired in the U.S. In addition, outbreaks of malaria that were probably acquired through local mosquito-borne transmission

Imported Malaria Cases in the Mid-Atlantic U.S. in 1995	
Delaware	3
Maryland	11
New York City	238
New Jersey	21
Pennsylvania	17
Virginia	57
West Virginia	5
Source: Centers for Disease Control	

were identified during 1989–1992 (i.e., California outbreaks in 1988, 1989, and 1990; Florida in 1991; and New Jersey in 1991).

Symptoms of malaria include fever, shivering, pain in the joints, headache, repeated vomiting, generalized convulsions, and coma. Severe anemia (exacerbated by malaria) is often the attributable cause of death in areas with intense malaria transmission. If not treated, the disease progresses to severe malaria, a cause of death.

The Comeback Kid? According to an Oct. 6, 2000, report from the National Institute of Allergy and Infectious Diseases Symptoms, malaria is considered a reemerging disease globally, due largely to the spread of drug-resistant parasite strains, decay of health care infrastructure, and difficulties in implementing and maintaining vector control programs in many developing countries. As a result of the spread of drug-resistant parasites and insecticide-resistant mosquitoes, in many respects there are fewer tools now to control malaria than existed even 20 years ago.

The *Infectious Disease News* ran this report dated February, 1998:

ORLANDO, Fla. - Due in large measure to increased antibiotic resistance, air travel and changes in the environment and population make-up, malaria transmission may be on the rise again in the U.S.

Centers for Disease Control and Prevention (CDC) epidemiologists said outbreaks in New Jersey, Texas, California, and New York are early warning signs that the reemergence of malaria could become a public health problem. Some of the signs are hotter and more humid weather, an influx of recent immigrants from malaria-endemic areas, and the lack of proper diagnosing and reporting of suspected malaria by health officials.

"Since malaria is something that hasn't been seen in this country for many years,

doctors presented with it should immediately treat the patient and report their findings to the local health department," said Lawrence Barat, MD, epidemiologist at the Division of Parasitic Diseases of the CDC. "Malaria, if caught early, can be stopped before it spreads."

In August 1998, the Associated Press ran this release:

Rare Malaria Case in U.S. State of Virginia

Monroe Hall, Virginia, USA–A 63-year-old woman contracted malaria, prompting U.S. federal health investigators to search for the source of the often-fatal disease. It is the first time the disease has been transmitted by mosquito in the U.S. since 1996 and the first time in the mid-atlantic state of Virginia in 50 years, according to the U.S. Centers for Disease Control and Prevention. "This is a rare situation," said Holly Williams, an epidemiologist with the center's Division of Parasitic Disease. The woman, whose name was not disclosed, is recuperating at home following an eight-day hospital stay. She doesn't remember being bitten by a mosquito but lives near swampy woods where they are common.

The bottom line is that malaria, by far the world's most important tropical parasitic disease according to the World Health Organization, may be staging something of a comeback in the U.S. Worldwide, malaria kills more people than any other communicable disease except tuberculosis. Malaria is a curable disease, however, if promptly diagnosed and adequately treated.

Malaria is transmitted by *Anopheline* mosquitoes that are found throughout North America, the number and type of which determine the extent of transmission in a given area. Transmission of malaria is affected by climate and geography, and often coincides with rainy seasons.

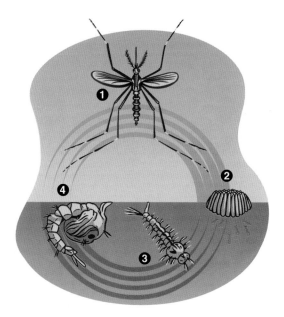

*The adult mosquito **(1)** lays a clutch of eggs in water **(2)**. The eggs hatch into larvae **(3)** which eventually grow into the tranistional pupa stage **(4)**. Finally, the mosquito emerges from the pupal case as a fully developed adult **(1)**.*

Although at present malaria poses no viable threat in the mid-Atlantic region, it is vitally important that you take a malaria prevention medicine if you are traveling to a country where malaria is prevalent. Your doctor can prescribe one for you. Some anti-malarial drugs produce minor side effects such as nausea and dizziness, but the alternative of contracting the disease (and potentially bringing more of it into the U.S.) is a critical one to consider.

MOSQUITO LIFE CYCLE

Now that we have a clearer picture of the damage mosquitoes can accomplish with their probing snouts, how can we stop them in their feather-light tracks?

There are 174 different species of mosquitoes in the U.S., all of which live in specific habitats and bite different types of animals. Despite these differences, all mosquitoes share some common traits, such as a four-stage life cycle. After the female mosquito obtains a blood meal (male mosquitoes do not bite), she lays her eggs directly on the surface of stagnant water, in a depression, or on the edge of a container where rainwater may collect and flood the eggs. The eggs hatch and a mosquito larva or "wriggler" emerges. The larva lives in the water, feeds, and develops into the third stage of the life cycle called a pupa or "tumbler." The pupa also lives in the water, but no longer feeds. Finally, the mosquito emerges from the pupal case and the water as a fully developed adult, ready to bite.

We All Need Water: Interrupting the Life Cycle by Eliminating Mosquito Breeding Sites

All mosquitoes require water to reach adulthood, so the best single thing you can do to reduce mosquitoes around your home is to make

sure there is no standing water in which they can reproduce. The best time to hunt for stagnant water is after a rainstorm or after you water the lawn. With diligence, you can interrupt the life cycle that produces a new generation of blood-suckers every 7 to 12 days.

- Remove containers such as soda cans, tires, buckets, plastic sheeting, or other water-catchers from areas surrounding your home.
- Do not allow water to remain in flowerpot bases or pet dishes for longer than a week.
- Clean gutters, downspouts, roofs, etc., to remove leaves and other debris that may hold standing water.
- Change water in birdbaths and children's wading pools at least once a week.
- Tree holes or stumps can often hold water. Drain them by drilling or fill them with sand or earth.
- Water your landscaping so standing water will not accumulate for more than a few days. Fill in any depressions that tend to hold water.
- Inspect animal water troughs and the surrounding ground for larval mosquitoes (they look like their name, "wigglers") and change the water if necessary.
- Stock your garden pool or ornamental pond with mosquito predators such as the top minnow *(Gambusia affinis)* or the common goldfish.
- Check to make sure that covers on boats or pools do not retain water.
- Cover rain-collecting barrels with a 16-mesh screen.

Container-breeding mosquitoes usually have a territory of about a city block, so make your cleanup a neighborhood effort with this idea in mind: If it holds water, get rid of it. Dense vegetation serves as resting sites for adults, so trimming it back will help to reduce the population, too, as will keeping the grass in check. In *Outwitting Critters: A Humane Guide for Confronting Devious Animals and Winning*, Bill Adler, Jr. advises, "Then there are the bug zappers, which are indiscriminate in their effect, and kill all insects. When you're sitting in the backyard listening to the rapid *zip!* of the zapper, you're hearing good insects go up in smoke. The zapper's light also attracts all the bugs in the neighborhood to your yard. If you want to use a zapper, give one as a present to a neighbor a few houses away."

WAYS TO AVOID MOSQUITO BITES

- Stay away from swampy, marshy areas where mosquito populations are high, but if you must go, use head nets, long sleeves and long pants. Mosquito-proof jackets made of tight mesh, with covering for your entire head, and pants can be found at outdoor specialty stores.
- Apply repellents, such as DEET or Permanone (containing permethrin) to your clothing, taking care to follow the application instructions. (See more on DEET below.)
- If you don't want to use a DEET-based repellent, look for alternatives such as Avon's Skin-So-Soft, or natural-based applications with lemongrass and pennyroyal. Others in this group include allspice, bay, camphor, cedar, cinnamon, citronella, geranium, lavender, nutmeg, peppermint, pine, and thyme. These may have some repellent properties, but they are limited in effectiveness in

Mosquitoes can breed in almost any standing water, particularly in pockets of collected, undisturbed rainwater. Popular breeding sites around the home include ornamental ponds **(A)**, *neglected pools* **(B)**, *hot tubs* **(C)**, *wading pools* **(D)**, *open boats* **(E)**, *dripping fauctes* **(F)**, *abandoned toys* **(G)**, *clogged gutters* **(H)**, *flowerpots* **(I)**, *wheelbarrows* **(J)**, *and birdbaths* **(K)**.

comparison to DEET. An extract of eucalyptus oil, though, does have the potential to become a promising alternative to DEET.

- Citronella products such as candles provide some help, but if a breeze is blowing their effectiveness is compromised.
- "Backyard foggers" do work temporarily, but like zappers, they are wiping out the good, as well as the bad and the ugly, not to mention that you are breathing the deterrent, too.
- Make sure your window and door screens are "bug tight."
- Use yellow "bug lights" out-

doors to reduce insect attraction to lighted areas.

The Dirt on DEET

DEET (chemical name: diethyl-meta-toluamide) is the active ingredient in many insect repellent products, and it is used to repel biting pests such as mosquitoes and ticks, including ticks that may carry Lyme disease. Every year, approximately one-third of the U.S. population uses DEET. Products containing DEET currently are available to the public in a variety of liquids, lotions, sprays, and impregnated materials (e.g., wristbands, which are of dubious

value in repelling insects). Formulations registered with the EPA for direct application to human skin contain from 4–100% DEET.

DEET is designed for direct application to human skin to repel insects, rather than kill them. After it was developed by the U.S. Army in 1946, DEET was registered for use by the general public in 1957. As of April 1998, approximately 230 products containing DEET are currently registered with the EPA by about 70 different companies.

Some people are concerned about the human health implications of using DEET. After evaluation, however, the EPA's regulatory division has concluded that as long as consumers follow label directions and take proper precautions, insect repellents containing DEET do not present a health concern. Part of this evaluation rests on the belief that human exposure is expected to be brief; long-term exposure is not expected. Based on "extensive toxicity testing," the EPA believes that the normal use of DEET does not present a health concern to the general population.

If you are comfortable with going chemical, Dr. Paul Auerbach on outdoorhealth.com has this advice:

Choose a product with one or more of these four active ingredients:
- N,N-diethyl-3-methylbenzamide (DEET)
- butyl 3,4-dihydro-2,2-dimethyl-4-oxo-2H-pyran-6-carboxylate (Indalone)
- 2-ethyl-1,3-hexanediol (EHD; Rutgers 612)
- dimethyl phthalate (DMP)

Good choices include:
- Ben's 100 (100% DEET)
- Cutter spray (18% DEET, 12% DMP)
- Cutter stick (33% DEET), Cutter cream (52% DEET, 13% DMP)
- Muskol spray (25% DEET)
- Muskol lotion (100% DEET)
- OFF spray (25% DEET)
- Deep Woods OFF cream (30% DEET)
- Deep Woods OFF liquid maximum strength (100% DEET)
- 6-12 Plus spray (25% EHD, 5% DEET)
- Repel spray (40% DEET)
- Sawyer Products' Gold (16.6% DEET plus MGK 264 synergist) is an effective lotion that can be applied to skin to repel ticks, mosquitoes, biting gnats and flies, and fleas. Sawyer Controlled Release DEET Formula is advertised to provide 24-hour protection and to minimize absorption of DEET by using an encapsulating protein to keep the chemical off the skin.

Take note! Do not use repeated applications or concentrations of DEET greater than 15% on children under the age of 6 years. In adults, 75–100% DEET may cause skin rash and, rarely, serious adverse neurological reactions.

Safe Use of DEET Repellents
The following safety regulations from the EPA indicate that although DEET is an effective repellent as a chemical substance it is nothing to be trifled with.
- Do not apply over cuts, wounds, or irritated skin.
- Do not apply to hands or near eyes and mouth of young children.
- Do not allow young children to apply DEET products.
- Do not use under clothing.
- Do not spray in enclosed areas.
- Do not spray repellent directly onto face. Spray it on your hands first, and then rub it on your face.
- Do use just enough repellent to cover exposed skin and/or clothing.

- Do avoid breathing a repellent spray and do not use it near food.
- Do avoid over-application of DEET products.
- Do wash treated skin with soap and water after returning indoors.
- Do wash treated clothing before wearing it again.

Use of DEET may cause skin reactions in rare cases. If you suspect that you are or your child is having an adverse reaction, discontinue use of the product, wash treated skin, and call your local poison control center (see list in the back of this book) or physician for help. If you go to a doctor, take the repellent container with you.

Children and Insects

- Apply an insect repellent regularly to the child's skin if in an area where bites are a risk (note that repellents are not effective against stinging insects). Use a repellent with the lowest possible concentration of DEET or use a natural repellent without DEET.
- Dress the child in light-colored clothing thick enough that insects can't bite through it.
- Teach the child to be respectful of bug's homes; this may mean not turning over rocks and logs (or doing so carefully and only with adult supervision), and not disturbing spiderwebs.
- Teach the child to shake out shoes and clothing before putting them on, especially if the shoes and clothes have been sitting outdoors.
- Teach the child to freeze ("play statue") when he or she is being investigated by stinging insects so that the child doesn't frighten the insect into stinging.
- Keep tent screens zipped, opening them only to enter and exit the tent.

- Have the child sleep enclosed in a mosquito net if in an area where mosquitoes are especially numerous or persistent.
- Shake out the child's sleeping bag or bedding before going to sleep. Have the child wear shoes at all times, especially after dark when insects are likely to be around.
- Coating the skin with mud also acts as a repellent, as does cigar smoke.
- Apply repellent to children yourself so that it doesn't get on their hands or in their mouths or eyes. Keep repellent off of a child's hands so they don't rub it in their eyes or get it in their mouths.
- Do not apply insect repellent to infants.
- Do not apply insect repellent underneath clothing.
- Wash insect repellent off of the skin after bites are no longer a threat.

Public Spraying to Control Mosquitoes

If you live in areas where massive mosquito control has become a governmental concern, you may occasionally have ULV (Ultra Low Volume) spray trucks rumble through your neighborhood, spreading chemical repellent—or maybe your pesticide is delivered via airmail. The EPA has evaluated the risks of human exposure to these compounds such as malathion and naled, and has determined them to be from 100 to 10,000 times below an amount that would pose a health concern. Their estimates projected several spraying events over a period of weeks, and also, you might be interested to learn, factored in the assumption that a toddler would eat some soil and grass during that interval, too. Although the EPA is not worried about your overexposure to such compounds, they do recommend the following:

- Listen and watch for announcements about spraying and remain indoors during the application in your area.
- If you have chemical sensitivities or think the spraying might aggravate an existing health problem, contact your doctor or you local health department to take special measures to avoid exposure.
- Close your windows and turn off window air conditioners when spraying is taking place.
- Do not let children play near truck-mounted applicators when they are in use.

seaboard from Maine to Florida, west to Texas, and north to Nebraska.

• SIZE
0.2 inch.

• DESCRIPTION
Its body is golden brown with smoky-colored wings (females have spotted wings) and a feathery thorax.

• HABITAT
The golden salt-marsh mosquito lives adjacent to salty or brackish water.

• COMMENTS
Its larvae, which feed on algae, are also found in unused swimming pools.

GOLDEN SALT-MARSH MOSQUITO
Ochlerotatus sollicitans

HOUSE MOSQUITO
Culex pipiens

SUBSPECIES:

Black salt-marsh mosquito
Aedes taeniorhynchus

• DANGER
This mosquito is a carrier for diseases such as encephalitis.

• ABUNDANCE & RANGE
It is found along the Atlantic

• DANGER
The house mosquito is a carrier for diseases such as encephalitis.

• ABUNDANCE & RANGE
It is found throughout the U.S., with a northern and southern subspecies in these respective areas.

• SIZE
0.2 inch.

• DESCRIPTION
It has a brown probiscus (mouth-parts) and wings. Its abdomen is banded white and brown.

• HABITAT
This mosquito lives near stagnant water such as ponds, lakes, and swamps. Larvae are found in foul-water receptacles, sewage, and waste-contaminated runoff.

• COMMENTS
This is the most common night-flying mosquito and a common pest.

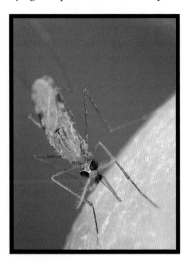

MALARIA-CARRYING MOSQUITO
Anopheles **spp.**

• DANGER
It is potentially lethal as a malaria vector.

• ABUNDANCE & RANGE
This mosquito is common through-out the U.S.

• SIZE
0.2 inch.

• DESCRIPTION
Slender legs on a dark brown body with pale hair on the head. When touching down, it executes a "head-stand" with its hind legs in the air.

• HABITAT
This mosquito is found in areas of human habitation and in deciduous and mixed forests.

• COMMENTS
The few recorded cases of malaria transmission in the mid-Atlantic U.S. make this species a very mar-ginal threat to human health

SNOW MOSQUITO
Aedes communis

• DANGER
It is potentially lethal as a malaria vector.

• ABUNDANCE & RANGE
This mosquito is common through-out the northern U.S.

• SIZE
0.25 inch.

• DESCRIPTION
Brown body has dark and light bands on top of the abdomen. The wings are brown-scaled.

• HABITAT
This mosquito is found in shady forests.

• COMMENTS
This mosquito is active in cold weather, even when snow is on the ground.

Summer Mosquito

Ochlerotatus atlanticus

• DANGER

This mosquito is a possible carrier for diseases such as encephalitis.

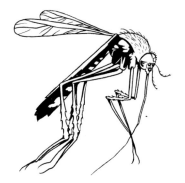

• ABUNDANCE & RANGE

It is found from New Jersey south to Florida and west to Texas.

• SIZE

0.2 inch.

• DESCRIPTION

Thorax, abdomen, wings, and legs are dark brown. The thorax has a light-colored stripe in the center.

• HABITAT

The summer mosquito lives in the vicinity of standing, shallow water.

• COMMENTS

Summer rains that increase the standing water breeding locations increase population. A related species, *Aedes aegypti,* is not common but is the carrier of dengue in the tropics.

Tree-Hole Mosquito

Aedes triseriatus

• DANGER

This mosquito is a carrier for diseases such as LaCrosse encephalitis.

• ABUNDANCE & RANGE

It is found throughout the eastern U.S.

• SIZE

0.25 inch.

• DESCRIPTION

The tree-hole mosquito is black to brown with white streaks and patches on head and thorax. Abdomen has dark and light bands.

• HABITAT

It is found in tree holes in mature woodlands.

• COMMENTS

This is the most widely distributed species of tree-hole breeders.

FLIES

"Wouldn't hurt a fly," the saying goes, but if you've had big or little buzzing biters attack you, it's easy to wonder where in the world that saying originated. Flies belong to the *Diptera* ("two winged") order, the group of insects with one pair of flight wings. They do have a second pair of "wings," though, knobby organs used for flight stability called halteres. North America has about 16,300 of the world's 86,000 known species, with many still awaiting discovery. Thousands of species are known only from fossils, the oldest of which, a limoniid crane fly, is some 225 million years old. Members of the order *Diptera* include mosquitoes and midges, as well as flies.

You'd have to go to the Arctic poles to escape them, so commonplace are flies. They destroy our food, especially grains and fruits, and they can also be superior disease carriers, as well as aggravating biters, depending on the species. On the positive side, they are important in pollination and as a food supply for other animals. On the dark positive side, the blue bottle fly *(Calliphora vomitoria)*—also called the common blow fly—keeps wounds sterile while feeding on such wounds, but they do retard healing when doing so (surprise!).

LOW LIFE

You've seen them land on your sandwich, but try not to think about where those fly feet have been before that. It's as bad as you think it is: flies subsist on various organic substances, including excrement. This makes them transmitters of germs for infectious diseases such as cholera, dysentery, diarrhea, typhoid fever, salmonellosis, hepatitis, and poliomyelitis.

Most fly species reproduce in dry areas, with breeding promoted by warm temperatures, so summertime is party time for flies. They lay up to 2,000 eggs, mostly in manure, feces, compost heaps, and some species deposit them on protein-rich substances such as meat. These eggs grow to become white maggots, larvae typical of the *Diptera* order that are soft, legless, and look headless. Probably to your horror, you may have discovered them in the cat litter box in summer if you were negligent in freshening it. If you don't tightly secure and cover your garbage, you'll also offer the best possible habitat for flies to reproduce. Consider that they can complete their development in 7 to 14 days, and it's a quick turnaround to a fly problem that is out of control.

There is good reason to reduce the fly population. Adult houseflies, for example, feed on a wide range of liquid waste but can eat solid foods, such as sugar. To digest solid foods, houseflies liquefy food by regurgitating. During feeding, they also defecate on the food. No wonder then that each housefly can easily carry over one million bacteria on its body. They are passive transmitters of disease, carrying pathogens on their bodies that "hitch a ride."

TO PREVENT PASSIVE DISEASE TRANSMISSION BY FLIES:

- Cover food as much as possible on picnics.
- Eliminate breeding areas such as garbage piles and spilled animal feed.
- Bury all dead animals.
- Compost carefully, being sure never to put animal feces, meat scraps, or other animal products in a compost pile.

BITING FLIES

Other varieties of flies, such as deer and horseflies, spread trouble by biting to feed on small amounts of blood from several animals in succession. The biters are almost always the females in search of a protein meal needed to carry on the reproduction of the species. As it is with mosquitoes, every time a biting fly takes a blood meal, it injects a small amount of salivary fluid to help prevent coagulation within and around its mouthparts. This fluid contains proteins which act as allergens, resulting in swollen, itchy welts. A more generalized anaphylactic reaction, though fortunately rare, can occur in a few individuals who are hypersensitive. Some species of biting flies seem to have more allergenic saliva than others. Black flies may be worse than others in this regard.

American horseflies and deerflies may also transmit bacteria that cause tularemia, an infection transferred from an animal to a human that is most often transmitted by ticks and rabbits. Normally it is not possible to catch the disease from other humans. Biting flies have also been linked to the transmission of anthrax, but this is so rare in the U.S. your chances of contamination by biting flies are virtually nonexistent.

Black Flies

Also known as buffalo gnats and turkey gnats, black flies are small, bloodsucking insects slightly less than 0.25 inch long with a stout-bodied and hump-backed appearance. They are much more of a pest in the northern reaches of the U.S., but they are found as far south as Florida. Legendary for their bite, black flies have piercing and sucking mouthparts similar to those of mosquitoes.

Thanks to wing beats of around 300 times per second, mosquitoes will warn you of their presence, but black flies are like stealth bombers. Typically, several will hover maddeningly around your head while they take turns striking. They are prone to strike out of your range of vision—behind your ears, on your scalp, or inside your collar. Though they favor the head just beneath the hat rim, all exposed parts of the body are subject to attack. Black fly bites are bigger than mosquito bites, they sometimes bleed due to anti-coagulants in the insects' saliva, and these bites itch longer and more persistently. Livestock, pets, poultry, and wildlife are also severely irritated by these flies.

Their biting season occurs in spring and early summer just as the weather tempts humans outside. Their numbers, as well as their tendency to bite, increases as sunset approaches, but they do not bite after dark. Some species of black fly females, fresh from their underwater cocoons in cold streams, must have blood to create their eggs (from mammals or birds)—a system that is 180 million years old. Other phases of their life cycles pose no imposition on humans or on other mammals whatsoever.

Although there are cases of black fly bites inducing anaphylactic shock, the vast majority of bites are merely aggravating, and in the U.S. black flies are not known to transmit diseases to humans.

Beyond lack of disease transmission, black flies offer another plus as described by Stewart Edward White in his 1903 book, *The Forest*:

. . . [The black fly is to be complimented because] he holds still to be killed. No frantic slaps, no waving of arms, no muffled curses. You just place your finger calmly and firmly on the spot. You get him every time. In this is great, heart lifting

joy. It may be unholy joy, perhaps even vengeful, but it leaves the spirit ecstatic. The satisfaction of murdering the beast that has had the nerve to light on you just as you are reeling in almost counterbalances the pain. . . .

Signs of Black Fly Bites

- Punctures that may bleed.
- Immediate pain, swelling (welt), and redness that is frequently intense and persistent.
- Sores that may persist for weeks.
- Multiple bites can produce swollen lymph glands, particularly in children.

Avoiding Black Fly Bites

- Avoid areas along rivers and streams during late spring and early summer, though black flies cross hills and may be found miles from their lowland breeding sites.
- Take refuge indoors or in a car. When trapped inside something, black flies concentrate on escape, not on feeding.
- Tuck pants cuffs into your socks and button shirts up. Black flies cannot bite through clothing, but they will crawl under it to bite in such aggravating spots as the ankles and waist.
- Wear light-colored clothing such as white or yellow.
- Avoid blue, purple, brown, and black clothing.
- Blue jeans without holes that are tucked into socks might be better than pale trousers because they may attract the flies away from your head.
- Use insect repellents. Spraying a DEET-based repellent on your jacket will likely discourage most black flies from crawling under one's shirt or into one's hair.

Sue Hubbell, a fine writer and beekeeper by trade, discovered that a nylon (not cotton) bee suit with a zip-pered veil and cowhide gloves are just right for black-fly season in Maine during the months of May and June. Might be worth a try, though note that nylon won't absorb DEET.

Deerflies and Horseflies

Both of these biters will feed on humans, but it's more likely a deerfly that's biting you, and more likely a horsefly after your livestock. Both generally resemble a housefly, but the deerfly is slightly larger than a housefly, and the horsefly can start to take on sci-fi proportions when they reach over an inch in length. Deerflies come in late spring to early summer. Horseflies are more of a late summer phenomenon. Both types of flies are potential vectors of such diseases as anthrax, tularemia, anaplasmosis, hog cholera, equine infectious anemia, and filariasis, and perhaps Lyme disease, according to the *New England Journal of Medicine* in 1990.

Not a delicate date at all, the deerfly rams her sharp, knifelike jaws into your skin, leaving no doubt she has arrived for that blood Slurpee she craves to get her reproductive wheels spinning. The bite is painful and can leave a mark of blood after feeding on us, cattle, horses, mules, hogs, dogs, deer, and other warm-blooded animals. The anticoagulant they inject to keep the blood flowing is what triggers our histamines that cause the stinging response to their bites.

Miniature female winged vampires, adult deerflies emerge from the soil in late May or early June, ready to rock and roll. They frequently attack humans along summer beaches, near streams, and at the edges of moist, wooded areas. When bitten by deerflies, some people suffer severe lesions, high fever, and even general

disability. These symptoms are allergic reactions to hemorrhagic saliva poured into the wound to prevent clotting while the fly is feeding. A person can become increasingly sensitive to repeated bites.

Deerfly and Horsefly Bites

- They are more likely to occur on warm, sunny days when there is little or no wind.
- They are less likely to occur when the temperature drops slightly or when a breeze arises.
- They can be repelled with DEET-based solutions carefully applied according to instructions, although permethrin-based repellents applied only on clothing usually last longer.
- Mesh jackets treated with repellents that slip on over regular outdoor clothing can be very effective when a strong repellent is applied. Store the jacket in a sealed plastic bag.
- Gloves offer good protection.
- Buttoned-up and tightly woven, long-sleeved shirts and long pants can also help.
- Light-colored clothing is preferred to dark.
- Area repellents with citronella or naphthalene are helpful to repel deerflies and mosquitoes in or near a patio, yard, tent, or cabin.
- Providing daytime shelter for humans and animals is important as horse and deerflies do not appear to bite much at night.

Deerfly Bites

- Deerflies seem to be attracted to moving objects and dark shapes.
- Bites are likely to occur around the face and neck.
- As many as four to five flies may simultaneously attack.

Horsefly Bites

- Horseflies are usually attracted to shiny surfaces, motion, carbon dioxide, and warmth.
- Horseflies may attack while you are swimming in a pool.

Treatment for Fly Bites

- Take oral antihistamines, such as benadryl.
- Apply ice to affected areas.

CONTROLLING FLIES

- Do not accumulate piles of garbage and rotting substances where flies will eat and breed.
- Do not leave food or meals uncovered.
- Do keep kitchens and cooking utensils clean.
- Do use insect repellents to provide effective protection against biting flies.

BED NETTING PROTECTION

Horseflies, black flies, sand flies, deerflies, gnats, and other assorted nuisances may not be driven away by insect repellents. At such times, fashion has to fall by the wayside, and a head net (not a hair net) may be invaluable during times of high mosquito infestation. Netting can be an excellent defense, especially at night. If you use a bed net, be certain that it is free of holes and has its edges tucked in. The net needs to be woven to a tightness of 18 threads per inch (6 to 7 per centimeter). Tighter mesh may hinder ventilation, and a net that has been dipped in an insecticide, usually permethrin, is more effective. Note that fleas and chiggers are generally not deterred by bed nets.

AMERICAN HORSEFLY

Tabanus americanus

• DANGER
Their bites are painful with remote chances of transmission of tularemia.

• ABUNDANCE & RANGE
They are found throughout the U.S. east of the Rocky Mountains.

• SIZE
0.75 to 1.25 inches.

• DESCRIPTION
The horsefly's body is large and broad with a brown–black thorax and dark red-brown abdomen. Wings are smoky. Eyes are large and green.

• HABITAT
They are found near standing water such as ponds, marshes, and swamps.

• COMMENTS
According to Ross H. Arnett, Jr., "The Declaration of Independence was signed July 4, 1776, instead of a later date that would have permitted further discussion because the horse-flies in Philadelphia were biting so fiercely at the time that the delegates decided to adjourn just to get away from them." (Arnett, 2000, p. 870.)

After being quickly sliced by knifelike mouthparts and receiving an anticoagulant via saliva, horsefly wounds may continue to bleed. Repeated attacks may cause serious weakening of livestock due to loss of blood.

BLACK FLY

Simulium **spp.**

• DANGER
The black fly has a painful bite.

• ABUNDANCE & RANGE
It is found throughout the eastern U.S. south to Florida, but is more common in northern latitudes.

• SIZE
0.1 to 0.2 inch.

• DESCRIPTION
It is stout black or dark brown with short antennae, humped thorax, and short legs.

• HABITAT
The black fly is found close to running water in forests and mountains.

• COMMENTS
It is also called the buffalo gnat or turkey gnat. It carries a parasitic worm in other parts of the world that causes blindness, but this fly is

not a vector for disease in the U.S. Worst bites occur in late spring and early summer.

DRONE FLY
Eristalis tenax

DEERFLY
Chrysops **spp.**

• DANGER
Its painful bite has a remote chance of transmitting tularemia.

• ABUNDANCE & RANGE
It is found throughout the U.S.

• SIZE
0.25 to 1 inch.

• DESCRIPTION
Wings have distinctive brownish-black pattern. Body is black with yellow-green markings.

• HABITAT
The deerfly is found in damp woodlands, suburbs near water, meadows, and roadsides, especially with standing water.

• COMMENTS
This fly is active from May to September. It can be distinguished from horseflies, who have either clear or black wings or very small markings.

• DANGER
These are carriers of intestinal myiasis (maggot infestation).

• ABUNDANCE & RANGE
They are found throughout the U.S.

• SIZE
0.6 inch.

• DESCRIPTION
The drone fly resembles a honeybee but lacks a waist between the thorax and abdomen. Movement also imitates honeybee. Body is dark brown to blackish.

• HABITAT
Adults are found in meadows, fields, and on flowers, especially daisies. Larvae, called rat-tailed maggots, are found in polluted water, on wet carrion, and in open latrines.

• COMMENTS
They are active in summer months. *Note: Readers be forewarned that the following comment is "tough to stomach."* "The adult flies may lay their eggs on soiled human bodies; for example in

vomit around the mouth of a child, or in mucus. The eggs are swallowed and the larvae grow in the intestinal tract where they may actually feed on living tissue." (Arnett, and Jacques, 1981, #331.) This intestinal myiasis may also result from ingesting food contaminated with eggs or larvae, and may produce cramps, nausea, vomiting, and diarrhea. Within a short time, however, the organisms are destroyed by gastrointestinal juices and passed in the feces.

• **HABITAT**

They are found on exposed and/or rotting food and manure.

• **COMMENTS**

These are aptly named, as 98% of flies in your house are houseflies.

HOUSEFLY
Musca domestica

• **DANGER**

These are mechanical transmitters of typhoid fever, cholera (not a threat in the U.S.), dysentery, pinworms, hook-worms, tapeworms, and salmonella.

• **ABUNDANCE & RANGE**

They are found worldwide, for prac-tical purposes.

• **SIZE**

0.1 to 0.25 inch.

• **DESCRIPTION**

The housefly has red eyes and clear wings on a gray body with four black stripes on the thorax.

MIDGES

NOSEE'UMS

Biting midges of the *Ceratopogonidae* family are also called sand flies, nosee'ums, punkies, mouse flies, and flying teeth. The smallest of the biting flies—less than 0.25 inch long—they look (under a microscope) like short-legged mosquitoes. They are so small you probably won't be aware of them until they have started to feed on you. They can be intensely aggravating, leaving a painful red bump that seems out of proportion to their size. After your immune system becomes sensitized to these bites, reactions may become worse. After repeated assaults, you may develop blisters or small sores. As usual, it's the females that are feeding on you, but not all biting midges go after humans. Some feed on other insects, pollen, and nectar.

Nosee'ums live most often near salt marshes, ponds, or streams, and by some accounts they stay within 100 yards or so of their breeding area, where their eggs are laid in gelatinous masses on the water surface. So, the farther you can get from the water source, the less likely you are to be bitten. That, plus insect repellent, is about your only line of defense against them.

They are vectors for filariasis, a parasitic disease caused by microscopic, threadlike nematode worms that only live in the human lymph system (in other mammals, these worms are transmitted by mosquitoes rather than biting midges). In its severest form, also usually as a result of mosquito bites, lymphatic filariasis causes elephantiasis—dramatic swelling of limbs (usually the leg) and genitals (usually the scrotum). It affects over 120 million people in 73 countries throughout the tropics and subtropics of Asia, Africa, the Western Pacific, and parts of Central and South America, but according to the CDC, you cannot get the worms in the U.S. So in this country, nosee'ums are just an aggravation, and not a serious threat to well-being.

SALT MARSH PUNKIE

Culicoides furens

• DANGER
The punkie's bite is severe.

• ABUNDANCE & RANGE
It is found throughout the U.S. near coastal areas.

• SIZE
0.1 to 0.2 inch.

• DESCRIPTION
They resemble tiny black flies. They have dark bodies with white markings on the thorax.

• HABITAT
Punkies are found near ponds and streams. Larvae are found in salt marshes.

• COMMENTS
They're considered a serious local pest.

CATERPILLARS

One of the great romantic stories of nature is how the lowly "worm" transforms into a spectacular, ephemeral paradigm of grace, beauty, and flight. Of course, this is the story of the metamorphosis of butterflies and moths, who begin life as eggs and then become caterpillars. After shedding their skins, these caterpillars either spin a cocoon if they are to evolve into a moth, or find a safe hiding place if to become a butterfly. A final skin shedding reveals the pupa (from the Latin for girl or doll), an outer shell with no head or feet. Inside this shell, the final metamorphosis into a winged wonder will occur.

During the larval stage, a caterpillar is a creature with a mission: eat, survive, and transform. As a part of its protective equipment, some caterpillars possess stinging spines or hairs. These sharp spines are hollow and sometimes connected to venom glands (venom flows on contact); or, similar to glass fibers, the hairs break off and lodge in skin easily, causing pain like a needle prick.

Individual reactions to these "stings" vary from mild discomfort (itching, redness, swelling, and a raised rash) to severe pain. At the extreme end, some people may experience severe swelling, nausea, and generalized systemic reactions, occasionally requiring hospital treatment. In some cases, entrance of hairs into the eye can cause blindness.

Just touching a hairy or spiny caterpillar can cause skin irritation, so wash well with soap and water after contact with a caterpillar, and don't touch your eyes, nose, or mouth until you do.

AVOIDING CATERPILLAR STINGS

Stings (we'll use the term for convenience, though caterpillar spines are not true stingers) generally occur when people accidentally brush against one of these caterpillars or when they attempt to remove it by hand from clothing or the body. Interactions usually occur in summer or obviously whenever the species is in the larval stage. Caterpillars are often found on leaves, vegetable plants, shrubs, and trees, and they are often encountered when harvesting sweet corn in late summer and early autumn. Wear long-sleeve shirts, trousers, and gloves when gathering the ears to reduce possible stings. When among trees, caterpillars may drop down on you.

When Trent was canoeing in North Carolina, he leaned forward to paddle under some overhanging trees. He felt something tickle down his back under his shirt, but at the time the rocks and the rapids had more of his attention. When he was able to stop, he found a caterpillar inside his shirt. He rid himself of the creature, but did not try to wash his back, sensing no immediate overt reaction. By that evening, however, the allergic response to the caterpillar's venom had taken effect. Several days later Trent was fine, but in the meantime he had swelling, a rash, and enough muscle soreness to make turning his head difficult. If he had been able to wash his back, or even rinse it, and perhaps apply ice when the swelling began, his caterpillar incident might have been less severe.

Be careful when attempting to brush caterpillars off. Never swat or crush by hand. Remove them carefully and slowly with a stick or other object. Never hand-pick these hairy, fuzzy, or spiny caterpillars except with heavy leather gloves if necessary.

Individuals, especially children, should be cautioned about handling or playing with any colorful, hairy, fuzzy caterpillars, since it is sometimes difficult to distinguish between harmless and venomous insect larvae. To be on the safe side, tell them if it is hairy or fuzzy and looks like a teeny, tiny hot dog, leave it alone.

TREATMENT FOR CATERPILLAR STINGS

Diagnosis is usually simple since a rash generally breaks out where the hairs or spines have made skin contact.

- Immediately apply and then remove adhesive or transparent tape over the sting site to remove broken hairs or spines. Repeat as necessary.
- Wash the affected skin area thoroughly with soap and water. This may help remove irritating venom.
- Promptly apply an ice pack and a baking soda poultice to help reduce pain and swelling.
- Household analgesics, such as aspirin, are not very effective in reducing pain and headache, but an oral antihistamine such as benadryl may help relieve itching and burning.
- Topical cortico-steroids may reduce the intensity of inflammatory reaction.
- Desoximetasone gel, a prescription topical steroid, applied twice daily to affected areas will help.
- Contact a physician promptly if severe reactions occur.
- Very young, aged, or unhealthy persons are more likely to suffer severe reaction symptoms.

IO MOTH CATERPILLAR
Automeris io

• DANGER
Their spines can penetrate skin to cause a painful sting.

• ABUNDANCE & RANGE
They are found across the eastern U.S.

• SIZE
3 inches long.

• DESCRIPTION
These caterpillars are green with reddish and white side stripes. Body segments have clumps of spines.

• HABITAT
They're common in woods, meadows, and cornfields and are found eating on a wide variety of foliage.

• COMMENTS
They spin cocoons in ground debris.

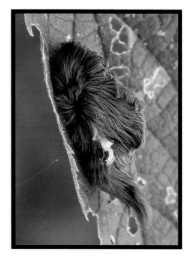

PUSS MOTH CATERPILLAR

Megalopyge opercularis

• **DANGER**
Their venomous spines can cause an allergic reaction.

• **ABUNDANCE & RANGE**
They are common from Maryland south to Florida and west to Texas.

• **SIZE**
1 inch in length.

• **DESCRIPTION**
Soft brown hair entirely covers this caterpillar.

• **HABITAT**
They are found in vegetation, including trees (particularly orange, pecan, almond, and persimmon), shrubs, and orchards.

• **COMMENTS**
Each spine or hair has its own supply of venom. Symptoms of reaction range from minor rash to severe allergic reaction, including fainting, nausea, and vomiting.

SADDLEBACK MOTH CATERPILLAR

Sibine stimulea

• **DANGER**
Spines cause sting on contact.

• **ABUNDANCE & RANGE**
These caterpillars are found from Massachusetts south to Florida and east to Louisiana.

• **SIZE**
1 inch.

• **DESCRIPTION**
It has a brilliant green body with dark brown ends and a highly distinctive dark brown oval, or "saddle" on its back encircled with white. It also has tufts of hairs (spines) along body sides.

• **HABITAT**
This caterpillar is found in gardens, woods edges, and orchards where it feeds on a wide variety of foliage.

• **COMMENTS**
Children, who may be especially drawn to these caterpillars because of their distinctive patterns, should be forewarned not to handle them.

TRUE BUGS

So what's a true bug? An old VW? Actually, entomologists really do have an order called "true bugs," or *Hemiptera*, which means "half wing." True bugs have forewings called hemelytra, leathery thick in the front, and transparent and membranous in the back. Another way to identify true bugs is by the way they fold their wings flat over their bodies, making an X-shape. They have sucking beaks to slurp juices, but most feed on plants. Another common trait is that most true bugs also have glands that dispatch a foul odor, e.g., the green stink bug. Most are terrestrial, but some are aquatic and can literally walk on water. The insects we're concerned with here are in the assassin bug family *(Reduviidae).* They will bite you in defense or in search of a blood meal, and the conenose or kissing bug is a vector for Chagas disease in South America, a parasitic infection that produces heart damage. Assassin bugs are named for the way they attack and "stab" victims, which is actually a bite.

IF YOU ARE BITTEN BY A BUG

- Wash the bite with soap and water.
- Apply topical relief such as Benadryl ointment, and/or . . .
- . . . take Benadryl orally if a stronger reaction such as increased swelling occurs.
- Bug bites are not known for producing anaphylactic shock, but it's always a good idea to monitor reactions of any encounter for the first hour or two.

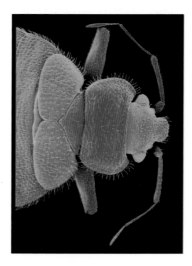

BED BUG
Cimex lectularius

• DANGER
Bed bugs bite. They have been implicated as but not proven to be disease carriers.

• ABUNDANCE & RANGE
They can be found throughout the U.S.

• SIZE
0.2 inch.

• DESCRIPTION
They are flat and reddish brown to purplish. They have short legs and stubby (vestigial) wings.

• HABITAT
They can be found in human dwellings, especially bedrooms, in all socioeconomic classes.

• COMMENTS
Each feeding bug makes several punctures. As the bugs' salivary fluid is not immediately irritating, their bites can go unnoticed for a period of time. After feeding, the nymphs and adults hide to be out of harm's way and can survive up to 15 months without food.

BLOODSUCKING CONENOSE

Triatoma sanguisuga

- **DANGER**

Conenose bites can cause severe allergic reactions.

- **ABUNDANCE & RANGE**

These are found from New Hampshire south to Florida.

- **SIZE**

0.5 to 0.75 inch.

- **DESCRIPTION**

They are black to dark brown with yellow-red markings (six spots).

- **HABITAT**

Conenose bugs are found in small animal nests.

- **COMMENTS**

They feed on bed bug, humans, and other mammals. Also known as the Mexican bed bug or the big bed bug.

MASKED HUNTER

Reduvius personatus

- **DANGER**

The masked hunter bites.

- **ABUNDANCE & RANGE**

It can be found in New York, Pennsylvania, New Jersey, and Delaware.

- **SIZE**

0.5 to 0.75 inch.

- **DESCRIPTION**

It is almost uniformly black, with a red cast, and has pale leg markings.

- **HABITAT**

The masked hunter is attracted to lights in early to midsummer.

- **COMMENTS**

It can bite humans on the lips, causing considerable swelling—hence its alternative name, "kissing bug."

WHEEL BUG

Arilus cristatus

• DANGER
The wheel bug can "stab" when handled.

• ABUNDANCE & RANGE
It is found throughout the eastern U.S.

• SIZE
1 to 1.25 inches.

• DESCRIPTION
The adult is black to grayish-brown. Nymph is deep red with black markings. The name derives from the semicircular arrangement of 8 to 12 tubercles (small, knoblike projections) resembling half a wheel.

• HABITAT
The wheel bug is found in meadows and fields with crops.

• COMMENTS
The perceived "stab" is actually a bite.

BEETLES

Fill in the blank: One of every three known animal species on the planet is a _____. If you guessed "beetle" you are a quick study, my friend. In the mud, on the mountains, at the poles, in the puddles, in the deserts, by the lakes—you name the habitat, and you find the beetles there. They are an incredibly diverse lot. They would have to be to inhabit such various ecologies, but they can be recognized by their tough, armorlike wings that close to form a straight line down their backs. These leather-like front wings, the elytra, cover and protect the real flying wings underneath them.

Beetles have some other significant things in common. Many share a defensive maneuver wherein they can emit funky odors and even acid. They are pests who make life more difficult (the boll weevil who obliterates cotton crops) and pals who amuse us with their imminently practical lives (the dung beetle who lays her eggs in the balled-up mass of other animals' dung). They all use antennae for touch and smell, and of especial interest to us, they all have biting mouthparts.

There are just a few beetles who will bite if handled. Another species, the black blister beetle, has earned its middle name. Within its blood is a poison, cantharidin, which blisters human skin on contact and is extremely irritating to mucous membranes. Cantharidin in powder form is used to remove warts (do not try this at home), and it also goes by the nickname "Spanish fly." Although this substance is billed as an aphrodisiac, in fact it is deadly poison when ingested. So potent is this toxin that horses have died because they ingested dead beetles trapped inside bales of hay. The toxicity is in relation to the size and health of the horse, but some cases suggest that as few as 100 beetles can be fatal. This number of insects seems more menacing in light of the fact that blister beetles, only about 0.5 inch in length, tend to congregate in large colonies.

PREVENTING YOUR HORSE FROM FATALLY INGESTING BLISTER BEETLES

- Learn how to identify the species of blister beetles.
- Grow your own alfalfa and maintain complete control over management practices, if possible.
- Because blister beetle populations are not large until mid-to-late summer, set aside first and often second cutting hay for use in feeding horses or consider purchasing first cutting hay from neighbors to use as horse feed.
- Watch for beetles as you cut hay; some species "swarm" in front of the harvester. If they do, stop and let the beetles disperse before continuing.
- Crimping and other conditioning increases the number of beetles that remain in the swath prior to baling. If possible, try to cut the alfalfa and put it in swaths that can be straddled by the tractor to avoid crushing beetles in the windrow.
- Eliminate weeds and cut the alfalfa before it reaches advanced bloom stages. Flowering plants attract the beetles that feed on alfalfa and weed pollen.
- Insecticide treatments are available but must be applied with pre-harvest intervals in mind. If you treat with insecticides, be sure to allow enough time so that dying beetles fall out of the canopy to the ground where they burrow into the soil. Do

not treat fields at peak bloom to avoid bee kills and losses to other beneficial species. Contact your local agricultural extension agent to assess your risk for the best control methods for your area.

IF YOU ARE BITTEN BY ANY SPECIES OF BEETLE

- Wash the affected area with antibacterial soap and water.
- Apply topical antibacterial ointment.
- Biting beetles are not known to transmit disease, but watch for signs of infection, and contact your physician if complications arise.

IF YOU ARE BLISTERED BY CONTACT WITH A BEETLE

- Gently wash the affected area with antibacterial soap and water, taking care not to break the blister.
- Treat as you would a burn with antibacterial cream. Blisters may take several weeks to heal.

BOMBARDIER BEETLE

Brachinus **spp.**

• DANGER
These beetles can emit a vapor capable of staining human skin.

• ABUNDANCE & RANGE
They are found throughout the U.S.

• SIZE
0.25 to 0.6 inch.

• DESCRIPTION
They have a distinctive two-toned body coloration with a golden brown head, prothorax, legs, and antennae. The bulk of the body is a dark blue that may have a metallic cast.

• HABITAT
They are often found under logs or rocks, near temporary pools of fresh water by lakes or alongside rivers in floodplains.

• COMMENTS
The defensive spray that can cause staining is a liquid emitted from the beetle's anal glands.

GOLD-AND-BROWN ROVE BEETLE

Ontholestes cingulatus

• DANGER
This rove beetle has sharp mandibles that can inflict a painful bite if the beetle is handled without due care.

• ABUNDANCE & RANGE
They are found throughout the U.S.

• SIZE
0.5 to 0.75 inch.

• DESCRIPTION
A dark brownish body that has black hairs forming a spotty pattern on the head, thorax, and abdomen. Yellow-golden hairs form a point at the end of the abdomen.

• HABITAT
This beetle is found in the woods on mushrooms or flowers, or especially where carrion is near.

• COMMENTS
Adults eat maggots, thereby reducing the fly population.

STRIPED BLISTER BEETLE

Epicauta vittata

• **DANGER**

This one is potentially lethal to horses (and humans!) if ingested. Blood contains a burning agent, cantharidin, that can blister human skin on contact.

• **ABUNDANCE & RANGE**

The striped blister beetle is found throughout the eastern U.S.

• **SIZE**

0.3 to 0.6 inch.

• **DESCRIPTION**

Black and dull yellow stripes run the length of the the elytra (protective forewings) and two black spots are on the dull yellow-orange head.

• **HABITAT**

It is found in pastures, fields, and croplands, including on tomato and potato plants, plus a variety of weeds.

• **COMMENTS**

Larvae feed on grasshopper eggs, which mature into potential crop pests.

SHORT-WINGED BLISTER BEETLE

Meloe angusticollis

• **DANGER**

Can exude liquid drops from its legs that can cause blisters.

• **ABUNDANCE & RANGE**

This beetle is found across the northern U.S.

• **SIZE**

0.5 to 0.6 inch.

• **DESCRIPTION**

Its uniformly dark blue to near-blue-black body is stocky and strong.

• **HABITAT**

A beetle found in agricultural fields and meadows.

• **COMMENTS**

According to the *National Audubon Society's Field Guide to North American Insects & Spiders,* this beetle feigns death by falling on its side when it is disturbed.

Six-Spotted Tiger Beetle

Cicindela sexguttata

- **DANGER**
This beetle bites if handled.

- **ABUNDANCE & RANGE**
It is common throughout the eastern U.S. from late spring through fall.

- **SIZE**
0.5 to 0.6 inch.

- **DESCRIPTION**
A brilliant metallic green, the tiger beetle usually has six white spots on forewings (elytra).

- **HABITAT**
It is found along roadways and paths in deciduous or mixed woods and in open sandy areas in fields.

- **COMMENTS**
Adults will "accompany" trail walkers for several yards, flying ahead, and then pausing as if waiting for the approaching walkers to "catch up."

Carolina Sawyer

Monochamus carolinensis

- **DANGER**
The Carolina sawyer bites if handled.

- **ABUNDANCE & RANGE**
It is found throughout the eastern U.S.

- **SIZE**
1 inch.

- **DESCRIPTION**
Antennae are considerably longer than body, which is narrow, elongated, and grayish brown. Forewings (elytra) have whitish markings.

- **HABITAT**
This beetle lives in forests, especially pine, spruce, and fir where larvae bore in.

- **COMMENTS**
Adults are attracted to lights at night.

SPIDERS

SPINNING THE STORY

Perhaps spiders can generate such strong responses in us because they loom large in our symbolic understanding of the world. In Egyptian, Babylonian, Greek, Norse, Hindu, Buddhist, Japanese, Oceanic, African, Caribbean, and Native American cultures, to name a few, the creature that is smaller than a human hand and usually about the size of penny or less, has held a revered position for millennia. In myth, spiders are portrayed as no less than the Great Mother, the great weaver of fate, the creator of the world who spins the thread of life from her body and attaches humanity to it, binding people together as one. The core of her web is the cosmic hub, whose rays, like the sun, extend outward to life.

A SHY PERSONALITY AND A KILLER BODY

Maybe it happens in your dreams, but in reality spiders will not chase you. (Jumping spiders can leap 20 times their own length to capture food, but they are not going to make a flying leap at a human.) In fact, spiders as a whole are seldom aggressive, generally biting only when threatened or injured. They do bite when ordering dinner, but we're not on their menu. They are interested in liquified flies and other similar arachnid culinary delights, and they down many pounds of mostly insects every year. Even if they did want to turn the tables on us and wrap their tiny little mouths around our big succulent thighs, the low level toxicity of their venom is negligible for humans.

Spiders are most easily recognized by their four pairs of legs divided into seven segments. Like other arachnids, spiders possess a cephalothorx and abdomen, but they also have a "waist" or pedicel, a body configuration which scorpions, mites, and daddy longlegs do not possess. Although variety among spiders is great, most have eight simple (not compound) eyes that are in two or three rows. Below the eyes are two small jaws, the chelicerae, that end in fangs. Venom produced in these glands empties into the fangs through a duct. That venom is released when spiders want to paralyze or kill prey.

HOW DO SPIDERS PREY?

Silently. Almost all spiders are poisonous, or more accurately venomous. This means they bite their victims and inject a venom, most often one that essentially breaks down the prey so that the spider can then eat it in its "pre-digested" form, though what happens next varies. Most spiders then puncture the insect's exoskeleton, pump in that digestive enzyme that liquifies the "innards," and then suck that soup right into their stomachs, leaving just a mere shell of what

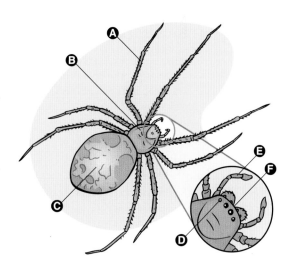

Typical spider anatomy: eight legs **(A)**, *cephalothorax* **(B)**, *abdomen* **(C)**, *eight simple eyes* **(D)**, *two feelers* **(E)**, *and mouth parts* **(F)**.

once was probably a viable six-legger. Other spiders use their jaws to grind their prey to a pulp before they spray it with digestive juices and then suck it up.

WHICH SPIDERS HAVE DANGEROUS BITES?

Many spiders do bite, but for the most part their bites are insignificant. However, just as bee and wasp stings may trigger allergic reactions in some people, the same can be true for spider bites. Young children, the elderly, and hypersensitive individuals are more likely to react strongly to a spider bite. Encounters between people and spiders are usually accidental and occur when the spider's web or nest is disturbed. There are 3,000 spider species in North America, but only black widows, recluses, hobos, and tarantulas are chief causes for concern, and only black widows live in the mid-Atlantic region.

Of the four types of spiders to be concerned about, each will produce different effects. Generally speaking, black widows make you ill overall, brown recluses and hobo spiders make the tissue at the bite site rot (the hobo might also give you a whopper headache), and tarantulas inflict a minor wound comparable to a wasp sting. Also note that the urticating hairs on tarantulas' abdomens can also cause irritation to skin, mucous membranes, and particularly the eyes.

REDUCING SPIDER POPULATIONS

Spiders are overwhelmingly beneficial creatures, and we owe them gratitude for eating the many insects that feed on the flowers, shrubs, and other plants in our gardens and natural areas. Many folks, however, still just don't want them in the general vicinity. Keep in mind, though, that

if you spray chemicals to reduce general spider populations, you may actually increase your number of pests by also destroying the spider's natural enemies.

Although not all spiders build webs (some hide and some just hang out), web-building spiders are most likely to show up in areas where insects are abundant, e.g., around woodpiles, porch lights, windows, or water sources such as spigots. (It's always about food and water in the end.) Knocking down these webs with a broom or burst of water from a garden hose will provide adequate regulation. Outdoor pesticide applications for spiders are largely unnecessary and should be avoided.

On occasion, you will find spiders on objects or in areas that have been left undisturbed, including sandboxes or even children's toys. Check these items periodically for signs of spiders. For obvious reasons, don't spray pesticides around sandboxes or other play areas unless you absolutely have to.

Likewise, if you have spiders indoors, that means they are getting the survival substances they need, such as insects. If you work to reduce the insects, the spider population in your house will decline, too.

You can also:
- Knock down webs.
- Vacuum along baseboards, in corners, and under furniture.
- Clean bookshelves periodically.

If you're concerned that more spiders will show up (or hatch from an unseen egg sac), then you could resort to applying an insecticide along baseboards, in corners, and inside storage closets, but be sure to select a pesticide that is labeled for use against spiders indoors. Always read the insecticide label for complete instructions on how and where to use the product.

Treating your crawl space is an option, but exercise extreme caution when applying pesticides in such confined areas without adequate ventilation and personal protection. For these reasons, crawl space treatments are often best left to pest control professionals. Again, your county agricultural agent can advise you on the latest and wisest methods for large-scale problems.

GENERAL RULES FOR AVOIDING SPIDER BITES

- Check for spiders before sticking your bare hands into dark corners or areas.
- Wear work gloves when handling boxes, firewood, lumber, and other items that have been stored/stacked undisturbed for some time.
- Before wearing, shake stored clothing vigorously to dislodge any spiders and inspect the clothing carefully.

WHAT TO DO IF YOU THINK YOU HAVE BEEN BITTEN BY A VENOMOUS SPIDER

- Remain calm. The chance that your wound will prove fatal is extremely remote. The 1998 annual report of the American Association of Poison Control Centers attributed only three deaths nationwide to spiders. In 1997, there were none.
- Carefully apply ice or a cold pack to decrease pain, though ice should not be applied directly to the skin.
- Collect the specimen, if possible, for a positive identification. If you can't easily do this, do try to get a good look at the spider, and if possible get a family member, neighbor, coworker, or friend working on the identification, too.
- Seek medical attention and/or contact your local poison control center immediately (see the list in the back of this book).

Before calling emergency facilities, try to determine the following information:
- Patient's age, weight, and condition.
- Time the bite occurred.
- Area where the bite occurred.
- Identity of the spider, if possible.

Poison Control (listed in the back of this book) will help you determine what steps to take next.

If I am Bitten, How Serious Will the Bite Be?

The answer to this question depends on factors like:
- Species of spider.
- Area of the body where the bite occurs.
- Amount of venom injected.
- Depth of the bite.

Black Widow Spiders

The intrigue of it all: "She mates, she bites, he dies, and now she is . . . the widow . . . the black widow of death!" Sounds like a promo for a Hitchcock horror movie, doesn't it? Indeed, many people do find the thought of black widow spiders spine-tingling. They are probably one of the first "deadly" creatures that children learn about, coloring the coal-black bodies and the infamous reddish-orange hourglass on their bellies.

The male is shy and rarely seen by humans, and although the female does attack the male after he has fulfilled his reproductive duties, this does not happen in every case. Of course they kill other creatures in search of food, but females are generally not aggressive unless they perceive a threat or are guarding an egg sac.

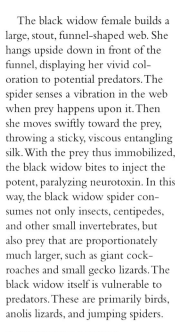

The black widow female builds a large, stout, funnel-shaped web. She hangs upside down in front of the funnel, displaying her vivid coloration to potential predators. The spider senses a vibration in the web when prey happens upon it. Then she moves swiftly toward the prey, throwing a sticky, viscous entangling silk. With the prey thus immobilized, the black widow bites to inject the potent, paralyzing neurotoxin. In this way, the black widow spider consumes not only insects, centipedes, and other small invertebrates, but also prey that are proportionately much larger, such as giant cockroaches and small gecko lizards. The black widow itself is vulnerable to predators. These are primarily birds, anolis lizards, and jumping spiders.

INQUIRING MINDS

It's only within the last 100 years or so that any spiders were considered venomous. Prior to that, it was thought impossible that such a small creature could have such a big impact on a human. Then, according to entomologist Paul Hillyard, the London Natural History Museum's "spiderman," a stouthearted southerner, took a bold step:

The American arachnologist W. J. Baerg, of Fayetteville, Arkansas, made a brave gesture to scientific inquiry when in 1922 he arranged for himself to be bitten by a black widow. He survived the bite but suffered considerably and reported later: "The first test proved very difficult and ended in failure; it is not always easy to make the black widow bite. The second test resulted in all I could wish. The spider dug into the third finger of the left hand and held on till I removed her about 5 or 6 seconds later. The pain at first was faint but very soon began to increase into a sharp piercing sensation. In less than one hour the pain had reached the shoulder and within two hours the chest was affected; the diaphragm seemed

partially paralysed, breathing and speech became spasmodic. After five hours, the pain extended to the legs, and after nine hours, I was taken to hospital. A severe nausea and excruciating pain not only kept me awake but kept me moving throughout the night." (Hillyard, 1994, p. 70.)

WHY DO THEY BITE?

Normally, the black widow will curl up into a ball and drop to the ground if she has nowhere to run, defensive only if she is guarding her egg sac. Otherwise black widows are shy by nature and bite only when trapped or sat on.

HOW TO AVOID BLACK WIDOW BITES

Black widows can be found almost anywhere in the Western hemisphere. The key words are "dark" and "damp" places.

Their favorite spots outside are:
- Woodpiles.
- Under boards.
- In dense plant growth.
- Tree stumps.
- Trash piles.
- Storage sheds.
- Fruit and vegetable gardens.
- Stone walls.
- Under rocks.
- In electrical, water, and telephone equipment boxes.
- In drainage pipes.
- In sheds, barns, well houses, and root cellars.

Although they are not as prevalent as they once were, outhouses are another legendary place for black widows, where the genitals seem especially vulnerable. Curiously, some sources say not even urinating men are exempt. (Makes you want to wait until you get home, doesn't it?)

Their favorite places inside are:
- Closets.
- Garages.

- Crawl spaces.
- Beneath appliances.
- Under furniture.
- Inside boxes.
- Inside seldom-worn shoes.

To reduce your chances of a bite:
- Discourage your children from playing in either rock piles or woodpiles.
- If you are working outside in the yard in big piles of logs or leaves, wear gloves.
- Shake out blankets and clothing that have been stored in the attic or the basement, or if they have been in a closet but not used for a long time. This applies even if the clothes have been stored in a closed cedar chest.
- Especially if you keep your shoes in a mud room or garage, shake them out before putting them on.
- Clear away old furniture, tires, and other junk from yard areas. This will not greatly influence black widow populations, but it will help reduce habitat for this spider (and will also improve the neighborhood!).
- Because they prefer closed, dark places such as water meter compartments and crawl spaces, construct barriers to inhibit entrance to these areas. Screen openings and plug holes and crevices with steel wool or other material.
- Most spiders have little defense against insecticides, and black widows are no exception. Apply an insecticide to the habitats frequented by these spiders when you detect an infestation. For the common black widow, spot treat directly on the web where the spider is found or suspected. Since the vast majority of spiders and other arthropods are either harmless or beneficial, treat only if you have an infestation or if you find one inside your home.

SYMPTOMS OF A BLACK WIDOW'S BITE

The bold spider experimenter Mr. Baerg endured many classic symptoms of a black widow bite, and also typically, he did not die. Note, too, that it was not easy to induce the animal to attack. The effects of a black widow's bite are systemic, that is, felt throughout the body, and the symptoms below make respect for the spider easily understood:
- Initial pain similar to a pinprick at the bite that changes to a numbing pain of the affected area.
- Muscle cramps, particularly of the abdomen and back.
- Muscle rigidity in the shoulders, back, and chest.
- Muscle pain.
- Muscle twitching.
- Increased perspiration.
- Increased salivation.
- Chest muscle spasms and/or respiratory difficulty.
- Swelling or drooping eyelids.
- Facial swelling.
- Skin temperature over bite is warmer than surrounding area.
- Skin rash or itching.
- Nausea and/or vomiting.
- Restlessness.
- Anxiety.
- Headache.
- Numbness and tingling of the palms of the hands and bottoms of the feet.
- Dizziness.
- Pain in the lymph nodes.
- Drooling.
- Fever.
- High blood pressure.
- Men may develop an erection.
- Children may cry persistently.
- Pregnant woman may develop uterine contractions and premature labor.

The characteristic cramping abdominal pain may be associated with pain in the flanks, thighs, or chest and be confused with acute

appendicitis, renal stones, or acute myocardial infarction.

Will I Immediately Know I Have Been Bitten?

Maybe or maybe not. The puncture may just feel like a pinprick, but two tiny red spots may help you confirm the fact of a bite. If you've only got one puncture mark, it's very likely an insect bite, but to be safe you should still monitor for the symptoms above. The wound may also appear as a bluish red spot, surrounded by a whitish area.

TREATMENT FOR A BLACK WIDOW SPIDER BITE

- Apply ice packs to the bite. Place ice (wrapped in a washcloth or other suitable covering) on the site of the bite for 10 minutes and then off for 10 minutes. Repeat this process. If the patient has circulatory problems, decrease the icing time to prevent possible damage to the skin.
- Immediately transport the victim to a medical facility.

Once the victim is in the hospital, the doctor will have a number of therapies to use:

- Intravenous muscle relaxant medicines for muscle spasms and/or anti-hypertensive drugs for elevated blood pressure.
- Pain medicine.
- An antivenin, called "ANTI-VENIN (LATRODECTUS MACTANS)" or black widow spider antivenin, for the most severe cases. It is available only through a physician and should be administered, if necessary, as soon as possible after the bite occurs. It will be administered by injection.

On outdoorhealth.com, Dr. Paul Auerbach, author of *Wilderness Medicine,* recommends the following:

If you will be unable to reach a hospital within a few hours and the victim is suffering severe muscle spasms, you may administer an oral dose of diazepam (Valium), if you happen to be carrying it. The starting dose for an adult who does not regularly take the drug is 5 milligrams, which can be augmented in 2.5-milligram increments every 30 minutes up to a total dose of 10 milligrams, so long as the victim remains alert and is capable of normal, purposeful swallowing. The starting dose for a child age 2 to 5 years is 0.5 milligrams; for a child age 6 to 12 years the starting dose is 2 milligrams. Total dose for a child should not exceed 5 milligrams; never leave a sedated child unattended.

Small children must receive antivenin as soon as possible and be treated in a hospital. Evacuate if you are camping, especially if symptoms do not begin to subside after 24 hours or if the person bitten is under the age of 16, of small body weight, or elderly.

Considerations Prior to Using the Antivenin

- Tell your doctor if you have ever had an allergic reaction to black widow spider antivenin, to horses, or to any products of horse origin. You should also tell your doctor if you are regularly exposed to horses. Black widow spider antivenin contains horse serum.
- Tell your doctor if you have any other allergies, such as allergies to preservatives.
- Tell your doctor if you are pregnant. Envenomation by the black widow spider may result in miscarriage if left untreated.
- Tell your doctor if you are breast-feeding. It is unknown if the antivenin passes into the breast milk. Most medicines do pass into breast milk in small amounts, but

many of them may be used safely while breast-feeding.

- Tell your doctor if you are using any other prescription or nonprescription (over-the-counter/OTC) medicine.

Possible Side Effects of the Black Widow Antivenin

Confer with your doctor immediately if any of the following occur:

- Difficulty in breathing or swallowing.
- Hives.
- Itching, especially of feet or hands.
- Reddening of skin, especially around ears.
- Swelling of eyes, face, or inside of nose.
- Unusual tiredness or weakness, especially if it is sudden and/or severe.

These side effects below may occur, but they usually do not need medical attention. Do check with your doctor, though, if any of the following side effects continue or are debilitating:

- Feeling of discomfort.
- Fever.
- Inflammation of joints.
- Muscle aches.
- Rash.
- Swollen lymph glands.

There may also be other side effects, so consult with your doctor if you are concerned.

LIKELIHOOD OF DEATH FROM A BLACK WIDOW BITE

Death in a normally healthy individual is very rare. Full recovery usually takes about a week. Untreated, most people recover without help over the course of eight hours to two days. However, very small children and elderly victims may suffer greatly.

The common thinking is that the venom of a black widow spider is 15 times more potent than that of a rat-

tlesnake, but the tiny amount injected is so minute their bites are not as likely to be fatal—three or four times less fatal by some estimates.

BLACK WIDOW
Latrodectus mactans

• DANGER
The black widow is potentially lethal, but fatalities are rare.

• ABUNDANCE & RANGE
It is common throughout the mid-Atlantic, but it is more common in the southeastern U.S.

• SIZE
Its body is 0.3 inch long.

• DESCRIPTION
The female (biter) body is black. The spherical abdomen has a red hourglass pattern on its underside.

• WEB
The black widow web is funnel-shaped, with an irregular weave, and is found in sheltered sites.

• HABITAT
Black widows can be found in dark and damp areas such as among fallen branches and under any object (inside or out) likely to trap moisture, such as trash.

• COMMENTS

Probably the most feared spider, the black widow will attempt to escape rather than bite unless it is guarding an egg mass.

TICKS

If you live almost anywhere except inside a shopping mall or the equivalent, there's a host of ticks lurking and looking to hitch a ride on you to their next stage of life. These quiet, sneaky bloodsuckers top the "worst critter on earth" list of many people, and with good reason. At least with mosquitoes, who also bear serious diseases, you can see and hear them coming, but with ticks you look down and there they are— already crawling on you or dug in, dragging in their wake prolonged itching at best and disease at worst.

There are soft body ticks and hard body ticks, and although you might think that a "softbody" (filled with your blood) is the one to worry about, don't. They are not usually carriers of disease and are more prone to attack birds and mammals that have regular resting places. Of the hard body type, there are three species to be concerned about because of the diseases they carry.

TICKS TO TRACK

The **deer tick,** also known as the **black-legged tick** *(Ixodes scapularis)* was at one time considered to be two species, but is now understood as one species that is distributed across the midwest and eastern U.S. In the northern reaches, populations at all stages feed on humans and animals. The deer tick is the primary vector for Lyme disease *(Borrelia burgdorferi)* and human granulocytic ehrlichiosis (HGE).

The **lone star tick** *(Amblyomma americanum)* is so named after the dramatic white spot on the female's back. This spot is actually iridescent, and so it can appear as different colors depending on the light. All stages of this tick will feed on humans and domestic animals. Their larvae are known as "seed ticks"—they're that tiny—and are encountered in masses on vegetation, potentially resulting in hundreds of individual bites on one person. The good news is that if these little suckers don't get a blood meal, they will die after a killing frost in the fall. This species is known to transmit human monocytic ehrlichiosis (HME or *Ehrlichia chaffeensis*) and is found in the eastern half of the U.S. south of New York.

The **wood tick**, also known as the **dog tick** *(Dermacentor variabilis)* will feed on humans and domestic animals only in its adult stage. Immature stages typically feed on small rodents. This species can transmit Rocky Mountain spotted fever (RMSF or *Rickettsia rickettsi*) and is found in North America east of the Rocky Mountains and also in some western states such as California. The good news is that only 3–5% of adult ticks in RMSF areas carry the organism.

In the end, though, it probably makes more sense to be familiar with the symptoms of the diseases that the ticks carry rather than worry about which species it was that bit you. The important things to do always are:

- Remove ticks as soon as possible, which means checking twice a day or more if you are outside in areas where they are likely to be looking for a host.
- Be watchful for symptoms of the diseases ticks carry, and seek medical attention right away if you think you have contracted a tick-borne illness.
- If you find yourself at the doctor's office with some of the symptoms listed below, be sure to remember to tell your doctor if you've been bitten by or exposed to ticks lately. The faster you are correctly diagnosed for tick-borne illnesses, the better

are you chances of full recovery. Time is of the essence.

TICK LIFE CYCLE

Ticks typically have four life stages—egg, larva, nymph, and adult. Except for the egg stage, each phase must have a separate animal host to complete its development, which may span two to three years. Blood-swelled mature females leave their hosts and lay a single mass of 3,000 to 6,000 eggs. These hatch into larvae that are just 0.025 inch in length. Right after hatching, these starving-for-blood larvae climb onto the nearest vegetation and wait for a warm-blooded animal to pass by. After grasping the feathers or hair of the unsuspecting beast, the young ticks insert their mouthparts and hook into the skin. After a two- to three-day blood feast, the tick larvae drop off their host and begin to molt into nymphs. Ticks at this stage of life may survive the winter (hence, the problem presented by relatively mild winters), but at first blush of spring, they must feed again as soon as possible. After they do, they dismount their host again and molt into adults, who likely will idle through the winter again before emerging—hungry as ever—in the spring, and with a

Lone star tick larvae are small enough to hide on a U.S. penny.

need not only to eat, but also to mate. They feed on the next host, and then the cycle is set to repeat now that the female is ready to lay eggs again.

HOW TICKS FEED

Ticks cut an entrance into a host's skin and insert their mouthparts. This feeding tube, the hypostome, has several rows of curved barbs that serve to anchor the tick to its host. This is why tick removal must be executed with gentle, steady care so as not to detach the tick head from the body. Blood is then pumped up by a muscular pharynx, and special glands secrete an anticoagulant in order to prevent the host's blood from clotting during the lengthy feeding period.

TICK REMOVAL

- Grasp the tick just behind the point of attachment with a fine-point tweezers and pull straight out using slow, steady pressure until the tick is dislodged.
- Do not twist the tick as you remove it.
- Wash the bite area and apply an antiseptic.
- Do not use the unsafe, antiquated methods of applying gasoline, mineral oil, alcohol, kerosene, camp stove fuel, Vaseline, fingernail polish remover, or a match, a recently extinguished match head, or other hot object to the tick prior to removal. These practices are likely to make the tick

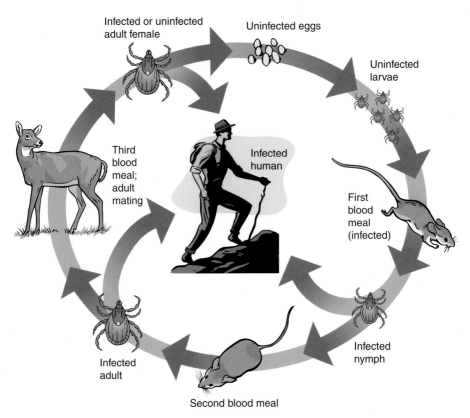

Ticks transmit a variety of diseases by feeding on infected and uninfected hosts throughout their life cycle.

struggle and vomit infectious fluids into the bite site. (Tick barf!)

- For deeply embedded ticks, apply the insecticide permethrin (such as in Permanone), swabbing both the upper and lower sides of the tick with cloth or tissue. After 10 to 15 minutes, you should be able to pull the tick free. Carefully check the bite site for remaining head- and mouthparts, and gently scrape them away using a sharp edge, such as a knife blade.

- If you use your fingers, grasp the tick using tissue paper or cloth. Children, elderly persons, and immuno-compromised persons may be at greater risk of infection and should especially use this procedure because infectious diseases carried by tick fluid agents may enter through mucous membranes or breaks in the skin. This is the same reason not to crush ticks with your fingers.

- Nymphs, which are also known as "seed ticks," are sometimes present in such numbers that the U.S. Forest Service recommends removal by ripping them off your skin with a strip of duct tape before they can effectively burrow in.

TICK DISPOSAL

We know a friend who has such a war with ticks she used to keep a trophy jar filled with alcohol on her kitchen counter so she could readily see and show off to visitors how many of those "little bastards" she had pulled off herself and her dogs, some of which were quite large from engorging. In a junior-high-science sort of way, it was fascinating, but it didn't do much for the appetite. Still, her methodology was correct.

- Dropping them in alcohol is the surest, safest way to kill them.
- You can flush them down the toilet, but flush them right away.

They will crawl out if you don't. We're not sure if they survive the trip through the sewage treatment plant, (they're probably mutating for an *X-Files* episode as you read this), but we can't live with a jar of them. It's just a personal preference. Another friend sends them down her kitchen drain to save water.

- Burn them *after* you've removed them from your body.

- Don't try to mash them with your fingers. First, it's disgusting. Second, it's hard to do, especially if they are small. Third and most importantly, there is a slim chance that if they are carrying infection, it may enter your body if you have a small cut on your finger.

- If a single tick bite is a rare event for you, you may want to save the tick in a jar should you later develop disease symptoms. Preserve the tick by either adding some alcohol to the jar or by keeping it in the freezer. Identification of the tick may facilitate the physician's diagnosis and treatment. For those who find multiple ticks on them in any given season, however, this archival method is of less value in diagnosis.

WHEN AND WHERE TICKS ARE FOUND

- Ticks are present from early spring, as early as March in warmer areas, and they remain active until after the first freeze.

- Ticks love high grasses and brushy areas that provide shade and moisture. They hold on to a blade of grass with back legs, which leaves their forelegs available to grab a hold on anything passing by. Ticks can also be found in trees, and they can drop down on you.

- Ticks are common near stables, kennels, barns, or any other areas in which animals are kept.

REPELLING AND DISCOURAGING TICKS

- When in a tick-infested area, a good prevention is an insect repellent; however, consider using a product designed to be applied to clothing rather than your skin.
- Tuck pants cuffs into boots or socks and wear long sleeves and light-colored clothing, which makes it easier to spot ticks. Some experts recommend putting tape around the area where pants and socks meet for added protection. Some people wrap small tick-prevention dog collars around their ankles on the **outside** of the pants tucked into socks.
- Stay to the center of hiking paths and avoid grassy and marshy woodland areas.
- Inspect yourself and your children for clinging ticks after leaving an infested area several times a day if the situation warrants it. Pay special attention to the hairy parts of the body and where clothing is snug against it. The sooner you remove a tick, the less chance it has to start spreading infections. When you get home, definitely inspect yourself carefully. Use a mirror to check difficult-to-observe parts of your body.
- If you suspect ticks in your clothing, wash them as soon as possible and use your dryer on a high heat setting.
- Ticks cannot easily tolerate direct sunshine, so keeping your grass cut short is one means of discouraging them in your yard. It also discourages rodents (a common host) from nesting. At its critical life stages, a tick must have a blood meal or die, so anything you can do to break that life cycle is a worthwhile endeavor.

- Sealing cracks and crevices inside and out can reduce entry points and hiding places.
- Dogs and cats are common carriers of ticks, but fortunately there are excellent products available from your veterinarian that, when used regularly, can virtually eliminate these parasites from your pets and ultimately from you. Some products are geared more toward tick prevention than others, so be sure to talk to your vet about all the options. Your animals will thank you, and you won't have to resort to "bombing" the inside of your house every summer, a practice with its own problems, risks, and inconveniences.
- In some cases, creating a barrier around your yard by removing leaves and laying down a path of wood chips (two to four feet wide) has reduced tick populations by 44–88%.
- Insecticides that contain permethrin can reduce ticks infestations by 90%. Permanone is 0.5% permethrin. This is for spray application to clothing and is reported to be an excellent tick repellent.
- Guinea fowl (also known as "ginnies" and "peeps") will eat ticks, so if you want a flock, check your local civic ordinances and then go for it. They also make excellent "watch dogs" as they will raise a ruckus when strangers approach your yard.
- Check with your local county agricultural agent if you have more ticks than you think you can take. He or she can recommend infestation treatments best suited to your area and needs.

Special Considerations about Deer Ticks

Because deer ticks transmit Lyme disease, here are a few extra facts:

- Deer ticks are most active from April through October.
- Deer ticks are hard to see. Nymphs are dot-sized, and adults can be smaller than a sesame seed.
- If you discover a tick, do not panic. The evidence suggests that an infected tick does not usually transmit the Lyme organism during the first 24 hours.

DISEASES TICKS CARRY

It seems that nobody champions ticks. As one scientist said, "We are trying to come up with new ways to kill these little suckers as fast as we can. They are on mankind's hit list, not on the endangered species list."

A major reason to minimize the world's tick population is the diseases they spread. Although your chances of contracting a tick-borne disease are extremely small, do not underestimate the power and prevalence of these tiny, insidious creatures. The most common tick-borne diseases in the southeast are Rocky Mountain spotted fever (RMSF—very similar to tick fever), human erlichiosis, tick paralysis, tularemia, and Lyme disease, all of which you can contract in the mid-Atlantic region.

As a rule, if children are discovered to have ticks, it is a good idea to write the information down and keep it for several months. Many tick-borne diseases do not show symptoms immediately, and the incident may be forgotten by the time a child becomes ill with a tick-borne disease.

Rocky Mountain Spotted Fever

Rocky Mountain spotted fever (RMSF) is the most severe tick-borne rickettsial illness in the U.S. This disease is caused by infection from the bacterial organism *Rickettsia rickettsii* that is transmitted through the bite of an infected tick. The American dog tick *(Dermacentor variabilis)* and Rocky Mountain wood tick *(Dermacentor andersoni)* are the primary vectors of Rocky Mountain spotted fever bacteria in the U.S.

Rocky Mountain spotted fever is a seasonal disease that occurs generally throughout the months of April through September. Over half of the cases occur in the south Atlantic region of the U.S. (Delaware, Maryland, Washington, D.C., Virginia, West Virginia, North Carolina, South Carolina, Georgia, and Florida). The highest incidence rates have been found in North Carolina and Oklahoma. Although this disease was reported most frequently in the Rocky Mountain area early after its discovery, relatively few cases are reported from that area today.

Rocky Mountain spotted fever was first recognized in 1896 in the Snake River Valley of Idaho and was originally called "black measles" because of the characteristic rash. It was a dreaded and frequently fatal disease that affected hundreds of people in this area. By the early 1900s, the recognized geographic distribution of this disease grew to encompass parts of the U.S. as far north as Washington and Montana and as far south as California, Arizona, and New Mexico. In response to this severe problem, the Rocky Mountain Laboratory was

Average Annual Incidence of Rocky Mountain Spotted Fever by Age Group, 1993–1996	
Age Group	Cases per Million
0–4	1.5–2.0
5–9	2.5–3.0
10–19	1.0–1.5
20–29	0.5–1.0
30–39	1.0–1.5
40–49	1.0–1.5
50–59	1.0–1.5
60–69	1.0–1.5
>70	1.0–1.5
Source: Centers for Disease Control	

established in Hamilton, Montana, a facility now run by the National Institute of Allergy and Infectious Diseases, National Institutes of Health.

Rocky Mountain spotted fever remains a serious and potentially life-threatening infectious disease today. Despite the availability of effective treatment and advances in medical care, approximately 3–5% of individuals who become ill with Rocky Mountain spotted fever still die from the infection. However, effective antibiotic therapy has dramatically reduced the number of deaths caused by Rocky Mountain spotted fever. Before the discovery of tetracycline and chloramphenicol in the late 1940s, as many as 30% of persons infected with *R. rickettsii* died.

The disease affects about 800 people each year in the U.S. It is most commonly seen from April through September but can occur any time of year during warm weather. RMSF can be difficult to diagnose in the early stages, and without prompt and appropriate treatment it can be fatal.

In 1998, the Associated Press released this story about a fatal episode of RMSF in South Carolina:

Tick-bite fever kills woman

SPARTANBURG, S.C. — A Spartanburg woman has died of a rare fever several weeks after being bitten by an infected tick. Authorities believe Jane Clark Varnavas, 36, was infected in late April. She died Sunday.

"If she had been hit by a car or had cancer, I could have understood it," said her mother, Alice Clark. "With a little bug, it is hard to understand how this could happen." Ms. Varnavas initially developed flu-like symptoms. She was tired and had no energy, relatives said. Then she got a rash on her arms, and her conditioned worsened. Her 17-year-old son found her collapsed on the living room floor May 7. Within days, her body swelled to three times its normal size. Infections developed all over her body, and she could not breathe without a respirator. Doctors diagnosed her after a series of tests. "Rocky Mountain spotted fever never entered our minds," said Myrna Hutchinson, one of Ms. Varnavas' sisters. "We had been dealing with ticks all of our lives, and we never thought she would die from it."

Symptoms of Rocky Mountain Spotted Fever Patients infected with *R. rickettsii* usually visit a physician in their first week of illness, fol-

Seasonal Distribution of Reported Cases of Rocky Mountain Spotted Fever, 1993–1996				
Month	1993	1994	1995	1995
January	0–20	0–20	0–20	0–20
February	0–20	0–20	0–20	0–20
March	0–20	0–20	0–20	0–20
April	0–20	0–20	20–40	20–40
May	40–60	20–40	40–60	80–100
June	20–40	40–60	60–80	80–100
July	40–60	40–60	60–80	40–60
August	20–40	20–40	40–60	40–60
September	0–20	0–20	20–40	20–40
October	0–20	0–20	0–20	0–20
November	0–20	0–20	0–20	0–20
December	0–20	0–20	0–20	0–20

Source: Centers for Disease Control

lowing an incubation period of about 5 to 10 days after a tick bite. The early clinical presentation of Rocky Mountain spotted fever is often nonspecific and may resemble many other infectious and noninfectious diseases.

Initial symptoms may include:
- Fever.
- Nausea.
- Vomiting.
- Muscle pain.
- Lack of appetite.
- Severe headache.

Later signs and symptoms include:
- Rash.
- Abdominal pain.
- Joint pain.
- Diarrhea.

Three important components of the clinical presentation are fever, rash, and a previous tick bite, although one or more of these components may not be present when the patient is first seen for medical care. Rocky Mountain spotted fever can be a severe illness, and the majority of patients are hospitalized.

The rash first appears two to five days after the onset of fever and is often not present or may be very subtle when the patient is initially seen by a physician. Younger patients usually develop the rash earlier than older patients. Most often it begins as small, flat, pink, non-itchy spots (macules) on the wrists, forearms, and ankles. These spots turn pale when pressure is applied and eventually become raised on the skin. The characteristic red, spotted (petechial) rash of Rocky Mountain spotted fever is usually not seen until the sixth day or later after onset of symptoms, and this type of rash occurs in only 35–60% of patients with Rocky Mountain spotted fever. The rash involves the palms or soles in as many

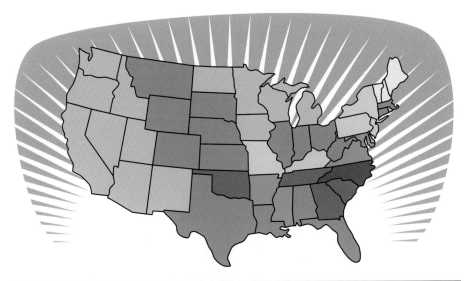

None	Minimal	Very Low	Low
Moderate		High	Very High

Rocky Mountain spotted fever disease assessment: cases reported by state, 1994–1998.

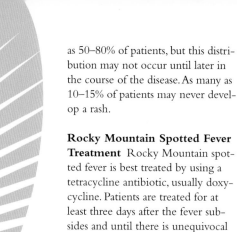

as 50–80% of patients, but this distribution may not occur until later in the course of the disease. As many as 10–15% of patients may never develop a rash.

Rocky Mountain Spotted Fever Treatment Rocky Mountain spotted fever is best treated by using a tetracycline antibiotic, usually doxycycline. Patients are treated for at least three days after the fever subsides and until there is unequivocal evidence of clinical improvement.

Infection with *R. rickettsii* is thought to provide long lasting immunity against re-infection. However, prior illness with Rocky Mountain spotted fever should not deter persons from practicing good tick-preventive measures or visiting a physician if signs and symptoms consistent with Rocky Mountain spotted fever occur, especially following a tick bite.

Rocky Mountain Spotted Fever's Potential After Effects Treated in a timely manner with antibiotics for a standard 5 to 10 days, RMSF can be cured with no long-term health problems. However, if not properly treated, an acute Rocky Mountain spotted fever infection can leave the following in its wake:

- Partial paralysis of the lower extremities.
- Gangrene requiring amputation of fingers, toes, arms, or legs.
- Hearing loss.
- Loss of bowel or bladder control.
- Movement disorders.
- Language disorders.

These complications are most frequent in persons recovering from severe, life-threatening cases, often following lengthy hospitalizations.

Human Ehrlichiosis

Human ehrlichiosis is a tick-borne illness that is caused by an extremely small type of bacteria known as

"ehrlichiae." Human ehrlichiosis is a generic term for a group of diseases that invade and live within white blood cells. These diseases are closely related to *rickettsiae,* the type of bacteria that cause Rocky Mountain spotted fever (RMSF).

Ehrlichiosis was first recognized in 1935 as a disease of dogs (canine ehrlichiosis) caused by *Ehrlichia canis*. In the 1960s, a number of military guard dogs stationed in Vietnam died from this disease. The first diagnosed case of human ehrlichiosis occurred in 1986 in a 51-year-old man from Detroit who had been exposed to ticks in a rural area of Arkansas. In 1990, the agent of human ehrlichiosis was isolated from the blood of a U.S. Army reservist at Fort Chaffee, Arkansas. The new species of ehrlichiae was named *E. chaffeensis* and the specific disease that it causes has been designated "human monocytic ehrlichiosis" (HME).

In 1994, another type of human ehrlichiosis was recognized following a report in the *Journal of the American Medical Association* of 12 cases of an ehrlichial illness that occurred in Minnesota and Wisconsin from 1990 through 1993. Two of those patients died from complications and secondary infections. This most recently recognized type of ehrlichiosis has been designated "human granulocytic ehrlichiosis" (HGE). Since that time, many additional cases of HGE have been diagnosed.

Both HME and HGE are tick-borne. The HME vector is the lone star tick, *Amblyomma americanum*. The major vector for HGE is the black-legged or deer tick *(Ixodes scapularis)*. Both species are found in the mid-Atlantic region, so it is possible to contract human ehrlichiosis in this area.

A Soldier's Story The following account by Peter Jaret appeared on WebMD.com:

June 19, 2000 — The 22-year-old soldier wasn't worried. He had been bitten by a few ticks while out on military maneuvers, but that wasn't unusual for soldiers at the base in Tennessee. Even when he developed a fever, he wasn't alarmed. But instead of getting better, his condition steadily worsened. . . . The diagnosis was a tick-borne disease called ehrlichiosis.

"We had him on three powerful antibiotics to treat the infection. And by all rights he should have recovered," said the doctor assigned to the case. "He didn't. Within hours the young man's lungs and liver began to fail. His blood clotted in his veins. Two days after he was admitted, he went into seizures and died."

Ehrlichiosis was first discovered in the 1980s. In 1998, four people in Oklahoma who had been infected with a form of this disease long thought to afflict only dogs were diagnosed. According the September 15, 1999 issue of The New England Journal of Medicine, *four more human cases turned up in 1999 in Missouri, Oklahoma, and Tennessee.*

Symptoms of Human Ehrlichiosis

The two forms of human ehrlichiosis, HGE and HME, are similar enough to be discussed together here.

Symptoms begin in 1 to 21 (average 7) days following infection, and they resemble those of Rocky Mountain spotted fever. They vary greatly in severity, ranging from an illness so mild that no medical attention is sought, all the way to a severe, life-threatening condition. The most common symptoms are:
- High fever.
- Headache.
- Chills.
- Muscular aches and pains.

But may also include:
- Nausea.
- Vomiting.
- Loss of appetite.
- An overall feeling of bodily discomfort.

Rash is rare, but when present it may resemble the spotted rash of RMSF, although it is usually less prominent and more variable in appearance and location. Since ehrlichiae invade white blood cells, the body's immune system is compromised. That lessens the body's ability to fight other infections so complications can quickly arise, and in the most severe cases kidney or respiratory failure occurs. There have been a number of deaths associated with both HME and HGE.

Treatment for Human Ehrlichiosis

Blood tests can confirm the diagnosis. The antibiotic doxycycline is very effective for treating both HME and HGE, and when treated early both forms can be completely defeated. However, because human ehrlichiosis can be so severe or even deadly, it is very important to obtain early diagnosis and treatment, as it is with all the tick-borne illnesses.

Tick Paralysis

The cause of this disease, often affecting children and pets, is a neurotoxin produced in the ovaries of female ticks. It enters the host while the tick is engorging for up to six to seven days. The result is gradual paralysis from the legs upwards, and death can result in humans if the tick is not properly removed in time.

To repeat: As a rule, if children are discovered to have ticks, it is a good idea to write the information down and keep it for several months. Many tick-borne diseases do not show symptoms immediately, and the incident may be forgotten by the time a child becomes noticeably ill.

Signs and Symptoms of Tick Paralysis
- History of exposure to ticks through camping, a tick-infested area, dogs, or other animals.
- Finding a tick, especially attached at the back of the neck at the hairline.

- Unsteady jerky body movements and gait (ataxia).
- Muscle weakness beginning in the lower extremities and progressing upwards.
- Breathing difficulties.

Treatment of Tick Paralysis

Contact your health care provider immediately. Removal of the tick should produce full and rapid recovery, but follow-up care may be necessary.

Tularemia

Tularemia is a bacterial disease occurring in both animals and humans caused by the bacteria *Fransicella tularensis,* and it is most commonly associated with rabbits. People can become infected with tularemia from the bite of infected ticks of several species, including the wood tick, dog tick, and the lone star tick, and less commonly from the bites of flies or mosquitoes. People also may be infected from handling the carcasses of infected animals, from eating improperly cooked meat from infected animals, from contaminated water sources, and from inhalation of dust from contaminated soil, hay, or grain. Very, very rarely a person may be infected via the bite wound of an animal that has a contaminated mouth from eating an animal that had tularemia. In the summer, people are at risk for tularemia through tick bites.

In the U.S., there are about 150 to 300 cases per year, with the highest incidence east of the Mississippi during the winter when cottontail rabbits are hunted. Hunters are more at risk in the winter months if they handle the carcasses of infected animals. Tick bite infections are highest in the Midwest during the summer months when ticks are common, but there has been a steady decline in cases of tularemia (by whatever means of infection—bite, ingestion, inhalation) since 1939.

Symptoms of Tularemia

Symptoms develop within 1 to 14 days, usually within 3 to 5 days.

- Tularemia is usually recognized by the presence of a skin lesion and swollen glands, sometimes at the point of infection. These may be accompanied by the sudden onset of high fever.
- Ingestion of the organism may produce a throat infection, intestinal pain, diarrhea, and vomiting.
- Inhalation of the organism may produce a fever alone or combined with a pneumonia-like illness.

Treatment of Tularemia

If you think you have tularemia, contact your physician right away. Upon diagnostic confirmation through laboratory tests, you can take antibiotics for the disease. Long-term immunity follows recovery, but re-infection has been reported. Without therapy, fatality rates are 5% (ulceroglandular) to 30% (pneumonic). The mortality rate is about 6% or fewer than 20 people per year.

Preventing Tularemia

- Wear rubber gloves when skinning or handling animals, especially rabbits.
- Cook wild game, especially rabbit and squirrel meat, thoroughly before eating.
- Avoid bites of flies and ticks by the use of protective clothing and insect repellents, and check for ticks frequently.
- Avoid drinking untreated water.
- Instruct children not to handle any sick or dead animals.

Lyme Disease

The most commonly reported vector-borne disease, Lyme disease is caused by infection with the spirochete *Borrelia burgdorferi,* transmitted to humans by infected deer ticks (*Ixodes scapularis*) and black-legged

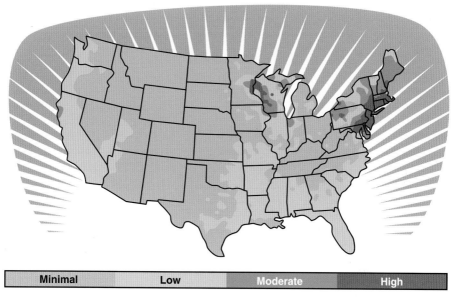

| Minimal | Low | Moderate | High |

Lyme disease risk: areas of predicted transmission.

ticks *(I. pacificus).* Lyme disease bacteria are maintained in the blood systems of small rodents and are not transmitted from person to person. For example, you cannot get infected from touching or kissing a person who has Lyme disease, or from a health care worker who has treated someone with the disease. Having had Lyme disease doesn't protect against re-infection.

Where is Lyme Disease Concentrated in the U.S.? Lyme disease is the leading cause of vector-borne infectious illness in the U.S., with about 15,000 cases reported annually, but the disease is greatly underreported. Based on cases reported to the Centers for Disease Control, during the past ten years 90% of cases of the highly focused Lyme disease occurred in ten states, five of which are in the mid-Atlantic scope of this book.

The name of the disease finds its origin in Lyme, Connecticut, where numerous cases were diagnosed.

The majority of reported cases had onsets of disease in June, July, or August, corresponding with the seasonal feeding activity of nymphal deer ticks in the northeastern U.S. In addition, June, July, and August are the months when humans most commonly engage in outdoor activities. Researchers believe that a majority of human cases result from nymphal tick

Lyme Disease

State	90% of Cases Reported 1989–98	Annual Incidence per 100,000 persons
New York	39,370	21.6
Connecticut	17,728	54.2
Pennsylvania	14,870	12.3
New Jersey	13,428	16.9
Wisconsin	4,760	9.3
Rhode Island	3,717	37.5
Maryland	3,410	6.8
Massachusetts	2,712	4.5
Minnesota	1,745	3.8
Delaware	1,003	14.0

Source: *Centers for Disease Control*

Average Annual Incidence of Reported Cases of Lyme Disease by Age Group and Gender, 1992–1998		
	Cases per 100,000	
Age	Male	Female
0–4	3–4	3–4
5–9	6–7	5–6
10–14	5–6	4
15–19	3–4	2–3
20–24	2–3	2
25–29	2–3	2–3
30–34	3–4	3–4
35–39	4–5	4–5
40–44	5–6	5–6
45–49	6–7	6–7
50–54	7–8	7
55–59	6–7	6
60–64	6	5–6
65–69	6–7	5–6
70–74	6–7	5–6
75–79	6–7	4–5
80–84	5–6	3–4
85+	3–4	2–3

Source: Centers for Disease Control

attachment. Because the attached nymph is approximately the size of a poppy seed, it might not be noticed, and therefore, not removed before disease transmission occurs.

Lyme disease is rarely, if ever, fatal.

Who Is at Risk? Children ages 5 to 9 and adults ages 45 to 54 statistically have the greatest incidence of Lyme disease. Probability is higher for males, especially in the 5- to 19-year-old and over 60 age brackets. As you might expect, risk of Lyme disease increases with increasing exposure to wooded, brushy, or overgrown grassy areas in endemic regions.

Symptoms of Lyme Disease
Within days to weeks following a tick bite, 80% of patients will have a red, slowly expanding "bull's-eye" rash (called erythema migrans), accompanied by:
- General tiredness.
- Fever.
- Headache.
- Stiff neck.
- Muscle aches.
- Joint pain.

If untreated, weeks to months later some patients may develop:
- Arthritis, including intermittent episodes of swelling and pain in the large joints.
- Neurologic abnormalities, such as asepticmeningitis, facial palsy, motor and sensory nerve inflammation (radiculoneuritis), and inflammation of the brain (encephalitis).
- Rarely, heart problems.

Treatment of Lyme Disease
Lyme disease can usually be treated successfully with standard antibiotic regimens, although severe cases can have effects that linger or reoccur over a period of years.

Lyme Disease Vaccine LYMErix has been shown to be safe and effective in preventing Lyme disease in people ages 15 to 70. After three doses, its maker SmithKline Beecham claims it reduces the risk of definite Lyme disease by 78% and risk of asymptomatic infections by 100%.

Administered by injections on a 0, 1, 12 month schedule (e.g. January, February, January), LYMErix may produce local injection-site reactions including redness and swelling, flu-like symptoms, and joint and muscle pain. As with any vaccine, LYMErix may not protect all individuals. To ensure optimal protection, it is important that you receive all three doses. Existing data suggest boosters might be needed.

Recommendations from the CDC Regarding LYMErix Vaccine

Who Should Consider the Vaccine:

- Persons ages 15 to 70 years whose exposure to tick-infested habitat is frequent or prolonged.

People Who May Consider the Vaccine:

- Persons ages 15 to 70 years who have some exposure to tick-infested habitat but whose exposure is neither frequent nor prolonged.

Not Recommended For:

- Persons whose exposure to tick-infested habitat is minimal or none.
- Persons who reside, work, or recreate in areas of low or no risk.
- Children under the age of 15.
- Pregnant women.

DEER TICK

Ixodes scapularis

• DANGER
This tick is potentially lethal as a carrier for human granulocytic ehrlichiosis (HGE) and Lyme disease.

• ABUNDANCE & RANGE
It is found across the midwestern and eastern U.S as far north as Maine.

• SIZE
Unengorged, it is 0.1 inch in length; engorged, 0.2 inch.

• DESCRIPTION
Deer ticks are dark brown to black in color, and they often have black legs.

• HABITAT
The deer tick is found in wooded or grassy areas.

• COMMENTS
Also known as the black-legged tick, this creature was at one time considered to be two species, but it is now understood to be one species. The distribution of *I. scapularis* is linked to the distribution and abundance of its primary reproductive host—white-tailed deer. Only deer or some other large mammal are apparently capable of supporting high tick populations.

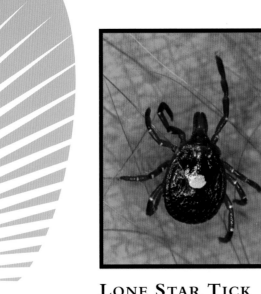

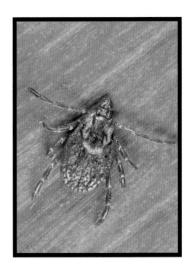

LONE STAR TICK

Amblyomma americanum

• DANGER
This tick is potentially lethal as a carrier for erlichiosis.

• ABUNDANCE & RANGE
It is found in the eastern half of the U.S. south of New York.

• SIZE
Unengorged, 0.2 inch; engorged, 0.5 inch.

• DESCRIPTION
Its oval, flattened body is reddish brown but becomes slate gray when engorged. Single whitish-to-silvery spot on the female's back gives the species its common name.

• HABITAT
The lone star tick is found in grasslands and wooded areas.

• COMMENTS
Masses of larvae found on vegetation are called "seed ticks" indicating their minute size, which is smaller than the letters in the word "liberty" on the U.S. penny.

WOOD TICK

Dermacentor variabilis

• DANGER
The wood tick is potentially lethal as a carrier for Rocky Mountain spotted fever and tick fever.

• ABUNDANCE & RANGE
It is found in North America east of the Rocky Mountains, and also in some western states such as California.

• SIZE
Unengorged, 0.2 inch; engorged, 0.6 inch.

• DESCRIPTION
The body is oval and flattened. Color is brown with whitish to grayish markings, often with silvery hue.

• HABITAT
These ticks are numerous along roads, paths, and trails, especially in grasses.

• COMMENTS
Between the larvae, nymphs, and adults, the wood tick or "dog tick," as it is also known, is active from late March until about mid-September.

MITES

Mites are minute arachnids, ranging from near invisibility to 1+ inches. Most usually measure 0.125 inch or less in length. Together with their buddies the ticks, who also share the *Acarina* order, these creatures comprise more than 30,000 known species worldwide, and the National Audubon Society estimates there are probably at least one million species yet to be identified. Mites' bodies resemble those of ticks—oval, elongated, and unseparated into cephalothorax and abdomen.

Many mites are beneficial—preying on aphid eggs, for example, or chowing down on other insects. But there are a couple of mites worthy of examination here. Both are parasitic at some point during their four-stage life cycle (egg, larva, nymph, adult), and, more importantly, both can make you itch enough to think you are going to lose your mind. We are speaking, of course, of chiggers and scabies.

Chiggers

"I'm hosting a party Friday night."
"Really. Well, I'm hosting a chigger colony."
—"In Defense of Mosquitoes,"
a story by Vicki Edwards

The word chigger reportedly comes from the Wolof (African) word "jiga," and Caribbean islanders call tropical sand fleas "chigoes," probably a linguistic mutation from the same African origin. They also go by the name of red bugs because they are, in fact, orange-red in color, if only you could see them with your naked eyes, which you usually don't—and that's part of the problem. They cling to

you, do their dirty work, and split probably before you even know they paid you a visit. Chiggers resemble tiny, tiny ticks, and it's a rare person who has not experienced their invidious itch. They don't do anything more serious, however, than drive you crazy.

Chiggers are so well-known that internationally respected artist Red Grooms immortalized them with a caricature on his "Fox Trot Carousel" located in downtown Nashville. The chigger ride on this working carousel is an anatomical digression from the real thing, but Red has captured the mean-spirited heart of the beast. His chigger looks like a bloated science-fiction-sized mosquito on LSD, with bloodshot eyes, a long probing snout, and a definite attitude.

Chiggers are the larvae of the harvest mite, those creatures that look like small, velvety red spiders you see on the soil surface when turning the garden during the warm days of springtime. Around this time of year, these adults lay eggs in the soil that hatch into the larval chigger.

Although the harvest mite adults and most immature stages are completely harmless, the larval stage is a parasite on many animals: rodents, birds, poultry, rabbits, livestock, snakes, and toads, as well as humans. Chiggers move very quickly on the ground, and they can rapidly crawl onto your feet or legs. On board the necessary host for the protein meal for its next stage of life, the chigger usually moves about until it reaches a place where it is somewhat confined. Vexing locales such as around ankles, under socks, behind knees, in the groin or armpit, and anywhere that elastic meets skin are desirable. Chiggers can wander for hours on a host, selecting just the right real estate before settling down to feed.

In about 3 to 24 hours after initial feeding by the chigger, and depending

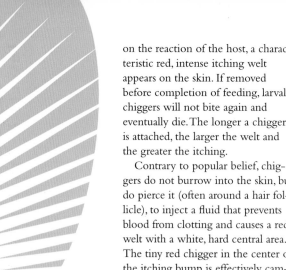

on the reaction of the host, a characteristic red, intense itching welt appears on the skin. If removed before completion of feeding, larval chiggers will not bite again and eventually die. The longer a chigger is attached, the larger the welt and the greater the itching.

Contrary to popular belief, chiggers do not burrow into the skin, but do pierce it (often around a hair follicle), to inject a fluid that prevents blood from clotting and causes a red welt with a white, hard central area. The tiny red chigger in the center of the itching bump is effectively camouflaged by the inflamed tissues. When our bodies produce histamines to combat this anticoagulant fluid, the itching begins. After a belly full and a beer (just kidding), the chigger drops from its host and goes into the ground for an inactive stage. In the fall, it becomes a bright red adult which has four pairs of legs and spends its winter in the ground.

ARE THERE CHIGGERS THERE?

To check out whether an area is infested with chiggers, place six-inch squares of black paper vertically in the grass. These will become covered with chiggers that will look like tiny yellow or pink dots moving around if chiggers are present. In the southern U.S., chiggers are active throughout the year where continuous development occurs. They are found in clumps, which is why you can get overwhelmed by them, and your party mate may be left unscathed.

Chigger Country

Chiggers are basically "bags of water" needing high humidity to keep from drying out and dying. They are most likely to be found in areas where vegetation is thick and where there is an abundance of moisture and shade:

- At woodland borders.
- Along the periphery of swamps.
- In shrub thickets.
- In un-mowed areas of lawn.
- In thick layers of pine straw, leaf litter, or thatch.

PREVENTION OF CHIGGER BITES

- Chiggers are attracted to their host by carbon dioxide, so stop breathing. (Hello?)
- Eliminate shade to help reduce the number of chiggers in an area.
- Keep your lawn trimmed to prevent favorable breeding sites and reduce populations.
- Keep outdoor walkways tidy.
- Eliminate tall weeds and shrubs—particularly berry patches that furnish food for rodent and bird hosts of mites.
- Chiggers don't like DEET, so you can apply those types of repellents to shoes, socks, pants cuffs, ankles and legs, and around your waist (on the outside of your clothes only).

TREATMENT OF CHIGGER BITES

- Don't wait for the red welt or the itch. Chiggers are easily dislodged by gentle rubbing, even if attached. If you have been in "chigger country," bathing immediately after exposure and lathering your entire body with soap several times and scrubbing with a washcloth may reduce the number of bites. If you cannot bathe immediately after walking in a chigger-infested area, rubbing yourself down with a towel or cloth may be of benefit.
- Wash your clothes to prevent re-infection. To the extent that chiggers are like ticks, they may require a high-heat dryer cycle to kill them.

- To relieve itching, over-the-counter lotions and ointments containing antihistamine and/or hydrocortisone formulated with an anti-itch remedy such as lidocaine or benzocaine may be helpful. "Painting" bites with clear nail polish to destroy the chigger is probably not effective because by the time the bite itches, the chigger is probably no longer there, and you don't want to hold on to that sucker anyway, do you?
- Oral antihistamines may help, too.

Other (untested by the author) remedies include:

- A home remedy using meat tenderizer (papain—without salt) or baking soda, fashioned into a paste and rubbed onto the welt has been known to reduce itching.
- Sponging vinegar or a diluted solution of bleach (1 part bleach: 10 parts water) on welts has also been reported, by some, to help reduce itching.
- Repeated scratching of the welt may cause additional wounding of the skin and result in secondary infection, so try not to scratch (right!) and keep the welt area clean.
- If a severe reaction develops, consult your physician.

Scabies

Scabies is an infestation of the skin with the microscopic mite *Sarcoptes scabiei*. Infestation is common, found worldwide, and affects people of all races and social classes. Scabies spreads rapidly under crowded conditions where there is frequent skin-to-skin contact between people, such as in hospitals, institutions, childcare facilities, and nursing homes.

This mite is about the size of a pinhead and can live only two to three days at room temperature apart from the human body. It burrows into the outer layer of skin and lays eggs that hatch in three to five days. After hatching, the newly formed mites leave the burrow, move to other skin surfaces, and repeat the cycle.

MORE THAN A HANDSHAKE

Scabies is spread by direct skin-to-skin contact with a person already infested with scabies. Contact must be prolonged (a quick handshake or hug will usually not spread infestation), but infestation is easily spread to sexual partners and household members. Infestation may also occur by sharing clothing, towels, and bedding. People with weakened immune systems and the elderly are at risk for a more severe form of scabies, called Norwegian or crusted scabies.

Once away from the human body, mites do not survive more than 48 to 72 hours. When living on a person, an adult female mite can live up to a month.

Diagnosis is most commonly made by looking at the burrows or rash. A skin scraping may be taken to look for mites, eggs, or mite fecal matter to confirm the diagnosis. Typically, there are fewer than 10 mites on the entire body of an infested person; this makes it easy for an infestation to be missed.

SYMPTOMS OF SCABIES

- For a person who has never been infested with scabies, symptoms may take four to six weeks to begin. For a person who has had scabies, symptoms appear within several days. There is no immunity to an infestation.
- Pimple-like irritations, burrows, or rash of the skin large enough to see with the naked eye, especially on the webbing between

the fingers; the skin folds on the wrist, elbow, or knee; or the penis, the breast, or shoulder blades. The burrows look like grayish-white lines or tracks that zigzag on the skin surface.

- Intense itching, especially at night and over most of the body.
- Sores on the body caused by scratching that can sometimes become infected with bacteria.

CAN YOU GET SCABIES FROM YOUR PET?

The Centers for Disease Control say no. Pets have a different kind of scabies mite (also called mange). If your pet has mange and they have close contact with you, the mite can get under your skin and cause itching and skin irritation. However, this type of mite dies in a couple of days and does not reproduce. You may itch for several days, but you do not need to be treated with special medication to kill the mites. Until your pet is successfully treated, though, mites can continue to burrow into your skin and cause you to have symptoms.

TREATMENT OF SCABIES

Anyone who is diagnosed with scabies should be treated, as well as his or her sexual partners and persons who have close, prolonged contact to the infested person. If your health care provider has instructed family members to be treated, everyone should receive treatment at the same time to prevent re-infestation. Several lotions are available to treat scabies. Lindane is a popular treatment, although it is not a good treatment for children who have sensitive skin. Permethrin cream and crotamiton cream are also popular treatments for scabies. Ask your doctor which treatment is right for you. Always follow the directions provided by your physician or the directions on the

package insert, but the general drill is:

- Apply lotion to a clean body from the neck down to the toes and leave overnight (eight hours).
- After eight hours, take a bath or shower to wash off the lotion. Put on clean clothes.
- All clothes, bedding, and towels used by the infested person two days before treatment should be washed in hot water and dried in a hot dryer.
- A second treatment of the body with the same lotion may be necessary 7 to 10 days later.
- Pregnant women and children are often treated with milder scabies medications.

Itching may continue for two to three weeks, and does not mean that you are still infested. No new burrows or rashes should appear 24 to 48 hours after effective treatment. Your health care provider may prescribe additional medication to relieve itching if it is severe.

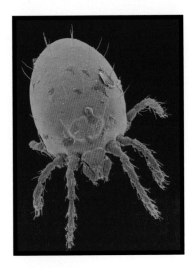

CHIGGER

Trombicula **larva**

• DANGER
Chiggers cause intense itching.

• ABUNDANCE & RANGE
They are found along the Atlantic coast through the midwest and into the southwestern U.S.

• SIZE
0.1 inch.

• DESCRIPTION
They are six-legged as larvae and colored red to pale yellow or white, and eight-legged and red as adults.

• HABITAT
They are common in fields, especially during the autumn.

• COMMENTS
Chiggers are most abundant in areas that support thickets or scrub-type vegetation and where the ground is undisturbed, supporting many rabbits, other rodents, and various small host animals. They are generally eliminated automatically by habitat destruction in areas that are heavily populated or intensively farmed. In new urban subdivisions, however, chiggers may persist in lawns for several years.

SCABIES-CAUSING MITE
Sarcoptes scabiei

• DANGER
They cause intense itching.

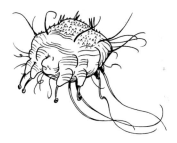

• ABUNDANCE & RANGE
They are found worldwide.

• SIZE
Fuggetaboutit. They are invisible to the naked eye.

• DESCRIPTION
Ditto.

• HABITAT
They live on the human body.

• COMMENTS
No comment.

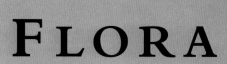

FLORA

VEGETABLE VIOLENCE

For all the splendid variety of the plant world that nourishes us body and soul, there are a surprising number of species that are variously toxic to ingest. Others are skin irritants such as the familiar sumacs (poison ivy, oak, and sumac) and the lesser-known troublemakers such as nettles.

These are the only two ways to get in trouble with plants: ingesting them (including inhalation) and touching them. Having said that, the paths to those troubles are not always as clearly marked as you might think, and the consequences of veering off the safe course may prove extremely aggravating or even fatal. It's one thing to set yourself purposefully before a final serving of deadly nightshade berries with a perfectly chilled exceptional chardonnay, and it's another to roast a wiener innocently on a stick of oleander and slosh it down with a canned diet drink, but they both lead to the same place. When you get there, you'll probably be "knock, knock, knockin' on heaven's door."

By far, however, the most likely plants you'll encounter that will give you troubles are poison ivy, oak, or sumac, so we'll devote the bulk of this chapter to them after we address the wisdom of taste testing.

TO INGEST OR NOT TO INGEST: IS THAT THE QUESTION?

No, it isn't the question. ***Never even consider eating vegetation you are not familiar with, especially wild mushrooms of any kind.*** From azaleas to yew trees, the natural world has many species that can prove mildly or fatally injurious to you and your pets. Reactions include severe vomiting; slow or irregular heartbeat; blurred vision; inability to urinate; convulsions; coma; and death, among many others. It is especially important to teach your children never to put a plant in their mouths without first asking an adult if that plant is safe. As is so often the case, children can find danger in the most unlikely places. A child can become seriously ill from biting into a daffodil bulb or drinking the water out of a vase holding a bunch of lilies-of-the-valley.

FLORA TOXIC TO INGEST

The following incomplete inventory indicates the number of common flora species that are potentially harmful for you (or your pets ★) to ingest. The point of this partial list is to indicate that there are many dangers in the plant kingdom and to encourage you strongly to refrain from "just tasting." We're not trying to put you at odds with the natural world, but it is easy to be misled by plants—one part may be edible while another is poisonous, and there are no obvious rules of thumb.

Take tomatoes for example. Their red luscious fruit is loved all over the world, but ingesting their leaves can make you ill. The potato tuber is another world staple, but again the green parts of the plant can make you sick. *Venomous Animals and Poisonous Plants,* a Peterson Field Guide by Steven Foster and Roger Caras, is a good reference for those curious to learn more about which parts of which plants are dangerous. Again, we list these species here as a signpost that plants are not to be casually ingested.

All the plants or trees on this list do not spell "d-e-a-t-h," but some do, and all will generate various degrees of discomfort based on the amount ingested and the condition (age, size, general health) of the person who has eaten them. Some species on this list may also be medicinal or forage plants under some circumstances, at some dose, but that's a decision best left to the experts given the risks involved.

(★ = also toxic to pets)

- American nightshade
  (*Solanum americanum*)
- Atamasco lily
  (*Zephyranthes atamasco*)
- Azalea *(Rhododendron* spp.*)*★
- Avocado *(Persea americanca)*★
- Barilla *(Halogeton glomeratus)*
- Black locust *(Robinia pseudoacacia)*
- Black nightshade
  (*Solanum nigrum*)
- Blue-green algae
  (*Cyanophyta* spp.*)
- Bracken fern
  (*Pteridium aquilinum*)
- Buckeyes *(Aeseulus* spp.*)*★
- Bunchflower *(Melanthium* spp.*)*
- Caladium *(Caladium* spp.*)*★
- Carolina all-spice or bubby bush
  (*Calycanthus floridus*)★
- Castorbean *(Ricinus communis)*
- Chinaberry tree *(Melia azedarach)*
- Chokeberry *(Prunus* spp.*)*
- Climbing nightshade
  (*Solanum dulcamara*)
- Cocklebur *(Xanthium* spp.*)*
- Coral beam *(Erythrina herbacea)*
- Crow poison *(Zigadenus densus)*
- Cypress spurge
  (*Euphorbia cyparissias*)
- Daffodil *(Narcissus* spp.*)*★
- Deadly nightshade
  (*Atropa belladonna*)
- Death camus *(Zigadenus* spp.*)*
- Dumbcane *(Dieffenbachia* spp.*)*★
- Dutchman's breeches
  (*Dicentra* spp.*)
- Ergot *(Claviceps* spp.*)*
- European bittersweet
  (*Solanum dulcamara*)
- False hellebore *(Veratrum* spp.*)*
- False Sago palm *(Cycas revoluta)*★
- Fly poison
  (*Amianthemum muscaetoxicum*)
- Foxglove *(Digitalis purpurea)*
- Groundsel *(Senecio* spp.*)*
- Halogeton *(Halogeton glomeratus)*
- Horse chestnut *(Aeseulus* spp.*)*★
- Iris *(Iris* spp.*)*
- Hydrangea *(Hydrangea* spp.*)*

- Hyacinth *(Hyacinthus orientalus)*★
- Jack-in-the-pulpit
  (*Arisaema* spp.*)
- Jimsonweed *(Datura stramonium)*
- Lamb's-quarters
  (*Chenopodium album*)
- Larkspur *(Delphinium* spp.*)*
- Lily-of-the-valley
  (*Convallaria majalis*)
- Locoweed
  (*Astragalus* spp. or *Oxytropis* spp.*)
- Lupine *(Lupinus* spp.*)*
- Mayapple *(Podophyllum peltatum)*
- Milkweed *(Asclepias* spp.*)*
- Mistletoe *(Phorodendron* spp.*)*
- Monkshood *(Aconitum* spp.*)*
- Mountain laurel *(Kalmia* spp.*)*
- Oaks *(Quercus* spp.*)*
- Oleander *(Nerium oleander)*★
- Onion *(Allium cepa)*★
- Philodendron
  (*Philodendron* spp.*)★
- Pigweed *(Amaranthus* spp.*)*
- Poison hemlock
  (*Conium maculatum*)
- Poison ivy
  (*Toxicodendron radicans*)
- Poison oak (eastern)
  (*Toxicodendron toxicarium*)
- Poison sumac
  (*Toxicodendron vernix*)
- Pokeweed *(Phytolaccca americana)*
- Potato *(Solanum tuberosum)*
- Precatory bean *(Abrus precatorius)*
- Red maple *(Acer rubrum)*
- Rhododendron
  (*Rhododendron maximum*)★
- Rhubarb *(Rheum* spp.*)*
- Rosary pea *(Abrus precatorius)*
- Sensitive fern *(Onoclea sensibilis)*
- Skunk cabbage
  (*Symplocarpus foetidus*)
- Snake plant or mother-in-law's
  tongue *(Sansiveira* spp.*)*★
- Snow-on-the-mountain
  (*Euphorbia marginata*)
- Spurge nettle
  (*Cnidoscolus stimulosus*)
- Star-of-Bethlehem
  (*Ornithogalum umbellatum*)
- Stinging nettle *(Urtica* spp.*)*

- Sweet clover *(Melilotus* spp.*)*
- Sweet pea *(Lathyrus* spp.*)*
- Thorn apple *(Datura stramonium)*
- Tomato *(Lycopersicon esculentum)*
- Tung-oil tree *(Aleurties* spp.*)*★
- Water hemlock *(Cicuta* spp.*)*
- White snakeroot
  (Eupatorium rugosum)
- Wild bleeding heart
  (Dicentra spp.*)*
- Wisteria *(Wisteria* spp.*)*
- Wood nettle *(Laportea canadensis)*
- Yesterday, today, and tomorrow
  (Brunfelsia spp.*)*★
- Yellow jessamine
  (Gelsemium spp.*)*
- Yellow oleander *(Thevetia* spp.*)*★
- Yew *(Taxus* spp.*)*★

CHRISTMAS CHEER

You may note that poinsettias are not on the list of toxic flora above. Widely reported to be highly toxic, the common variety sold widely at Christmas time is not poisonous to people or animals. The confusion stems from the fact that this red flowering beauty is a branch member of the African milk plant family, which does have some extremely lethal specimens. In African folk culture, these deadly specimens are sometimes referred to as "husband medicine" for women who want to "cure" themselves of their attachment.

Mistletoe, however, is another package altogether. All parts of mistletoe are considered potentially toxic, but the berries are especially to be avoided as they have caused death in humans. Children, in particular, might be attracted to sample the small white spheres.

STICK OF DEATH, ANYONE?

Oleander *(Nerium oleander)* is a prime example of the toxic potential lurking even in suburban yards. This commonly cultivated ornamental evergreen shrub is widely used as colorful hedging along driveways

and property borders. Oleander's deadly properties, however, have been known since ancient times. All parts of the plant are poisonous; if ingested, one leaf is potent enough to kill an adult. The special problem that arises with oleander is that its long, strong, straight branches, when stripped of their leaves, seem like nature's perfect hot dog or marshmallow roasting tool. So if you're on a picnic, be sure to watch where you or your children pick up sticks, because the wrong choice can prove very sickening if not fatal.

SNEEZES AND WHEEZES

Allergic reactions to pollen (allergic rhinitis) produce the typical symptoms of sneezing, nasal discharge (runny nose), congestion, and an itchy nose and throat. Seasonal allergic rhinitis occurs during pollen seasons in the spring, summer, and fall. Perennial allergic rhinitis has the same symptoms, but they occur year-round and are triggered by molds, dust, mites, feathers, and animal dander. The common name "hay fever" was coined about 150 years ago because reactions of this type were frequent during the hay harvesting season, but hay is usually not the allergen that causes the difficulties.

Although goldenrod *(Solidago* spp.*)* and pine *(Pinus* spp.*)* are often mistaken for allergy culprits, ragweed *(Ambrosia* spp.*)* is a much more likely offender. In late summer or early fall, ragweed pollen arises to cause misery for many. Ragweed is found throughout the lower 48 states on dry fields, pastures, roadsides, and construction sites, and you can find ragweed on every other continent except Antarctica. Ragweed pollen is just about impossible to avoid because it is so small, entering your home through tiny cracks. If your doors or windows are open to savor the last of summer, you can guess the results. One plant can generate one million grains of pollen, but fewer than 1,000 grains in your bedroom can trigger an allergic reaction. Just about all you can do is resort to over-the counter, prescription, or natural substances to try to alleviate the symptoms.

PLANTS AND CHILD FIRST AID

The *Poisons and Antidotes Sourcebook* (2nd ed.) by Carol Turkington is an excellent resource that every home should have. It offers this advice if you think your child has eaten a plant:

- Stay calm and check your child for adverse reactions.
- Determine how much of the plant and what part (berries, stem, etc.) your child has eaten.
- Remove any uneaten plant material from the child's mouth. Check the mouth for redness, blisters, swelling, irritation, and cuts.
- Observe for allergic reactions: blotchy, red skin; swelling; breathing problems; nausea and diarrhea.
- Identify the plant. If someone else is in the house, send him or her to a nursery to identify the plant if you don't know its name.
- Call the poison control center (see the back of this book for listing of regional centers). Report any adverse reactions and give age and weight of child.
- If told to go to a hospital, take the plant or a sample with you.
- If your child is too young to speak, retrace the child's steps and check for any damaged plants. If there is plant material in the mouth, try to match it with a plant in the area.

Safe Plants

Turkington has thoughtfully compiled the list of safe plants below so that your home and gardens can still

It takes less than a thousand grains of pollen from ragweed (Ambrosia spp.) to cause an allergic reaction. A single ragweed plant can generate a million grains of pollen.

be beautiful and trouble-free if you are the parents of young children:

- African violet
- Aluminum plant
- Aspidistra
- Aster
- Baby's tears
- Begonia
- Bird's nest fern
- Boston fern
- Bougainvillea
- California poppy
- Camellia
- Christmas cactus
- Coleus spider plant
- Creeping Charlie
- Dahlia
- Dandelion
- Easter lily
- Gardenia
- Impatiens
- Jade plant
- Lipstick plant
- Magnolia
- Marigold
- Nasturtium
- Norfolk Island pine
- Pepperomia
- Petunia
- Poinsettia
- Prayer plant

- Purple passion
- Rose
- Sensitive plant
- Swedish ivy
- Tiger lily
- Umbrella tree
- Violet
- Wandering Jew
- Wild strawberry
- Zebra plant

POISON IVY, POISON OAK, AND POISON SUMAC

Billy Ward got it right when he wrote the classic lyrics for "Poison Ivy," the Coasters' 1959 #1 R&B hit. Sometimes it seems like "an ocean of calamine lotion" won't begin to be enough when poison ivy gets under your skin, driving you mad with its relentless itch. Estimates vary, but somewhere between 50–85% of Americans can relate to Billy Ward's time-honored tune because they are allergic to poison ivy, oak, and sumac—three cousins of the cashew family that in combination are found virtually throughout the lower 48 states. This trio is reported to be the single most common cause of allergic reactions in the U.S. That means millions (estimates range from 2 to 50 million) of folks each year have a painful, irritating contact dermatitis (varying degrees of itching, swelling, redness, and blisters) in reaction to urushiol, an oil that is in all parts of the plants: leaves, stems, berries, and especially the sap.

Urushiol is a clear or slightly yellow resin; its name comes from the Japanese word for "lacquer." While the urushiol is slightly different in the three plants, it is similar enough so that people who have an allergic reaction to one will have an allergic reaction to another. For this reason, what we say about poison ivy here will also apply to the other two species unless otherwise indicated. The profiles at the end of this chapter will help you to identify them individually.

Leaves of Three?

Actually, it isn't leaves you are counting, but leaflets; nonetheless, this is a good place to start identifying the poison cashew crew. The famous "leaves of three, let it be" is good rule to follow, but some plants don't always play by the rules. Poison sumac, for example, has 7–13 leaflets. To avoid these itch-producing plants, here's a quick overview:

Poison Ivy

- Grows around lakes and streams in the eastern U.S., but also favors mixed forest grounds and forest edges.
- Can be a woody, hairy, rope-like vine, a trailing shrub on the ground, or a free-standing shrub.
- Normally has three leaflets (groups of leaves all on the same small stem coming off the larger main stem), but may vary from groups of three to nine.
- Has leaves that are green in the summer and red in the fall.
- Has yellow or green flowers and white berries.

Poison Oak

- Found in the eastern U.S. as a low shrub, generally in well-drained, upland sites. In the west (along the Pacific coast), this plant may grow as a vine but usually is a shrub.
- Has hair on its fruit, stem, and leaves.
- Has oak-like leaves, each with three leaflets.
- Has clusters of yellowish berries.

Poison Sumac

- Found in the eastern U.S. and grows in boggy areas; also found in bay swamps and the margins of ponds.

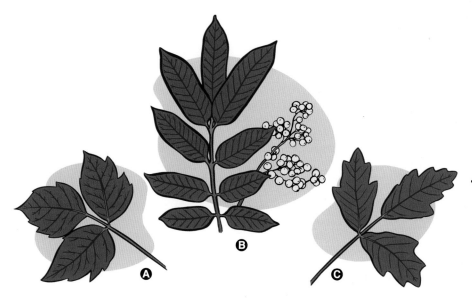

Poison ivy has three wide leaflets **(A)**; *poison sumac has 7 to 13 smooth-edged leaflets* **(B)***; and poison oak has three oak-like leaflets* **(C)**.

- Appears as a rangy shrub up to 15 feet tall.
- Has 7 to 13 smooth-edged leaflets.
- Has glossy pale yellow or cream-colored berries.

HOW DO YOU GET POISON IVY?

You can get contact dermatitis from poison ivy only by coming in contact with the urushiol (sap) that is released when the plant is bruised or crushed. Although that sounds easy enough to avoid, the plant is delicate and easily bruised on contact—with anything. "Poison oak, ivy, and sumac are very fragile plants," says William L. Epstein, M.D., professor of dermatology, University of California, San Francisco. "Stems or leaves broken by the wind or animals, and even the tiny holes made by chewing insects, can release urushiol."

Here's a typical scenario of how you might "mysteriously" get poison ivy: You use a garden tool to work around an area that has poison ivy, and the tool touches the plant. You clean the tool with a cloth (you always clean all your tools after using them, don't you?), and then wipe your hands and arms with that cloth. Chances are you will get poison ivy. Why? The urushiol contaminates anything it touches: clothing, tools, sports and camping equipment such as sleeping bags, and even some of your dearest friends as you will understand from the following story.

Edith wasn't sure if she was allergic to poison ivy when she started clearing the overgrown yard of her first home purchase. Fairly aware of the "leaflets of three" guiding principle, she was careful about touching the plants directly and always wore gloves and long sleeves when working in the yard. She had already tried to target the worst patches of poison ivy with Round-Up, which kills plants by absorption through the leaves, but some remained. In the early fall, she started to rake the yard. It was still

hot, and when she started to perspire, she wiped the side of her face and brow with her sleeve. What she didn't know was that poison ivy leaves were in the bundles she was lifting and that they had touched her shirt-sleeves. She awoke the next morning to a red, swollen, puffy, itching face that had developed dermatitis in reaction to the urushiol. The fact that the oil was on the tender skin of her face made the situation worse. Urushiol had been transferred from her shirt to her face as she repeatedly wiped the sweat away with her shoulder and forearm. Her allergic reaction was so severe she could barely see out of one eye, so she had to resort to a round of steroids prescribed by a doctor to diminish her body's strong reaction. Edith vowed to be more careful of contact in the future, and she was. She was innocently (and quite mistakenly) relieved when winter took its toll on the remaining plants, thinking that at last, like the ticks, they were out of her life until spring. She was lucky the rest of that year and was extremely careful to avoid plant contact when doing yard work that next spring, summer, and fall until . . .

The next winter when freezing temperatures had been the norm for weeks, she awoke one morning to a disturbingly familiar itching, swelling, and general aggravation on the inside of her lower arms. She wondered, "Poison ivy? In February, when I haven't done any yard work for months?" Yes, it was poison ivy. She had gotten it by loving some of her furry best friends. Although she had eradicated almost all of the plants in her fenced-in yard, her cats still went into the neighboring woods where the understory was a virtual carpet of poison ivy quite recognizable in the spring and summer. The cats picked up the oil on their fur, and when she picked up the cats to carry them with bare arms, she contacted the

urushiol just as if she had had direct contact with the plant itself, so another systemic round of poison ivy ensued. The good news is that Edith didn't have outbreaks on her hands because the skin of the palms (and soles) is thicker, so the oil does not usually penetrate these areas.

In another example, Joan also contracted a serious bout of poison ivy when her clothes touched the clothes of her husband Bob after he had been mountain biking. Although Bob had no sensitivity to the plant, his clothes carried the oil home to Joan, who had left the house that weekend only to go shopping for quilt fabric at the mall. Bummer.

Points of Contact

To reiterate, contact with urushiol can occur in three ways:

- Direct contact—touching the sap of the toxic plant.
- Indirect contact—touching something to which urushiol has spread. The oil can stick to the fur of animals, to garden tools or sports equipment, or to any objects that have come into contact with a crushed or broken plant.
- In another form of indirect contact, airborne urushiol particles, such as from burning plants, may come in contact with your skin or respiratory system.

When Can You Get Poison Ivy?

As we see from Edith's story, you can get poison ivy at any time of year. The urushiol is more potent in the spring and summer when the plants are most vibrant, but the dead of winter will do just fine, too. The oil also has real staying power, remaining active for up to a year or more on the surface that was touched. So a hunter who had the oil on his camouflage jacket last year can get poison ivy again this year before he even steps out of the house—just by putting on his jacket.

Paddlers and Others, Step Lively

Poison ivy—and its cousin poison oak—have an insidious way of wreaking havoc on the simplest adventure, be it a hike in the woods or a picnic in a park. Even when water is the dominant environment, poison ivy may lurk along river-banks, so paddlers need to be alert, too. The damage is usually done while traipsing to put-ins and away from take-outs, while scouting or portaging when your concentration is more focused on rocks and rivers than rash-causing flora. Countless waterways hide the vicious vine along their shores. Watch your step—and add calamine or some other soothing option (see below) to your equipment list.

RELATIVE SENSITIVITY TO POISON IVY

The poison ivy rash can affect almost any part of your body, especially in places where your skin is thin, such as on your face or on the inside of your arms. It's less likely to manifest on the thicker-skinned areas (such as palms and soles).

Sensitivity may occur after only one exposure, but usually people develop sensitivity to poison ivy, oak, or sumac only after several encounters with the plants, sometimes over many years. About 85% of all people will develop an allergic reaction when adequately exposed to poison ivy.

Sensitivity varies from person to person. People who reach adulthood without becoming sensitive have only a 50% chance of developing an allergy to poison ivy. Sensitivity to poison ivy tends to decline with age. Children who have reacted to poison ivy will probably find that their sensitivity decreases by half in young adulthood without repeated expo-

sure. People who were once allergic to poison ivy may even lose their sensitivity later in life. Some people are very sensitive to poison ivy, developing a severe rash with blisters and extreme swelling on their face, arms, legs, and genitals. Such severe cases need medical treatment sooner rather than later.

When assessing whether or not to get medical treatment, consider:

- If you have had strong reactions in the past, you are likely, but not guaranteed, to have strong reactions in the future.
- The characteristics of the rash outbreak, including location (as above), degree of severity, and amount of body affected. Even if the rash does not appear to be severe, the greater the area affected, then the greater the need for medical care.

AVOIDING EXPOSURE TO POISON IVY

The American Academy of Dermatology recommends that whenever you're going to be around poison ivy—trying to clear it from your yard or hiking in the woods—wear long pants and long sleeves, and, if possible, gloves and boots. And must we add, don't wipe with vegetation? Drip dry.

IF YOU HAVE BEEN EXPOSED TO POISON IVY

Because urushiol can penetrate the skin within minutes, there's no time to waste if you know you've been exposed. "The earlier you cleanse the skin, the greater the chance that you can remove the urushiol before it gets attached to the skin," says Hon-Sum Ko, M.D., an allergist and immunologist with the Food and Drug Administration's Center for Drug Evaluation and Research. Cleansing may not stop the initial outbreak of the rash if more than 10 minutes has elapsed, but it can help prevent further spread.

If you've been exposed to poison ivy, oak, or sumac, if possible, stay outdoors until you complete the first two following steps:

- First, cleanse exposed skin with generous amounts of isopropyl (rubbing) alcohol. Don't return to the woods or yard the same day. Alcohol removes your skin's protection along with the urushiol, and any new contact will cause the urushiol to penetrate twice as fast. The resin is soluble in alcohol, and some say that beer or other alcoholic beverages will help remove the resin from the skin. If you have none of these substances, go to the next step.

- Wash skin with cold water. Do not scrub with a brush. Remove rings, bracelets, and such before washing hands. Wash jewelry. First rely more on rinsing and less on soaping because immediately after contact the soap might increase distribution of the fresh urushiol.

- A solution of baking soda and water may also be helpful. If the oil has been on the skin for less than six hours, thorough cleansing with cold water and strong soap, repeated three times, will usually prevent reaction.

- Third, take a regular shower with soap and warm water. Do not take a bath, because that will only distribute the oil all over your body.

- Clothes, shoes, tools, and anything else that may have been in contact with the urushiol should be wiped off with alcohol and water. The palms of the hands rarely break out in a rash because of the thickness of the skin, but hands can still be contaminated with the plant's oil. The problem with getting the oil on your hands is that you carry it to other surfaces. Touch

yourself anywhere and the rash spreads. You rub your cheek, scratch your ear or your back, go to the bathroom, or pull off your socks—and you've spread the oil to all those spots. Wear gloves when handling contaminated clothing or tools and then discard the hand covering.

- The oil can also travel around on your clothes. Contaminated clothing should be washed separately. Once you've showered and washed all contaminated areas and articles, the rash can no longer spread to other parts of your body or to anyone else. Make sure you wash all clothes and shoes with hot water and a strong soap. If you bring the clothes into your house, be careful that you do not transfer the urushiol to rugs or furniture. You may also dry-clean contaminated clothes. Bathe pets who have come in contact with poison ivy, oak, or sumac because the sap can stay on them for days.

- Because urushiol can remain active for months, wash camping, sporting, fishing or hunting gear that was in contact with the oil.

Tec Labs Solutions

God and the doctors know (notice they are different), we've had some strong reactions to poison ivy. While there are many good products on the market to help folks through the event, personal experience has led us to Tec Labs products. Their Tecnu® Outdoor Skin Cleanser "decontaminates laundry, pets, and tools," as well as you. Clearly Calagel is their answer to calamine lotion. Aside from being an effective itch stopper, it doesn't make you look like a pink flaking alien with a weird case of psoriasis. The company's website (www.teclabs inc.com) explains that Tec Lab "has been protecting consumers and

industrial workers for over 20 years...
The flagship Tec Labs product, Tecnu, was developed in 1961 during the cold war era by chemical engineer Dr. Robert Smith as a waterless cleanser for removing radioactive dust from the skin and clothing. His wife accidentally discovered that Tecnu would remove poison plant oils after exposure to poison oak and ivy. (Talk about industrial strength!)

The Tec Labs website has good information on the poison ivy product line, as well as on the company's other repellents. You can find a list of distributors there, or you can call (800) ITCHING to find out where you can buy Tec Lab products.

No product, including Tecnu, will make the experience just disappear, but the company's soap and gel can really help.

Symptoms of Poison Ivy Contact Dermatitis

If you don't cleanse quickly enough, or your skin is so sensitive that cleansing didn't help:
- Redness, rash, and swelling will appear in about 12 to 48 hours. A characteristic pattern is a line of reaction, as if you had made a streaking mark with a pen or pencil tipped with the allergen oil.
- Blisters and itching will follow.
- Blisters will peak about five days after exposure, then break and ooze clear fluid, crust over, and eventually heal in another week or two, even without treatment.

For those rare people who react after their very first exposure, the rash appears after 7 to 10 days.

Treating the Rash and Itch

Because they don't contain urushiol, the oozing blisters are not contagious, nor can the fluid cause further spread on the affected person's body. Nevertheless, don't scratch the blis-

ters because your fingernails may carry germs that could cause an infection in the open sores.

The rash doesn't spread across the body and will only occur where urushiol has touched the skin. However, the rash may seem to spread if it appears over time instead of all at once. This is either because the urushiol is absorbed at different rates in different parts of the body or because of repeated exposure to contaminated objects, such as urushiol trapped under the fingernails.

The rash, blisters, and itch normally disappear in 14 to 20 days without any treatment, but most people need some itch relief.
- For mild cases, wet compresses or soaking in cool water may be effective.
- Oral antihistamines (such as over-the-counter remedies like Benadryl) can also relieve the itching.
- Over-the-counter topical hydrocortisone compounds (such as Cortaid and Lanacort) with 1% or less of hydrocortisone are generally not considered to be effective.
- For severe cases, prescription topical corticosteroid drugs can halt the reaction, but only if treatment begins within a few hours of exposure.
- A tepid bath with oatmeal or colloidal Aveeno (see below) can help. If your skin's too sore for you to go to the store, run some uncooked rolled oats through the blender till you have a fine flour. Sprinkle that in the bath and get in it — reportedly it substantially reduces the itching.
- For those who prefer more natural alternatives, jewelweed (untested by the author), applied by rubbing the plant on affected areas, is commonly listed as an in-the-field treatment to break

down the urushiol. It almost goes without saying that you need to be absolutely sure you know your jewelweed before you use it. You can also purchase a line of jewelweed products (such as soap) from the Alternative Nature Online Herbal website at altnature.com. We haven't tried this soap, but it sounds worth investigating. Rhuli anti-itch gel made with camphor is another general (bites, stings, etc.) transparent itch treatment favored by those who prefer "alternative medicine." Rhuli is good, but Tecnu's Clearly Calagel (see above) is tougher. Both are found at drugstores.

- Naturopathic remedies include jewelweed juice, which is contained in "Oak-Away." This product also contains mugwort, goldenseal, comfrey, and chickweed. Both (untried by this author) "Oak-Away" and the homeopathic formula "Hyland's PoisonIvy/Oak" are available at health food stores. A homeopathic remedy worth trying as a preventative contains Rhus toxicodendron 6X (poison ivy/poison oak), Croton tiglium 6X (croton oil), and Xerophyllum 6X (basketgrass flower).
- A short-term but effective fix is a really hot bath or shower. Heat releases histamine, the substance in the skin that causes itching. Extremely hot water will cause intense itching as the histamine is released, but the itching subsides as the skin becomes depleted of histamine.
- If you have had severe reactions in the past and know you have been exposed, it's a good idea to contact medical help, such as your dermatologist, as soon as possible after a new exposure. He or she can help to lessen the effects of

Poison ivy in spring.

your body's allergic reaction before it gets "carried away."

- Severe reactions can be treated with prescription oral corticosteroids, such as prednisone. Oral corticosteroids may be especially appropriate if the rash is on the face, genitals, or covers more than 30% of the body. The drug must be taken for several days, commonly 10 to 14 days. Topical steroid creams are less effective than oral systemic treatment, but the oral varieties can make you feel like Arnold Schwarzenegger, all armored up and no place to annihilate.
- The FDA recommends a number of OTC (over-the-counter) products to help dry up the oozing blisters:

  aluminum acetate
  (Burrows solution)
  baking soda
  Aveeno (oatmeal bath)
  aluminum hydroxide gel
  calamine
  kaolin
  zinc acetate
  zinc carbonate
  zinc oxide

Poison ivy in fall.

Poison ivy in winter.

PREVENTIVE MEDICINE?

The FDA has recently approved some barrier cremes (bentoquatam). Our friends at Tec Labs (see above) have created a barrier solution to be applied **before** exposure, when you know you're going into poison ivy country. We don't know how effective it is, but based on the company's reputation, it's worth a try. If it is effective, it's a real breakthrough because preventative measures have been sought for decades. Two other (author untested) barrier products are Ivy Block and Work Shield.

Prescription pills can provide immunization, but this treatment takes months to achieve reasonable hyposensitization. It also has a track record of some substantial side effects, such as skin problems, stomach problems, fever, inflammation, and convulsions. For these reasons, only folks (such as firefighters) who have a lot of contact with poison ivy as a course of duty are the best candidates. Contact your dermatologist for more information.

GOOD RIDDANCE

There are really only two solutions for ridding your surroundings of poison ivy: chemical and manual.

Herbicides can chemically do the job, but the FDA advises that the two herbicides most commonly used for poison ivy—Round-Up and Ortho Poison Ivy Killer—will kill other plants as well. Spraying Round-Up (active ingredient glyphosate) on the foliage of young plants will kill the poison ivy, but if the poison ivy vine is growing up your prize rhododendron or azalea, for example, the Round-Up will kill them too.

Joseph Neal, Ph.D., associate professor of weed science at Cornell University, advises, "Ortho Poison Ivy Killer (active ingredient triclopyr), if used sparingly, will kill poison ivy, but not the trees it grows around. Don't use it around shrubs, broad-leaf ground cover, or herbaceous garden plants. It is possible to spray the poison ivy without killing other plants if you pull the poison ivy vines away from the desirable plants and wipe the ivy foliage with the herbicide, or use a shield on the sprayer to direct the chemical."

If you don't want to use chemicals, manual removal will get rid of the ivy, but you must be diligent and get every bit of the plant—leaves, vines, and roots—or it will sprout again. Obviously, manual removal has its own hazards. Wear plastic gloves over cotton gloves when pulling the plants. Plastic alone isn't enough because the plastic rips, and cotton alone won't work because after a while the urushiol will soak through.

Check local regulations to see how the plants can be safely and legally disposed of. Urushiol will break down with composting, but the plants must be chopped into small pieces first, which just adds to your risk of exposure.

Never burn poison ivy. The smoke is also toxic and can irritate the noses, throats, lungs, eyes, and faces of those who come in contact with it.

SHAPE SHIFTERS FOR ALL SEASONS

Poison ivy can have different forms. It grows as a crawling vine, a climbing vine, or low shrub. Poison oak, with its leaflets resembling oak leaves, is a low shrub in the East and can be a low or high shrub in the West. Poison sumac grows to a tall shrub or small tree.

Because they are year-round hazards, know how to recognize these toxic plants in all seasons. In the early fall, the leaves can turn colors such as yellow or red when other plants are still green. The berry-like fruit on the mature female plants also changes color in fall, from green to off-white, and in the winter the plants lose their leaves. In the spring, poison ivy has yellow-green flowers.

CONTACT URTICARIA

No, this isn't a commando's directive in a B-grade science fiction film. "Urticaria" is from the Latin word for nettle, a plant with toothed leaves covered with hairs that have a stinging fluid. The other Latin root at work here is "uro," the word for "burn," in the sense of a chafing, irritating, rubbing sore. Contact urticaria occurs when you touch plants such as nettles whose broken hairs then inject a stinging toxin into your skin. The most common causes of contact urticaria in the U.S. are from rubbing against or handling stinging nettles, spurge nettles, bull nettles, or wood nettles. Although the sensation is unpleasant, the effects are usually not serious nor long-lasting. Prevention is best achieved through awareness of the nettle-type plants and subsequent avoidance. If necessary, antihistamines such as Benadryl may be useful, but in situations of extreme anaphylactic reactions, epinephrine administration (as from a bee sting kit) is required.

POISON IVY
Toxicodendron radicans

• DANGER
Exposure to poison ivy causes mild to severe (including systemic) contact dermatitis for allergic individuals.

• ABUNDANCE & RANGE
Poison ivy is common throughout the eastern U.S.

• SIZE
Size varies depending on the form of the plant.

• DESCRIPTION
It may take the form of a ground cover trailing vine, a climbing vine with hairy rope-like stem, or rarely as a low shrub. Leaves are alternate (not directly opposite each other on the stem) with three leaflets. The plant has green flowers in June and July. Fruits are white and smooth or hairy from August to November. Leaves are green in summer, red in fall. Poison ivy loses its leaves in winter.

• HABITAT
Poison ivy grows in fertile, well-drained soil in the woods and at their margins; along structures suitable for climbing, such as stone walls; and at the water's edge on rock-strewn shores of rivers and lakes, or on the flood plains of streams.

• COMMENTS
Poison ivy is often confused with seedlings of box elder *(Acer negurdo)*. Box elder is a maple, and maples have opposite leaves, whereas poison ivy has alternate leaves. Three other common plants are often mistaken for poison ivy: hog peanut, Virginia creeper, and the seedlings of Manitoba maple. Manitoba maple seedlings have three leaflets, but the leaves grow in pairs, with the stalks opposite each other on the stem. Poison ivy has three leaflets with pointed tips; the stalks of the leaves do not grow from the same point on the stem; the stem is woody, and the plant may have creamy yellow-green flowers or clustered waxy berries that are green to yellow. Hog peanut has three leaflets, but the stem is not woody. Flowers are white to lilac-colored. Virginia creeper has five leaflets and produces blush-colored berries.

EASTERN POISON OAK
Toxicodendron toxicarium

• DANGER
Eastern poison oak causes mild to severe (including systemic) contact dermatitis for allergic individuals.

• ABUNDANCE & RANGE
It is common in the eastern U.S.

• SIZE
This plant grows to three to six feet in height as an upright shrub.

• DESCRIPTION
Poison oak is an upright bushy shrub that sometimes takes on a vine-like appearance. Branches are rigid and smooth. Leaves are alternate and compound with three leaflets that are oval-shaped or evenly lobed, shiny, and reminiscent of oak leaves. Fruit is white and smooth.

• HABITAT
It grows in sandy soils in acid woods, sometimes near lakes.

• COMMENTS
Unlike poison ivy, poison oak is never a climbing vine. Three other common plants are often mistaken for poison oak: hog peanut, Virginia creeper, and the seedlings of Manitoba maple are

similar and easily confused. Poison oak has three leaflets with rounded tips; the stalks of the leaves do not grow from the same point on the stem; the stem is woody, and the plant may have creamy yellow-green flowers or clustered waxy berries that are green to yellow. The center leaves resemble oak leaves. Hog peanut has three leaflets, but the stem is not woody. Flowers are white to lilac-colored. Virginia creeper has five leaflets and produces blush-colored berries. Manitoba maple seedlings have three leaflets, but the leaves grow in pairs, with the stalks opposite each other on the stem.

POISON SUMAC

Toxicodendron vernix

• DANGER
Exposure causes mild to severe (including systemic) contact dermatitis for allergic individuals.

• ABUNDANCE & RANGE
This plant is common in the eastern U.S.

• SIZE
Poison sumac grows to 6 to 20 feet.

• DESCRIPTION
Poison sumac grows as a small tree or shrub with alternate pinnately (feather-patterned) compound leaves of 7 to 13 smooth-edged leaflets. It has smooth, white fruit from August to November.

• HABITAT
Poison sumac tends to grow in wet soil near standing water, such as peat bogs, swampy pine woods, bay swamps, edges of ponds, or acidic creek bottoms.

SPURGE NETTLE

Cnidoscolus stimulosus

• DANGER
This plant stings on contact.

• ABUNDANCE & RANGE
Spurge nettle is found from Virginia south to Florida and west to Texas.

• SIZE
The plant grows up to 39 inches in height.

• DESCRIPTION
This perennial, tubular white herb is covered with stinging hairs on leaves and stems. Three to five lobed leaves are alternate, simple, and palmate (in a radial pattern like fingers from a palm). The fruit is a three-seeded capsule.

• HABITAT

The spurge nettle is found in forests or natural areas in sandy woods; weedy in disturbed areas (altered by humans), and along roadsides and old fields.

• COMMENTS

Contact causes only minor, short-lived skin irritation, usually only about 30 minutes, but a dull purple stain may linger for almost a month. Also known as "tread softly" and by the charming sobriquet of "finger rot."

• HABITAT

Stinging nettle grows in moist thickets and waste areas.

• COMMENTS

The lower stems especially have stinging hairs that break off on contact and inject a burning chemical mixture into the skin. The sensation may last for up to an hour.

STINGING NETTLE
Urtica dioica L.

• DANGER

This plant stings on contact.

• ABUNDANCE & RANGE

Stinging nettle is found throughout much of the U.S, and it is commonly found in the eastern U.S.

• DESCRIPTION

This perennial has four angled stems. Lower stems have stinging hairs. Leaves are roughly heart-shaped. Greenish flowers bloom from June to September.

• SIZE

It grows to one to four feet in height.

AT THE
SEASHORE

IT CAME FROM THE DEEP

For just about everybody, the open grace of beach, sea, and sky is irresistible. Walking, wading, and swimming in the ocean are surely ancient pastimes that our earliest ancestors probably enjoyed as much as we do. Poking about to see what the tide has brought, dancing away from the water's edge, and feeling buoyed by the surge of surf are definite pleasures. But as calming and delightful as a seaside interlude can be, there are some hazards to consider.

It's easy to imagine the dangers of the deep—creatures that boggle the mind with their adaptations to the cold, dark depths, creatures that could stalk your nightmares if you only knew what to call them. However, there are life forms to beware at the very edge of the water, on the beach, and within easy swimming distance of the shore. Certainly sharks are the most obvious of these, and that's why we cover them first; but there are also jellyfish, such as the Portuguese man-of-war, and rays whose tails have powerful stingers that can inflict burning wounds. You are much more likely to encounter a stinging jellyfish or a ray than you are a biting shark. A few other less well-known species bear mentioning, too, such as fire worms, red sponges, and predatory mollusks with mildly venomous dart-like teeth. (Who knew?)

All of the species discussed in this chapter will be those you might encounter while walking, wading, swimming, and surfing at the beach. Dangers encountered diving and snorkeling from an anchored boat in deeper waters, such as the extremely rare cases of barracuda attack, are not included here.

SHARKS

OLD BEACH BUDDIES

Sharks have probably been attacking people as long as sharks and people have shared the water. These superb predators were first chronicled in written form about 2,300 years ago by Aristotle, but he didn't explore the phenomenon of shark attack, preferring instead to dwell on the amazing attributes of this fish that has remained unchanged for 400 to 450 million years. Where lives and livelihoods are bound to the sea, various marine cultures have both venerated and cursed this mysterious creature for its beauty and power. In dryer inland regions, though, it seems only the grisly man-eating abilities of the fish have made it into the abiding consciousness. The word "shark," for example, is thought to derive from the German "schurke," meaning "villain" or "scoundrel."

NAKED FEAR

Face it. Although it's a reality the vast majority of life on earth faces every waking and sleeping moment, we humans don't like the idea of being eaten alive (or dead, for that matter). Our rules say we may eat just about anything, but heaven help the species that might eat us. Then there's the awful truth: there we are in the ocean, literally "out of our element," maybe even "in over our heads," virtually naked, and here comes the massive dorsal fin "knifing" through the water, and not a rifle in reach! Egads! Of course, fear and loathing are all we have left—until we substitute knowledge.

Sharks are, of course, quite worthy of our respect and even our praise. This passage, from *The Old Man and the Sea* by Ernest Hemingway, hints at the magnificence and power of a mako shark:

He was a very big Mako shark, built to swim as fast as the fastest fish in the sea and everything about him was beautiful except his jaws. His back was as blue as a sword fish's and his belly was silver and his hide was smooth and handsome. He was built as a sword fish except for his huge jaws which were tight shut now as he swam fast, just under the surface with his high dorsal fin knifing through the water without wavering. Inside the closed double lip of his jaws all of his eight rows of teeth were slanted inwards. They were not the ordinary pyramid-shaped teeth of most sharks. They were shaped like a man's fingers when they are crisped like claws. They were nearly as long as the fingers of the old man and they had razor-sharp cutting edges on both sides. This was a fish built to feed on all the fishes in the sea, that were so fast and strong and well armed that they had no other enemy.

MAGNIFICENT AND MYSTERIOUS

Sharks, along with rays, are members of the *Chondrichthyes* class, whose name from the Greek means cartilage and fish. Because their skeletons are made of cartilage they are distinct from another evolutionary branch of marine life, the bony fishes. Sharks, though making up only 1% of all fishes, are a testament to the sublime success of evolution. As highly evolved as they are now, they "got it right" 400 or so million years ago, and they remain essentially unchanged.

Fifty percent of all sharks attain a length somewhere between 6 and 39 inches, and most sharks pose no threat at all to humans. We are larger than 80% of all sharks.

The business end of a shark has rows of teeth that are connected by soft tissue and replaced continually. Various breeds of shark have

The shark has several rows of teeth which are continually replaced throughout its lifetime. No tooth fairy wants to get assigned to "shark detail" … it really bites.

differently shaped teeth suited to various needs. By no means are all sharks built to shred human thighs; many shark species are comparatively sedentary and some have flat teeth that are suited for grinding the shells of their favorite food, mollusks.

When a shark feeds, its mouth, located on the underside of its cigar-shaped body, undergoes an unusual transformation. The upper jaw is attached to the skull by ligaments and tissue. When taking prey, the jaw is literally thrust forward out of the body, enabling the shark to take large bites.

The shark's sense of smell is one of its most legendary features, and it is likely that sharks can track a scent in the water over many miles. A shark's hearing is probably directional and is used to help it locate struggling fish. Reports indicate that sharks can hear much lower-frequency sounds in the water than humans can, and they sometimes react to loud noises underwater from several miles away. With eyes on the sides of their heads, sharks have a wide range of vision that becomes appreciably effective when the object of examination or prey is within close range. (It is also interesting to note that the infamous "dead" eye of the shark is often a boon to human sight, taking on new life when shark corneas are used in transplant operations.) It seems that sharks do have a sense of taste, as some are noted to prefer certain types of food over others. According to shark attack records, you will be glad to know that humans do not rank high on sharks' list of culinary delights. One of the most interesting capabilities of sharks is that of electro-sensation. Sharks can locate nearby life forms through special organs called the ampullae of Lorenzini. Located about the mouth and eyes, these organs enable sharks to read the weak electrical aura of another creature even when it is buried in the sand.

For all that is known about sharks, much more is unknown. They are prime examples of the many creatures who possess types of intelligence and aptitudes that will likely be perpetually beyond our comprehension. In some ways, this is understandable as

The shark's upper jaw normally rests just below the skull (**1**)*. As the shark's mouth opens to bite, the upper jaw detaches from the skull* (**2**)*.*

sharks roam and rule in a world that is quite foreign to us in spite of our fascination with it. Our magnetic attraction to the sea and its creatures is an old story, often told in literature and film.

HOLLYWOOD HORROR SHOW

Think back to 1975. Can you hear the menacing movie music? Can you remember the poster with the hapless woman about to be horribly consumed by a 50-foot sharkskin rocket (it was supposed to be a Great White, which actually grows to only 24 feet) about to soar straight out of the deep, straight for her? The hugely popular 1974 book *Jaws* by Peter Benchley and the subsequent movie directed by Steven Spielberg did more to set the world's nerves on edge about sharks than any other single event in the history of human-shark relations. A dramatic but relatively infrequent natural tragedy was catapulted into public consciousness and lodged there as securely as when Ahab finally harpooned Moby Dick. Ahab went down with the whale in a one-on-one contest to the finish, but nowadays on a worldwide average sharks kill about six of us and we kill about 12 million of them each year.

Nowadays Peter Benchley campaigns actively on behalf of sharks. "Sharks have become much more victims than villains," he asserts. To make a status-laden bowl of shark fin soup, over the years millions of sharks have been stripped of their fins and then dumped back in the ocean to die. This activity, however, is now banned by some countries including the U.S. Driftnets and longlines set for tuna threaten worldwide shark populations, too. Some shark species face difficulties "pupping" (delivering their live-born young) in polluted inshore waters, another threat to shark populations the world over. Several species face extinction such as the dusky and sandbar sharks— whose populations have dropped 80% in the last ten years.

THE LIKELIHOOD OF SHARK ATTACK

In 1958, the U.S. Navy started to compile records of shark attacks worldwide. This archive has now become known as the International Shark Attack File (ISAF), and it is managed by the Florida Museum of Natural History, affiliated with the University of Florida in Gainesville.

While records are incomplete because 100% reporting is not achieved for a variety of reasons— some of them economic and related to tourism—the ISAF does have a wealth of strong data that suggests your exposure to shark attack is extremely small, even if you swim or surf in shark-inhabited waters every day. There is no question, however, that if you're not in the water, you're definitely not going to be bitten.

The summer of 2001 seemed to disprove the distant likelihood of attack. Two deaths along the Virginia and North Carolina coasts over Labor Day weekend—when warm waters attract both bathers and sharks—and 11 attacks in Florida for the year as of September 17, 2001 set off old fears of *Jaws*. Most of these attacks received a lot of media attention, particularly because tragically one child died and another went into an extended coma. Experts concur, however, that although the Virginia and North Carolina attacks are atypical for their northerly latitude, the summer of 2001 was typical for attacks overall. Concurring with George Burgess of the ISAF, Erich Ritter of the Global Shark Attack

File in Princeton, NJ commented, "It just happens … It's just a regular year."

WHY SHARKS ATTACK

The bottom line is the frequent refrain: nobody knows for sure. Sharks are wild creatures, and wild creatures are unpredictable. That said, there are observable patterns of attack that indicate the motive of the shark's apparent predation on humans. The information below considers unprovoked attacks. ("Provoked" attacks are often triggered by unusually stupid human tricks that go horribly awry, such as divers pulling on a shark's tail, hand feeding, etc. Enough said.)

TYPES OF SHARK ATTACKS

There are basically three versions of unprovoked human-shark encounters:

"Hit and Run" Attacks

- By far the most common type of attack.
- Typically happen close to the shore in the swimming and surfing zone, where a shark may be trapped between sandbars during low tide. Another common area of attacks is at the edge of steep drop-offs, where food sources are plentiful.
- Occur under conditions that diminish visibility, including breaking surf, cloudy water, and strong currents. In its search for regular food, a shark must rely on quick instincts and movements to be successful under such situations.
- Made more likely by humans splashing and swimming in comparatively uncoordinated fashion so as to seem like a wounded fish—typical shark prey. Shiny jewelry, contrast-colored bathing suits, and contrasting skin color from tanning,

(especially the bottoms of the feet) may send additional mixed signals to a shark whose traditional food sources may have some of these attributes.

- Have an element of surprise. The victim seldom sees the attacker.
- Involve a single bite or gash, pointing to a case of "mistaken identity": the human for a conventional source of food, such as a seal, fish, or turtle. (From an underwater point of view, a human lying on a surfboard with limbs dangling over the edges bears a remarkable resemblance to a sea turtle.) Sharks may also release after a single bite because they've determined that the human is simply too large to tangle with, and therefore the shark defers and swims away. Another theory is that these attacks are unrelated to food acquisition but instead are a form of expressing social dominance.
- Usually result in comparatively minor lacerations on the leg below the knee.
- Typically not life-threatening.

A Great White Encounter

Although we are focusing on dangers to swimmers and this is written about a diver, Marco Flagg, who sustained shark bites, Ken Kurtis' charming and highly anthropomorphic account of an attack makes the "Hit and Run" scenario come alive from a great white shark's point of view:

" A Reply and Another Perspective of the Shark Attack on Marco Flagg, Filed by Bruce, G.W.S."

Abstract

I have been given a copy of the account of Marco Flagg and the shark attack on 6/30/95, which was posted in the rec.scuba newsgroup on 7/7/95. I wanted to share some thoughts with those of you who read Mr. Flagg's thorough account.

Basic Facts

Exactly as Mr. Flagg described them.

About myself

I'm a 17-year-old Great White Shark. In fact, I'm the shark that mistakenly bit Mr. Flagg. (In Great White Shark society, we don't like to use the word "attacked" when it was a mistake.) I was born in 1978 off of the Farallon Islands and spend most of my time in that area with an occasional foray down to the Monterey area. One summer I got as far south as Anacapa Island off of Oxnard, but that was only because there was a rumor of some yellowtail tuna and some blue whales in the area. Too much work. The tuna are fast and the whales are huge so I came back north. But I digress.

Chronological Incident Report

I was cruising around the Pt. Lobos area. I hadn't eaten in two days and was hoping to find some sea lion pups venturing into the water. I was patrolling the area at about 50 feet down when I detected some motion to my left. I really didn't get a good glimpse, but it was a fast-moving dark object and I thought I'd hit the pinniped jackpot. Using my lateral line to sense the movement of my intended, I circled back around. As I approached (from below and behind—just like I was taught by my parents), it seemed to me the sea lion was heading for the surface, perhaps to take a breath of air. I gave a good twitch of my tail and opened my mouth. It was only as I closed down that I realized something was terribly wrong. I tasted metal, and I know that sea lions aren't made of metal. On top of that, I detected an electrical current in the water (which throws off my senses somewhat). I thought, "Oh, shit," and within maybe two seconds I opened my jaws, let go, and swam off.

Comments

Do you realize how embarrassing this is for me? Here I am, an apex predator, top of the food chain, and I can't distinguish the difference between a sea lion and a scuba diver. I can't even begin to tell you all the taunting I've taken from the other sharks in the area.

But even worse are the psychological repercussions. Mr. Flagg, I am so sorry for the problems I caused and all I can tell you is that I'm delighted that you were not seriously injured. For a few days after the mistake (not attack) I lost my appetite. I mean, I'm an eating machine—it's what I do. And mistakes happen, but we Great Whites pride ourselves on the fact that these mistaken identity problems occur infrequently. We really don't want to eat any of you. We're just doing what nature compels us to do.

Final Thoughts

Again my profound apologies. And I'm terribly sorry that your friend lost both his scooter and his video camera, but another shark I know said they were delicious. All I can tell you is that we in the shark community are working very hard to avoid these problems and we'll do our best to make sure this doesn't happen again.

Finally, in parting, if any of you reading this know of a nice, plump, juicy sea lion—would you please send him my way?

This "Incident Report" was playfully provided by Ken Kurtis at Reef Seekers Dive Company in Beverly Hills, who wishes everyone safe diving (and watch out for those G.W.S.es!).

"Bump and Bite" Attacks

- Less common, but often result in more severe injuries and more fatalities than "hit and run" assaults.
- Generally take the form of the shark first circling the victim (often a diver, but sometimes a swimmer near shore) and then

bumping the human prior to attack. This suggests that the bump phase is an assessment, since the shark obviously has no hands to "get the feel" of another creature in the water.

- Much more likely to involve severe multiple bites and repeat attacks, and thus more likely to result in death.
- Suggest a feeding or hostile function rather than a case of mistaken identity.

"Sneak" Attacks

- Differ from "bump and bite" attacks only in that there is no preliminary stage of aggression. The shark comes out of nowhere, is not seen in advance, and sets to work for whatever reason with quick, repeated efficiency.

FREQUENT FEEDING FRENZY?

H. David Baldridge, author of the classic *Shark Attack* and former director of the U.S. Navy's International Shark Attack File, has carefully examined attack data and concluded that the "feeding frenzy" phenomenon is actually fairly rare. He writes, "Only about one-fourth of all attack victims received wounds of a nature

and number to suggest that hunger might have provoked the attack. Sharks repeatedly strike their victims in a wild, frenzied fashion only about 4% of the time." (Taylor & Taylor, 2000, p. 243).

WHO IS BITING WHOM

Any sharks larger than us (approximately six feet or more in length) are a potential threat, but three species in particular are responsible for most attacks on people:

- Great White *(Carcharodon carcharias)*
- Tiger *(Galeocerdo cuvier)*
- Bull *(Carcharhinus leucas)*

All of these are widely found, attain a large size (six feet or more), and regularly consume large prey such as turtles, marine mammals, and fishes, among others. These species probably are responsible for a large portion of "bump and bite" and "sneak" attacks. Globally, the great hammerhead *(Sphyrna mokarran)*, shortfin mako *(Isurus oxyrhynchus)*, oceanic whitetip *(Carcharhinus longimanus)*, Galapagos *(Carcharhinus galapagensis)*, and certain reef sharks (such as the Caribbean reef shark, *Carcharhinus perezi)* have also been implicated in these kinds of attacks.

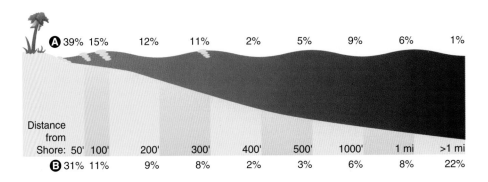

The total percentage of people who swim at the noted distance from shore **(A)** *versus the percentage of where shark attacks occur* **(B).**

Some sharks adopt threatening or aggressive body posturing by bringing the head up and arching the back **(A)**, *as well as making wide sweeps with the tail* **(B)**.

In "hit and run" attacks, the sharks are seldom seen and therefore difficult to identify. A large number of species might be involved, but the data is not conclusive. Florida evidence, where 20 to 30 of these types of attacks occur per year, suggests that the blacktip *(Carcharhinus limbatus),* blacknose *(Carcharhinus acronotus),* and possibly spinner *(Carcharhinus brevipinna)* sharks are the major culprits in this region.

THE POINT OF VIEW OF AN OLD SCHOOL "CHUM"

In college, we knew a fellow who had lost his leg below the knee to a shark while playing in waist-deep water off the Florida coast. Doug was philosophical about his childhood loss. "It wasn't the shark's fault. After all, I had entered the shark's world. He didn't come into mine."

This sort of balanced appraisal is not uncommon among shark attack survivors, some of whom go on to champion the fish that is now hunted and hated to the point of endangerment for some species. Despite their losses, these people understand the vital role sharks play as dominant predators in the great scheme of marine (and therefore planetary) health.

WATER DEPTH CHART

Shark attacks frequently occur surprisingly close to shore. The opposite illustration reveals that 51% of 570 analyzed attacks occurred less than 70 yards from the water's edge, which is where about two thirds of ocean swimmers and waders are found.

BODY BEHAVIOR

Some sharks have been observed displaying various defensive body postures and motions. Notably, the gray reef shark sometimes exhibits an exaggerated swimming style before attack: arched back, pectoral fins pointed down rather than parallel with the shark's trunk, combined with a curved tail. Another defensive behavior that may signal attack is "tail cracking," whereby the shark swims to a threat and then turns quite suddenly with the quick flick of its tail that produces an audible cracking sound. Such behaviors may

Shark Attacks by Activity	
Surfers/windsurfers	43%
Swimmers/waders	38%
Divers/snorkelers	11%
Body surfers	2%
Kayakers	2%
Other	4%
Source: International Shark Attack File	

be described as "agonistic"—striving for effect. In general, however, it's very difficult at best to know for certain what the animal is trying to communicate at any given time—aggression and threat, or appeasment and avoidance.

SHARK ATTACK STATS

The ISAF reports that there were 65 *worldwide* alleged shark attacks on humans in 1999, and 58 of these proved to be "unprovoked"; that is, they occurred in the shark's habitat without human provocation. These figures are consistent with recent compilations: 54 attacks in 1998; 60 in 1997; and an annual average of 54 in the 1990s which logged the highest

number of shark attacks. These numbers are consistent with the continual upward swing throughout the past century. The ISAF relates that, "The number of shark attacks transpiring in a given year is directly correlated to the amount of human time spent in the sea." *Of these 58 worldwide attacks in 1999, only 4 were fatal, which is roughly half the decade's yearly average of 7.*

Twenty-five of these 58 attacks occurred in Florida, where many miles of shoreline intersect with many tourists and locals who partake of water recreation, often year-round.

Putting Shark Attack in Perspective

The ISAF has done a masterful job in making it clear where the real risks are. Check out these tables on injuries due to home improvement or animal bites in New York—they really help put sharks in their place.

REDUCING THE RISK OF SHARK ATTACK

Although these statistics support the fact that the relative risk of a shark attack is very small, there are things you can do to better your odds:

- If you are new to the area, seek local advice about the frequency and types of sharks.
- Spearfishing is asking for shark trouble. The blood and struggling movements of the fish are a siren to sharks seeking food.
- Always stay in groups since sharks are more likely to attack a solitary individual.
- Do not wander too far from shore—this not only isolates you, but places you far away from assistance.
- Avoid being in the water during darkness or twilight hours when sharks are most active and have a competitive sensory advantage.
- Do not enter the water if bleeding from an open wound or if

A Comparison with the Number of Injuries Associated with Home Improvement Equipment in 1996	
Equipment	**Number of Injuries**
Nails, screws, tacks, and bolts	198,849
Ladders	138,894
Toilets	43,687
Pruning, trimming, edging	36,091
Chain saws	13,458
Pliers, wire cutters, and wrenches	15,957
Manual-cleaning equipment	14,386
Power grinders, buffers and polishers	13,458
Buckets and pails	10,907
Room deodorizers and fresheners	2,599
Toilet-bowl products	1,567
Paints or varnish thinners	1,549
Shark injuries and deaths in the U.S.A.	18
Source: © International Shark Attack File	

Shark Injuries Compared to the Number of Biting Injuries Occurring Annually in New York City

Biting Injury	1981	1984	1985	1985	1987
Dog bites human	12,656	10,593	9,809	8,870	8,064
Human bites human	*	1,589	1,591	1,572	1,587
Cat bites human	826	*	879	*	802
Wild rat bites human	60	*	311	*	291
Squirrel bites human	81	*	*	*	95
Hamster bites human	52	*	*	*	*
Rabbit bites human	37	*	*	*	*
Raccoon bites human	18	*	*	*	11
Horse bites human	18	*	*	*	*
Gerbil bites human	17	*	12	*	*
Lab rat bites human	15	*	9	*	*
Monkey bites human	11	*	*	*	*
Snake bites human	8	*	4	*	*
Bat bites human	7	*	4	*	*
Ferret bites human	5	*	5	*	7
Guinea pig bites human	5	*	*	*	*
Parrot bite human	5	*	6	*	*
Blue jay bites human	2	*	*	*	*
Spider bites human	*	*	2	*	*
Skunk bites human	1	*	*	*	3
Parakeet bites human	1	*	*	*	*
Opossum bites human	1	*	*	*	*
Sea lion bites human	1	*	*	*	*
Lion bites human	1	*	*	*	*
Ocelot bites human	1	*	*	*	*
Lion fish stabs human	1	*	*	*	*
Shark injuries and deaths in the U.S.A.	12	14	12	6	13

Source: © *International Shark Attack File*

* Information not available. Source of New York City biting injury data: New York City Health Department statistics quoted by U.P.I. (1982), A.P. (1986), and Newsday (1988). Source of shark attack data: International Shark Attack File, February 3, 1998. From the web pages of the International Shark Attack File [www.flmnh.ufl.edu/fish], courtesy of George H. Burgess, Director ISAF.

menstruating—a shark's olfactory ability is acute.

- Avoid wearing shiny jewelry because the reflected light resembles the sheen of fish scales.
- Avoid waters with known effluents or sewage and those being used by sport or commercial fisherman, especially if there are signs of bait fishes or feeding activity. Diving seabirds are good indicators of such action.
- Do not swim where rivers join the sea as sharks have been known to enter freshwater sources.
- Do not assume porpoise sightings indicate the absence of sharks—both often eat the same food items.
- Use extra caution when waters are murky, and avoid uneven tanning and bright-colored clothing—sharks see contrast particularly well.
- Refrain from excess splashing and do not allow pets in the water because of their erratic movements.
- Exercise caution when you are

occupying the area between sandbars or near steep drop-offs—these are favorite hangouts for sharks.

- If baits are being used to attract sharks, such as around a jetty, make sure you are up-current of the bait as sharks will follow the current-carried smell many miles.
- Do not enter the water if sharks are known to be present and evacuate the water if sharks are seen while there. And, of course, do not harass a shark if you see one!
- If you do see a shark, do not panic. Sharks are curious animals and may simply want to investigate the area.
- Never try to touch, corral, or surround a shark. It may attack simply because it feels cornered and threatened.
- Where possible, maintain eye contact with the shark. This will diminish the likelihood of attack.
- In close quarters, sometimes a punch on the shark's nose will cause it to retreat, but if possible your slow and steady retreat is a much safer option.
- Sharks are wild, unpredictable animals. They will naturally defend themselves if they perceive a threat.

Shark Repellent

Many varieties of shark repellent have been devised through the years, and one finally seems to be genuinely promising. SharkPOD™ is based upon the fact that sharks are very sensitive to electrical fields. Pores in their snouts enable them to detect electrical signals of extremely low voltage (approximately one millionth of a volt per centimeter). SharkPOD generates an electrical field to repel sharks approaching from any direction. Correctly used, the electrical field is not strong enough to cause

any discomfort to humans. However, the field is far greater than sharks can tolerate. In field tests, sharks were repelled from 12–22 feet away. We haven't tried SharkPOD, but it has good endorsements, so if you've got the $1,080 list price, SharkPOD is manufactured by POD Holdings SA under license from the Natal Sharks Board, Durban, South Africa.

All trade inquiries should be addressed to:

POD Holdings Limited
P.O. Box 74072
Rochdale Park 4034
KwaZulu-Natal, South Africa
Fax: +27-(0)31-566-0481
Tel: +27-(0)31-566-0480
Contact: Theo Meyer
meyer@sharkpod.co.za

Of course, one shark repellent is absolutely guaranteed or double your money back for the cost of this book: dry desert sand. Lie down in it and you will be safe.

Fishing Encounters

If you unintentionally catch a shark:
- Take care not to injure yourself. Struggling, captured creatures are panicked and provoked.
- If the shark attempts to bite your boat, this is not an attempt to sink the boat to attack the humans on board. The biting response is based on fear, curiosity, or a search for food.
- Bring the shark close, but keep enough of distance so that its teeth are not a threat, and cut the line as close to the hook as safety permits.
- Do not use barbs, gaffs, or other implements that will injure the shark.
- Resist any temptation to remove the hook. You may injure yourself or the shark, which might die later from the stress of the event. Use hooks made of regu-

lar (not stainless) steel. These will rust fairly quickly in the ocean environment and thereby not pose a permanent problem for the shark. Hooks and wire leaders can cause entanglement problems for sharks that can lead to suffocation or death by slow starvation.

- Learn which species of sharks are harmful. Just because you have mistakenly hooked a shark is no reason the fish should be left out of water to die. Sharks are a vital element of the ocean ecosystem that must not be eliminated purely on the basis of lack of knowledge, fear, or cruelty. A dead shark is not the only good shark.

Note about other fishes: We have not included information about other potentially dangerous species of fish in this section because fish in general move rapidly away from human contact. People fishing, however, should be cautious around such species as the sea catfish that has sharp dorsal and pectoral spines that can cause puncture wounds, and the toadfish that has powerful jaws and will bite.

FIRST AID FOR SHARK ATTACK

- Remove the victim from the water as soon as possible so as to deter the arrival of more sharks attracted by blood. While so-called feeding frenzies are rare, it makes sense to remove the possibility of repeat attacks.
- Shock and loss of blood are the primary reasons that shark attacks prove fatal. Apply pressure to reduce bleeding and secure emergency medical help immediately.
- Even small bites or scratches from a shark carry the risk of serious infection. After *any* encounter with a shark, no matter how seemingly inconsequential, seek professional medical care.

BLACKTIP SHARK
Carcharhinus limbatus

• DANGER
These sharks are potentially lethal. They are variously reported as "harmless unless provoked or feeding" and "the most frequently identified attacker in Atlantic waters."

• ABUNDANCE & RANGE
They are found along the Atlantic and Gulf coasts, and the Pacific coast along southern California.

• SIZE
20 inches at birth. Matures to 6 to 8 feet.

• DESCRIPTION
These sharks are fusiform (tapering to the ends) and slender, with gray back and white belly. All fin tips are black in youth, and all but the pectoral fin fade with age. Snouts are long and pointy with serrated, erect, sharp front teeth. The blacktip is similar to the **spinner shark** *(C. brevipinna)* which has a sharper snout and smoother lower teeth.

• HABITAT
They live at the surface above continental shelves and frequently in shallows along sandy beaches, bays, and rocky coasts in warmer months.

• COMMENTS

They often swim in packs of 6 to 12. The **spinner** is noted for its leaping, spinning stunts in pursuit of food or when hooked.

BULL SHARK

Carcharhinus leucas

• DANGER

The bull shark is potentially lethal. Despite the reputation of the great white, this is perhaps the most dangerous of the sharks. It has probably executed more attacks on humans than it has been credited with because it is often confused with other requiem sharks.

• ABUNDANCE & RANGE

It is found along the Atlantic and Gulf coasts, and freshwater rivers with sea outlets, such as the Mississippi River where it has been found as far as 1,750 miles upstream.

• SIZE

22 to 32 inches at birth. Matures to 11 feet.

• DESCRIPTION

The bull shark is fusiform (tapering to the ends) with gray back and white belly. It has a short distinctive snout with strongly serrated teeth.

Eyes are small. Broad, large pectoral fins have pointed tips. The first dorsal fin is much larger than the second.

• HABITAT

They are never far from shore.

• COMMENTS

The bull shark is omnivorous and will eat anything it can capture. It tolerates highly salted as well as fresh water, so it is able to traverse rivers inland.

GREAT HAMMERHEAD SHARK

Sphyrna mokarran

• DANGER

The great hammerhead is potentially lethal to humans.

• ABUNDANCE & RANGE

This shark makes its home in Atlantic, Gulf, and Pacific coastal waters.

• SIZE

Matures to 11.5 feet.

• DESCRIPTION

The dominant feature is a distinctive hammer-shaped head (depressed and laterally extended) with eyes at the ends of the lateral expansions that yield vision in all directions, as well as good depth perception. The shark's body is elongate and stout with gray-brown top color grading to paler cream below.

• SIMILAR SPECIES
The **scalloped hammerhead** *(Sphyrna lewini)* is quite comparable, though slightly larger (maturing to 13+ feet). Reports vary more on the danger posed to humans by scalloped hammerheads, as opposed to the more aggressive great hammerhead. However, scalloped hammerheads are no gentle giants—they are known to attack their own kind.

• HABITAT
Hammerheads live near the surface. The young are more likely to be found nearer the coast and often enter shallow bays and estuaries.

• COMMENTS
These sharks are voracious predators.

SAND TIGER SHARK
Carcharias taurus

• DANGER
These are potentially lethal and have been known to attack humans.

• ABUNDANCE & RANGE
Sand tigers are found along the Atlantic coast from Maine south to Florida, and they are commonly found north of North Carolina. Although somewhat rare in the Gulf of Mexico, they are occasionally found along the waters from west Florida to Texas.

• SIZE
3+ feet at birth. Matures to 10+ feet.

• DESCRIPTION
Sand tiger sharks have stout, light brownish-gray bodies that are paler on their belly. They have two large dorsal fins of roughly equal size.

• COMMENTS
Found in shallow bays and sandy coastal waters, the tiger shark is not regarded as aggressive, but it will attack people if provoked. They can hover motionless in the water because of their ability to hold air in their stomachs, and they swim with an open mouth, exposing three rows of large teeth.

which sometimes cause it to land unexpectedly in fishing boats.

SHORTFIN MAKO SHARK

Isurus oxyrinchus

• DANGER

These are potentially lethal and have been known to attack humans.

• ABUNDANCE & RANGE

They live along the Atlantic coast from Cape Cod south, the Gulf of Mexico, and the Pacific coast.

• SIZE

2 to 2.5 feet at birth. Matures to 13 feet.

• DESCRIPTION

Their streamlined and spindled shape is perfectly adapted for long-distance travels (up to 36 miles a day) and bursts of speed (22 mph). This shark has a long, conical snout and long, slender teeth that are visible even when mouth is closed. Body color is gray-blue to deep blue on top with a white belly. It has short pectoral fins and a crescent caudal (tail) fin.

• COMMENTS

Made famous by Ernest Hemingway's classic, *The Old Man and the Sea*, this shark has a superior reputation among sport fishermen for its stamina, speed, and leaping abilities,

TIGER SHARK

Galeocerdo cuvier

• DANGER

The tiger shark is potentially lethal and has reportedly attacked humans. Some compare it to the white shark for its voracious nature.

• ABUNDANCE & RANGE

It is found along the Atlantic and Gulf coasts, most often in southern Florida.

• SIZE

20 to 30 inches at birth. Matures to 18 to 24 feet.

• DESCRIPTION

This shark is named for the black or dark gray vertical "tiger" stripes occurring along its sides that disappear with age. Its barrel-shaped body tapers to a slender form as its reaches the long, pointed caudal (tail) fin. The snout is short, blunt, and rounded with deeply notched and sharply serrated teeth that can cut through the bodies of sea turtles.

• HABITAT

It lives near the surface offshore and in coastal waters.

• COMMENTS

Slow swimmers, they are nevertheless capable of short bursts of speed. They are rarely seen and are notorious scavengers—eating virtually anything that falls overboard.

WHITE SHARK

Carcharodon carcharias

• DANGER

The white shark is potentially lethal and a known human attacker. Considered the most dangerous shark, it is the dominant species of legend in literature and film.

• ABUNDANCE & RANGE

It is found along the Atlantic, Gulf, and Pacific coasts, but this shark is now relatively rare due to overfishing. It has protected status in some parts of the world.

• SIZE

3 to 4 feet at birth. Matures to 21 to 24 feet.

• DESCRIPTION

The white shark's stout, torpedo-shaped body is gray, blue-gray, or slate brown on top and a grayish-white or cream below. The snout is conical and equipped with triangular, pointed, serrated teeth distinguished by symmetry in upper and lower jaw. Eyes are black. Second dorsal fin is much smaller than the first.

• COMMENTS

Awesome for its sheer size, the white, "Great White," or "White Death," as it as variously called, is a supreme and fearless predator that feeds on fishes, crabs, sea otters, seals, and sea lions. Although it has been responsible for human deaths on the eastern U.S. coast, great white attacks on humans along the Pacific coast are much more common because the Pacific's cooler waters support such great white favorites as sea lions, thereby attracting more of this species.

RAYS

FLAT-OUT BEAUTIFUL

Think of rays and skates (known together as batoid elasmobranchs) as nearly two-dimensional fishes. They are related to sharks (another elasmobranch) and diverged from them at about the time of the dinosaurs, roughly 200 million years ago. Aside from being very flat in form, rays and skates differ from sharks in the fact that they glide through the massive water weight of the ocean by using their greatly enlarged pectoral fins, which curve gracefully from near the head and resemble wings. Skates pose us no problems in the U.S., but with rays, an encounter can be shocking or stinging.

When not gliding through the water, most rays often rest in the soft sand or muddy shores. By "ruffling" their "wings," they can settle down and quickly submerge their bodies. This mastery of hiding in plain sight, where only their eyes may remain visible, contributes unavoidably to human-ray interactions. Swimmers or waders sometimes inadvertently step on a stingray or an eagle ray, whose venomous tails will whip up in defense to deliver a painful injury. An electric ray has powerful muscles near its head that can produce an electrical charge to stun its prey or to defend itself. The Atlantic torpedo has been known to generate up to 220 volts of electricity, but we can be grateful to know that it does not have a reputation for injuring humans.

Unless they are escaping danger, most rays move slowly along the bottom, feeding on fish and invertebrates with mouths that are on the undersides of their bodies. Rays vary somewhat in body shape and size, and

Rays are often found just inches from the waterline—sometimes actually behind waders and swimmers who assume such creatures live only in deeper water.

electric rays are distinguished by a rounded (almost disclike) shape. They range from one to six feet in length. Eagle rays, the ones that you sometimes see flying out of the water, have a shape wider than it is long with a distinct tail. Take our word for it that rays' bodies are smooth and soft. You don't want to know this firsthand because rays are only dangerous when disturbed through contact.

While not studied as much as their glamorous cousins the sharks, rays are known to be complex animals with rather large brains and well-developed sensory systems. They are social creatures, and they will sometimes congregate in groups of hundreds or thousands of individuals, resting in confined spaces on top of each other. So especially for safety purposes, if you see one ray, assume there are more nearby. Your chances, by the way, of encountering a ray are much greater than those of coming "nose-to-nose" with a shark.

DO THE SHUFFLE

Rays are often found within inches of the water's edge, so use care not to startle them lest they sting or shock you. Rather than striding across the ocean floor, slide your feet gently in the sand as you walk. Rays will detect your presence in this way and will be happy to levitate gracefully away like some kind of elegant spacecraft. Except for the Pacific electric ray, these fishes are quite nonaggressive. Their defensive responses are understandable when you consider that no one likes to be stepped on.

THE BUSINESS END

The sting—or stinging spine—of a ray is actually an adapted dorsal fin on top of the tail. The edges of stings are serrated, hard, and flattened to a point at the tip. The serration can cause lacerating damage if driven into a victim, and sometimes pieces

of a sting break off in the wound and must be removed. For this reason, it is common for stingray wounds to be x-rayed (no pun intended). Narrow grooves running the length of the underside of the sting supply the venom, which is normally contained by a thin skin covering the whole structure. When the skin is ruptured, the venom is released.

Symptoms of Stingray Stings

A stingray does its damage by lashing upward in self-defense with a muscular tail-like appendage that carries up to four sharp, sword-like stings. The stings are supplied with venom, so the injury is both a deep puncture (or laceration) and an envenomation. The pain from a stingray wound can be mild to excruciating and accompanied by bleeding, weakness, vomiting, headache, fainting, shortness of breath, paralysis, collapse, and, occasionally, death. Most wounds involve the feet and legs because unwary waders and swimmers tread upon the creatures hidden in the sand.

Folklore attests to the stingray's power: a tree was expected to die by withering after a sting was scraped along its trunk. The kernel of truth here is that the sting is a potent force. The venom can prove lethal, especially if the sting punctures a vital organ, but fatalities are rare. It does affect the cardiovascular system and can even cause irregular heart rhythms with potentially extremely serious results.

- Barbed tail may produce laceration leading to significant bleeding (hemorrhage).
- Immediate pain at the site of injury intensifies over 30 to 90 minutes, subsiding gradually over 6 to 48 hours depending on the amount of venom delivered.
- Venom affects the cardiovascular system (heart and blood vessels) and can cause both peripheral

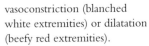

vasoconstriction (blanched white extremities) or dilatation (beefy red extremities).

- The venom may also cause arrhythmias (irregular heartbeats) or even asystole (the heart may stop beating altogether).
- The venom can act on respiratory centers in the brain and cause a slowing of respiration.
- Convulsions may develop from the venom's effect on other brain centers.

First Aid for Stingray Stings

If someone is struck by a stingray, immediately do the following:

- Rinse the wound with whatever clean water is available and immediately immerse the wound in hot water—as hot as the victim can tolerate without scalding (110 to 113° Fahrenheit or 43.3 to 45° Celsius). This may provide some pain relief because the venom contains a water-soluble protein that is destroyed by heat. Most often it is necessary to soak the wound for 30 to 90 minutes. Gently extract any obvious piece of stinger.
- Gently scrub the wound with soap and water. Do not try to sew or tape it closed; doing so could promote infection.
- Apply a dressing, and seek medical help. If professional medical help is more than 12 hours away, start administration of an antibiotic (ciprofloxacin, trimethoprim-sulfamethoxazole, or doxycycline) to oppose *Vibrio* bacteria.
- Administer appropriate pain medication.

Note to Fishermen about First Aid for Scorpion Fish Stings

The pelvic, dorsal, and anal fin spines of these species contain a painful venom. Detailed profiles of the nearly 30 individual types of scorpion fishes in North America is beyond the reach of this book, but the first aid procedures are the same as they are for stingray stings. If you are on a fishing boat that doesn't have hot water, look for a microwave to heat a damp towel for the wound. Note that scorpion fish are also known as "sculpin" in fisherman lingo; also, lionfish (a common aquarium fish) are relatives of the scorpion fish and treatment for their sting is the same. Stonefish are South Pacific relatives, but they are much more dangerous (there is an antivenom for their sting).

FISHING ENCOUNTERS

If you unintentionally catch a ray:

- Take care not to injure yourself. Struggling, captured creatures are panicked and provoked.
- Bring the ray close, but keep enough distance so that its sting is not a threat and cut the line as close to the hook as safety permits.
- Many rays have soft skin. Do not use barbs, gaffs, or other implements that will injure the ray.
- Resist any temptation to remove the hook. You may injure yourself or the ray, which might die later from the stress of the event. Use hooks made of regular (not stainless) steel. These will rust fairly quickly in the ocean environment and thereby not pose a permanent problem for the ray. Hooks and wire leaders can cause entanglement problems for rays that can lead to suffocation or death by slow starvation.

ELECTRIC STINGRAY SHOCK

The species likely to be encountered by barefoot anglers and waders produces only a mild electric shock. Although some people have been knocked down, this result is likely produced by the surprise factor more than the amount of electrical discharge, and no medical treatment should be necessary. (But a cold beer might taste really great!)

SPOTTED EAGLE RAY
Aetobatus narinari

• DANGER
Venomous spine can deliver a stinging defense when the ray is stepped on.

• ABUNDANCE & RANGE
This most common of the eagle rays is found along the Atlantic and Gulf coasts.

• SIZE
Up to 9 feet in width, but 6 feet is more common.

DESCRIPTION
Its distinctive pattern of regularly spaced white spots on its pink-to-greenish back make it easy to identify, as does the flattened snout that gives it its apt nickname of "duck-bill" ray.

• HABITAT
It lives near shore in waters less than 200 feet deep.

• COMMENTS
This is an extraordinarily graceful creature that "soars" by slowly "flapping its wings" (pectoral fins). Powerful and agile, it can accelerate rapidly and deftly. Adults may play near the surface where they can sometimes be seen leaping out of the water. A loner, the spotted eagle ray socializes to spawn and migrate.

COWNOSE RAY
Rhinoptera bonasus

• DANGER
Venomous spine can deliver a stinging defense when the ray is stepped on.

• ABUNDANCE & RANGE
The cownose ray is found along the Atlantic and Gulf coasts.

• SIZE
Up to 3 feet wide.

• DESCRIPTION
This ray is brown above and cream-colored below with a moderately concave head front.

• HABITAT
It lives on the bottom of the inshore shelf and in shallow bays.

COMMENTS

This ray burrows in the sand, especially during the day, and feeds at night. It can conceal almost all of its body in seconds by "ruffling" its pectoral fins and sinking into the ocean floor. A popular large aquarium specimen, it is known for its gentle, inquisitive, and social nature.

SOUTHERN STINGRAY

Dasyatis americana

• DANGER

Potentially but rarely lethal venomous spine can deliver an especially strong stinging defense when the ray is stepped on. Tail spines are razor sharp on larger species and can render significant lacerations to human flesh.

• ABUNDANCE & RANGE

Primarily a southeastern species found along the Gulf and Atlantic coasts, this ray is sometimes washed in by storms and found north of Cape Hatteras, North Carolina.

• SIZE

Up to 5 feet wide.

• DESCRIPTION

This ray's form is a rhomboid-shaped disk with rounded corners. Based on surroundings, its color varies from gray to olive to light brown. It lacks a dorsal fin.

• HABITAT

It lives in bays and close to shore, sometimes within two to three feet of the surf's edge.

JELLYFISH AND THEIR RELATIVES

HEARTLESS

Exquisite, exotic, enchanting, and sometimes envenomating. . . . We call them jellyfish, and some are notorious for their painful stings. Jellyfish stings, however, are not personal. How could they be? "Jellies" literally have no heart, no brain, no blood, no gills. Basically they are hollow bells with one or more mouths on a central oral surface. Their trailing tentacles trap and stun nourishment, making jellies very efficient predators. This probably helps explain why they have existed for more than 650 million years.

FLOAT LIKE A JELLY, STING LIKE A JELLY

The umbrella-like form of an adult jellyfish is called a medusa, named after the Greek gorgon Medusa, whose hair was a nest of writhing snakes. If you've ever been stung by a jelly, most likely a Portuguese man-of-war or a sea nettle in the U.S., then you know they are formidable to tangle with.

Jellies are carried by the wind, waves, and currents, but they can also swim efficiently using jet propulsion by expelling water from their hollow bell. Expulsion in one direction means travel in another. To the untrained eye it appears that jellies are aimless floaters, but they are actually always trolling for food using their long following tentacles that can wrap around swimmers unaware. On these tentacles are stinging cells that consist of a capsule with sensory hair and a nematocyst, which actually stings, captures, and

subdues prey. When the sensory hairs are triggered by an animal's motion, the nematocyst fires its toxin like a harpoon. This process happens in milliseconds, which makes it one of the fastest workings in nature, according to the National Aquarium in Baltimore.

The Portuguese Man-of-War

Infamous for its sting and aided by a mysterious and legendary name, the Portuguese man-of-war is found in tropical waters; along the eastern U.S. coast, this common jelly is carried northward by the Gulf Stream of the Atlantic Ocean. This is the jellyfish that most often entangles saltwater lovers. Its 3- to 12-inch-long gas-filled bladder floats as much as six inches above the water and it trails tentacles up to 60 feet long. It is often difficult for swimmers to identify and avoid the ethereal blue, pink, or violet chamber's long extremities that can mean long-stinging effects. Sea turtles feed on the man-of-war, and these turtles seem to be particularly attractive to sharks, who might mistake a human swimming on a surfboard in murky water for just another tender turtle stuffed with jellies. So when you see evidence of man-of-wars on the beach, read signs about their presence, or hear from lifeguards or locals that they are "currently" in the area, you now have a second reason (sharksbeing the first) to stay out of the water.

Sea Nettles

The sea nettle runs second to the man-of-war in frequency of marine misadventure in the U.S. Looking like an ethereal mushroom, the sea nettle is especially common in the Chesapeake Bay area, but with its two species (*Chrysaora quinquecirrha* on the eastern and Gulf coasts and *C. melanaster* on the west coast) taken

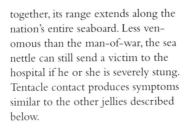

together, its range extends along the nation's entire seaboard. Less venomous than the man-of-war, the sea nettle can still send a victim to the hospital if he or she is severely stung. Tentacle contact produces symptoms similar to the other jellies described below.

WASHED UP?

When you find a jelly washed up on the beach, do not touch it. The nematocyst may still be able to fire because tentacles can retain their venom for months, even if they appear to be dried out and withered.

Although they are feared by swimmers, jellies can be useful to many people. After jellies have been dried and de-salted—don't try this at home—some people consider them a culinary delicacy . . . delicious, low-fat, low in calories and salt, and rich in nutrients. Jellies are also providing promising research avenues for cancer and heart disease.

STING CITY

Often, jellies are found floating together by the thousands, and their stings can cause a range a symptoms from mild rashes to death. The most deadly of them is the box jellyfish (*Chironex fleckeri*) found off the coast of northern Australia and in the Indo-Pacific ocean. It contains one of the most potent animal venoms known—more potent than cobra venom—that can result in death in less than five minutes from cessation of breathing, abnormal heart rhythms, and profound low blood pressure (shock).

Death by jellyfish sting is very rare in U.S. coastal waters, but such stings may still create painful interruptions in a pleasant vacation. Stings can range in severity depending on the species, size, geographic location, time of year, and other natural factors. Some people who are especially sensitive to the toxin can have severe allergic reactions following a stinging encounter, so it is important to monitor health conditions after a sting.

Symptoms of Jellyfish Stings

- Stinging pain on contact ranging from mild to intense.
- The appearance of red welts that look like whip marks on the skin formed by swollen tissue that may itch intensely. Welts can last for minutes or hours.
- Blisters and ulcerations may follow, especially if the sting is unattended.
- Recurrent episodes of swelling may persist for four to six weeks.

Severe Symptoms Requiring Immediate Medical Attention

- Excruciating pain.
- Severe blistering with generalized illness (nausea, vomiting, shortness of breath, muscle spasms, low blood pressure, etc.).

General Jellyfish Sting First Aid

- If the victim has a large area involved (an entire arm or leg, face, or genitals), is very young or very old, or shows signs of generalized illness (nausea, vomiting, weakness, shortness of breath, chest pain, and the like), seek help from a doctor.
- If a child has placed tentacle fragments in his mouth, have the child spit out as much saliva as possible, and then rinse out the mouth with fresh or salt water. If salt water is used, try to prevent the child from swallowing it because this can trigger nausea. If there is already swelling in the mouth (muffled voice, difficulty swallowing, enlarged tongue and lips), do not give anything by mouth, protect the airway, and rapidly transport the victim to a hospital.

Portuguese Man-of-War Sting First Aid

The following recommendations are from the book *All Stings Considered: First Aid and Medical Treatment of Hawaii's Marine Injuries* by Craig Thomas, M.D. and Susan Scott, ©1997, University of Hawaii Press.

Note: It is not safe to generalize about jellyfish sting treatment across species because nematocysts vary among species. Stings on the continental U.S. coast are likely to be from the Portuguese man-of-war, so this information should cover the great majority of situations.

1. Pick off any visible tentacles with a gloved hand, stick, or anything handy, being careful to avoid further injury. Do not try to scrape away tentacles as this will cause more nematocysts to fire.

2. Rinse the sting thoroughly with saltwater (preferable) or freshwater to remove any adhering tentacles.

3. Applying ice for pain control may help.

4. Irrigate exposed eyes with copious amounts of room temperature tap water for at least 15 minutes. If vision blurs, or the eyes continue to tear, hurt, swell or are light sensitive after irrigating, see a doctor.

5. For persistent itching or skin rash, try 1% hydrocortisone ointment four times a day, and one or two 25mg diphenhydramine (Benadryl) tablets every six hours. These drugs are sold without prescription. Diphenhydramine may cause drowsiness. Don't drive, swim, or surf after taking this medication.

Questionable Treatments for Jellyfish Stings

- Although formerly considered effective, vinegar is no longer recommended for Portuguese man-of-war (PMOW) stings. In a laboratory experiment, vinegar dousing caused discharge of nematocysts from the larger *(P. physalis)* man-of-war species. The effect of vinegar on the nematocysts of the smaller species (which has less severe stings) is mixed: vinegar inhibited some, discharged others. Accordingly, vinegar has been abandoned as a treatment for PMOW stings in Hawaii and Australia. Those wishing to confirm and explore this shift in treatment can consult the book *All Stings Considered* (as above). In it, the authors cite published journal articles supporting this and other recommendations.

- No studies support applying heat to Portuguese man-of-war stings. Studies on the effectiveness of meat tenderizer, baking soda, papain (papaya), or commercial sprays (containing aluminum sulfate and detergents) on nematocyst stings have been contradictory. It's possible these substances cause further damage. In one U.S. Portuguese man-of-war fatality, lifeguards sprayed papain solution immediately on the victim's sting. Within minutes, the woman was comatose, and later died.

- Alcohol and human urine may be harmful on Portuguese man-of-war stings.

- Most Portuguese man-of-war stings disappear by themselves, sometimes within 15 or 20 minutes. Because of this, even harmful therapies often appear to work. A key concept in the first aid of any injury is: Do no harm. Therefore, avoid applying unproven, possibly harmful substances on stings.

See a Doctor If:

- Pain persists.
- Rash worsens.

- Overall ill feeling develops.
- A red streak develops between swollen lymph nodes and the sting, or if either area becomes red, warm, and tender.

Few Portuguese man-of-war stings cause life-threatening reactions, but this is always a possibility. Some victims are extremely sensitive to the venom; a few have allergic reactions. Consider even the slightest breathing difficulty or altered level of consciousness a medical emergency. Call for help and use an automatic epinephrine injector if available.

• DESCRIPTION
A thick, resilient hemisphere colored milky blue or yellow. Eight deep notches on the tan margin contain the sense organs. The cannonball, jelly ball, or cabbage jellyfish as they are sometimes called has no tentacles.

• HABITAT
It floats near the shore.

• COMMENTS
Occurs in huge swarms, estimated at up to two million creatures, especially in the Gulf of Mexico. Probably the most common jelly found between Cape Hatteras and Cape Canaveral.

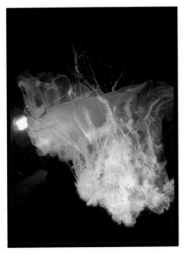

CANNONBALL JELLYFISH
Stomolophus meleagris

• DANGER
These jellyfish are very mildly venomous and usually not very harmful to people.

• ABUNDANCE & RANGE
They are found along the U.S. Atlantic coast and in the Gulf of Mexico from Florida to Texas.

• SIZE
5 inches high and 7 inches wide.

LION'S MANE
Cyanea capillata

• DANGER
These are highly venomous. Contact with tentacles produces severe burns and blisters. Extensive or prolonged encounters can result in muscle cramps and death from breathing difficulties.

• ABUNDANCE & RANGE
They are found in the Atlantic and Pacific oceans.

• SIZE
2 feet high and 8 feet wide.

• DESCRIPTION

The world's largest jellyfish has a saucer-shaped bell that varies in color with age and size from yellow-pink to reddish to yellow-brown in specimens smaller than 18 inches. Darker red-brown is typical for sizes beyond 18 inches. More than 150 disorderly bunches of tentacles trail a transparent bell that appears extremely fragile. A jumble of reddish-orange to tawny brown ruffled appendages are also attached to the bell.

• HABITAT

The lion's mane floats near the surface.

• COMMENTS

It was made famous in "The Adventure of the Lion's Mane," a story by Sir Arthur Conan Doyle, wherein Sherlock Holmes solves the mystery of a homicide in a tide pool.

MOON JELLYFISH

Aurelia aurita

• DANGER

This jellyfish is mildly venomous. Contact produces an itching rash that may persist for several hours.

• ABUNDANCE & RANGE

It lives in the Atlantic and Pacific oceans.

• SIZE

Up to 3 inches high and 16 inches wide.

• DESCRIPTION

Translucent white, the moon jellyfish is saucer-shaped with numerous fringelike tentacles and four symmetrical, opaque white petal-like lobes radiating from the center.

• HABITAT

It floats near shore near the surface.

• COMMENTS

This jelly is commonly found on beaches after being washed up by high tide or storms.

PORTUGUESE MAN-OF-WAR

Physalia physalis

• DANGER

The man-of-war is highly venomous and contact with tentacles can produce stinging red welts. Extensive exposure to this, one of the most powerful marine poisons, can produce breathing difficulties, nausea, muscle spasms, and, in extreme cases, death. Even after the animal lies dead on the beach, it can still inflict burns and blisters.

• ABUNDANCE & RANGE
It lives along the Atlantic coast of Florida to the Gulf coast of Texas, but has been driven ashore by storms as far north as Maine.

• SIZE
Float is 12 inches long, 6 inches high, and 5 inches wide.

• DESCRIPTION
The Portuguese man-of-war's gas-filled iridescent pale blue or pink float changes shape to "sail" with the prevailing winds. Beneath the float are dense clusters of polyps and tentacles of various lengths up to 60+ feet.

• HABITAT
It lives on the surface of the sea

• COMMENTS
The Portuguese man-of-war is responsible for most stinging jellyfish encounters for swimmers, surfers, and waders.

irritation, but extreme exposures may require hospitalization.

• ABUNDANCE & RANGE
It lives along the Atlantic coast and Gulf coast with an abundant concentration in Chesapeake Bay.

• SIZE
5 inches high and 10 inches wide.

• DESCRIPTION
The sea nettle is pink with radiating red stripes, but the Chesapeake Bay form is smaller and whiter. Forty tentacles are attached to a symmetrical bell that gives an overall appearance of a fragile, translucent mushroom.

• HABITAT
It floats near the surface.

• COMMENTS
The sea nettle benefits the Chesapeake Bay oyster crop by feeding on oyster predators.

FEATHERED HYDROID
Pennaria tiarella

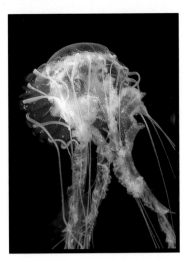

SEA NETTLE
Chrysaora quinquecirrha

• DANGER
The sea nettle is mildly venomous; tentacle contact produces an itchy

• DANGER
This species is venomous and delivers a mild sting on handling.

• ABUNDANCE & RANGE
It lives along the Atlantic and Gulf coasts.

• SIZE
6 inches high and 6 inches wide.

• DESCRIPTION
This creature is a jellyfish, but it does not match the traditional image of a gelatinous or air-filled mass. The hydroid resembles a "feathery," small, open-styled shrub with tough stems that are yellow-tan to black. A whitish-pink pod-like head is surrounded by thin tentacles.

• HABITAT
It lives in shallow water below the low-tide line, where it attaches itself to solid objects such as pilings and coral.

OTHER SEASHORE WILDLIFE

Barnacles

None are venomous, but these crustacean cousins of shrimp, lobsters, and crabs do have sharp edges. When you are poking about the rocks or steadying yourself alongside a piling, beware you don't get cut. If you do, treat the laceration with antiseptics and monitor for signs of infection.

Sea Slugs

Sea slugs are gastropods that have protective shells they shed with maturity. Some nudibranches, as they are also called, rely on stinging cells to subdue prey. The **red-gilled nudibranch** *(Coryphella verrucosa)* is one such animal; it is found among seaweed and hydroids near the low tide line and out to deep water along the northeast Atlantic coast, from the Arctic south to New York. This

191

translucent gray-white slug is about an inch long and along its back are orange or reddish white-tipped projections. Try to avoid stepping on these, as they will sting if you do so.

Shrimp and Squid

CLAWS AND JAWS

Common sense will tell you that messing with the delicious blue crabs in the shallow surf or the ubiquitous ghost crabs scuttling along the beach carries its own risks. Just ask any dog who has gotten its soft fleshy jowls a little too close what one of those pincers can do. It's a safe bet that anything with claws can give you a nip.

Common Mantis Shrimp *(Squilla empusa)* At 10 inches long and 2.5 inches wide, this shrimp resembles a flat shrimp in form, but is green to bluish in color. It is found along the Atlantic and Gulf shores at the low-tide line and below, where it burrows in the sand or mud. Known as the "shrimp snapper," its large jack-nife-like appendage can make a quick cut into human flesh.

Brief Squid *(Lolliguncula brevis)* This little guy is only 3 inches long and 1.25+ inches wide. The brief squid has reddish-purple spots on a cream-white body, and it is found on the Atlantic coast south of Maryland and along the Gulf coast in bays and inlets, where it is often captured for food and bait. The squid can bite if handled.

MAMMALS

THE MOST DANGEROUS GAME

We often like to forget the fact that we are mammals—warm-blooded creatures with body hair and females with mammary glands that secrete milk to nourish young. You might think that other mammals pose the greatest danger to you, and in one sense you would be dead right about that: we humans are by far the most dangerous mammals on earth. The FBI's 1999 *Crime in the U.S.* reported 16,974 murder and non-negligent manslaughter victims in 1998, whereas for the same period the American Association of Poison Control Centers, one precise yardstick of encounters, reported zero fatalities from exposure to animals including bats, cats, dogs, foxes, raccoons, rodents, lagomorphs (rabbits and hares), skunks, and other mammals.

There are approximately 400 mammal species in the U.S. (including marine varieties), and of these there are only 11 nationwide that should cause you any concern at all: bats, bears, elk, feral pigs, mountain lions, moose, opossums, porcupines, raccoons, shrews, and skunks. Bears loom large in the minds of many outdoor people, even those who live in parts of the U.S. where bears are no longer found. We'll spend a good portion of this chapter helping you sort out the bear facts, but keep in mind that the statistics are clearly on your side even when it comes to this able-bodied, magnificent predator. For instance, the black bear (the only bear found in the mid-Atlantic) has been deemed responsible only for a single human death (May 2000) in the entire history of the highly visited Great Smoky Mountains National Park, where the species can be routinely seen.

That said, it is a very foolish person indeed who engages any wild animal. Make no friendly assumptions about nor overtures toward any wild species, including dogs you don't know. Even field mice will bite, and they can carry disease and cause infection, so when you are tempted to rescue one from the jaws of your house cat, take the time to grab a dish towel first to shield your hands. The panicked mouse will draw blood if it can—a perfect example of how seemingly innocent meetings can take a nasty turn with a wild animal whose instincts drive an agenda quite different from yours.

Basically, mammals can affect you in a limited but powerful number of ways: bites, charges, sprays, punctures if you live in porcupine territory, disease, and auto accidents.

BITING MAMMALS

When threatened or angered, we are all likely to use "any means necessary" to communicate our needs and passions. Most people can identify to some degree with the statement "I just snapped." Other mammals, unable simply to slam a fist on the table in vexation, can snap, too. In this section, we'll talk about the kinds of encounters you might have in your home and neighborhood.

Again, we want to stress the extreme unlikelihood of your encounter with the teeth of a wild animal unless you do something foolish—and our intent is to minimize that possibility. It is impossible, though, and not even desirable to take the risk out of dangerous or deadly encounters with animals. Such encounters are inescapable in nature. Animal expert Stephen Herrero argues the point about bears, but it applies to all wild animals: "You've got to have some tolerance to risk. You reduce it to zero, you've reduced the bears to zero, too."

"WILD THANG, I THINK YOU MOVE ME"

In nature, it's always good to expect the unexpected. Just ask former President Jimmy Carter. Some of you may recall that he was attacked by a rabbit while vacationing in Plains, Georgia. While fishing from a canoe in a pond, he spotted a rabbit with a real attitude swimming furiously toward him. Though the rabbit's problem was never identified precisely, Carter later speculated that the highly agitated lagomorph was fleeing a predator. Whatever the case, the rabbit was clearly troubled. "It was hissing menacingly, its teeth flashing and nostrils flared and making straight for the President," a press account said. Fortunately for all, Carter deflected the frenzied beast with his canoe paddle before the Secret Service was forced to plug the bunny to save the prez. The moral of the story is: It's a jungle out there, and rightly so. "En garde!"

FIRST, CROSS THESE OFF YOUR WORRY LIST

Larger wild cats such as bobcats, lynx, mountain lions, and panthers are among the most able, wily, stealthy predators on earth, but you need not fear them as you go merrily along your way. The reasons for this are several. First, generally speaking, their numbers have been severely diminished due to loss of habitat, poaching, hunting, and deliberately caused extermination due to a general misunderstanding of their place in the big ecological picture. Second, they are shy and reclusive, and should you ever see one in the wild, count yourself a lucky and rare human. Third, they would have no reason to attack you viciously on general principles, and they are not established carriers of such diseases as rabies that would initiate aberrant, aggressive behavior. Fourth, almost without exception these cats look to other places and faces for victuals, but death-by-cat does happen. There have been seven fatalities attributed to mountain lions, for example, in the last decade—but there are no mountain lions in the east. Generally, we're just too big, dangerous, and maybe noisy and social to fool with as food. If you are really worried about a cat attack, travel in a group.

Much of the same applies to the wild canines, the coyotes and wolves. While there is still plenty of hot debate over wolves and livestock predation, and small mammals including pet cats do "disappear"

where coyotes (and big cats) are prevalent, attacks on humans from these *Canidae* are extremely rare—less than one fatality per year, and again these incidents occurred in the western U.S. Lastly, all were triggered by human thoughtlessness.

Put simply, when it comes to canines and felines, the danger of a "close encounter of the fang kind" is greatest at home. Our companion animals, domestic dogs and cats, are many, many times more likely to inflict bites than are their wild country cousins. Good samaritans who are trying to help an injured dog or cat, even if it is their own pet, should be especially cautious. If it can be accomplished safely, injured dogs should be muzzled; otherwise it might be better to wait for animal control assistance.

BITING THE HAND THAT PETS YOU

The joys of sharing life with a pet can enrich your days beyond measure. Research amply documents that pets relieve anxiety in times of stress, as well as teach important lessons about life and responsibility. At any stage of our lives, animals enlighten us with vital, important, and positive messages, but they can have a special influence on a child's development. A pet's unconditional affection provides emotional continuity and perhaps even a lifeline for a child.

On the cautionary side however, according to a 1996 National Center for Injury Prevention and Control report, 4.7 million people, or 1.8% of the U.S. population, are bitten by dogs annually. During the ten years prior (1986–1996) the number of dog bites *requiring medical care* rose from 585,000 to 800,000, a whopping 37%. During that same period, the number of dogs kept as pets increased only 2%. Cat bites are estimated at 700,000 annually. The

National Medical Society calculates that 1% of all emergency room visits are from animal bites, with dogs accounting for 80–90% and cats 15–20%. The difference may be due to the fact that dog bite damage is readily apparent, while cats may simply sink a single puncture wound that seems innocuous enough at the time of injury. Cat bites, however, are much more likely to develop serious infection because of the types of bacteria they carry in their mouths. With all this biting going on, it seems practical and prudent to prevent the situations that tend to provoke our furry buddies.

Most bite victims are children between the ages of 5 and 14, and they are likely to be bitten on the face. Because their natural exuberance may easily startle, overexcite, or threaten a pet, children should be instructed from a very early age on how to handle themselves around dogs and cats. Biting is a natural response for dogs and cats, so the responsibility falls to us—children and adults—to learn how to safely be around them.

All that said, let's put this in perspective. Dog attack fatalities remain extremely rare. Children are at much greater risk of drowning in a backyard suburban pool, or being murdered by a close relative or caregiver than they are of being killed by what will always be "man's best friend." More people are killed each year in the U.S. by either bees or lightning than by dogs, and this perspective should not be lost in an upswell of anti-dog hysteria. As for specific breeds, one vet reports that "It's much more likely for me to have to muzzle a cocker spaniel or chihuahua for a routine exam than it is to muzzle a pit bull or Rottweiler."

Guidelines for Preventing Cat and Dog Bites

Some of the directions below may seem overly cautious to dedicated animal lovers who generally make friends easily with dogs and cats. We have given you these more careful, extensive instructions, however, because reported biting incidents are on the rise. We want to give you every tool you may need for those encounters that turn menacing.

- Teach your children to apply the golden rule to animals. Respect for another creature is a valuable lesson animals have to offer, so make sure your child knows that a family pet is not simply another fuzzy toy, but a creature who has needs and wants very similar to his or her own. Therefore, teach children that if an animal doesn't come to them, leave it alone. Animals that are handled gently are much more likely to respond in kind.
- Do not approach strange dogs or cats. If an animal is on a leash, ask the human if you may pet the dog or cat. Especially avoid a dog that is on a chain or tied up. Avoid contact with free-roaming animals.
- Always be gentle in your voice, touch, and movement around the animal.
- Do not approach dogs or cats quickly. If you startle them, they may run or attack.
- Don't pull on a cat's or dog's tail, ears, or neck, or physically harass the animal in any way.
- Teach children not to tease dogs or cats with sticks, food, or any other objects. Older children can be taught the fine line between teasing and playing with an animal and can learn the warning signs when playing turns into something more dangerous. Teasing even during play will

unintentionally frustrate the dog or cat and may lead to biting.
- Growling is a dog's warning to stop whatever you are doing, but some dogs will bite without warning. Also cease and desist if a cat begins growling, snarling, hissing, or arching its back.
- Keep close watch on children when dogs or cats are in the same vicinity.

Preventing Cat Bites

- Many bites take place when a well-intentioned person tries to pick up or pet a stray cat. Any animal who is scared, perhaps starving, or feels cornered is likely to bite. When dealing with stray or feral kitties, be careful and wear gloves, or at minimum use a cloth or towel as a bite barrier.
- People are frequently bitten or scratched when they try to stop a fight between cats, or try to comfort a cat that is scared. A person in the wrong place at the wrong time can be a victim of a cat's redirected aggression. The cat is not actually mad at the person, but because the cat has already been aroused and is angry or fearful, it may attack any person or thing that comes near it.
- When a cat is cornered, forcing your attention on it will leave it no choice but to fight.
- Cats who are declawed may be more apt to become biters because one of their prime defense mechanisms for protection and escape has been eliminated. This point is controversial, but still worthy of consideration. If you feel you must declaw a cat, perhaps you should consider more carefully having a cat as a pet.
- Sometimes petting a cat on certain parts of its body will trigger

an instinctive reaction to bite or scratch. One area, especially for un-neutered males, is around the base of the tail. Another is the stomach. If your cat grabs or begins to bite your arm or hand while you are petting its stomach, do not immediately try to withdraw it as this will only excite the cat's instincts. Stop moving and wait for your cat to lose interest in this perceived threat.

Preventing Dog Bites

- Use reason in selecting a dog. Consider the traits of the breed and how well they will match the care, training, and supervision you can give it. Though a dog with a highly aggressive temperament may seem good for home security, it may not be compatible with small children who do not fully understand the dog's need for boundaries.
- When buying puppies from breeders, ask to see the parents of the dog to assess their temperaments.
- There is some consensus that properly weaned puppies should be separated from their dams and placed in their new homes at seven weeks of age for proper socialization. Prematurely separated puppies fail to be properly socialized by their dam and litter-mates. Yet delaying the process is thought by some experts to foster "pack" mentality and behavior, as well as interfere with the bonding to the new human family.
- When acquiring dogs of any age from the local animal shelter, try to determine how the animal interacts with other dogs, cats, and people of various ages and sizes. This can lessen the chance of an unsuitable match.

- Properly socialize puppies, especially between 4 and 16 weeks of age, in order to prevent excessive fear and aggression toward strangers when they are adults. Young dogs need to learn how to be comfortable around other dogs, too, so take your puppy (on a leash at first) to places where he or she can learn to feel at ease around other dogs. *However, and this is important, contact with other dogs should be avoided until three weeks after the puppy completes a puppyhood vaccination series.* Distemper and parvo viruses still kill a lot of unvaccinated dogs.
- Puppies naturally use their teeth when playing, but they must be discouraged from doing so on people even during play. Their chewing and "mouthing" should be corrected with a sharp "NO" and the chewing redirected to an appropriate chew toy.
- Puppies and dogs should not be allowed to use their teeth when taking treats out of hands. To discourage this, offer the treat inside a closed fist. Only allow the dog to take the treat after it has gently nudged with its muzzle. Do not hold the treat above the dog's head, which would encourage it to jump up and grab the treat out of your hand.
- Teach your child about any dangerous neighborhood animals and avoid routes where dogs are known to chase pedestrians or cyclists. Dogs are often prompted by motion, such as a person running or riding a bike.
- Dogs are also motivated by noise and are more likely to bite when the person yells or screams. If you do speak, do so in a low, firm voice.
- If an unleashed dog does approach your child, teach the

child not to panic, but to stand with hands at his sides while being as quiet and as still as possible. Let the dog sniff, and speak in a calm low voice to the animal. The dog will probably move away and the child can then also move away.

- If a dog starts to growl or show signs of aggression, back away. Do not turn and run, as you may trigger the dog's natural chase instinct. You may try to slowly back away. If this movement makes the dog more assertive or aggressive (moving toward you, growling, snarling), then you must stand still and very slowly move your hands and arms to protect your chest and neck. In this situation, only back away after the dog has left.

- Avoid eye contact with the dog because the dog may perceive this as a challenge. Stare straight ahead if you encounter a dog running loose. If a dog approaches you, do not stare at it, i.e. do not make direct eye contact. Instead, watch its movements out of the corner of your eye.

- If a dog approaches or runs toward you, stand still. You cannot outrun a dog. Running away will encourage the dog to chase you. Keep your movements and actions low-key and your voice firm but subdued.

- If you happen to be in a situation where a menacing stray dog approaches you aggressively, stand very still with your hands to your side and feet together. Or if you're on the ground, lay on your side, tucking your chin and knees to your chest and placing a fist over each ear. Be like a rock. If a dog knocks you down, do not move. Lie on your stomach and cover the back of your neck with your hands.

- Do not let children stick their fingers or hands through a fenced enclosure to pet a dog. Likewise, stay clear of dogs in parked cars or tied by a leash. The dog may feel especially defensive of its territory under these confining conditions.

- Never enter a fenced yard containing a dog if the owner is not there, and even then, not without the owner's permission.

Dog Fights

Trying to break up fighting dogs is a quick, sure, and easy way to get bitten. Instead of reaching into a swirling mass of flying fur and gnashing teeth, try making an unexpected loud noise like honking a car horn. That may startle the animals into separating. Turning the hose on the dogs is another option, but some report limited effectiveness with this method. Otherwise, be patient, stay out of the way, and hope for the best.

Human Infants in a Home with Cats or Dogs

Sadly, many people automatically assume that having an animal in the home is incompatible with bringing home a new baby, so they "dispose" of their pet by giving it away or taking it to a shelter where odds are good it will be killed. This is simply not necessary. With a small amount of effort, your animal can adapt quite well to the presence of the child in the house, perhaps even coming to its aid in times of need. Stories of how dogs and cats like to "watch over" young children are quite common. You should never, however, leave an infant (or a young child) alone with an animal, especially a dog. You may think the risk of danger is low, but the stakes are far too high for gambling.

All that said, most animals will adjust with ease to the new arrival.

Throughout this book, we try to give you every possible tool for success, but please do not misread this amount of topic coverage as an indicator of the likelihood of trouble. The longstanding human-animal bond is mutually rewarding and beneficial, and the odds are excellent that your creatures will adapt just fine.

Regarding Cats and Dogs

- To begin the transition of bringing a newborn into the house, send something home from the hospital as soon as possible that smells of the baby. Let the dog or cat sniff this so that when the baby comes it will not be quite so strange or interesting. You can augment this by letting the animal smell the other aromas associated with newborns such as lotions and powders.

- When you come home from the hospital, have someone else carry the baby into the house. Your pet will have missed you in your absence, and this way you can devote some critical first minutes with your dog or cat to reassuring them that they still hold a special place in your heart.

- Remember that along with your baby, your dog or cat needs you, too! Spare at least a few minutes every day for special attention to your pet.

- You can't keep your infant and your pet apart forever, so let them meet as soon and as often as possible. Give the animal plenty of treats during this introductory time so that it will associate being in the presence of the baby as a pleasant experience and nothing to worry about.

- Each new experience you have with the baby (crying, feeding, bathing, etc.) is also a new experience for your pet, so simply let your pet see what the commotion is about. If you exclude pets, you may initiate resentment toward the child.

- It is essential for your child's safety that you teach him or her not to mistreat animals in any way, for even the slightest cruelty might provoke a trusted pet. An old woman wise in the ways of animals observed, "I bet they get headaches and have bad days, too."

Regarding Cats

- Pregnant women should avoid coming into contact with the cat's litter box because it is a source of toxoplasmosis, an infection caused by a protozoan that can cause mental retardation in newborns. (Another source is handling or eating raw meat, which pregnant women are also advised to avoid.) Pregnant women should have their partners change the litter box. If you must do it yourself, wear gloves and a mask as the protozoan responsible for toxoplasmosis can be airborne. Scoop the litter boxes of indoor/outdoor cats daily to decrease or even eliminate the risk of "toxo"; the infective life-cycle stage requires at least a day after being shed by the cat to become infectious.

- It's a myth that cats will inadvertently suffocate a baby while sniffing for milk on the baby's lips, or that cats will attack an infant when it cries, thinking another cat is in the house. (It's much more likely that a cat will run from such a wailing.) After a period of adjustment, you may find your cat cuddled up with your child. This is a classic illustration of a cat seeking warm, lazy comfort (for which cats are notorious)—not the beginning of a coup on the crown prince. If this behavior is a concern, use netting over the crib to prevent the cat's entry.

Regarding Dogs
- You have months of foreknowledge that a child is coming, so use the time to prepare the dog by establishing proper behavior boundaries.
- If the dog sleeps with you, you may want to train it to stay off the bed for those times that the newborn will be with you there.
- If a dog jumps freely on the furniture when it pleases, it could inadvertently leap onto the baby one day.
- Train your dog to respond to basic commands properly. It will be extra difficult to carry a baby around and have a dog that completely ignores you when you need it to sit-stay or down-stay, for example.
- Dogs who jump up on people can easily and inadvertently injure a baby carried in someone's arms.
- You might need to leave a room with the baby, leaving the dog behind. Make sure your dog already accepts being left in one room while you are elsewhere in the house.
- On the first encounter after arriving home from the hospital, greet the dog without the baby in your arms (as above) and then perhaps put it outside while you get the baby settled. Then bring the dog back inside on leash, and let it satisfy its curiosity in the new arrival. Because babies are essentially boring, the dog will probably quickly lose interest. Someone might want to play a quick game with the dog or take it for a walk fairly quickly after the homecoming to lower the already high energy level of the house on such an important day.
- Without the proper attention, it is possible, though not likely, that your pet will become jealous of your newborn. To reassure your old friend, spend some time on the floor with your baby on your lap. Without pressuring your pet, invite her or him to come to you for some affection. This will give the animal a chance to satisfy its curiosity about the baby and diminish its concern over being replaced. Don't, however, force closeness.
- All dogs do not immediately comprehend an infant as a human. Most dogs will adapt with no problems, but if your dog has a reputation by breed or temperament toward aggression, or is especially prone to bringing down small prey, be especially watchful until you know how the new relationship is sorting itself out. Because you will never leave the infant alone with the dog, this should not prove to be a problem.
- You're at a critical stage of child-dog relations when babies start learning how to move around. Children are fascinated with the dogs, moving towards them and sometimes cornering a dog who has no means of escape. Babies grab things, including the dog, to pull themselves up, and they may fall on sleeping dogs or grab the dog's toys away. Be especially sensitive to your dog's needs at this time. You may have to keep the dog's toys off the floor while the child is "loose" to prevent possessiveness.
- An excellent page of the Family Dog Training web site (www.familydogonline.com/babies.htm) goes into greater detail about further precautions.

If You Are Bitten by a Cat or Dog

If you or a child is bitten by a dog or cat, seek medical aid as soon as possible. Try to remember the circumstances of the attack, the description of the animal, and if possible, obtain the owner's name and address. Later, when you speak to the owner, try to ascertain whether the animal is current in its rabies vaccinations. All of this information may be useful in treating the injuries.

A Special Note About Cat Bites

Cats' mouths, especially, carry a lot of bacteria, so any time a tooth breaks the skin, infection is a possibility. People whose immune systems are compromised, whether they have an infection or the HIV virus, are more likely to develop complications from a cat bite, *but even fully healthy individuals should take extra care with a cat bite.* The puncture nature of a cat bite (dog bites tend more toward a flesh tear) makes the wound both difficult to clean and highly susceptible to infection that can even lead to a need for amputation in severe circumstances. If it's a very superficial wound, clean it well with running water for 10 to 15 minutes and use an antibacterial soap. Be sure you actually clean the wound. Just pouring on alcohol does not do that, and in the words of our veterinary expert reviewer, "Pouring alcohol on the wound would burn like hell!" He further advises to apply over-the-counter triple antibiotic ointment or Betadine ointment to the wound, if possible, before seeking treatment.

Very promptly seek medical attention for any bite or scratch wound that is deep, reddened, swollen, painful, or draining. Your physician may recommend a round of antibiotics and a tetanus shot if yours is not current. That may sound like a hassle, but it beats losing your hand.

Cat Scratch Fever

Cat scratch fever is a bacterial infection that can cause painful swelling in the lymph nodes, fatigue, headache and joint pain, seizures, and other symptoms. It is caused by *Rochalimaea hensleae,* a bacillus picked up in the soil. It appears to be mainly transmitted by a bite or scratch from kittens, although mature cats and occasionally dogs will transmit the disease. Persons with compromised immune systems are more likely to have an adverse reaction. Certainly, not all cat scratches are of concern, and cat scratch fever generally goes away on its own after lasting two to four weeks with lymph node symptoms. If necessary, it can be treated with antibiotics.

Who is Biting Whom?

A study in El Paso, Texas reviewed a random sample of dog and cat bites and found the following:

- 89.4% of cat bites were provoked, and the victims were mostly female (57.5%) and adult (68.3%).
- 44.6% of dog bites were provoked, and the victims were more likely to be male (65.6%) and children (63%).

These results likely indicate ownership and interaction patterns more than they do gender or age "bite preference" for the animals involved, but they do indicate that dogs frequently bite without obvious provocation, and that young boys should be taught to behave with sensitivity for their own well-being (and just to be nice).

Dog Bite–Related Fatalities

On September 15, 2000, the journal of the American Veterinary Medicine Association, *Vet Med Today*, issued a special report, "Breed of Dogs Involved in Fatal Human Attacks in the United States between 1979 and 1998." During this 20-year period of

Dog Bite–Related Fatalities 1979–1998	
Breed of Dog	**Fatalities**
Purebred	
Pit bull–type	66
Rottweiler	39
German shepherd	17
Husky-type	15
Alaskan malamute	12
Doberman pinscher	9
Chow chow	8
Great Dane	7
Saint Bernard	7
Crossbred	
Wolf-dog hybrid	14
Mixed breed	12
German shepherd	10
Pit bull–type	10
Husky-type	6
Rottweiler	5
Alaskan malamute	3
Chow chow	3
Saint Bernard	1

Source: American Veterinary Medicine Association

study, there were more than 300 deaths from dog bite–related injuries; most victims were children. This grim scenario is probably due in part to the simple fact that it is easier for a dog or a group of dogs to overcome a smaller rather than a larger individual. *But remember, as we stated above, children are at much greater risk of drowning in a backyard suburban pool, or being murdered by a close relative or caregiver, than they are of being killed by what will always be "man's best friend."*

Based on data collected from the Humane Society of the United States and media accounts, the following information was gleaned:

- At least 25 breeds of dogs were involved in dog bite–related fatalities (DBRF) from 1979 to 1998. Pit bull–type dogs and Rottweilers were involved in more than half of these deaths,

but breeds responsible for DBRF have varied over time and have included dachshunds, a Yorkshire terrier, and a Labrador retriever.
- 58% involved unrestrained dogs on their owners' property
- 24% involved unrestrained dogs off their owners' property
- 17% involved restrained dogs on their owners' property
- <1% involved restrained dogs off their owners' property

The study, while acknowledging the inability to calculate breed-specific bite rates, said, "Finally, it is imperative to keep in mind that even if breed-specific bite rates could be accurately calculated, they do not factor in owner-related issues. For example, less responsible owners or owners who want to foster aggression in their dogs may be drawn differentially to certain breeds. Despite these limitations and concerns, the data indicate that Rottweilers and pit bull– type dogs accounted for 67% of the DBRF in the United States between 1979 and 1998. It is extremely unlikely that they accounted for anywhere near 60% of dogs in the United States during that period and, thus, there appears to be a breed-specific problem with fatalities."

Another study indicates that dog bites that required medical attention were more likely to be caused by un-neutered, chained, male dogs. This is another reminder to weigh carefully the needs and abilities of owners and prospective pets, as well as yet another reason to neuter animals who are not part of a purebred breeding effort.

The short interpretation is that, yes, pit bulls and Rottweilers bear close watching, to be sure, but many other breeds under various conditions can be lethally dangerous as well. In the final analysis, it again comes down to us to treat animals with the care they need and the respect they deserve—for their safety and ours.

WILD ANIMAL ENCOUNTERS

Breaking and entering isn't just for human beings anymore. An eighty-year old widow in Washington Township, Ohio, was startled when a rambunctious deer smashed through her living room picture window. She fled out the front door, and she later admitted she "must have held the door open for him, because he bounded out the front door" too. Even that story pales before another incident in Jeffersonville, Kentucky, when a manic deer crashed through a school window to terrorize a roomful of kindergartners:

They screamed as the deer broke a large window pane and bounded over tables, ran to a sink in the back of the classroom, leaped over a counter, and smashed into the blackboard, before breaking two more windows on its way out, about a minute later. … The deer injured itself when it crashed through the window and hit the blackboard, leaving a large bloody spot.

These cases may be bizarre, but they do illustrate that anything can happen with wildlife; that's why it's called "wild." Of course, these instances and the unusual events you can catch on TV are not the norm, but here are a few directions to reduce further your chances of a dangerous encounter.

Minimizing Wild Encounters

Common sense dictates these (obvious) guidelines:

- Animals will not generally attack unless provoked, starving, or ill. Provocation can include physical abuse, crowding, or frustrating the creature (as when you entice it with edibles and then withhold the food).
- Do not corner or handle wild animals. Many wild animals can-

not tolerate the stress of a human encounter. Your interference may cause their death or your injury.
- Do not approach young offspring when the elder animals are in attendance. (See "Aid to the Wounded or Abandoned" below.)
- Do not disturb a feeding animal, and give it and the surrounding territory a wide berth. You cannot know how much that meal may mean to the animal who may be quite ready to defend this essential component of life.
- Do not disturb animals who are mating. Among other things, it's stupid, discourteous, and potentially damaging to you, them, and their species in the long run.
- Do not separate fighting animals using your bare hands. If separation is really necessary—say, if your dog is tangling with a raccoon—drive the animals apart using a long stick or club while keeping a good distance from the heavy action. A loud noise such as a car horn may help to startle the animals apart.

Heavenly Help for Animal Attacks Pray to St. Vitus, the patron saint for the prevention of animal attacks, as well as the protector of actors, comedians, comediennes, Czechoslovakia (now the Czech Republic and Slovakia), dancers, dogs, epileptics, lightning, and storms. (I'm not making this stuff up.)

Treatment for Animal Attacks

The basic field treatment for all animal bites and maulings is the same, regardless of the animal type that may produce different types of wounds and risks of infection.

- Apply pressure to stop any brisk bleeding.
- Clean the wounds well by flushing all injuries that have broken the skin with at least two quarts

of disinfected water, scrubbing with mild soap, and flushing again.

- If you are carrying povidone iodine (Betadine) solution 10% (not soap or scrub); benzalkonium (Zephiran) liquid 1% antiseptic; or, in a pinch, Bactine antiseptic (benzalkonium 0.13%), rinse the wound with one of these for one minute (to help kill the rabies virus), then rinse away the solution until there is no discoloration of the wound.
- Unless it is absolutely essential for rescue, minimize the risk of infection by not sewing or taping closed any animal bite. If a large tear is present, the wound edges can be held together with tape and wraps. Apply a thin layer of antibacterial cream into the wound.
- If the victim is more than five hours from a physician, administer antibiotics, and especially if the bite is from a cat (domestic or wild), administer an antibiotic as soon as possible.

AID TO THE WOUNDED OR ABANDONED

Encounters with injured or potentially abandoned wildlife are a part of modern life for most people. It can be heart-wrenching trying to determine what to do, and your choices may put you at risk depending on the species and the circumstances. You should leave larger wounded wild mammals, such as raccoons and opossums, to the wildlife care experts (See appendix for contact information). *Do not attempt to capture them yourself.*

You should almost always secure professionally trained care for any animal you do rescue by transporting it yourself to a facility or by summoning wildlife personnel while you isolate or watch the whereabouts of the creature.

Professional care is almost always a "must" for several reasons:

- It is illegal for private individuals to possess or treat wildlife without a permit issued by appropriate state or federal agencies.
- Professionals can administer the proper diet as well as care. Unsuitable diet and handling can often lead to unnecessary fatalities.
- Through a lack of knowledge and proper equipment, you may expose yourself and your family to disease.

The Humane Society of the United States offers the following advice on their useful website (www.hsus.org):

If you have found a wild animal that you think is injured or orphaned, immediately call one of the following resources for assistance. Most can be located fairly easily through your local telephone directory.

- A local wildlife rehabilitator.
- Your local animal shelter.
- Your local animal control agency.
- A local wildlife/exotic animals veterinarian.
- Your local nature center.
- A local wild bird store.
- Your state wildlife management agency.

Describe the animal and its physical condition as accurately as possible and carefully follow the instructions you are given. Signs that a wild animal needs help:

- Bleeding.
- Vomiting.
- Shivering.
- Evidence of a dead parent nearby.
- A featherless or nearly featherless bird (nestling) on the ground.
- A wild animal presented to you by a cat or dog.
- An apparent or obvious broken limb.

Many animals who appear to be orphaned are not. Here are some tips

to help you know when not to rescue a baby animal. Unless one or
more of the signs mentioned above is
present, *do not attempt to rescue an animal in any of the following circumstances*:

- A fawn curled up in grass and
  approachable—its mother most
  likely out of sight but nearby
  and watching you.
- A bird who is feathered with
  some downy tufts and is hop-
  ping on the ground but unable
  to fly—it is a fledgling and its
  parents are probably nearby.
- A rabbit who is four inches long
  with open eyes and erect ears—
  it is independent.
- An opossum who is seven inches
  or longer (not including the
  tail)—it is independent.
- A squirrel who is small but fully
  furred and able to climb—it is a
  juvenile but independent.

OPOSSUMS AND RACCOONS

These two critters are so commonly
found around human dwellings that
they bear mentioning. Odds are good
that if you have these nighttime ram-
blers poking about your environs,
you'll have no safety issues if you
don't engage or threaten them.

Of course, the opossum is the one
that looks like the biggest rat you have
ever seen. They're roughly the size of
house cats and top out at about 15
pounds. Opossums are primitive animals that date back to the dinosaur
age, which is remarkable because they
are notoriously dimwitted. But, hey,
survival of the species is the bottom
line, and they are great at it even if
they also have a high mortality rate at
all stages of life, only living for about
three years. What makes us interested
in them is that they have 50 sharp
teeth, more than any other mammal.
When they are threatened, sometimes
they feign death by "playing possum,"

A treed opossum (Virginia opossum)
bares its many teeth.

a proven defense even against the jaws of a Siberian husky in a fenced yard.

However, the *National Audubon Society Field Guide to North American Mammals* describes this vivid alternative opossum behavior: "More often, it tries to bluff its attacker by hissing, screeching, salivating, opening its mouth wide to show all of its 50 teeth, and sometimes excreting a greenish substance." It can also emit smelly stuff from its anal glands. So, if you find a possum in your garage ransacking your pet food (they eat just about anything, which is why they continue to thrive), don't get in there and start whacking away with the broom, trying to corner or to capture it. The very fine book, *Living with Wildlife: How to Enjoy, Cope with, and Protect North America's Wild Creatures Around Your Home and Theirs,* recommends that you "use bright lights, make loud noises by banging pans, rustling paper, opening/closing doors, or playing radios; and/or squirting water to frighten them away." After the opossum leaves, take better care to store your edibles more securely. Another potential troubling situation might arise with a female who is trying to defend her young, so fully assess any situation to the best of your ability.

Raccoons, of course, are the masked bandits who are quite, quite clever, as well as exceptionally dexterous. They can grow to more than three feet in length and weigh up to almost 50 pounds. Television ads that show them entering a house by turning the doorknob and then opening the refrigerator to raid for snacks before flopping on the sofa are not far-fetched. According to *Living with Wildlife,* if you find a raccoon in your house, close the doors to other rooms and open all the windows and doors you can to give the raccoon an easy exit. Don't try to lure it out with food, as this will reinforce the food association that might prompt the raccoon to return.

Alarmed and anxious raccoons can cause extensive damage. If the animal doesn't leave in a reasonable amount of time, then call the local wildlife authorities. Don't try to handle the animal yourself. Raccoons are strong, and they have sharp teeth and claws. Warning signs of an aggressive raccoon include growling, snarling, hissing, a lowered head with flattened ears, bared teeth, and bushed-out neck and shoulder fur. (You probably could've guessed that, right?)

Raccoons are formidable, and most predators know that to engage one can mean a losing fight to the death. A raccoon, for example, can dispatch a single dog, which is probably why coon hunters use packs of dogs in their pursuit. Raccoons, however, are not normally aggressive animals unless they are cornered, mating, or with young. They do carry a roundworm, *Baylisascaris procyonis,* in their dung. While not harmful to the raccoon, this organism is potentially very injurious to other mammals, including humans. For this reason, and also because the raccoon is a primary rabies carrier in many southeastern states, it is unwise to entice these admittedly charming creatures with food.

THWARTING OPOSSUMS AND RACCOONS

- Do not leave pet food or trash outdoors at night.
- Pick fruit and garden crops when they are ripe, and do not leave rotten fruit or crops on the ground.
- Eliminate brush piles, dilapidated buildings, and holes under concrete slabs.
- Raccoons, opossums, and skunks (!) will easily enter a house through the pet door, so secure them at night.

For more solutions to various scenarios involving these backyard buddies, consult *Living with Wildlife: How to Enjoy, Cope with, and Protect North America's Wild Creatures Around Your Home and Theirs* by the California Center for Wildlife with Diana Landau and Shelley Stump. Bill Adler, Jr.'s *Outwitting Critters: A Human Guide for Confronting Devious Animals and Winning* is another good resource.

OPOSSUM
Virginia opossum

• DANGER
The opossum can bite if cornered.

• ABUNDANCE & RANGE
It is common throughout the eastern U.S.

• SIZE
Up to 40 inches in length, including a 10- to 20-inch prehensile, hairless tail. Weighs up to 14 pounds.

• DESCRIPTION
About the size of a house cat, the opossum has silvery "grizzled" hairs covering black hairs below. Its pinkish nose is long and pointed.

• SIMILAR SPECIES
This marsupial, unique to North America, has no comparable cousin.

• DIET
Omnivorous, the opossum eats insects, small mammals, bird eggs, grain, fruit, and carrion.

• REPRODUCTION
Opossum litters, produced two or three times a year, are comprised of tiny young with up to 14 members—each about the size of a honeybee.

• HABITAT
Opossums are found in suburban areas, farmlands, and forests, usually near water.

• TRAITS
They are generally not aggressive but will defend themselves if cornered. They are nocturnal and solitary, and they are often killed on the highway as they attempt to feed on carrion.

COMMON RACCOON
Procyon lotor

• DANGER
The raccoon can bite if cornered. Because the animal can be a carrier of rabies, the bite is potentially fatal.

• ABUNDANCE & RANGE
It is common throughout the U.S., but is not found in pockets of the Rockies and the southwestern U.S.

• **SIZE**

Up to 37 inches in length, including a tail of 8 to 16 inches.

• **DESCRIPTION**

The raccoon is distinguished by its black mask and black-ringed tail on a grayish-brown body. It has a pointed snout.

• **SIMILAR SPECIES**

It has no comparable species in the mid-Atlantic. The ring-tail and white-nosed coati are found in other regions.

• **DIET**

The raccoon's omnivorous diet includes grain, nuts, berries, rodents, insects, crayfish, bird eggs, and carrion.

• **REPRODUCTION**

One litter per year of usually four young are delivered in the spring.

• **HABITAT**

The raccoon is highly adapted in suburban areas, and is also found near water in forests, bottom lands, and in rocky outcroppings.

• **TRAITS**

Nocturnal, curious, and extremely dexterous, the raccoon is not aggressive but will fight ferociously if cornered or to defend itself.

SHREWS

Shrews are intense, active, nervous creatures who resemble mice, but they have long, slender snouts that house needle-sharp teeth, and five-clawed toes on their forefeet, whereas mice have four toes on their forefeet. The shrew is a burrower who darts about constantly in search of food to satisfy its extremely high metabolism. It is generally a solitary animal that will fight viciously to defend itself or its nest.

There are more than 30 species of shrew in North America, but only two deserve special mention here. The short-tailed shrews (southern and northern) are unique among mammals because they produce a poison in their salivary glands that paralyzes earthworms and snails. While this substance is not similarly dangerous to humans, the bite from these shrews in particular can be painful and swollen for several days.

SOUTHERN SHORT-TAILED SHREW

Blarina carolinsiensis

• **DANGER**

Its painful but nonlethal bite can cause significant swelling.

•**ABUNDANCE & RANGE**

In the mid-Atlantic region, this shrew is found in Maryland and south into eastern Virginia.

• **SIZE**

Seldom over 4 inches in length.

• **DESCRIPTION**

The shrew is mouselike with a gray body and short tail.

- **SIMILAR SPECIES**

The northern short-tailed shrew is
larger, and the least shrew is brownish in color.

- **DIET**

A shrew's daily fare may include
earthworms, insects, spiders, snails,
slugs, salamanders, small or young
birds, snakes, rabbits, and mice.

- **REPRODUCTION**

Breeding begins in midwinter and
continues into fall. After three weeks
gestation, 3 to 10 young are born.
Females may produce two to three
litters per year.

- **HABITAT**

Shrews are found in almost any
landscape with vegetation.

- **TRAITS**

Using its powerful snout and
forefeet, this mole-like creature
makes burrows in the earth about
one inch wide. It is active day and
night to satisfy its voracious appetite,
and it is aggressive when handled.

NORTHERN SHORT-TAILED SHREW

Blarina brevicauda

- **DANGER**

Its painful but nonlethal bite can
cause significant swelling.

- **ABUNDANCE & RANGE**

Very commonly found in northern
Virginia north to Maine and west to
Nebraska.

- **SIZE**

Grows to 5 inches, making it the
largest shrew in North America.

- **DESCRIPTION**

This shrew is solid gray and mouselike with very small eyes.

- **SIMILAR SPECIES**

The southern short-tailed shrew is
smaller, and the least shrew is also
smaller and brownish in color.

- **DIET**

A shrew's daily fare may include
earthworms, insects, spiders, snails,
slugs, salamanders, small or young
birds, snakes, rabbits, and mice.

- **REPRODUCTION**

Four to eight young are born after
three weeks of gestation. Birth usually occurs from spring into fall, but
can occur year-round.

- **HABITAT**

Shrews are found in almost any
landscape with vegetation.

- **TRAITS**

Using its powerful snout and
forefeet, this mole-like creature
makes burrows in the earth about
one-inch wide. It is active day and
night to satisfy its voracious appetite,
and it is aggressive when handled.

- **COMMENTS**

This shrew is likely North America's
most common mammal.

BEARS

"The bear's price is everything," is the closing line of a Ted Hughes poem, and indeed a bear encounter may cost you everything, including your life. The power of the bear has been acknowledged among humans since Neolithic times when we constructed shrines and altars to the Master Bear and buried bear bones beside us, no doubt to give us unparalleled capabilities for the next world. The heavens themselves declare the power and glory of the beast—the nucleus of the constellation Ursa Major, Latin for "Great Bear," is the Big Dipper, the first star pattern that children look to and one that lasts a lifetime. Because they hibernate and bring forth new life in the spring, bears are also associated with resurrection and inspiration.

Bears can inspire, all right, especially if you find yourself face to face with one of the earth's most imposing predators and North America's largest carnivore. There are only eight species worldwide of this magnificent animal, and only three species inhabit the North American continent: polar bears, grizzly bears, and black bears. In the lower 48 states, you need only be concerned with grizzlies and black bears, and only black bears are found in the mid-Atlantic states. For grizzlies, you must head to the Rockies, especially around Yellowstone National Park, and the extreme northwestern states. Black bears are found in many more areas of the continental U.S., and in territories where the two species overlap, it definitely behooves you to know how to identify the bear you are looking at because that information could save your life. In the interest of natural history, we'll give you some general information about both species—but when it comes to encounters, *be aware that what we advise here about black bears does not apply to grizzly bears, and if you try to employ the wrong type of protection—playing dead with a black bear, for example— you will likely be mauled to death.*

Having sufficiently scared you (again, perhaps), we should add our frequent refrain: your chances of any kind of deeply dangerous bear encounter are very slim. As author Kevin Van Tighem puts it in his fine work *Bears,* "The risk of a car accident on the way to bear country far outstrips the risk of a close-range encounter with a bear, but it's the bear that worries us as we hurtle down the pavement at 100 kilometres (62 miles) per hour." (Van Tighem, 1999, p.11)

There are many human-bear encounters every year, and most result in nothing more than a peak experience and a good story. Take Bob, for instance, a veteran mountain-biker who enjoys all types of terrain, even the flatter distances of central Florida where black bears are still plentiful enough to warrant bear crossing signs along two-lane roads. As our intrepid peddler rounded a blind corner in the woods, he rammed into the back end of a black bear who was simply minding his or her own business. If someone rammed us in the butt with a speeding bicycle, we'd be rather cross and quick to anger. To be sure, Bob didn't waste any time finding out. He quickly did an about-face and pedaled like his life depended on it. The bear was gracious enough not to charge after him. Bob was, of course, lucky (or unlucky, depending on your point of view), but this story is indicative of the fact that most bear encounters do end peacefully.

THE DIET TO DIE FOR

Along with dogs, to whom they are anciently related, bears are mostly carnivorous (though technically omnivores). This means they have sharp, long canine teeth for puncturing and ripping flesh, as well as molars to slice, shred, and grind. Before your palms start sweating, you should know that both grizzlies and black bears are considered opportunistic carnivores, eating vegetation most of the time, taking advantage of meat, fish, and insect supplies as they can (see table below).

In order to sustain their weights—300 to 900 pounds for grizzlies and 200 to 600 for black bears—they must consume great quantities of food—especially prior to the winter hibernation, when they do not eat, urinate, or defecate. A bear who begins hibernation when it is seriously underweight is likely to die during the winter. So, although we all love and need food, the bear has an especially large appetite and a serious food agenda during the warmer months and especially approaching fall.

A note about hibernation and reproduction: Although bears do not eat or eliminate during the winter months, they remain warm and rouse easily, sometimes leaving the den during a winter warm spell. Cubs are born during the hibernation period and are nursed by the mother in the den for several months. Bears reproduce slowly. Beginning with a pair, the maximum theoretical increase in 10 years is 8 grizzly bears and 15 black bears. This slow reproduction rate magnifies the potential tragedy and far-reaching effects of human encounters that result in a bear's death.

This deep need for tremendous quantities of food puts the bear on a collision course with people, many of whom act thoughtlessly. The short

explanation is, "A fed bear is a dead bear."

When you are hungry, what do you do? Are you more likely to walk to the fridge, open it, and pull out the makings of a ham sandwich? Or will you take the time and energy to locate and bring down a pig? Bears are notoriously smart, capable, and curious. They learn very quickly where the easy pickings are. In too many instances, that means in the campground, at the garbage dump, or along the roadside.

What's the harm, you ask? The harm is that as bears come to associate food with people, they lose their fear and become gradually more aggressive—grizzlies more so than black bears. Although bear trapping and relocation is often used to try and remove nuisance bears from areas of human frequency, it is seldom a viable solution. Many bears will return to their home range or simply get into trouble with humans again near where they have been relocated. Through no fault of their own, by far the most common outcome of this tragic scenario is that the bears are shot to death. They simply went to the fridge to see if they could find something quick, easy, and satisfying to eat.

The Canadian Ministry of Environment said it perfectly, "Every person who contributes to habituating bears by feeding them, by leaving garbage at campsites or along road, by not handling food properly, by not taking care of fruit trees, pet foods, barbecues or other attractants around the home or farm, is responsible for the loss of bears."

BEAR FACTS

Bear Size

Black bears average four to six feet in length and weigh 200 to 600 pounds. Grizzlies are 5.5 to 7.5 feet

Typical Bear Diet				
	Vegetarian	Meat	Fish	Insects
Black Bear	75%	15%	<1%	10%
Grizzly Bear	80%	10%	5%	5%

Source: Bears, Kevin Van Tighem

in length and weigh anywhere from 300 to 900 pounds. Although they are not found in the lower 48 states, we can't help but let you know that polar bears grow up to 11 feet!

Bear Color

Both black bears and grizzlies come in different colors. This is especially confusing, of course, when it comes to the "black" bear. The black bear does appear black most often in the eastern U.S., but it can appear brown. In the southwest, black bears are most frequently brown or even blond. Grizzlies, too, can range from almost radiantly blond, reddish blond, or light brown to medium to dark brown or even black. Both individual black and grizzly bears exhibit a variety of patterns and possible shades in their coats. Grizzlies are named for their "grizzled" coat that is frequently flecked with gray or white hairs, multiplying the possibilities of grizzly appearance.

Black or Grizzly?

Neither size nor color is a good gauge to distinguish the two species, for large black bears can be bigger than small grizzlies. Habitat can provide a clue: grizzlies favor more open country and black bears favor forested areas, but these guidelines don't provide a hard and fast rule either. The best way to differentiate black bears from grizzly bears is to examine the shape and proportion of the body and head. Kevin Van Tighem characterizes the two species in these ways:

Black bear attributes:
- Comparatively larger, more elongated ears.
- Snout and forehead run together in more of a straight line.
- Smooth throat.
- Little or no hump at the shoulders. Rear end seems higher than shoulders.
- Dark claws that are generally not noticeable.

Comparison of grizzly bear and black bear body types.

5.5–7.7'
300–900 lb.

4–6'
200–600 lb.

Grizzly bear attributes:

- Comparatively smaller, more rounded ears.
- Snout extends from a dish-shaped face.
- Sports rough hairs on the throat beneath the chin.
- Has a pronounced hump at the shoulders. In adults, shoulders seem higher than rump.
- Long, frequently pale-colored claws.

(Van Tighem, 1999, p. 33)

Depending on the angle at which you sight a bear, it may still be difficult to determine which species you are looking at. If you are in a part of the U.S. that has both species (not the eastern U.S.) and you cannot be sure, it is better to assume you are encountering a grizzly, which means you will be more cautious in a variety of ways (detailed in the Northwest and Rockies volumes of this *Dangerous Wildlife* series).

Bear Senses and Smarts

The Native American saying goes, "A pine needle fell. The eagle saw it. The deer heard it. The bear smelled it." Bears have a legendary, phenomenal sense of smell. They can smell carcasses or newborn wild ungulate calves such as elk from several miles away. Often they can be seen standing on their hind legs sniffing the offering of the breezes. Although bear hearing and sight are certainly adequate for the job, the sense of smell is what directs bears to food sources, both appropriate and inappropriate. For this reason, it is good to be aware of where you are in relation to wind direction when in bear country should you see them before they see you. And don't kid yourself about "hiding" food in your tent.

As for intelligence, bears learn rapidly and remember for a long time. For example, black bears have shown the ability to discriminate among small forms such as squares, triangles, and circles, and they retained this knowledge throughout an eight-month study. For all we know, those bears are still mulling over those sublime, quintessential forms. This quick study/long memory aspect of bear behavior comes in handy when bears want to learn which campsites, trails, and roadsides have the best, easiest eat treats.

In his concise manual, *Safe Travel in Bear Country*, Gary Brown assesses bear psychology:

Bears learn rapidly and are quite capable of reason. Their curiosity, combined with an excellent memory, is the crux of the bears' intelligence. They learn and remember from a single experience—the location of a food source, a threat, a trap, or a rifle shot. They display cunning minds; they bluff, chose alternatives, avoid problems, outwit humans, retreat in the face of odds (human impacts, dominant bears). They are resourceful. (Brown, 1996, p. 22)

Bear Strength and Speed

"Strong as a bear" is quite a compliment indeed. A provoked bear can knock you 10 to 15 feet with one blow, and because the bear is also an enormously agile animal, be on the attack again before your body stops rolling. Grizzly bears have the power and skills to bring down a mature ungulate, such as an elk, and then crack its leg bones like so much hard candy to get at the marrow. In addition to their crushing jaws, black and grizzly bears' claws are superior tools to rip prey or dig a bear-sized hole; they can also finesse backpacks, open door latches, and handle foods. To say that bears are swift is an understatement, as they can attain speeds of 25 to 40 miles per hour, which makes them capable of outdistancing Olympic sprinters. True, they can maintain these top speeds only for short distances, but their general stamina is extraordinary. One source reports a bear running for 10 miles without a break. Don't be fooled into thinking that their running skill applies only on flat terrain. Despite their seemingly lumbering style, bears are just as agile moving uphill, downhill, or sideways on a slope. *You cannot outrun a bear, and it is a grave mistake to try.* Basically, bears have it all over us in the physical attribute department. Even young bears only six months old are a formidable match for human beings. As for the grown-ups, bear expert Stephen Herrero puts it graphically, "Trying to physically subdue an enraged adult black or grizzly bear is like wrestling with a tank."

Bear Personalities and Moods

Different bears have different personalities. Bears can be angered, but this is not the norm. It is true that black bears generally pose less of a threat to humans than do grizzlies. Black bears seem to be astonishingly tolerant of "stupid human tricks," but you should never take it for granted that black bears will not attack; they have been responsible for human fatalities. They are first and foremost bears, remember, with copious measures of power, agility, and speed. Grizzlies are notorious for their ferocity, but as we have said, most human encounters with either species end peacefully.

Bears are curious. Sometimes they seem to initiate encounters because they simply want to know if packs, coolers, tents, cans, and people are edible. In this scenario, curiosity can kill more than the cat—very curious and aggressive bears usually end up being shot. This is a tragedy with potentially larger ramifications as arguably quintessential and sublime bear traits are removed from the creatures' gene pool as a result of the killing.

Bears like to play, but they become loners. Both grizzlies and black bears have a reputation for "horsing around," a vital part of their social and physical development as cubs. Except for breeding females who have their cubs with them, however, bears are essentially solitary animals. You don't need to worry about packs of bears ganging up on you. One will do just fine, thanks.

Bears are maternal. Grizzlies have a stronger reputation for maternal protection than do black bears, but both will protect their young. Especially with grizzlies, if the mother even *perceives* you to be a threat to her young, she is likely to let you know it in a big, scary way. This means that the old adage, "Don't come between a mother bear and her cub," is insufficient. Instead, "Don't go anywhere remotely near a mother and her cub" should be your guide. This fierce, protective nature in mother bears likely stems from two facts: bears reproduce very slowly, and probably more to the point, adult males have been known to kill and eat cubs. (It's a tough, unsentimental world when it comes time to honor mother bear, too, as cubs have been known to eat a mother shortly after she has been killed by someone else.)

Bear Habitats and Rhythms

Generally speaking, on the North American continent, bears can be found between sea level and 10,000 feet. Because they like to climb trees for safety and to nap, black bears are creatures of the forest, which may be deciduous, coniferous, mixed, or swampy. Grizzlies, who do not look to trees for cover, haunt mixed forests, areas such as meadows that are treeless or nearly so, and arctic or alpine tundra. A bear has a home range: for an adult male black bear, approximately 43 square miles; for an adult male grizzly, 23 to 879 square

miles; for females, somewhat smaller ranges. The bear roams this home range in search of food. This territory can encompass various terrains, so both species of bears can be spotted in most of the habitats mentioned above (no grizzlies in swamps). As they move throughout their ranges, bears can negotiate almost any type of topography, including steep ridges and cliffs, strong rivers, and thick vegetation.

Roving for food, however, bears are likely to take the path of least resistance. This means they often take to hiking trails, roads, developed areas, and along shorelines: the same places that humans often travel, camp, and picnic. Bears are traditionally active from dusk to dawn, but when they are searching for food and find daytime exploits that pay off, they will be active then, too. Bottom line: any time of day you may find bears out and about.

Superb swimmers, bears can be found in streams, lakes, and ponds where they escape insects, cool down, swim, play, and, of course, drink.

Black bears are terrific tree climbers, and they will take to the trees to feed, rest, and hide. For this reason, climbing a tree is not a good escape from a black bear. Grizzlies are not terrific tree climbers, but they *can* climb trees and will ascend many feet if they are sufficiently motivated by hunger or, especially, anger.

Bears like to nap and often take time throughout the day for various periods of rest. These resting sites are typically near food sources and often have a commanding view. Black bears might snooze in trees, on the ground in grassy areas, or in conifer needles. Grizzlies are found in similar terrestrial nests (not in trees), including shallow depressions dug in soil or snow.

In most climates, bears hibernate from some portion of October through March. In warmer areas, such as subtropical Florida, they may not hibernate at all. Grizzlies den in snow accumulation areas on slopes of 25 to 45 degrees and sometimes as steep as 60 degrees, which makes the likelihood of hikers or skiers stumbling upon them remote. Black bears, however, normally den on the forest floor, sometimes forming a hollow against a log or under the roots of trees, but they are not particular. In southern pine woods, they may just gather up some leaves in a pile and sleep in the pile. Sometimes in the mountains, black bears prefer a large hollow tree. Typically the tree has an opening up high and the bear climbs up, in, and then down into the tree. They may den in a pile of rocks or logging slash. Typically, injuries do not occur near black bear dens, again perhaps because the creature is usually tolerant.

Black Bears

Once common throughout the country, black bears now live in the Appalachian Mountains, in parts of Arkansas, in Florida's national forests and wildlife refuges in the central regions, and along the Gulf of Mexico's borders with Florida, Alabama, Mississippi, and Louisiana. In the north and east, they are found from Maine south into New York and Pennsylvania.

How many black bears are there? Today, for example, biologists estimate that about 1,500 to 2,000 bears inhabit Florida, where just a century ago there were approximately 12,000. That's an old pattern of disappearance. As early as 1809, Davey Crockett was complaining about the bear numbers being lower than he had hoped. Today, with an estimated population of 400,000 to 750,000 in North America, the black bear is the most common species of bear in the U.S.—but it's still listed as threatened in Mississippi, Louisiana, and Texas. A relatively healthy population lives in the Great Smoky Mountains National Park, where an unusual tragedy occurred.

MANSLAUGHTER AND MAYHEM

The May 23, 2000, newspaper headline said it all: "Bears' attack stumps experts: Killing humans is out of character." A 50-year-old woman and experienced Smokies hiker, Glenda Ann Bradley, was hiking by herself while her companion veered off to go fishing. When he returned to locate her, he found her dead near the trail with a mother bear and her cub standing guard. The bears were killed and an autopsy confirmed they were the attackers, but no motivation was officially attributed to the death, the first fatality from a bear in the park's 66-year history. The best informal speculation was that the somewhat underweight bear was simply hungry. She had been tagged for research purposes two years before and had no history of aggression.

The fact that this is a unique event is a remarkable testament to the black bear's mostly peaceable nature. In a park with 10 million visitors per year—some of them who do quite stupid things like feed bears food from their hands; chase cubs through the woods with video cameras; and surround bears who have taken refuge in trees—a black bear has plenty of reasons to become provoked. Bear-sighting traffic jams and minor auto offenses are a way of life in the park's popular Cades Cove driving loop.

But black bears have killed people and are capable of inflicting nearly unthinkable wounds. The following account was reprinted in *Bear Attacks* by Stephen Herrero, who decided to include this gruesome story by Jim East of a hunter's encounter in his book "because of the casual manner

with which many people treat black bears." We include it for the same reason.

East recounted the story of a seasoned hunter named Pitka. After dropping the black bear with one shot and then waiting to confirm that it was dead, Pitka made a tremendous mistake by approaching the bear with nothing but his knife.

He was three yards away when the bear rolled to its feet and leaped on him. It knocked him unconscious with one blow, which proved a merciful happening. When he came to he was lying on the ground, the bear was standing over him, he could feel its fur against his arms and smell its foul breath. The bear's face was only a foot from his, but the luckless Indian no longer had a face. . . . He had taken incredible punishment. The entire right side of his face from the eye across to the nose and down to the chin had been torn away. The right eye was ripped out of the socket, and he could barely distinguish light with the left. His nose was torn off, with cartilage sticking out of raw flesh. The right cheek and part of the left were gone, and his mouth was so mangled he could not manage a drink of water. Three teeth were left in the jaw; the rest were dangling loose. All the torn flesh and skin of his face were hanging down beneath his chin like a grisly, bloody bib, and the pain in his head was beyond description.

Somehow Pitka survived. His wife found him near death more than fifty hours after the attack. He spent a total of ten months in the hospital and was left crippled and mutilated. As the Indian said later, "What remained was not a very good face, but it was better than none." (From Ben East's Bears, *1977. Book Division of Times Mirror Magazines, Inc., p. 53. Reprinted in Herrero, 1985, p. 103–104.)*

If you are cheering the bear over the hunter, you are not alone, but you are missing the point of the

story: black bears are formidable animals not to be trifled with. Now that we have your attention . . .

THE MOST DANGEROUS BLACK BEAR SCENARIO

Although they account for perhaps only one death every four years or so throughout North America, black bears do kill people. Typically these deaths do not come from bears habituated to human food and garbage. Instead, bears in wilder, truly remote areas who have very little or no experience with humans sometimes regard them as prey. In years of crop failure or drought where human foodstuffs are suffering, you can bet that bears will be affected by shortages, too. Thus general climactic conditions can help you estimate the probability of this extremely rare occurrence. Take note of where you are and what you are doing. Solo individuals who are in remote areas picking berries (a bear's delight), walking, or fishing are the ones who are most at risk for this type of extremely rare predatory attack.

Herrero's study, focusing on the period from 1900 to 1980, published as part of his landmark *Bear Attacks: Their Causes and Avoidance*, revealed the following:

- When people die from black bear attacks, predation seems to be the motive in 90% of the attacks (18 of 20 cases).
- Only 1 of the 20 deaths occurred within a national park where food conditioning is most common, evidence that food-conditioned black bears (but not grizzlies) can learn to coexist with humans with almost no fatalities.
- Half of the victims were under the age of 18, and five of them, or 25%, were under 10 years of age. Three of the five were playing outdoors.

- Nine of the 20 victims were adult males, obliterating notions of only younger and smaller people falling victim.
(Herrero, 1985, p. 105–106)

FIGHTING OFF A BLACK BEAR

Although in some rare cases children have fallen prey to these animals, even they can fend off black bears. If you are actually attacked by such an animal, do the following:

- Fight the bear with the closest weapon—a heavy stick, a rock, an axe, anything at hand. Fists and feet will do if nothing else is available.
- Head for shelter if it is very nearby, continuing to fight and yell.
- Do not run if shelter is not in the immediate vicinity. Black bears can easily outrun humans.
- Do not seek safety by climbing a tree. The black bear is easily a better climber than you are.
- Do not play dead—or in short order you will likely not have to "play."

Although fighting back seems like an impossible success story, it really is your best bet when it comes to black bear attacks. Still, the odds of your ever needing to do this are very, very remote. Remember, Herrero's study found only 20 fatalities in 80 years, and only one of those occurred inside a national park.

AVOIDING AND AVERTING BAD ENCOUNTERS WITH BLACK BEARS

The circumstances surrounding any bear attack are crucial factors in determining your most appropriate response. For this reason, the best tool you have to avoid dangerous or deadly bear encounters is your brain. Don't scoff at this asset, especially since compared to the bear's overwhelming physical superiority, it may be your only natural advantage. We can't, of course, guarantee your success with these recommendations, but they have expert statistical weight on their side.

- Do not presume that you will have the leverage of a firearm with which to dispatch the bear and therefore disregard these ad-monitions and recommendations.
- Your chances of being attacked around campsites by any black bear are extremely small. During a 19-year study of bear/camper encounters in the Boundary Waters Canoe Area Wilderness in Minnesota, only two injuries were reported in 19 million visitor-days. The study included the year 1985, when bear nui-sance activity was at a record high. The two injuries were by one bear on September 14 and 15, 1987. The bear was killed the next day.
- Don't feed or pet black bears. By further habituating them to humans you are inviting injury to yourself and almost certain death ultimately to the majestic creatures that you are so eager to admire.
- If a bear attacks in a place where it is likely habituated to people, e.g. a campground or roadside, assume first that the bear is attacking because it feels crowd-ed. In this case, simply back up slowly and give the wild animal the room it demands. *Always give bears an escape route!*
- The bear may be attacking because it wants your food. Give the bear what it wants. An expe-rienced "bear person" may feel equipped to try to get the bear to back down by displaying loud and/or conspicuous gestures such as raising arms and yelling or beating pots and pans. The evidence, however, indicates that once a bear has become aggres-sive to get food, stopping that bear is a difficult proposition. Once the bear has actually start-ed to eat your picnic's contents, the bear's dispersal is less likely (and, doubtless, your dispersal is more likely).

- In such an event, take shelter by backing slowly into your car or other suitable enclosure and sum-mon a ranger or a similar author-ity when safe and practicable.
- Certainly a tent is no place to hide from a black bear who has exhibited aggressive behavior.
- You can also make yourself appear as large as possible by raising your arms, jacket, pack or other object over your head.

GENTLE ENCOUNTERS WITH BLACK BEARS

Even if you have no food whatsoever, you may still encounter a black bear roaming about for victuals. If a bear sees you, it will run away or stop and observe you. If the bear stands up, that is not a signal of attack. It simply wants a better sniff or view. Stop your forward progress and begin speaking in low tones. ("Go away bear" might be an appropriate mantra.) Slowly back up and give the bear a wide berth and an escape route.

SUDDEN ENCOUNTERS WITH BLACK BEARS

We are happy to report that, unlike grizzlies, sudden encounters with black bears almost never lead to injury. What is much more likely is an aggressive display that might make you think your time has come, but the numbers say you will live to see another day. If you startle a bear, assume first that the bear will make an aggressive move. Stop in your tracks and then start backing up slowly, per-haps talking to it in a low voice. When startled, black bears are likely to exhibit the same behavior they use to scare other bears from feeding areas:

- Swatting the ground with a front paw or slapping the ground or trees.
- Making loud, blowing noises accompanied by clacking teeth, lunging, laid-back ears.
- Initiating a short charge toward you.
- A less common sound is the resonant "voice" of a bear used to express intense emotions (fear, pain, and pleasure), including strong threats. Black bears with ready escape routes seldom use this threat toward people. Grunts, on the other hand, are nonthreatening communication to cubs, familiar bears, and sometimes people.

All these sounds and actions above are all done explosively, with effective results, as you might imagine. It is rare, however, for a black bear to attack a person during or after such a demonstration.

Even if a black bear does charge you at speeds up to 30 to 35 miles per hour, the odds are that the bear will either stop short of you or veer past you. Assuming you have not passed out from fright, your best bet is to stand your ground just as any tough bear would. Once the episode seems to have abated, and it may include several charges, slowly and carefully back away. Do not run. Repeat, do not turn and run. Again, do not climb a tree for safety as black bears can climb faster and higher than you can.

PEPPER SPRAYS

Capsaicin spray repellent usually persuades black bears to leave when it is sprayed into their eyes. Capsaicin, the active ingredient of cayenne peppers, has long been used by mailmen as a dog repellent. In more than 200 trials, no bear gave any sign of anger after being sprayed, sometimes repeatedly. Most immediately turned and ran, stopping eventually to rub

their eyes. The repellent irritates the eyes for several minutes but causes no injury. Even those natural resource personnel working in grizzly country have taken to carrying pepper spray.

The disadvantages of relying on spray are that you must be close enough to the bear to effectively use it, and as an airborne solution you cannot completely and accurately predict the strength and direction of the vapor. If you choose to carry pepper spray, it's best to have it in a belt holster or sheath where it's readily accessible (you don't want to be rummaging in your daypack while a bear is teething on your leg).

"FE, FI, FO, FUM, I SMELL THE DEODORANT OF AN ENGLISHMAN"

Because they use their phenomenal sense of smell to track potential food sources, you should take the following precautions when recreating in bear country.

- Perfumes, deodorants, moisturizing lotions, insect repellents, toothpaste, suntan lotions, and fragrant lip balms can attract bears, so leave strongly perfumed items at home and use care to store items safely. It's not that your cologne will make you personally irresistible to the black bear, it's that the cologne signals a human presence which the bear may have come to associate with a good, easy, quick source of food.
- Avoid strongly scented foods such as bacon, sausage, cheese, fish, or fresh meats.
- Gum, candy, and other snacks have appeal for bears, too.
- Even pop-top canned drinks can motivate a bear to open them up to see what's inside.
- Food smells can permeate tents, backpacks, and sleeping bags as

well as clothing, so use care to keep food in plastic bags to avoid unnecessary odor contamination.

HIKING IN BLACK BEAR COUNTRY

- If a warning sign is posted at the trailhead, officials are aware of the bear but do not consider it to be overly aggressive. Remember, though, bears are unpredictable. If you proceed, remember to make an extra effort announcing your presence to avoid the very scary bear behaviors described above. Tap on rocks with a hiking stick, wear a small bell, or yell just before you enter trail portions with extensive brush, along streams, or as you round a bend.
- If you do see a bear, stop and look for one or two cubs nearby. If you do see her cubs, slowly and deliberately back up, moving in whatever direction is necessary to communicate that you are no threat to the cubs.
- If you happen on a large dead animal that appears to have died in a struggle, leave the area immediately. A bear may be nearby and will likely be very aggressive in defending its kill.
- Similarly, take note of signs that may indicate carrion, such as circling vultures or the smell of rotting meat. Carcasses attract bears. Leave the area immediately.
- Constantly check ahead for bears in the distance. If you spot one who has not seen you, make a wide detour and leave the area immediately.
- Keep your children nearby and in sight.
- Free-running pets can anger a bear and then lead the angered bear straight back to you. Leave pets at home or keep them leashed.

- Hike in a group. You will naturally make more noise in a group and will discourage a bear charge by your sheer numbers.
- Be alert for signs of bears, including tracks; scat; overturned rocks; trees torn apart, clawed, bitten or rubbed; and fresh diggings or trampled vegetation.

CAMPING IN BLACK BEAR COUNTRY

- *Never feed a black bear!* Most injuries from black bears occur when people try to feed, pet, or crowd them. Bears will nip or cuff bad-mannered humans, as they will bad-mannered bears.
- Generally, a clean area is a bear-free area. In spring, summer, and fall, black bears are constantly roaming and searching for food. Finding none, they move on.
- Bypass campsites with bear tracks, scat, and human garbage. Bears are regular visitors there. If you must camp at such sites, keep a clean camp.
- Reduce or eliminate odors that attract bears. At the campground, store food in airtight containers in your RV or car trunk rather than in the passenger section of the car.
- Do not store food inside a soft-sided camper (pop-up trailer tent) as black bears can easily rip the sides open.
- Fish smells are a strong attractant for bears, so do not clean them in your campsite. Throw entrails into deep or fast-flowing water and/or double-bag fishy-smelling garbage.
- Keep grills, hibachis, and barbecues clean.
- In the backcountry, cook and eat well away from your tent, cleaning up immediately and thoroughly. Do not leave cooking

utensils, coolers, grease, or dish-water lying around.

- Strain your dishwater, putting the solids in with the garbage to be packed out, and then throw the strained water into a gray water (soiled water) pit or pit toilet, or dump the water away from your camp.
- Along with your food, store your garbage out of reach of bears.
- Pack out all your garbage. Do not bury garbage or throw it into pit toilets. Only paper and wood may be burned: plastics, tinfoil, and food items do not burn com-pletely. The remains will attract bears and leave an ugly mess.
- Store fragrant cosmetics such as toothpaste, deodorant, and insect repellent with your food, not inside your tent.
- Sleep in a tent—not under the stars. Most black bears will not enter a tent with people in it.
- When leaving camp, tie tent flaps open so bears can easily check inside.
- Wash food from your face and hands before going to bed, and hang clothing beyond reach of bears if it has food or cooking grease on it.
- Keep empty containers out of sight (in a car trunk or away from camp) or leave them open so bears can easily determine they are empty.
- Some campers experienced with black bears sometimes chase them away before the bears settle in to eat the entire supply of food. *If you take this approach, and it has its risks, make sure the bear has a clear escape route* and then yell, wave, and rush to no nearer than 15 feet of the bear. This is especially effective when several people do it together.
- Especially if you are alone, make noise, yell, clap your hands, bang pots, or throw rocks to scare away a bear.

BACKCOUNTRY FOOD STORAGE

Extra precautions are often necessary in isolated backcountry situations. For example, store your food in sealed plastic bags suspended from a line between two trees. Sometimes you will find that lines or horizontal poles 20 feet above the ground have been installed at some bear-prone campsites. Bears have been known to leap from tree trunks to snatch food bags, and large black bears can reach up nearly nine feet without jump-ing. Slinging the bag over a branch rather than a line or pole is even less likely to stop a bear because it can break small branches and climb out on large ones.

- Sling your food bags over a line or pole supported by two trees so that the bags hang five feet below it, at least 10 feet from the nearest tree trunk, and at least 12 feet above the ground.
- If a branch must be used, sling the bag far out on the tip of a branch larger than four inches in base diameter.
- Bears sometimes chew through ropes to get hanging food bags, so it is best to counterbalance the bag with a second one to avoid tying the rope where a bear can bite it. This parallel bal-ancing act shortens the amount of rope available to the bear. To retrieve counterbalanced bags, use a long stick to push one bag up so the other will descend to within reach.
- Where bears already know about hanging food bags, hang-ing it might be only a delaying tactic giving you time to protect it. Pans hung on the food bag will rattle an alert if a bear is after your foodstuffs.

224

- If food containers smell of food, hang them with the plastic food bags to prevent bears from carrying them off. Food odors in empty containers are minimized if the food, was packed first in plastic bags before being stored in a container.
- Campers, picnickers, and backpackers report that if black bears want food, they will sometimes commit "highway robbery," using threats or bluffs to get it.

LIVING WITH BEARS

If you reside in an area where bears live, take the following precautions to minimize interactions:

- Secure your garbage in bear-proof containers.
- Keep pet food indoors.
- Know that even birdseed can attract bears.
- Keep grills, hibachis, and barbecues clean.
- Use electric fences around gardens, beehives, livestock pens, and compost piles.

WOMEN AND BEARS

In tests, bears have shown interest in menstrual odors, but there is no record of a black bear attacking a menstruating woman. To be on the safe side, however:

- Use tampons instead of pads.
- Store the used materials with the suspended garbage sacks as described above.
- If you are worried about bears, plan your trip so that menstruation is not factor.

STUPID PEOPLE TRICKS

Dozens of injuries, some of them serious, have occurred when people pet or crowd black bears while feeding or photographing them. Under these circumstances, black bears may nip or cuff with little or no warning. People who tease bears with food have been accidentally injured when the bear

quickly tried to take the "bait." Fortunately, when escape is possible, black bears typically behave subordinately toward people. You should not, however, interpret this as a green light to interact foolishly with this wild animal. If you do you, you invite tragedy for yourself and especially for the bear. It's as simple as that.

BLACK BEAR
Ursus americanus

• DANGER
Bites and maulings are potentially lethal.

• ABUNDANCE & RANGE
In the eastern U.S., the black bear is found in northeastern states south into New York and Pennsylvania; in the Appalachian Mountains; parts of Florida, Louisiana, and Arkansas; and along the Gulf coast in national forests and wildlife preserves.

• SIZE
3 to 3.5 feet at the shoulder. Length, 4.5 to 6 feet. Weight to 600 pounds.

• DESCRIPTION
The black bear may also appear brown in eastern U.S. habitats.

• SIMILAR SPECIES

The grizzly bear, the black bear's nearest relative, is not found in the eastern U.S.

• DIET

The black bear is omnivorous, but its diet primarily consists of vegetation including twigs, berries, dandelions, buds, and the cambium layer of trees under the bark. Supplemental items include honey, insects, fish, and small to medium-sized mammals, including carrion.

• REPRODUCTION

Usually two young are born around January to February while the mother is in winter hibernation. She will nurse cubs before they emerge in the spring. The species reproduces slowly, usually only once every three years.

• HABITAT

Black bears are found in forests, swamps, and mountains where tree cover is abundant.

• TRAITS

More tolerant of humans than its other lower-48 western "cousin" the grizzly, this smart, powerful creature is capable of great cunning. Its strong sense of smell in search of food leads it to encounters with humans where habituation almost always leads ultimately to the obligatory death of the bear. "A fed bear is a dead bear."

CHARGING MAMMALS

CHARGE IT!

Many of us remember the charming opening shots of the early 1990s television show *Northern Exposure* where Morty the moose ambled placidly through the quaint streets of Cicely, Alaska. That bit of television magic is a little misleading. Moose and other ungulates (hoofed mammals) such as deer, elk, bison, and wild boar can pose a significant danger. Even though the odds of an encounter are quite infrequent, camera-happy campers and unsuspecting joggers, hikers, or hunters are sometimes victims of a defensive or offensive charge.

The unique danger these animals pose is their tendency to charge when threatened or crowded, especially at certain times of the year when females protect their young or during the rutting season when the males' aggression is at its peak. Even tame and/or captive white-tailed deer bucks can become aggressive during the rut when they have been known to view their human friends as rivals and attack them. Large ungulate females can use their hooves to kick and stomp on a victim, while bulls sometimes lower their heads and use their antlers as an offensive weapon. Hunters, of course, should be wary of animals they falsely presume to be dead.

As reported by the Associated Press in April 2000, in Yellowstone National Park visitors are twice as likely to be injured by bison as they are by grizzly bears. Since 1978, these seemingly placid beasts have charged people 81 times, and two people have died in the park since 1971 from bison attacks. Adult bison stand 5.5 feet at the shoulder and weigh between 1,000 and 2,000 pounds. When provoked (and nearly all attacks stem from provocation, such as when someone approaches too close in hopes of getting a good photo), bison can charge in a fast burst of about 20 miles per hour. As the AP report noted, "People have been butted, thrown into the air, gored, and trampled."

Depending on where you live, these ungulates bear watching out for. Moose are a northern New England and Rockies phenomenon, where they sometimes place their 1,200-or-so pounds in the middle of the road, or once in a blue moon charge a hapless woods walker. Elk live in the northwestern U.S., the Rockies, and down into the southwestern U.S., and they have been reintroduced recently into parts of the southeast in such areas as Tennessee and Kentucky, and even into Pennsylvania east of the Allegheny National Forest. Feral pigs, who can also muster a healthy charge, are found in the southeastern and western U.S., whereas their smaller cousins, the peccaries or javelinas, inhabit southern Texas and Arizona.

Elk

This majestic animal that once commonly ranged throughout most of the U.S. stands up to 5.5 feet tall at the shoulder, stretches to 8 feet in length, weighs up to 1,000 pounds, and can sport a rack of antlers spanning 5 to 6 feet. In the mid-Atlantic states, small pockets of elk still exist, most notably in Pennsylvania.

Elk have a remarkable ability to learn the situations in which humans will harm them. When undisturbed, they readily adjust to humans, as is the case in national parks if humans keep their distance. The most serious elk and human conflicts occur, however, when elk and autos clash and when people get too close to them. Although charging encounters may occur year round, the likelihood of an elk charging and injuring someone is greatest during the spring calving season (females) and fall rut (males) when elk are at the height of their aggressiveness.

In situations of conflict, elk retain a weak tendency to bite, but most commonly they will use their front hooves, or in the case of bulls, antlers that can sufficiently gore another elk or a (much smaller) human. To use its front legs to the fullest effect, the animal rises on its hind legs. Elk will also deliver a blow simply by raising a front leg and smacking an opponent or giving him a push.

SIGNS OF IMMINENT ELK AGGRESSION

The following signs and actions are behaviors elk display among themselves, and it follows that these are the types of warnings that should signal trouble for you, too.

- Rapidly raising a front leg.
- Snapping a front leg hard on the ground, producing an audible sound.
- Raising the head and forebody while orienting toward the opponent, plus laying back the ears.
- Elk cows, in particular, have the capacity to bite. In the threat mode with each other, this means retracting the upper lip to expose rudimentary canines, grinding the teeth, and uttering a soft hissing sound. In full intensity, the nose points almost upward, the eyes roll forward as if to maintain the slit of the pupil horizontally, and the tongue may protrude from the side of the mouth. Yet, instead of biting, this behavior is followed by a sudden leaping upward to flail with the leg.

- Threatening bulls will spring into a rush and either attempt to gore the opponent or terminate the rush with ground slapping the moment the opponent makes any movement to terminate contact, particularly if the latter averts its eyes. Elk do not often use a rush threat (a threatened charge, signaled by a short rush with head elevated).
- Bull elk with velvet-less antlers threaten by snapping the antlers forward at an opponent.
- Although cow elk do not have antlers, they may use a "horn threat" occasionally, and even butt an opponent.

Overt aggression certainly is not very common in elk, but it does flare up when the animals are excited or crowded, and thus denied freedom of action, something to keep in mind when observing them in the wild.

Asking an elk to dance is a faux pas: you should never find yourself close enough to a wild elk to fear its hooves or its teeth. If for some reason an elk charges you, which is quite, quite unlikely unless you are being almost unimaginably foolish, probably your best bet is to try to climb a tree. Since elk can run up to 35 miles an hour and are quite able swimmers, if you can't climb a tree or duck into a very nearby enclosure, it just might be time to invoke St. Vitus, that patron saint of animal attacks.

ELK
Cervus elaphus

• DANGER
Elk can injure humans by charging and causing automobile accidents.

• ABUNDANCE & RANGE
Elk are not common in the mid-Atlantic, but small herds do exist, most notably in Pennsylvania.

• SIZE
Height to 5 feet at the shoulder. Weight to 1,000 pounds.

• DESCRIPTION
An elk is a very large member of the deer family. It has a broad neck, slender legs, and a brown to tan upper body with darker underbelly. Rump and tail are whitish-yellow. Males have large antlers to five feet in diameter with many tines.

• SIMILAR SPECIES
Moose, the elk's nearest relative, are not found in the mid-Atlantic.

• DIET
Elk feed on vegetation including grasses, twigs, bark, and crops where available.

• REPRODUCTION
Mating season extends from August to November and is busiest in October

and November. A cow gives birth to one to two calves nine months later who weigh about 25 to 40 pounds at delivery.

• HABITAT

Elk are found in meadows, forest edges near water, and valleys.

• TRAITS

Elk are not particularly aggressive and do not have the moose reputation of contentiousness, but males in particular can inflict damage when aroused through crowding, especially during the mating season. The bull's bugle, a challenge to other bulls and a sign of domination to cows, commences with a bellow that changes quickly to a screaming whistle and finishes with grunts. Elk are primarily nocturnal, and they are particularly active at dawn and dusk. They are also known as "Wapiti," a Native American word for "white," in reference to the elk's light-colored rump and tail.

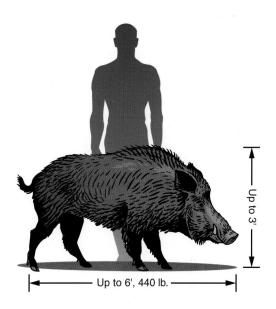

Large feral pig compared to human size.

Feral Pigs

Peter was paddling easily, blissfully taking in the early summer serenity of the filtered sunlight and the softness of the southern Louisiana swamp. "Ah, water, I love it," he mused, and then, perhaps by liquid association, he realized he needed to urinate. Selecting a stretch of firm ground, he gracefully climbed out of the canoe, still drifting mentally. Just as he was letting loose, Peter was startled, shocked, and a bit scared to find that a pack of about 20 to 30 wild pigs were charging straight for him, and they were, may we say, "pissed." Peter slung himself back in the boat in double time and started paddling with a vengeance, grateful to leave the hairy, horned defenders snorting and staring at him from the bank. What Peter didn't know at the time

was that the water was no impediment to the pigs. The wild porker pack could have easily swum after Peter but just decided to let him off easily that time.

How common is Peter's experience? We bet it's pretty rare, but in the world of the great outdoors you, too, could be chased by a wild pig or even a small herd of them. This doesn't seem like such a big deal when you think of domestic pigs, but feral pigs are a whole 'nother side o' bacon. For starters, they are much faster on their feet than domestic pigs, and they are good swimmers, too. But that doesn't really convey the essence of the beast. Here's how Gordon Grice describes them in his elegant, entertaining book, *The Red Hourglass: Lives of the Predators*:

A wild pig is quite a different animal than a captive one, and the captive pigs of today are much different than any, wild

or captive, that lived three hundred years ago. A wild pig, even when well fed, looks lean and razorbacked. It's long-snouted and hirsute. It rides high on thin legs. It has a set of tusks perfect for eviscerating other animals. Domestic pigs have tusks too, but most farmers trim them for safety reasons.

The tusks can amputate a human limb. Once, a friend of mine helped two friends trying to restrain a huge domestic boar so that its tusks could be cut. To control a pig, you put a loop of wire around its sensitive rooter (the flat disk at the end of its snout) and pull up. The pig holds still for fear of hurting itself. This boar caught on to the plan and tossed the men aside, refusing to let his nose be wired. One of the men decided to knock the boar unconscious so they could get on with the clipping. He swung a two-by-four at the boar's head. The boar bit it in half in midswing. The men apologized and left the pen. (Grice, 1998, p. 178)

PIGS IN PARADISE

The feral pig arrived in North America in 1893 when a herd of 50 animals was brought from Germany's Black Forest to a hunting preserve in New Hampshire's Blue Mountains. Other wild populations were released in 1910 and 1912 on the North Carolina and Tennessee border, and in the 1920s near Monterey and on Santa Cruz Island, California. The pure-blooded feral pig can still be found in the wild in North Carolina, Tennessee, California, and in hunting preserves in other states. Throughout their range, the undomesticated ones have also interbred with feral descendants of domestic pigs, who, it seems, return to their wilder ways within just a few generations.

A PIG WITH A POKE

Feral pigs, also known as wild boar or feral hogs, do exhibit many of the same behavioral characteristics as domestic pigs, such as wallowing in mud to protect themselves from the heat and from the sun's harmful rays. In contrast, wild boar are primarily active during twilight and during the dark hours of the day. Although much larger groups often exist, the social structure of wild populations usually consists of herds of about 20 sows, called "drifts," or "sounders." The males spend their time either alone or in small groups except for a brief period during breeding season, usually about January or February and then again in early summer. While the males are usually only aggressive during the rut, the females are territorial and very protective of their young during farrowing (birth) and for some time afterward.

Wild boar are potentially dangerous because of their size (up to six feet long, three feet high, and up to 440 pounds, though the vast majority are smaller) and their tusks (usually three to five inches long, though they can be up to nine inches long) that can slash flesh easily. Adults typically stand only one-and-a-half to two feet tall and forage in groups sometimes numbering more than a dozen. Like many animals, pigs are emboldened by the size of their group and are more aggressive towards humans en masse than when encountered singly or in groups of five or fewer. Even in groups, they don't often attack unless provoked. In order to ensure safety, however, they should not be approached for the first few weeks after having given birth, which might be a hard thing to know in advance of meeting one. The best advice we can give you is just to know they're out there, and they've got an agenda. It's the same as yours: survive and perpetuate the species.

REPRODUCTION

Though they may mate anytime, these wild pigs usually do so twice per year: summer and winter. After 16 weeks gestation, litters of 3 to 12 young are born with pale stripes on their sides that diminish with age.

HABITAT

They are found in swamps, mountain forests, ridges, and in scrub brush.

TRAITS

Usually found in herds of about 12, these pigs may band together to form groups of 50 individuals.

FERAL PIG
Sus scrofa

• DANGER
Feral pigs will charge.

• ABUNDANCE & RANGE
In the mid-Atlantic region, feral pigs can be found chiefly in West Virginia and Pennsylvania, but they are not abundant.

• SIZE
Height to 3 feet at the shoulder. Body 4 to 6 feet in length weighs up to 440 pounds.

• DESCRIPTION
Most feral pigs are black, sometimes with white, but color may also vary to brown or gray. Strong snout is framed by tusks three to nine inches long that are actually canine teeth that curl out and up. The tail always hangs straight.

• SIMILAR SPECIES
The domestic pig almost always has a coiled tail, is larger with a rounder body and shorter legs, but lacks tusks. Domestic and feral interbreeds show various characteristics of both.

• DIET
The feral pig is omnivorous.

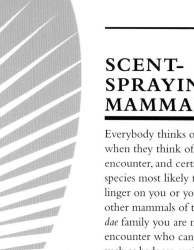

SCENT-SPRAYING MAMMALS

Everybody thinks of skunks first when they think of an odoriferous encounter, and certainly they are the species most likely to let their "love" linger on you or your pet. There are other mammals of the same *Mustedlidae* family you are much less likely to encounter who can also "let it fly," such as badgers, wolverines, minks, and weasels. For some of these species, the scent release is a form of marking and sexual attraction rather than defense, but a skunk's spray speaks clearly, saying, "Stay away!"

Skunks

Skunks of one kind or another are found throughout the U.S., with the striped skunk the one most commonly encountered. Skunks only spray when threatened; there are several accounts of peaceful coexistence between skunks and humans. It is true that de-scented skunks (this must be done at a very early age) make good pets, behaving similarly to cats. In the wild, though, the skunk you or your dog encounter will likely initiate defensive action rather quickly. Even so, skunks will probably first demonstrate the following behaviors before they send the spray (which is not urine) at you or Fido.

WARNING SIGNS BEFORE A SKUNK SPRAYS

- Bushing out its fur.
- Shaking its tail.
- Stamping the ground with its forefeet.
- Growling.
- Turning its head and spitting.

If a skunk turns its body into a U-shape or does a handstand (no kidding), run, run, run away. If a skunk aims its anus at you, get ready to dodge a 15-foot fan-patterned spray fired with precision accuracy. Skunks have teeth, and they can bite, but they rarely need to use them, so effective is their special formula.

A skunk's special formula is a yellow oil composed of thiols and thioacetate derivatives of these thiols, a substance stored in two walnut-sized glands with openings in the anus. Generally, a skunk can store enough for about five to six sprays, but because replenishment takes time, skunks are judicious about the spray and only fire when they feel they really need to. The human nose can detect skunk spray thiols at about 10 parts per billion, and anybody who has driven country roads with open windows knows it is a unique and powerful scent. It is so powerful and long-lasting, in fact, that the offending elements are chemically removed and the remaining substance is used in perfume manufacture.

DE-SKUNKING PETS: THE MYTH OF TOMATO JUICE

Bonnie is a nosy dog who has been "skunked" more than once. The first time, the spray was administered at such close range that Bonnie's white face fur was yellow. She received a good blast in the eyes, but seemed to have no blindness, temporary or otherwise. Flushing her face with water from a garden hose to reduce the concentration in her eyes was the first order of business. Next came the tomato juice treatment, which some people swear by. We thought it was just a messy failure.

William F. Wood of the Department of Chemistry at Humboldt State University agrees. "Bathing an animal in tomato juice seems to work because at high doses of skunk spray the human nose quits smelling the odor (olfactory fatigue). When this happens, the odor of tomato juice can easily be detected. A person suffering olfactory fatigue to skunk spray will swear that the skunk odor is gone and was neutralized by the tomato juice. Another person coming on the scene at this point will readily confirm that the skunk spray has not been neutralized by the tomato juice. To neutralize or deodorize skunk spray, the chemicals in the secretion must be changed to a different type of molecule. Tomato juice does not work."

Although, thank goodness, we haven't had a chance to try it lately, another chemist, Paul Krebaum concocted these chemically based "antidotes" to skunk spray:

Be careful not to get this solution in your pet's eyes.

For pets that have been sprayed, bathe the animal in a mixture of:

- 1 quart of 3% hydrogen peroxide (from drug store),
- ¼ cup of baking soda (sodium bicarbonate), and
- 1 teaspoon of liquid detergent.
- After 5 minutes, rinse the animal with water.
- Repeat if necessary.

The mixture must be used immediately and will not work if it is stored for any length of time. *Do not store in a closed container. The oxygen gas that forms could break the container.*

Note: This mixture may bleach the pet's hair. Rumor has it that a black Labrador became a chocolate after her deskunking treatment, but since fur grows out, the interval of a pleasant-smelling pet seems a small price to pay.

SKUNK SPRAY ON YOUR CLOTHES AND CLEAN-UP TOWELS AND RAGS

After conducting this pet treatment outside to prevent odor contamination in your house, wash your clothes and/or rags sullied in this procedure with one cup of liquid laundry bleach per gallon of water.

SKUNK SPRAY ON BUILDINGS AND DECKS

To sanitize the exterior of buildings, deck surfaces, etc., apply a solution of liquid laundry (Clorox®) bleach (one cup per gallon) *Caution: This may bleach the surface, so try it first on a small area if colorfastness could be a problem.*

The bleach must come in contact with the spot where the secretion was sprayed. Repeated applications may be necessary for large amounts of the skunk spray. *Do not use this solution on pets.*

SKUNK SPRAY OVER A LARGE AREA OR TRAPPED IN A HOUSE

Time and adequate ventilation alone will help. Sorry!

MINIMIZING SKUNK ENCOUNTERS

Beyond the spray factor, skunks are carriers of rabies. Here are some suggestions for discouraging their presence:

- Do not feed the skunks.
- Do not leave pet food outside or discard edible garbage skunks can access.
- Secure garbage containers.
- Keep pet doors closed at night to prevent illegal entry by a skunk.
- Keep fruit trees picked and do not leave rotted fruit on the ground.
- Skunks are attracted to birdseed and to the birds and rodents that use the feeder.

- If possible, eliminate outdoor sources of water.
- If a skunk wanders into your garage, leave an outside door open and let the skunk leave in its own good time.
- Securely enclose chickens, especially at night, making sure the fencing has no holes and that it extends six to eight inches underground to prevent skunks and other animals from digging under.
- To eliminate suitable nesting cavities, remove debris and brush piles or at least stack them neatly.

Living with Wildlife: How to Enjoy, Cope with, and Protect North America's Wild Creatures Around Your Home and Theirs by the California Center for Wildlife with Diana Landau and Shelley Stump and Bill Adler, Jr.'s *Outwitting Critters: A Human Guide for Confronting Devious Animals and Winning* are good resources for solutions to other skunk-related problems, such as when skunks want to live under your house.

STRIPED SKUNK
Mephitis mephitis

• DANGER
The main hazard skunks pose is spraying, but a bite is potentially fatal as the animal is a carrier of rabies.

• ABUNDANCE & RANGE
These skunks are common throughout the U.S. with the exception of the southern tip of Florida and a small corner of the southwestern U.S.

• SIZE
Up to 31 inches in length, including a tail of 5 to 9 inches.

• DESCRIPTION
They are black with two broad white stripes that begin as a cap on the head and run the length of the upper body and down the tail.

• SIMILAR SPECIES
The spotted skunk has more mottled black and white markings.

• DIET
The skunk is omnivorous, eating berries, insects, grubs, bird eggs, amphibians, and small mammals.

• REPRODUCTION
Breeding occurs February to April with litters of four to seven born in May.

• HABITAT
Skunks are found in suburbs, forests, grasses, and desert lands.

• TRAITS
Mother skunk is extremely protective of her young and will spray to defend. Both sexes generally give warning postures before powerful, foul-smelling, long-lasting spray is released.

EASTERN SPOTTED SKUNK

Spilogale putorius

• DANGER

Like the striped skunk, the eastern spotted sprays, and its bite is potentially fatal as the animal is a carrier of rabies.

• ABUNDANCE & RANGE

In the mid-Atlantic region, this skunk is in found in Virginia, West Virginia, Maryland, Delaware, southern New Jersey, and southern Pennsylvania.

• SIZE

Up to 22 inches in length, including a tail of 3 to 8.5 inches.

• DESCRIPTION

The eastern spotted skunk is black with various patterns of white markings on head and body. Tail is white-tipped.

• SIMILAR SPECIES

The striped skunk has marked patterning of stripes along its back.

• DIET

Primarily carnivorous, this skunk favors small mammals, but will also feast on grubs, insects, and berries.

• REPRODUCTION

Litters of two to six are born in mid-spring.

• HABITAT

These skunks are usually found near water in forests, farmlands, and brushy, rocky areas.

• TRAITS

The eastern spotted does not spray unless provoked and then turns its back to its opponent, performing a handstand to release the spray up to 12 feet.

PORCUPINES

Linguistically speaking, porcupines meander to us through Middle English, Middle French, and Old Italian, originating with the Latin for "pig prickle" (porcus + spina). They are not pigs, however; they are rodents, and they take the red ribbon for being the second largest rodent on the North American continent. (Beavers take the blue ribbon.) Porcupines can grow up to well over a yard in length including their tail, and they weigh in at up to 40 pounds. Most are much smaller, but it's not the size of the porcupine that makes it a worthy opponent. It's the 30,000 barbed quills that each animal packs that are of concern to you, and especially to your dog.

HEAVE HO? NO.

These quills can reach four inches in length. They are actually modified hairs attached loosely to the animal, and they are mostly hollow along the shaft. It is a myth that porcupines can "throw" their quills. When the animal is relaxed, the hair and quills lie flat and point backwards. When threatened, the porcupine draws up the skin of the back to expose quills facing all directions, and then it turns around to present its menacing, bristling back to its attacker. If further angered, the porcupine swings its tail, and if it makes contact with the enemy, the loosely attached quills are easily and often deeply embedded into the opponent. When you think how dogs often investigate with their face, you see the potential disaster clearly. The tail quills are the most dangerous because they can be driven in with the force of the tail's action.

QUILL REMOVAL

The quills are so tough to remove that the field treatment recommendation is to use pliers (!) or surgical hemostats (powerful clamps). It probably doesn't help to cut the end off the quill to "open the quill's vacuum" to make removal easier, although experts disagree on this point. Except in extreme conditions, don't try to remove the quills yourself. Instead, get your pet to your veterinarian quickly so that the removal can take place under anesthesia because extrication is very painful. Especially if your pet has a quill in its eye, do not attempt removal yourself, and get the animal to a vet without delay. Even if you do pull the quills yourself, make sure your animal sees a vet very soon after the event as antibiotics are frequently needed to stem infections.

Removal sooner rather than later is definitely advised, too, since the warm body temperature of the punctured victim causes the quills to expand, more securely lodging the inverted barbs in the animal. Left untreated, the quills can, in the right circumstances, actually work their way farther into the body, possibly eventually puncturing vital organs. More commonly however, a wild attacker will suffer a starving death as the quills embedded in the face and mouth make capturing and eating pray impossible.

THE GOOD NEWS

The good news is that porcupines are nocturnal, solitary, nonaggressive animals, and they would much rather retreat up a tree than fight. The best way to protect your animals is not to let them roam freely where porcupines live, especially not at night. Porcupines are strict vegetarians, and one sure sign of their presence are "niptwigs." These are tree branches that have been neatly gnawed off by the animal and then stripped of buds or leaves for food. Under such porcupine favorites as sugar maples, beech, basswood, aspen, and apple trees, it is common to find niptwigs littering the ground. Irregular patches of bark stripped from tree trunks are another sign.

COMMON PORCUPINE

Erethizon dorsatum

• DANGER

Puncture wounds from quills that can prove fatal (usually from infection) if left untreated. Dogs are much more commonly wounded than humans.

• ABUNDANCE & RANGE

In the eastern U.S., porcupines are found in Pennsylvania and New York and then north into New England. They are distributed throughout the western states.

• SIZE

32 inches to 49 inches in length including the tail. 7 to 40 pounds.

• DESCRIPTION

The porcupine has a small head on a large, chunky body with a high arching back and short legs. In the eastern regions, the animal is black or brownish; in western habitats, it is yellowish in color. Guard hairs cover the chest, and detachable quills cover the back and rump.

• SIMILAR SPECIES

None. The porcupine's distinctive quills set it apart.

• DIET

This creature is a strict vegetarian who subsists on leaves, twigs, bark, and other green material.

• REPRODUCTION

After mating in the fall, one young is born in the late spring.

• HABITAT

The porcupine can be found in coniferous, deciduous, or mixed forests; in desert territory, it favors scrubby areas with some trees.

• TRAITS

The slow, ambling porcupine relies on its quills for protection. It is not at all aggressive, and it only uses its formidable quills for defense.

• COMMENTS

Porcupines love salt and have been known to chew the wooden handles of tools for the salt residue left by human hands. Even though the porcupine is a climber by nature, it falls from trees fairly often, as evidenced by the one-third of museum specimen skeletons with bone fractures.

MAMMAL-BORNE DISEASES

Rabies

Rabies looms large on the radar of those folks who fear certain mammals. This preventable viral inflammation of the brain that affects mammals is most often transmitted through the bite of a rabid animal. The vast majority of rabies cases reported to the Centers for Disease Control and Prevention (CDC) each year occur in wild animals like raccoons, skunks, bats, and foxes. Domestic animals account for less than 10% of the reported rabies cases, and although most people are aware that domestic dogs and cats can carry rabies, you should also know that cattle and horses (and other equines) can, too. (As it has for many diseases and conditions, the CDC has an excellent series of web pages on rabies, and much of the information contained in this section is from that source: www.cdc.gov/ncidod/dvrd/rabies/introduction/intro.htm.)

Before 1960, the majority of rabies cases were in domestic animals. The principal rabies hosts today are wild carnivores and bats (but see the information below on bats before you start screaming at twilight). The number of rabies–related human deaths in the U.S. has declined from more than 100 annually at the turn of the century to one or two per year in the 1990s because modern prevention has proven nearly 100% successful. In the U.S., human fatalities associated with rabies occur in people who fail to seek medical assis-

tance, usually because they were unaware of their exposure. If you are an international traveler, however, you need to know that exposure to rabid dogs is still the cause of more than 90% of human exposures to rabies and of more than 99% of human rabies deaths worldwide. Exact global statistics are not known, but the bottom line is this: don't pet dogs you don't know when you are traveling, or for that matter, don't pet unknown dogs in your own neighborhood either.

SYMPTOMS OF RABIES

Rabies virus infects the central nervous system and ultimately causes death. Early symptoms of rabies in humans are nonspecific:

- Fever.
- Headache.
- General malaise.

As the disease progresses, neurological symptoms appear:

- Insomnia.
- Anxiety.
- Confusion.
- Slight or partial paralysis.
- Excitation.
- Hallucinations.
- Agitation.
- Hyper-salivation.
- Difficulty swallowing.
- Hydrophobia (fear of water).

Death usually occurs within days of the onset of symptoms. Once symptoms have appeared, the treatment for rabies is ineffective.

RABIES VACCINE AND IMMUNE GLOBULIN

There is no treatment for rabies after symptoms of the disease appear, but two decades ago, scientists developed an extremely effective new rabies vaccine regimen that provides immunity to rabies when administered after an exposure (post-exposure-prophylaxis) or for protection before an exposure occurs (pre-exposure

Rabies cycle in a common raccoon: **(1)** *The raccoon is bitten by a rabid animal, and the rabies virus enters through infected saliva.* **(2)** *The virus spreads through the nerves to the spinal cord and brain, incubating for 3–12 weeks, during which the raccoon shows no signs of illness.* **(3)** *When it reaches the brain, the virus multiplies rapidly, passing to the salivary glands; at this point, the raccoon shows signs of the disease and becomes rabid.* **(4)** *The infected animal usually dies within seven days of becoming outwardly sick.*

prophylaxis). Although rabies among humans is rare in the U.S., every year an estimated 18,000 people receive rabies pre-exposure-prophylaxis and an additional 40,000 receive post-exposure-prophylaxis.

Pre-exposure prophylaxis consists of three doses of rabies vaccine given on days 0, 7, and 21 or 28, and is recommended for:

- Persons in high-risk groups, such as veterinarians, animal handlers, and certain laboratory workers.
- Other persons whose activities bring them into frequent contact with the rabies virus or potentially rabid bats, raccoons, skunks, cats, dogs, or other species at risk of having rabies.
- International travelers likely to come in contact with animals in areas of constantly present dog rabies that lack immediate access to appropriate medical care.

Although pre-exposure vaccination does not eliminate the need for additional medical attention after a rabies exposure, it simplifies therapy by eliminating the need for human rabies immune globulin (HRIG) and decreasing the number of vaccine doses needed. This is of particular importance for persons at high risk of exposure to rabies in areas where immunizing products may not be available. It also minimizes adverse reactions to multiple doses of vaccine and may enhance immunity in persons whose post-exposure therapy might be delayed. Finally, it may provide protection to persons with nonapparent exposures to rabies.

Post-exposure prophylaxis (PEP) is indicated for persons possibly exposed to a rabid animal. Possible exposures include animal bites or mucous membrane contamination with infectious tissue, such as saliva.

PEP should begin as soon as possible after an exposure, but it is a medical urgency, not emergency. You should get medical care as soon as possible, but there is no need for panic and fear. There have been no vaccine failures in the U.S. (meaning, no one developed rabies) when PEP was given promptly and appropriately after an exposure. Physicians should evaluate each possible exposure to rabies, and as necessary, consult with local or state public health officials regarding the appropriate need for rabies prophylaxis.

In the U.S., PEP consists of a regimen of one dose of immune globulin and five doses of rabies vaccine over a 28-day period. Rabies immune globulin and the first dose of rabies vaccine should be given as soon as possible after exposure. Additional doses of rabies vaccine should be given on days 3, 7, 14, and 28 after the first vaccination. Current vaccines are relatively painless and are given in your arm, like a flu or tetanus vaccine. The days of the long needle into your stomach are long gone.

TRANSMISSION OF RABIES

Transmission of the virus usually begins when the infected saliva of a host is passed to an uninfected animal. Various routes of transmission include contamination of mucous membranes (i.e., eyes, nose, mouth), aerosol transmission, and corneal transplantations. The most common mode of rabies transmission, however, is through the bite and virus-containing saliva of an infected host.

After primary infection, the virus undergoes an eclipse phase in which it cannot be detected easily within the host, an interval that may last for several days or months. Following uptake into peripheral nerves, rabies virus is transported to the central nervous system (CNS). The incubation period is the time of exposure to onset of clinical signs of disease, and it may vary from a few days to several years—but it typically lasts one to three months. Dissemination of virus within the CNS is rapid, and it is during this period of cerebral infection that classic behavioral changes develop.

WHAT TO DO AFTER A POSSIBLE EXPOSURE TO RABIES

If you are exposed to a potentially rabid animal, wash the wound thoroughly with soap and water, and seek medical attention immediately. A health care provider will care for the wound and will assess the risk for rabies exposure. The following information will help your health care provider assess your risk:

- Geographic location of the incident.
- Type of animal that was involved.
- How the exposure occurred (provoked or unprovoked).
- Vaccination status of animal.
- Whether the animal can be safely captured and tested for rabies.

Steps taken by the health care practitioner will depend on the circumstances of the bite. Your health care practitioner should consult state or local health departments, veterinarians, or animal control officers to make an informed assessment of the incident and to request assistance. The important factor is that you seek care promptly after you are bitten by any animal.

RABIES LINKED TO SPECIES AND GEOGRAPHY

According to the most recent data collected by the CDC in 1998, 49 states, the District of Columbia, and Puerto Rico reported 7,962 cases of rabies in animals and one case in humans, down by 6.5% from the 1977 counts. (Hawaii is the only state that

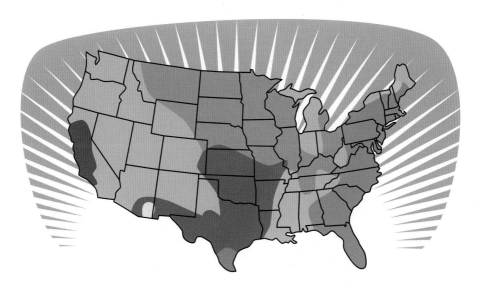

| Raccoon | Fox | Fox | Fox |
| Skunk | Skunk | Skunk | Coyote |

Major strains of the rabies virus in the continental United States. Rabies strains are indicated by primary carrier, but strains may be carried by different species. The variant of bat rabies is found throughout this range.

has never reported an indigenously acquired rabies case in humans or animals, so now when you're surfing you can quit worrying.) In line with previously indicated data, wild animals accounted for nearly 93% of reported cases of rabies in 1998.

The breakdown of reported cases in animals is as follows:

Raccoons 44.0%
Skunks 28.5%
Bats 2.5%
Foxes 5.5%
Other wild animals, including rodents and lagomorphs (rabbits) . . . .1.6%.

Domestic species accounted for 7.6% of all rabid animals reported in the United States in 1998, a decrease of 1.2% from the 610 cases reported in 1997 to 603 in 1998. In 1998, cases of rabies in dogs, cats, and cattle decreased 10.3%, 6%, and 4.9% respectively, whereas those in horses and mules increased 74.5%, compared to 1997 figures. Rabies cases in cats continue to be more than twice as numerous as in dogs or cattle. For a little bit more rabies trivia, Iowa reported the largest number of rabid domestic animals (70) for any state, followed closely by Pennsylvania (50).

SIGNS OF RABIES IN ANIMALS

Depending on where you live in the mid-Atlantic, you should be especially wary of skunks and raccoons that behave abnormally, though any mammal can have rabies.

Animals with rabies may act differently than healthy animals. Wild animals may move slowly or act tame. A pet that is usually friendly may snap at you and try to bite. Some wild animals that normally avoid porcupines, like foxes, raccoons, and skunks, may receive a face full of quills if they become rabid and try to bite these prickly rodents.

There are two common categories of rabies. One type is "furious" rabies.

Animals with this type are hostile, may bite at objects, and have an increase in saliva. In the movies and in books, rabid animals foam at the mouth. In real life, rabid animals look like they have foam in their mouths because they have more saliva.

The second and more common form is known as paralytic or "dumb" rabies. An animal with "dumb" rabies is timid and shy. It often rejects food and has paralysis of the lower jaw and muscles.

Other general rabies signs include:
• Changes in behavior.
• General sickness.
• Problems swallowing.
• Increased drool or saliva.
• Abnormally tame or sick wild animals.
• Biting at everything if excited.
• Difficulty moving or paralysis.
• Death.

WHAT HAPPENS IF A NEIGHBORHOOD DOG OR CAT BITES ME?

Although rabies is uncommon in dogs, cats, and ferrets in the U.S., you should seek medical evaluation for any animal bite. If the cat (or dog or ferret) appeared healthy at the time you were bitten, it can be confined by its owner for 10 days and observed, and no anti-rabies prophylaxis is needed. No person in the U.S. has ever contracted rabies from a dog, cat, or ferret held in quarantine for 10 days. If a dog, cat, or ferret appeared ill at the time it bit you or becomes ill during the 10-day quarantine, it should be evaluated by a veterinarian for signs of rabies and you should seek medical advice about the need for anti-rabies prophylaxis. The quarantine period is a precaution against the remote possibility that an animal may appear healthy but actually be sick with rabies. During the incubation period, which may last for weeks to months, the animal does not appear ill. A bite by the animal during the incubation period does not carry a risk of rabies because the virus is not in saliva. Only late in the disease, after the virus has reached the brain and multiplied there to cause an encephalitis (or inflammation of the brain), does the virus move from the brain to the salivary glands and saliva. Also at this time, after the virus has multiplied in the brain, almost all animals begin to show the first signs of rabies. Most of these signs are obvious even to an untrained observer, but within a short period of time, usually within three to five days, the virus has caused enough damage to the brain that the animal begins to show unmistakable signs of rabies. So, as an added precaution, the quarantine period is lengthened to 10 days total.

WHAT HAPPENS IF MY PET IS BITTEN BY A WILD ANIMAL?

Any animal bitten or scratched by either a wild, carnivorous mammal or a bat that is not available for testing should be regarded as having been exposed to rabies. According to the CDC, unvaccinated dogs, cats, and ferrets exposed to a rabid animal should be euthanized immediately. If the owner is unwilling to have this done, the animal should be placed in strict isolation for six months and vaccinated one month before being released. Animals with expired vaccinations need to be evaluated on a case-by-case basis. Dogs and cats that are currently vaccinated are kept under observation for 45 days.

RABIES-FREE ZONE

Small rodents (such as squirrels, rats, mice, hamsters, guinea pigs, gerbils, and chipmunks) and lagomorphs (such as rabbits and hares) are almost never found to be infected with rabies and have not been known to cause rabies among humans in the U.S. Bites by these animals are usually not considered a rabies threat unless the animal was sick or behaving in any unusual manner and rabies is widespread in your area. In all cases involving rodents, the state or local health department should be consulted before a decision is made to initiate post-exposure prophylaxis (PEP).

THE BAT RAP

Bats !
Bats go flying in the night,
Some give people a lot of fright,
Most people think they're very scary,
But most of them are just cute and hairy!
—By students Chelsea Reber & Hannah Hansen

From rain forests to deserts, bats play key roles in ecosystems around the globe—especially by eating insects, including agricultural pests. In rural and urban settings, bats can be observed at twilight, dipping and circling in a "loopy" flight pattern that resembles that of a butterfly more than a bird. In a given group of bat watchers, perhaps for lack of something more interesting to say, almost invariably someone will pronounce, "Bats carry rabies, you know." This is a true statement, but one that still requires a sense of proportion. Your risk of exposure is truly tiny, but if you do contract rabies from a bat, you may not know it until it is too late. For this reason and because bats are small enough to enter your house without your immediate knowledge, we will devote several pages to this animal's capacity to transmit rabies. *You should not construe this coverage to mean that all bats are dangerous. This is simply not true, and this false notion can deprive you of the pleasure of simply observing them in the wild.*

Of the 37 rabies-related human fatalities from 1981–1998 (which averages one to two per year), the majority (29 cases) had no known exposure to a potentially rabid animal.

Of these, 21 cases proved to have a bat variant of rabies, yet the victim had no record of a bat encounter. This story from the February 12, 1999, issue of *Morbidity and Mortality Weekly Report* will shed some light on the mystery of bat bites and rabies, the leading cause of human deaths from this viral infection.

On December 14, 1998, a 29-year-old inmate at the Nottoway Correctional Center in Nottoway County, Virginia, developed malaise and back pain while working on a roadside clean-up crew. He sought medical care at the prison on December 15, complaining of muscle pains, vomiting, and abdominal cramps, and was treated with acetaminophen. His clinical signs progressed to include persistent right wrist pain, muscle tremors in his right arm, and difficulty walking. On December 18, the patient was sent to a Richmond emergency department, where he had a temperature of 103° F (39.4° C). He initially was alert and oriented but had visual hallucinations. During the next 12 hours, he became increasingly agitated and less oriented. The patient's condition worsened, with hypersalivation, priapism, and wide fluctuations in body temperature and blood pressure. He was intubated and heavily sedated on December 20, and a diagnosis of rabies was first considered by the patient's physician on that date. Samples sent to CDC for testing on December 21 tested positive for a rabies virus variant associated with eastern pipistrelle bats (Pipistrellus subflavus) and silver-haired bats (Lasionycteris noctivagans). After the removal of all sedatives, the patient showed no purposeful movement and demonstrated loss of brainstem reflexes. He died December 31, 1998, in Richmond, Virginia, from rabies encephalitis caused by a rabies virus variant associated with insectivorous bats, the first case of human rabies in Virginia since 1953.

Family members, friends, and prison staff reported the patient had not indicated

any contact with or bite from an animal in recent months, and prison medical records did not document evidence of a bite or scratch. The patient lived at a work center that housed up to 160 inmates in two separate dormitories. He had worked around the prison on a farm repairing fence lines and feeding cattle, in a paper recycling facility, and along roadsides cleaning up trash and debris. No evidence of bats was found within the prison or on prison grounds, although inmates reported occasionally seeing bats flying near the outdoor lights in the summer. Several stray cats were reported to occasionally approach inmates at the facility; however, the patient was not known to have handled them.

The patient had been incarcerated at Nottoway for approximately six weeks after transfer from another correctional unit. At the other correctional facility, the patient worked inside the prison and on a road crew cutting brush and picking up trash along highways. No evidence of bats was found in the prison, and inmates reported that they had never seen bats inside the facility. Prison staff and inmates reported that they did not recall the patient ever being bitten by an animal while working and that he usually did not handle small animals found by the road crews. So how did he contract rabies?

A definitive history of an animal bite could not be established for this patient, and the most likely explanation is an unrecognized bat bite occurring either at the farm or recycling facility or while the patient was working on a road crew. Because the incubation period for rabies varies from several weeks to several months, he may have contracted rabies before his transfer to Nottoway.

Magic Bat Bites

The reasons for the preponderance of human rabies cases associated with bats remain speculative, but findings suggest that rabies can be transmitted after minor, undetected exposures. Insectivorous bats—such as those implicated in the human rabies deaths in the U.S.—have small teeth that may not cause an obvious wound in human skin. For this reason, it is important to treat persons for rabies exposure when the possibility of a bat bite cannot be reasonably excluded. In all cases where bat-human contact has occurred, the bat should be collected and tested for rabies if that scenario is both possible and safe. If the bat is not available for rabies testing, the need for a post-exposure prophylaxis (PEP), i.e., intervening injections, should be assessed by public health officials familiar with recent recommendations and outbreaks in the area.

Medical personnel should consider rabies as a diagnosis in any case presenting the acute onset and rapid progression of compatible neurologic signs, regardless of whether the patient reports a history of an animal bite. Although early diagnosis cannot save the patient, it may help minimize the number of other potential exposures and the subsequent need for PEP.

How Can I Tell If a Bat Has Rabies?

Rabies can be confirmed only in a laboratory. However, you should be suspicious of any bat that is:
- Active by day.
- Found in a place where bats are not usually seen, for example, in a room in your home or on the lawn.
- Unable to fly.
- Easily approached.

Bats such as these are far more likely than others to be rabid. Therefore, it is best never to handle any bat.

Children and "Injured or Orphaned" Bats

Bats can see at night.
But if a bat falls —Don't touch.
Bats hang upside down.
    —Bat Haiku by Quinn Franklin,
        3rd grader in Arkansas

Children are instinctively drawn to animals, especially those within reach. They will also show concern for creatures they perceive to be orphaned or injured. Bats found on the ground are likely to be ill, perhaps from rabies. For this reason, it is important to teach children what bats look like and not to approach or touch a bat lying on the ground.

What Should I Do If I Come in Contact With a Bat?

If you are bitten by a bat—or if infectious material (such as saliva) from a bat gets into your eyes, nose, mouth, or a wound, wash the affected area thoroughly and get medical advice immediately. Whenever both possible and safe, the bat should be captured and sent to a laboratory for rabies testing.

People usually know when they have been bitten by a bat, but, as we have seen, in rare cases they do not know because bats have small teeth which may leave marks that are not easily seen. In the following situations, the CDC cautions you to seek medical advice and have the bat tested even in the absence of an obvious bite wound:
- If you awaken and find a bat in your room.
- See a bat in the room of an unattended child.

In February 1995, the aunt of a four-year-old girl was awakened by the sounds of a bat in the room where the child was sleeping. The child did not wake up until the bat was captured, killed, and discarded. The girl reported no bite, and no evidence of a bite wound was found when she was examined. One month later, the child became sick and died of rabies. The dead bat was recovered from the yard and tested—it had rabies.

This tragic case demonstrates several points:

- This child's infection with rabies was most likely the result of a bat bite.
- Children sleep heavily and may not awaken from the presence of a small bat.
- A bat bite can be superficial and not easily noticed.
- The bat was behaving abnormally. Instead of hiding, it was making unusual noises and was having difficulty flying. This strange behavior should have led to a strong suspicion of rabies.
- If the bat had been submitted for rabies testing, a positive test would have led to life-saving anti-rabies treatment.

Remember, in situations in which a bat is physically present and you cannot reasonably rule out having been bitten, safely capture the bat for rabies testing and seek medical attention immediately.

When Are Bats Safe?

To repeat, most bats do not have rabies, especially those that are behaving normally (flying at dusk and dark). People cannot get rabies just from seeing a bat in an attic, in a cave, or at a distance. In addition, people cannot get rabies from having contact with bat guano (feces), blood, or urine, or from touching a bat on its fur, even though bats should never be handled!

You can also forget that urban folk tale about bats nesting in your bee-hive hairdo or dive-bombing your pompadour. It just doesn't happen.

What Should I Do If My Pet is Exposed to a Bat?

If you think your pet or domestic animal has been bitten by a bat, contact a veterinarian or your health department for assistance immediately and have the animal tested for rabies. Keeping vaccinations current for cats, dogs, and other animals is

the way to take the worry out of that scenario.

How Can I Keep Bats Out of My Home?

Some bats live in buildings, and there may be no reason to evict them if there is little chance for contact with people. However, bats should always be prevented from entering rooms of your home. For assistance with "bat-proofing" your home, contact an animal control or wildlife conservation agency. If you choose to do the "bat-proofing" yourself:

- Carefully examine your home for holes that might allow bats entry into your living quarters. Any openings larger than a quarter-inch by a half-inch should be caulked.
- Use window screens, chimney caps, and draft-guards beneath doors to attics; fill electrical and plumbing holes with stainless steel wool or caulking; and ensure that all doors to the outside close tightly.
- Additional "bat-proofing" can prevent bats from roosting in attics or buildings by covering outside entry points.
- Observe where the bats exit at dusk and exclude them by loosely hanging clear plastic sheeting or bird netting over these areas so that bats can crawl out and leave, but cannot re-enter. After the bats have been excluded, the openings can be permanently sealed.
- Remember that during summer, many young bats are unable to fly. If you exclude adult bats during this time the young may be trapped inside and die or make their way into living quarters. Thus, if possible, avoid exclusion from May through August.
- Most bats leave in the fall or winter to hibernate, so these are

the best times to "bat-proof" your home.

For more information about "bat-proofing" your home and plenty of other bat information, contact:

Bat Conservation International
P.O. Box 162603
Austin, TX 78716
(512) 327-9721
Fax: (512) 327-9724
Catalog orders and inquiries:
(800) 538-BATS
www.batcon.org

How Can I Safely Capture a Bat in My Home?

If a bat is present in your home and you cannot rule out the possibility of exposure, leave the bat alone and contact an animal control or public health agency for assistance. If professional help is unavailable, use precautions to capture the bat safely.

You will need:
- Leather work gloves.
- Small box or coffee can.
- Piece of cardboard.
- Tape.

When the bat lands, approach it slowly, while wearing the gloves, and place the box or coffee can over it. Slide the cardboard under the container to trap the bat inside. Tape the cardboard to the container securely and punch small air holes in the cardboard. Contact your health department or animal control authority to make arrangements for rabies testing.

If you see a bat in your home and you are sure no human or pet exposure has occurred, confine the bat to a room by closing all doors and windows leading out of the room except those to the outside. The bat will probably leave soon. If not, it can be caught, as described, and released outdoors away from people and pets.

The answer is not to kill any bat you can. Many local populations of

bats have been destroyed and many species are now endangered. This is a substantial loss to all, in part because bat studies have contributed to medical advances—including the development of navigational aids for the blind.

When people think about bats, they often imagine things that are not true. Bats are not blind, nor will they suck your blood—and most do not have rabies.

Preventing Bat-Transmitted Rabies

- Teach children never to handle unfamiliar animals, wild or domestic, even if they appear friendly. "Love your own, leave other animals alone" is a good principle for children to learn.
- Wash any wound from an animal thoroughly with soap and water and seek medical attention immediately.
- Have all dead, sick, or easily captured bats tested for rabies if exposure to people or pets occurs.
- Prevent bats from entering living quarters or occupied spaces in homes, churches, schools, and other areas where they might contact people and pets.
- Be a responsible pet owner by keeping vaccinations current for all dogs, cats, and ferrets; keeping your cats and ferrets inside and your dogs under direct supervision; calling animal control to remove stray animals from your neighborhood; and having your pets spayed or neutered.

Note on bat species: North America supports over 30 species of Vespertilionid bats ("vesper bats"), the family to which most bats belong. While it is difficult to discern individual species, bats as a group are easy to identify. The species profiled here represent but a small sample. All bats are thought to be capable of carrying rabies, so the precautions outlined in this chapter apply to all.

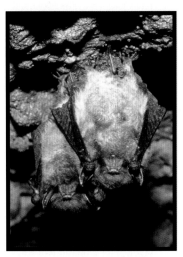

BIG BROWN BAT
Eptesicus fuscus

• DANGER
The bite of the big brown bat, a carrier of rabies, is potentially fatal.

• ABUNDANCE & RANGE
These bats are common throughout the U.S. except in parts of Florida and south central Texas.

• SIZE
3.5 to 5 inches in length.

• DESCRIPTION
One of the largest bats, it has a light to dark brown back with paler belly and fur on its wings. Wingspan is 10 to 13 inches.

• SIMILAR SPECIES
The evening bat is smaller, as are most other bats.

• DIET
Typical fare includes insects, primarily beetles, and especially agricultural pests.

• REPRODUCTION
Fall, winter, or spring mating usually yields a pair of young.

• HABITAT
Big brown bats prefer farmlands, forests, parks, urban areas, tunnels, caves, hollow trees, buildings, and under bridges.

• TRAITS
They are seen occasionally during the day, but more commonly emerge at twilight to pursue their prey. This bat is a boon to farmers in its maintenance of destructive insect populations. It can fly 40 miles per hour. Maternity colonies found in hollow trees, in buildings, or under bridges have up to 600 individuals.

EASTERN PIPISTRELLE BAT
Pipistrellus subflavus

• DANGER
Its bite is potentially fatal as it is a carrier of rabies.

• ABUNDANCE & RANGE
This bat is found in the eastern U.S. south to central Florida.

• SIZE
3 to 3.5 inches in length.

• DESCRIPTION
Red to light brown hairs are dark at base, light in the middle, and then

dark again at the tips. This is the smallest bat.

• **SIMILAR SPECIES**

Other myotises ("mouse-eared bats") lack tricolor arrangement on hair.

• **DIET**

Insects, primarily smaller species, are the eastern pipistrelle's typical fare.

• **REPRODUCTION**

A pair of young are born in June to July. Relatively small maternity colonies of 30 to 35 individuals are found in buildings and tree hollows.

• **HABITAT**

These bats are most commonly found in woodlands, especially near water, but will also roost in caves, tunnels, buildings, and in rock crevices.

• **TRAITS**

The eastern pipistrelle bat emerges in the early evening and flies slowly and erratically. During winter hibernation in mines or caves, their bodies are sometimes covered with water, which makes them seem to sparkle.

Tularemia

Tularemia, also known as rabbit fever, is a disease that can affect both animals and humans. It is caused by a bacteria, *Francisella tularemsis*. Although many wild animals are infected (hares, rabbits, squirrels, muskrats, beavers, deer), occasionally certain domestic animals can be infected (sheep and cats). The rabbit is the species most often involved in disease outbreaks, but the bacteria can also be found in ticks and deer flies.

Tularemia is a sporadic disease that occurs endemically, that is, outbreaks generally are restricted to a particular area or region. Since 1939, there has been a steady decline in the numbers of cases reported, and currently in the U.S., about 150 to 300 cases per year are seen.

The highest incidence of tularemia occurs in the Midwest during the summer months (when ticks are common) and east of the Mississippi during the winter (when cottontail rabbits are hunted).

WHO GETS TULAREMIA?

Hunters, trappers, or others who spend a great deal of time outdoors are at a greater risk of exposure to tularemia than people with other occupational or recreational interests.

HOW IS TULAREMIA SPREAD?

Many routes of human exposure to the tularemia bacteria are known to exist.

The common sources include:
- Inoculation of the skin or mucous membranes with blood or tissue while handling, dressing, or skinning infected animals.
- Contact with fluids from infected flies or ticks.
- The bite of infected ticks.
- Handling or eating insufficiently cooked rabbit or hare meat that can retain its power of infection even after being frozen for several years.

Less common means of spread are:
- Drinking contaminated water.
- Inhaling dust from contaminated soil.
- Handling contaminated pelts or paws of animals.

Tularemia cannot be spread from one person to another. Patients who recover from tularemia will develop a degree of immunity, but re-infection is possible.

SYMPTOMS OF TULAREMIA

Symptoms develop within 1 to 14 days, usually within 3 to 5 days.
- Tularemia is usually recognized by the presence of a skin lesion and swollen glands, sometimes at the point of infection. These

may be accompanied by the sudden onset of high fever.

- Ingestion of the organism may produce a throat infection, intestinal pain, diarrhea, and vomiting.
- Inhalation of the organism may produce a fever alone or combined with a pneumonia-like illness.

TREATMENT OF TULAREMIA

If you think you have tularemia, contact your physician right away. Upon diagnostic confirmation through laboratory tests, you can take antibiotics for the disease. Long-term immunity follows recovery, but re-infection has been reported. Without therapy, fatality rates are 5% (ulceroglandular) to 30% (pneumonic). The mortality rate is about 6%, or fewer than 20 people per year.

PREVENTING TULAREMIA

- Wear rubber gloves when skinning or handling animals, especially rabbits.
- Cook wild game (especially rabbit and squirrel meat) thoroughly before eating.
- Avoid bites of flies and ticks by the use of protective clothing and insect repellents, and check for ticks frequently.
- Avoid drinking untreated water.
- Instruct children not to handle any sick or dead animals.

Hantavirus

The hantavirus leads to Hanta Pulmonary Syndrome (HPS), a disease that can be fatal and is most commonly associated with the southwestern U.S. (especially the "Four Corners" area where the boundaries of New Mexico, Arizona, Colorado, and Utah conjoin). However, according to the CDC, as of Febru-ary 23, 2001, HPS has now been reported in 31 states, including Virginia, West Virginia, Pennsylvania, and New York. While these mid-Atlantic states log only one to four cases each (New Mexico leads the pack with 41 cases), three of the four known carriers of HPS, all rodents, are found in the mid-Atlantic.

HANTA HISTORY

In May 1993, an outbreak of an unexplained pulmonary illness occurred in the southwestern U.S. in the Four Corners area. A young, physically fit Navajo man suffering from shortness of breath was rushed to a hospital in New Mexico and died very rapidly. Reviewing the results of the case, medical personnel discovered that the young man's fiancé had died a few days before after showing similar symptoms, a piece of information that proved key to discovering the disease. As Dr. James Cheek of the Indian Health Service (IHS) noted, "I think if it hadn't been for that initial pair of people that became sick within a week of each other, we never would have discovered the illness at all."

An investigation combing the entire Four Corners region was launched by the New Mexico Office of Medical Investigations (OMI) to find any other people who had a similar case history. Within a few hours, Dr. Bruce Tempest of IHS, working with OMI, had located five young, healthy people who had all died after acute respiratory failure. Tests had failed to identify any of the deaths as caused by a known disease, such as bubonic plague. At this point, the CDC Special Pathogens Branch was notified. The CDC; the state health departments of New Mexico, Colorado, and Utah; the Indian Health Service; the Navajo Nation; and the University of New Mexico all joined together to confront the outbreak.

Remarkably, only six months later in November 1993, the specific hantavirus that caused the Four Corners outbreak was isolated. The Special Pathogens Branch at CDC used tissue from a deer mouse that had been trapped near the New Mexico home of a person who had gotten the disease and grew the virus from it in the laboratory. Shortly afterwards and independently, the U.S. Army Medical Research Institute of Infectious Diseases (USAMRIID) also grew the particular virus that was named Sin Nombre virus (SNV) from a person who had gotten the disease from a California mouse. This SNV is one of several similar viral infections that result in HPS, the condition that causes respiratory failure.

HPS Since the "First" Outbreak

After the initial outbreak, the medical community nationwide was asked to report any cases of illness with symptoms similar to those of HPS that could not be explained by

any other cause. Since 1993, researchers have discovered that there is not just one hantavirus that causes HPS, but several.

In June 1993, a Louisiana bridge inspector who had not traveled to the Four Corners area developed HPS. An investigation was begun, and the patient's tissues were tested for the presence of antibodies to hantavirus. The results led to the discovery of another hantavirus, named Bayou virus, which was linked to a carrier, the rice rat *(Oryzomys palustris)*. In late 1993, a 33-year-old Florida man came down with HPS symptoms; he later recovered. This person also had not traveled to the Four Corners area. A similar investigation revealed yet another hantavirus, named the Black Creek Canal virus, and its carrier, the cotton rat *(Sigmodon hispidus)*. Another case occurred in New York. This time, the Sin Nombre-like virus was named New York-1, and the white-footed mouse *(Peromyscus leucopus)* was implicated as the carrier.

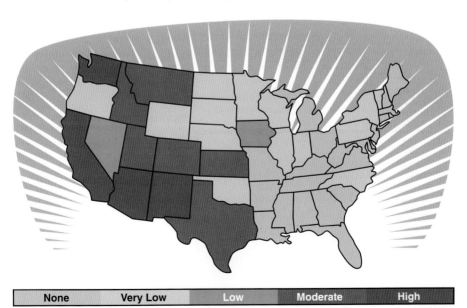

None | Very Low | Low | Moderate | High

Hantavirus pulmonary syndrome risk: 203 cases reported by state, 1994–2001. Source: Centers for Disease Control (information excludes data from 1993 outbreak).

Other early cases of HPS have been discovered by examining samples of tissue belonging to people who had died of unexplained adult respiratory distress syndrome, revealing that the earliest known case of HPS was that of a 38-year-old Utah man in 1959.

Obviously in retrospect, HPS is not a disease of Navajos, but the apparent initial concentration of the disease drew attention to that culture and revealed an interesting fact. While HPS was not known to the epidemiological and medical communities, there is evidence that it was known within Navajo medical traditions and was correctly associated with mice. Just as strikingly, Navajo medical beliefs concur with public health recommendations for preventing the disease.

Navajo Medical Traditions and HPS

In Navajo medical traditions, mice are considered the bearers of an ancient illness that even predates the bubonic plague in the Navajo region. Healers say that when mice enter the home and people come into contact with droppings and urine, the risk of infection arises. The illness enters through the mouth, the nose, or the eyes, and it usually attacks the strongest and

The wood mouse, *Peromyscus leucopus.*

healthiest of the Navajo people. Therefore, traditional medicine prescribes avoiding mice, keeping them out of the hogans, and isolating food supplies. Some of the Navajo elders had predicted the 1993 HPS outbreak. In addition, their oral tradition says that in 1918 and 1933–1934, there were similar outbreaks, after increases in rainfall produced increases in the piñon crop and the number of mice.

Why Did the Outbreak Occur in the Four Corners Area?

The key answer to this question is that during this period there were suddenly many more mice than usual. After a drought of several years, in early 1993 the Four Corners area received heavy snows and rainfall. These helped drought-stricken plants and animals to revive and grow in larger-than-usual numbers. The area's deer mice had plenty to eat, so they reproduced rapidly, generating ten times more mice in May 1993 than in May 1992. With so many mice, it was more likely that mice and humans would come into contact with one another, and thus more likely that the hantavirus carried by the mice would be transmitted to humans.

SYMPTOMS OF HPS

- Early (universal): fever, fatigue, muscle aches.
- Early (about half): headaches, dizziness, chills, abdominal problems.
- Late (universal): coughing, shortness of breath.

Ear ache, sore throat, and rash are very uncommon.

The incubation period (from contraction to symptoms) is unclear because there have been so few cases to study. On the basis of limited information, though, it appears that symptoms may develop between one and five weeks after exposure to potentially infected rodents and their droppings.

Four to 10 days after the initial phase of illness, the late symptoms of HPS appear. These include coughing and shortness of breath, with the sensation of, as one survivor put it, a "tight band around my chest and a pillow over my face" as the lungs fill with fluid.

TREATMENT OF HPS

As yet there is no specific treatment or "cure" for hantavirus infection. However, we do know that if the infected individuals are recognized early and are taken to an intensive care unit, some patients may do better. In intensive care, patients are intubated and given oxygen therapy to help them through the period of severe respiratory distress. If a patient is experiencing full distress, it is less likely the treatment will be effective.

If you have been around rodents and have symptoms of fever, deep muscle aches, and severe shortness of breath, see your doctor immediately. The earlier the patient is brought in to intensive care, the better. Be sure to tell your doctor that you have been around rodents—this will alert your physician to look closely for any rodent-carried disease such as HPS.

HOW IS HANTAVIRUS TRANSMITTED?

The short answer is that some rodents are infected with a type of hantavirus that causes HPS. In the U.S., deer mice, white-footed (or wood) mice, cotton rats, and rice rats are the rodents carrying hantaviruses that cause hantavirus pulmonary syndrome. These rodents shed the virus in their urine, droppings, and saliva. The virus is mainly transmitted to people when they breathe air contaminated with the virus. This happens when fresh rodent urine,

The deer mouse, *Peromyscus maniculatus.*

droppings, or nesting materials are stirred up. When tiny droplets containing the virus get into the air, this process is known as "aerosolization."

There are several other ways rodents may spread hantavirus to people:

- If a rodent with the virus bites someone, the virus may be spread to that person—but this is very rare.
- Researchers believe that you may be able to get the virus if you touch something that has been contaminated with rodent urine, droppings, or saliva, and then touch your nose or mouth.

The marsh rice rat, *Oryzomys palustris.*

- Researchers also suspect that if virus-infected rodent urine, droppings, or saliva contaminates food that you eat, you could also become sick.

These possibilities demonstrate why disinfecting rodent-infested areas is so important in preventing transmission of the virus because transmission can occur anywhere infected rodents reside. ***Common house mice do not carry hantavirus.***

Rodent Species That Carry Hantavirus

Two species of mice, the white-footed or wood mouse *(Peromyscus leucopus)* and the deer mouse *(Peromuscus maniculatus)* are known to carry the virus. These two species that range in size from 4.5 inches to 8.75 inches (excluding the tail) are very difficult to tell apart, in part because their color varies widely depending on location, which can range from woody, brushy areas to cultivated and open habitats.

Two species of rats, the marsh rice rat *(Oryzomys palustris)* and the hispid cotton rat *(Sigmodon hispidus)* are also carriers, ranging in size from 7.25 inches to 14.5 inches (excluding the tail). Although these are somewhat distinguished in color, the untrained eye they would have a difficult time discriminating between them in the grassy, weedy fields where they are found. (The marsh rice rat is, not surprisingly, also found in marshy areas.) The hispid cotton rat is not found in the mid-Atlantic region, but the other three species are.

Although transmission by bite may occur (wherein species identification would prove highly useful information), this form of infection is very rare. Because most transmission is airborne and the immediate physical presence of the animal is not in play (see above), you are better off noticing and avoiding mouse droppings and urine than you are trying to memorize minute species delineations. For this reason, we are not using our typical field guide entry information here but are happy to give you a look at these similar rodents.

Can You Get Hantavirus from Another Person?

No. The types of hantavirus that cause HPS in the U.S. cannot be transmitted from one person to another by touch, saliva, blood, or other bodily fluids.

Can You Get Hantavirus from Animals Other Than Rodents or from Insects?

No. The hantaviruses that cause HPS in the U.S. are not known to be transmitted by any types of animals other than certain species of rodents. You cannot get hantavirus from farm animals such as cows, chickens, or sheep, or from insects, such as mosquitoes, nor from dogs or cats. However, these pets may bring infected rodents into contact with people if they catch such animals and carry them home. Guinea pigs, hamsters, gerbils, and other such pets are not known to carry hantavirus.

The hispid cotton rat, *Sigmodon hispidus.*

WHAT KIND OF ACTIVITIES ARE RISKY?

Anything that puts you in contact with rodent droppings, urine, or nesting materials can place you at risk for infection.

- Opening up cabins and sheds or cleaning outbuildings that have been closed during the winter—such as barns, garages, or storage facilities for farm and construction equipment. Both activities mean you may directly touch rodents or their droppings and/or "stir up the dust," and when you touch or inhale them, you're at risk for infection.
- Hikers and campers can also be exposed when they use infested trail shelters or camp in other rodent habitats.
- Construction and utility workers can be exposed when they work in crawl spaces under houses or in vacant buildings that may have a rodent population.
- Cleaning in and around your own home and really stirring up dust can put you at risk if rodents have made it their home, too. When the weather turns cold, many homes can expect to shelter a few rodents.

Overall, the chance of being exposed to hantavirus is greatest when people work, play, or live in closed spaces where rodents are actively living.

Recent research results show, however, that many people who have become ill with HPS got the disease after having been in frequent contact with rodents and/or their droppings for some time. Many people who have become ill reported that they had not seen rodents or their droppings—at all. Therefore, if you live in an area where the carrier rodents such as the deer mouse are known to live, take sensible precautions before you do activities like those described above—even if you don't see any rodents or their droppings.

PRECAUTIONS FOR CAMPERS AND HIKERS IN THE AFFECTED AREAS

There is no evidence to suggest that travel into areas where HPS has been reported should be restricted simply because most usual tourist activities pose little or no risk of exposure to rodents, their urine, or droppings. However, outdoor enthusiasts who are active in areas where the disease has been reported should take precautions to reduce the likelihood of their exposure to potentially infectious materials.

- Avoid coming into contact with rodents and rodent burrows or disturbing dens (such as pack rat nests).
- Air out and then disinfect cabins or shelters before using them. These places often shelter rodents.
- Do not pitch tents or place sleeping bags in areas in proximity to rodent droppings or burrows or near areas that may shelter rodents or provide food for them (e.g., garbage dumps or woodpiles).
- If possible, do not sleep on the bare ground. In shelters, use a cot with the sleeping surface at least 12 inches above the ground. Use tents with floors or a ground cloth if sleeping in the open air.
- Keep food in rodent-proof containers.
- Promptly bury (or—preferably—burn then bury, when in accordance with local requirements) all garbage and trash, or discard in covered trash containers.
- Use only bottled water or water that has been disinfected by filtration, boiling, chlorination, or iodination for drinking, cooking, washing dishes, and brushing teeth.

- Do not play with or handle any rodents that show up at the camping or hiking site, even if they appear friendly.

PREVENTING HPS

Indoors

- Keep a clean home, especially kitchen (wash dishes, clean counters and floor, keep food covered in rodent-proof containers).
- Keep a tight-fitting lid on garbage, and discard uneaten pet food at the end of the day.
- Set and keep spring-loaded rodent traps. Set traps near baseboards because rodents tend to run along walls and in tight spaces rather than out in the open.
- Set Environmental Protection Agency–approved rodenticide with bait under plywood or plastic shelters along baseboards. These are sometimes known as "covered bait stations." Remember to follow product use instructions carefully since rodenticides are poisonous to pets and people, too.
- If bubonic plague is a problem in your area (see "Fleas" in the Insects and Arachnids chapter), spray flea killer or spread flea powder in the area before setting traps. *This is important.* If you control rodents but do not control fleas as well, you may increase the risk of infection with bubonic plague, since fleas will leave rodents once the rodents die and will seek out other food sources, including humans.
- Seal all entry holes 0.25 inch wide or wider with lath screen or lath metal, cement, wire screening, or other patching materials, inside and out.

Outdoors

- Clear brush, grass, and junk from around house foundations to eliminate a source of nesting materials.
- Use metal flashing around the base of wooden, earthen, or adobe homes to provide a strong metal barrier. Install so that the flashing reaches 12 inches above the ground and six inches down into the ground.
- Elevate hay, woodpiles, and garbage cans to eliminate possible nesting sites. If possible, locate them 100 feet or more from your house.
- Trap rodents outside, too. Poisons or rodenticides may be used as well, but be sure to keep them out of the reach of children or pets.
- Encourage the presence of natural predators, such as nonvenomous snakes, owls, and hawks.
- Remember that getting rid of all rodents may not be feasible, but with ongoing effort you can keep the population very low.

ANIMALS AND AUTOMOBILES

THINGS THAT GO BUMP IN THE NIGHT

We are by far the most dangerous mammal to each other and also to virtually all other animals. It's not just that we obliterate acres of wildlife habitat every day, often for asphalt. It's also that we smash critters with our cars as we motor through their lives, crossing their long-established patterns of migration, mating, and food gathering. This is certainly tragedy enough for the animals, but it can pose a genuine (even lethal) danger to you if you hit a good-sized mammal with your car.

Even an encounter with a relatively small mammal, such as a raccoon or a possum, can generate problems depending on your defensive driving strategies, and larger mammals such as horses or elk have obvious lethal possibilities for all concerned—but the most common and substantially damaging collisions are with deer.

OH, DEER!

Estimates place the white tail deer population in the U.S. at about one million around 1900. Today, in part because predators like the cougar and wolf have been removed from the food chain, there are more than 17 million. Deer have adapted remarkably well, foraging along forest edges and in forests with a significant understory of young trees, shrubs, and plants. Where wildlife managers once faced the problem of too few deer, they now face the problem of too many because deer love habitat comprised of agricultural lands alongside forests, and in many areas fewer people are hunting deer.

There are too many deer, indeed, if you have ever tried to dodge one with your car. Diana's story is typical.

I was driving home from a lovely dinner at a friend's home on a two-lane road in a fairly developed but still wooded suburban area. It was about midnight, late in the fall. I recall there wasn't much moonlight, but even if the moon had been shining like a streetlight I don't think I could have avoided the deer that bounded out of nowhere at a right angle to my car. Straight across the hood she dove. All I had time to see was the fur of her flank as she bounced across my car. I don't think I even had time to brake. I stopped and saw, to my extreme dismay, she was lying along the other side of the road. I tried to approach her to see how badly she was hurt, but before I could even get close she staggered to her feet, hobbling and dragging herself into the night and beyond my ability to help her. I called the police and the highway patrol and anybody else I could think of to try to find her and get her some help. Later I learned it's common for deer to stagger into the woods and die after they have been hit by a car. I remember her clearly and still have regret when I think about the accident, but I also recall how there was nothing I could do to prevent it. If she had wanted to "commit deer suicide," she couldn't have picked a better moment to plunge from out of the darkness into my car. I was really lucky. My car needed

1996 Automobile Collisions Resulting in Animal Fatalities		
State	**Fatal Crashes**	**Total Fatalities**
Delaware	1	1
Maryland	0	0
New Jersey	0	0
New York	7	7
Pennsylvania	5	5
Virginia	2	2
West Virginia	1	1

Source: National Highway Safety Traffic Administration, November 5, 1998.

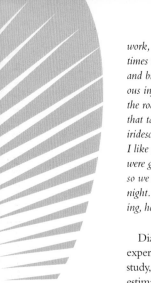

work, but the repair shop told me some-times deer slide right into the windshield and break through, causing death or serious injury for the driver. I always watch the roadsides intently now, looking for that taupe flash of flank or maybe that iridescent shining from any animal's eye. I like to think God knew the animals were going to need reflective eyes one day so we could see them from our cars at night. I'm always watching for that shining, hoping I never hit another animal.

Diana is far from alone in her experience. According to a Maryland study, the number of deer collisions is estimated to be 726,000 per year for the entire U.S. at a cost of $2 billion each year (Conover, 1997). That's an average of about 2,000 accidents per day, and the problem is multiplying. In Maryland, reported deer-vehicle collisions doubled from 1988 to 1996, causing nearly $10 million in property damage. Deer cause more than five percent of all reportable driving accidents across North Carolina, and such accidents are increasing at more than 10% a year in that state.

When Are You Most Likely to Hit a Deer?

- Between 60–75% of all deer collisions occur between 6 p.m. and 6 a.m.
- In clear weather.
- Roughly 75% of all deer collisions occur in late fall to early winter and in late spring to early summer.

Driving Defensively to Dodge Deer

- Be alert! Deer are most active at dawn and dusk. Drive slowly and cautiously, scanning the road and roadside, especially at sunrise and sunset when transitional lighting and shadows can play tricks on your vision.

- Also know that deer can try to cross busy roads in broad daylight, so always stay on guard.
- Even heavily populated suburbs may have deer who have lost more suitable habitat, so don't assume anything.
- Actively watch for deer where roads pass through wooded and agricultural areas.
- Deer crossing signs indicate where heavily used deer trails cross roadways. Slow down and watch for the eye-shine of deer near the road edges. At the very least, obey the speed limit, particularly at night in areas with deer crossing signs.
- Be especially cautious during seasons of high deer activity. October to January is the breeding season (and also includes hunting season when deer are motivated to move), and May to June is when yearlings are seeking new territories.
- Deer are often dazed or confused by vehicle headlights. If you see a deer along the roadside, reduce your speed, tap the brakes to alert other vehicles, and try to scare the deer by flashing lights or sounding the horn.
- Watch for other deer following the first one that you see. Many times, deer travel in groups.
- Removing vegetation from roadsides reduces the attraction for deer to feed there. Likewise, do not throw food refuse such as banana peels or apple cores from your car window. Their proximity to the road encourages wildlife of all kinds to search that margin for food.
- When you know a collision is unavoidable, experts recommend that you steer straight ahead to minimize losing control and colliding with oncoming traffic or hitting an object off the road.

Whistling for Deer

To reduce the number of deer-vehicle collisions, several manufacturers have developed "deer whistles" to mount on the front bumper of an automobile. The theory is that these whistles emit ultrasonic sounds that are frightening to deer, and they claim that their use will significantly reduce the rate of deer-vehicle collisions. Your insurance company may even offer a discount if you install this device on your automobiles.

Researchers at the University of Georgia and Texas A&M University, however, doubt the usefulness of these devices given the lack of information on deer hearing capabilities. Their findings suggest that deer whistles mounted on cars did not emit recordable sounds. When hand-held, these devices were capable of creating a high frequency sound in the 18 to 20 kilohertz range, but the researchers were unable to elicit any overt behavioral response by deer to these whistles, even when the deer were within yards of the devices.

Timothy J. Lawhern, a University of Wisconsin undergraduate at Madison, arrived at similar conclusions through a separate and perhaps more rigorous investigation of deer whistles. In the course of his research, Lawhern tested the whistles in the presence of seven species of the deer family, including 45 white-tailed deer. He looked for responses such as turning of ears or head, flinching, or looking in the direction of the sound. From this substantial survey he noted only one response, this from a single bull elk. At the shrill sound of the lower-pitched whistle (audible to human ears) the male elk charged the enclosing fence and crashed a two-by-four post. "In prolonged rage, he then bugled and urinated."

So, the usefulness of the deer whistle is in doubt, unless you potentially want to enrage a bull elk. (We recommend against this.) However, if you've hit a deer, you'd do almost anything to avoid a repeat experience. So if installing a whistle makes you more alert to deer, that's a good thing. On the other hand, if it lulls you into a false sense of security, that's a bad thing. Wildlife experts and officials agree that there is no substitute for driver education and awareness of the areas, seasons, and times of day of vulnerability. And every driver knows there are many more species than just deer that merit watching out for when you're driving. It's the least we can do for ourselves and for them.

TEXT PERMISSIONS & ACKNOWLEDGMENTS

REPTILES & AMPHIBIANS

Pages 17–18: First aid for snakebite text, courtesy Herpmed's Snakebite Emergency website: www.xmission. com/~gastown/herpmed/snbite.htm.

INSECTS & ARACHNIDS

Page 54: "A Pain Scale for Bee, Wasp, and Ant Stings," a scientific paper by Christopher K. Starr, courtesy of the *Journal of Entomological Science,* Wayne Gardner editor.

Page 58: "Sweet Sugar" bee sting story, courtesy RESCUE®'s website: www.traps.com/horrorstories.html.

AT THE SEASHORE

Page 165: Reprinted with permission of Scribner, a Division of Simon & Schuster, Inc., from THE OLD MAN AND THE SEA by Ernest Hemingway. Copyright 1952 by Ernest Hemingway. Copyright renewed © 1980 by Mary Hemingway.

Pages 168–169: "A Reply and Another Perspective of the Shark Attack on Marco Flagg, Filed by Bruce, G.W.S.", by Ken Kurtis, NAUI instructor and co-owner of Reef Seekers Dive Co., Beverly Hills, California.

Pages 172–173: International Shark Attack File data courtesy of the web pages of the International Shark Attack File (www.flmnh.ufl.edu /fish), courtesy of George H. Burgess, Director ISAF.

Pages 172–174: Advice on reducing the risk of shark attack is an augmented reprint, with emendations, from: Burgess, G.H. 1991. "Shark attack and the International Shark Attack File," pp. 101-105; cited in Gruber, S.H. (ed.), 1990. *Discovering Sharks,* American Littoral Society, Highlands, New Jersey.

Pages 187–188: Portuguese man-of-war sting information courtesy Craig Thomas, M.D., and Susan Scott, authors of *All Stings Considered: First Aid and Medical Treatment of Hawaii's Marine Injuries,* ©1997, University of Hawaii Press.

MAMMALS

Page 206: Katherine Ullmer. "Deer's intrusion shakes Washington Twp. grandmother," *Dayton Daily News,* 23 May 2001.

Page 206: Meghan Hoyer. "Deer bursts into class, scatters kindergart-ners," *Louisville Courier-Journal,* 18 May 2001.

Page 219: *Bear Attacks: Their Causes and Avoidance,* by Stephen Herrero. New York: The Lyons Press, 1988. Material reprinted by special arrangement with the Lyons Press.

Pages 229–230: Excerpt from *The Red Hourglass: Lives of the Predators* by Gordon Grice, published by Delta, 1999.

Pages 232–233: William F. Wood's debunking of the use of tomato juice versus skunk spray: www.humboldt.edu/ ~wfw2/livingwskunks.html.

PHOTOGRAPHY & ILLUSTRATION CREDITS

REPTILES & AMPHIBIANS

Page *xiv,* Northern Copperhead, *Agkistrodon contortrix mokasen.* Photo © Allen Blake Sheldon.

Page 4, snake head shapes, illustration © 2001 Carl Wiens.

Page 5, pit viper vs. cobra head shapes, illustration © 2001 Carl Wiens.

Page 5, Eastern Hognose Snake, *Heterodon platirhinos.* Photo © Ann and Rob Simpson.

Page 6, Scarlet Kingsnake, *Lampropeltis triangulum.* Photo by John Jensen.

Page 6, Northern Banded Watersnake, *Nerodia sipedon sipedon.* Photo © Allen Blake Sheldon.

Page 7, pit viper fang extension, illustration © 2001 Carl Wiens.

Page 10, Florida Pine Snake, *Pituphis melanoleucus mugitus.* Photo © Allen Blake Sheldon.

Page 11, Eastern Diamondback, *Crotalus adamanteus.* Photo © Allen Blake Sheldon.

Page 12, rattlesnake strike range, illustration © 2001 Carl Wiens.

Pages 18–19, rattlesnake bite series, photos © Sean Bush.

Page 21, snakebite first aid, illustration © 2001 Carl Wiens.

Page 22, Timber/Canebrake Rattlesnakes, *Crotalus horridus.* Photo © Allen Blake Sheldon.

Page 23, Timber/Canebrake Rattlesnake, *Crotalus horridus.* Photo © Kevin and Bethany Shank/ Dogwood Ridge Photography.

Page 24, Eastern Massasauga Snake, *Sistrurus catenatus catenatus.* Photo © Allen Blake Sheldon.

Page 25, Northern Copperhead Snake, *Agkistrodon contortrix mokasen.* Photo © Ann and Rob Simpson.

Page 27, Eastern Cottonmouth Snake, *Agkistrodon piscivorus piscivorus.* Photo © Ann and Rob Simpson.

Page 32, Common Snapping Turtle, *Chelydra serpentina.* Photo © Allen Blake Sheldon.

Page 33, Stinkpot/Common Musk Turtle, *Sternotherus odoratus*. Photo © Allen Blake Sheldon.

Page 34, Eastern Mud Turtle, *Kinosternon subrubrum subrubrum*. Photo by John Jensen, courtesy John Jensen/ Georgia Department of Natural Resources.

Page 36, Eastern American Toad; view of parotid gland, *Bufo a. americanus*. Photo © Allen Blake Sheldon.

Page 38, American Toad, *Bufo americanus*. Photo © Kevin and Bethany Shank/Dogwood Ridge Photography.

Page 39, Eastern Spadefoot Toad, *Scaphiopus holbrooki*. Photo by John Jensen.

Page 40, Fowler's/Woodhouse Toad, *Bufo woodhousii fowleri*. Photo © Allen Blake Sheldon.

Page 41, Two-Toed Amphioma, *Amphiuma means*. Photo by Barry Mansell.

Page 42, Slimy Salamander, *Plethodon glutinosus*. Photo by John Jensen, courtesy John Jensen/Georgia Department of Natural Resources.

INSECTS & ARACHNIDS

Page 44, Deer Tick, *Ixodes scapularis*. Photo by Scott Bauer, courtesy U.S. Department of Agriculture– Agricultural Research Service.

Page 47, insect vs. arachnid, illustration © 2001 Carl Wiens.

Page 50, honeybee sting, illustration © 2001 Carl Wiens.

Page 53, wasp and hornet nests, illustration © 2001 Carl Wiens.

Page 62, Bumblebee, *Bombus* spp. Photo © Allen Blake Sheldon.

Page 62, Mustached Mud Bee, *Anthophora abrupta*. Photo by Scott Bauer, courtesy U.S. Department of Agriculture–Agricultural Research Service.

Page 63, Honeybee, *Apis mellifera*. Photo © Kevin and Bethany Shank/ Dogwood Ridge Photography.

Page 63, Sweat Bee, *Halictus* spp. Photo by Scott Bauer, courtesy U.S. Department of Agriculture– Agricultural Research Service.

Page 64, Virescent Green Metallic Bee, *Agapostemon virescens*. Photo © Rob Curtis/The Early Birder.

Page 64, Baldfaced Hornet, *Vespula maculata*. Photo by Barry Mansell.

Page 65, European Hornet, *Vespa crabro*. Photo © Malcolm Storey, www.bioimages.org.uk.

Page 66, Paper Wasp, *Polistes* spp. Photo © Ann and Rob Simpson.

Page 66, Potter Wasp, *Eumenes fraternus*. Photo by Nathan G. Brockman.

Page 67, Sandhills Hornet, *Vespula arenaria*. Photo by Nathan G. Brockman.

Page 67, Yellow Jacket, *Vespula* spp. Photo © Allen Blake Sheldon.

Page 68, Black-and-Yellow Mud Dauber, *Sceliphron caementarium*. Photo by Nathan G. Brockman.

Page 68, Cicada Killer, *Sphecius speciosus*. Photo by Nathan G. Brockman.

Page 69, Common/Eastern Sand Wasp, *Bembix americana spinolae.* Photo by Nathan G. Brockman.

Page 70, Florida Hunting Wasp, *Palmodes dimidiatus.* Illustration © 2001 Chris Garrison.

Page 70, Great Golden Digger Wasp, *Sphex ichneumoneus.* Photo © Allen Blake Sheldon.

Page 71, Steel-Blue Cricket Hunter, *Chlorion aerarium.* Photo by Nathan G. Brockman.

Page 71, Thread-Waisted Wasp, *Ammophila* spp. Photo © Allen Blake Sheldon.

Page 72, Black Carpenter Ant, *Camponotus pennsylvanicus.* Photo © Allen Blake Sheldon.

Page 72, Common Eastern Velvet Ant/Cow Killer, *Dasymutilla occidentalis.* Photo © Ann and Rob Simpson.

Page 73, Lined Acrobatic Ant, *Cremastogaster lineolata.* Photo by Nathan G. Brockman.

Page 77, Head Louse, *Pediculus humanus capitis.* Photo © Dennis Kunkel Microscopy.

Page 78, Human Body Louse, *Pediculus humanus humanus.* Photo by Nathan G. Brockman.

Page 78, Pubic Louse, *Phthirus pubis.* Photo © Dennis Kunkel Microscopy.

Page 82, Human Flea, *Pulex irritans.* Micrograph by Janice Carr, courtesy Centers for Disease Control.

Page 83, Oriental Rat Flea, *Xenopsylla cheopis.* Photo © Dennis Kunkel Microscopy.

Page 84, mosquito feeding, illustration © 2001 Carl Wiens.

Page 87, arboviral encephalitis cycle, illustration © 2001 Carl Wiens.

Page 91, mosquito life cycle, illustration © 2001 Carl Wiens.

Page 93, mosquito breeding sites, illustration © 2001 Carl Wiens.

Page 96, Golden Salt-Marsh Mosquito, *Ochlerotatus sollicitans.* Photo by Nathan G. Brockman.

Page 96, House Mosquito, *Culex pipiens.* Photo by Nathan G. Brockman.

Page 97, Malaria-Carrying Mosquito, *Anopheles gambiae.* Photo by James Gathany, courtesy Centers for Disease Control.

Page 97, Snow Mosquito, *Aedes communis.* Illustration © 2001 Chris Garrison.

Page 98, Summer Mosquito, *Ochlerotatus atlanticus.* Illustration © 2001 Chris Garrison.

Page 98, Tree-Hole Mosquito, *Aedes triseriatus.* Photo by Nathan G. Brockman.

Page 103, American Horsefly, *Tabanus americanus.* Photo by Nathan G. Brockman.

Page 103, Black Fly, *Simulium* spp. Photo by J.F. Butler.

Page 104, Deerfly, *Chrysops* spp. Photo © Ann and Rob Simpson.

Page 104, Drone Fly, *Eristalis tenax.* Photo by Nathan G. Brockman.

Page 105, Housefly, *Musca domestica.* Photo by Nathan G. Brockman.

265

Page 106, Salt Marsh Punkie, *Culicoides furens*. Illustration © 2001 Chris Garrison.

Page 108, Io Moth Caterpillar, *Automeris io*. Photo by Barry Mansell.

Page 109, Puss Moth Caterpillar, *Megalopyge opercularis*. Photo © Ann and Rob Simpson.

Page 109, Saddleback Moth Caterpillar, *Sibine stimulea*. Photo © Ann and Rob Simpson.

Page 110, Bed Bug, *Cimex lectularius*. Photo © Dennis Kunkel Microscopy.

Page 111, Bloodsucking Conenose, *Triatoma sanguisuga*. Photo by B.M. Drees/Texas A&M University.

Page 111, Masked Hunter, *Reduvius personatus*. Photo by Nathan G. Brockman.

Page 112, Wheel Bug, *Arilus cristatus*. Photo © Ann and Rob Simpson.

Page 114, Bombardier Beetle, *Brachinus* spp. Photo © Rob Curtis/The Early Birder.

Page 114, Gold-and-Brown Rove Beetle, *Ontholestes cingulatus.* Photo © Rob Curtis/The Early Birder.

Page 115, Striped Blister Beetle, *Epicauta vittata*. Photo by Nathan G. Brockman.

Page 115, Short-Winged Blister Beetle, *Meloe angusticollis.* Photo © Rob Curtis/The Early Birder.

Page 116, Six-Spotted Tiger Beetle, *Cicindela sexguttata*. Photo courtesy Illinois Natural History Survey.

Page 116, Carolina Sawyer, *Monochamus carolinensis*. Photo by

Nathan G. Brockman.

Page 117, typical spider anatomy, illustration © 2001 Carl Wiens.

Page 123, Black Widow Spider, *Latrodectus mactans*. Photo © Ann and Rob Simpson.

Page 125, U.S. penny and tick larva illustration, © 2001 Carl Wiens.

Page 126, tick life cycle, illustration © 2001 Carl Wiens.

Page 137, Deer Tick, *Ixodes scapularis.* Photo by Scott Bauer, courtesy U.S. Department of Agriculture–Agricultural Research Service.

Page 138, Lone Star Tick, *Amblyomma americanum*. Photo © Ann and Rob Simpson.

Page 138, Wood Tick, *Dermacentor variabilis*. Photo by James Gathany, courtesy Centers for Disease Control.

Page 143, Chigger, *Trombicula* larva. Photo © Dennis Kunkel Microscopy.

Page 143, Scabies-Causing Mite, *Sarcoptes scabei*. Illustration © 2001 Chris Garrison.

FLORA

Page 144, Oleander, *Nerium oleander.* Photo by Paul Rebmann.

Page 149, Ragweed, *Ambrosia* spp. Photo by Daniel Reed/2bnThe-Wild.com.

Page 151, leaf comparison: ivy, oak, sumac, illustration © 2001 Carl Wiens.

Page 156–157, poison ivy seasonal series, photos © Ann and Rob Simpson.

Page 158, Poison Ivy, *Toxicodendron radicans.* Photo © Ann and Rob Simpson.

Page 159, Eastern Poison Oak, *Toxicodendron toxicarium.* Photo by Barry Mansell.

Page 160, Poison Sumac, *Toxicodendron vernix.* Photo courtesy U.S. Department of Agriculture.

Page 160, Spurge Nettle, *Cnidoscolus stimulosus.* Photo by Paul Rebmann.

Page 161, Stinging Nettle, *Urtica dioica* L. Photo © Ann and Rob Simpson.

AT THE SEASHORE

Page 162, Sand Tiger Shark, *Carcharias taurus.* Photo © Doug Perrine/Innerspace Visions.

Page 165, shark tooth fairy cartoon, illustration © 2001 Carl Wiens.

Page 166, shark jaw, illustration © 2001 Carl Wiens.

Page 171, shark body posturing, illustration © 2001 Carl Wiens.

Page 175, Blacktip Shark, *Carcharhinus limbatus.* Photo © Pierce and Newman.

Page 176, Bull Shark, *Carcharhinus leucas.* Photo © Doug Perrine/ Innerspace Visions.

Page 176, Great Hammerhead Shark, *Sphyrna mokarran.* Photo © Gary Adkison/Innerspace Visions.

Page 177, Sand Tiger Shark, *Odontaspis taurus.* Photo © Ben Cropp Productions/Innerspace Visions.

Page 178, Shortfin Mako, *Isurus oxyrinchus.* Photo © Bob Cranston/Innerspace Visions.

Page 178, Tiger Shark, *Galeocerdo cuvier.* Photo © Doug Perrine/Innerspace Visions.

Page 179, Great White Shark, *Carcharodon carcharias.* Photo © Saul Gonor/Innerspace Visions.

Page 180, stingray cartoon, illustration © 2001 Carl Wiens.

Page 183, Spotted Eagle Ray, *Aetobatus narinari.* Photo © Pierce and Newman.

Page 183, Cownose Ray, *Rhinoptera bonasus.* Photo by Curtis Krueger.

Page 184, Southern Stingray, *Dasyatis americana.* Photo by Ian Lauder.

Page 188, Cannonball Jellyfish, *Stomolophus meleagris.* Photo by Rodney Rountree/University of Massachusetts, Amherst.

Page 188, Lion's Mane, *Cyanea capillata.* Photo © Ann and Rob Simpson.

Page 189, Moon Jellyfish, *Aurelia aurita.* Photo © Ann and Rob Simpson.

Page 189, Portuguese Man-of-War, *Physalia physalis.* Photo © Ann and Rob Simpson.

Page 190, Sea Nettle, *Chrysaora quinquecirrha.* Photo © Ann and Rob Simpson.

Page 190, Feathered Hydroid, *Pennaria tiarella.* Photo © Pierce and Newman.

Page 191, barnacles, photo © Ann and Rob Simpson.

Page 191, Red-Gilled Nudibranch, *Coryphella verrucosa.* Photo by Erling Svensen.

Page 192, Common Mantis Shrimp, *Squilla empusa*. Photo by Jennifer Wortham.

Page 192, Brief Squid, *Lolliguncula brevis*. Photo by R.T. Hanlon/ National Resource Center for Cephalopods.

MAMMALS

Page 194, Common Porcupine, *Erethizon dorsatum*. Photo © Sharon Jansa.

Page 208, opossum showing teeth, photo © Ann and Rob Simpson.

Page 210, Opossum, *Virginia opossum*. Photo by Merle Austin, courtesy U.S. Fish and Wildlife Service.

Page 210, Common Raccoon, *Procyon lotor*. Photo © Ann and Rob Simpson.

Page 211, Southern Short-Tailed Shrew, *Blarina carolinensis*. Illustration © 2001 Chris Garrison.

Page 212, Northern Short-Tailed Shrew, *Blarina brevicauda*. Illustration © 2001 Chris Garrison.

Page 215, grizzly/black bear body types, illustration © 2001 Carl Wiens.

Page 225, Black Bear, *Ursus americanus*. Photo © Ann and Rob Simpson.

Page 228, Elk, *Cervus elaphus*. Photo courtesy U.S. Department of Agriculture.

Page 229, feral pig size, illustration © 2001 Carl Wiens.

Page 231, Feral Pig, *Sus scrofa*. Photo by Barry Mansell.

Page 234, Striped Skunk, *Mephitis mephitis*. Photo by John Collins, courtesy U.S. Fish and Wildlife Service.

Page 235, Eastern Spotted Skunk, *Spilogale putorius*. Illustration © 2001 Chris Garrison.

Page 237, Common Porcupine, *Erethizon dorsatum*. Photo by Barry Mansell.

Page 239, rabies cycle in raccoon, illustration © 2001 Carl Wiens.

Page 248, Big Brown Bat, *Eptesicus fuscus*. Photo courtesy U.S. Fish and Wildlife Service.

Page 248, Eastern Pipistrelle Bat, *Pipistrellus subflavus*. Photo by Robert Currie, courtesy U.S. Fish and Wildlife Service.

Page 252, Wood Mouse, *Peromyscus leucopus*. Photo © Kevin and Bethany Shank/Dogwood Ridge Photography.

Page 253, Deer Mouse, *Peromyscus maniculatus*. Photo © Ann and Rob Simpson.

Page 253, Marsh Rice Rat, *Oryzomys palustris*. Photo by Wayne Van Devender.

Page 254, Hispid Cotton Rat, *Sigmodon hispidus*. Photo © Ann and Rob Simpson.

SELECTED BIBLIOGRAPHY & RESOURCES

Readers seeking the most current information should take note of the copyright dates of the materials listed below. To construct this series, some older volumes listed below were consulted for general information. This list, designed to support this series of regional guides, may address species beyond your geographic area.

REPTILES & AMPHIBIANS

Behler, John L. and Deborah A. Behler. 1998. *Alligators and Crocodiles.* Stillwater, MN: Voyageur Press.

Behler, John L. and F. Wayne King. 1998. *National Audubon Society Field Guide to North American Reptiles and Amphibians.* New York: Alfred A. Knopf.

Conant, Roger and Joseph T. Collins. 1998. *A Field Guide to Reptiles & Amphibians: Eastern and Central North America.* The Peterson Field Guide Series. Boston: Houghton Mifflin.

Ettinger, Stephen J., D.V.M. and Edward C. Feldman, D.V.M. 1995. *Textbook of Veterinary Internal Medicine: Diseases of the Dog and Cat,* Philadelphia: W.B. Saunders Co.

Klauber, Laurence Monroe, and Harry W. Greene. 1997 *Rattlesnakes : Their Habits, Life Histories, and Influence on Mankind,* Berkeley: University of California Press.

Rubio, Manny. 1998. *Rattlesnake: Portrait of a Predator.* Washington, D.C: Smithsonian Institution Press.

Tennant, Alan, Richard D. Bartlett, and Gerard T. Salmon. 1999. *Snakes of North America: Eastern and Central Regions (Field Guide Series).* Houston: Gulf Publishing Company.

The Crocodile Specialist Group's link to all types of crocodilian information:
www.flmnh.ufl.edu/natsci/herpetology/brittoncrocs/cnhc.html

The University of Florida on alligators:
www.ifas.ufl.edu/agrigator/gators

The University of Georgia's Savannah River Ecology Lab on alligators:
www.uga.edu/~srel/gators.htm

INSECTS & ARACHNIDS

Arnett, Dr. Ross H., Jr. 2000. *American Insects: A Handbook of the Insects of America North of Mexico,* 2d ed. Boca Raton, Florida: CRC Press.

Arnett, Dr. Ross H., Jr. and Dr. Richard L. Jacques, Jr. 1981. *Simon & Schuster's Guide to Insects.* New York: Simon & Schuster, Inc., Fireside Books.

Berenbaum, May R. 1995. *Bugs in the System: Insects and Their Impact on Human Affairs.* Reading, Massachusetts: Perseus Books.

Hillyard, Paul. 1994. *The Book of the Spider: From Arachnophobia to the Love of Spiders.* New York: Random House.

Hubbell, Sue. 1993. *Broadsides from Other Orders: A Book of Bugs.* New York: Random House.

Milne, Lorus and Margery Milne. 1980. *National Audubon Society Field Guide to North American Insects and Spiders.* New York: Alfred A. Knopf.

Stokes, Donald. 1983. *Stoke's Guide to Observing Insect Lives.* Boston: Little, Brown and Company.

St. Remy Media Inc. 2000. *Insects & Spiders.* An Explore Your World Handbook (series). New York: Discovery Books.

Website devoted to brown recluse spider bites:
www.highway60.com/mark/brs

Survey of the hobospider:
www.hobospider.org

The American Mosquito Control Association:
www.mosquito.org

Commercial site with information on wasps, flies, ticks, mosquitoes, ants, etc.:
www.ungeziefer.de/en/fliegen-e.html

FLORA

Foster, Steven, and Roger Carras. 1994. *A Field Guide to Venomous Animals and Poisonous Plants: North America North of Mexico,* The Peterson Field Guide Series. Boston: Houghton Mifflin.

American Academy of Dermatology on poison ivy, oak, sumac, etc.:
www.aad.org/pamphlets

A broad source for alternative medicine applications:
www.healthy.net

AT THE SEASHORE

Boschung, Herbert T. Jr., James D. Williams, Daniel W. Gotshall, David K. Caldwell, and Melba C. Caldwell. 1997. *National Audubon Society Field Guide to North American Fishes, Whales and Dolphins.* New York: Alfred A. Knopf.

Meinkoth, Norman A. 1998. *National Audubon Society Field Guide to North American Seashore Creatures.* New York: Alfred A. Knopf.

Taylor, Leighton, ed. 1999. *Sharks.* The Little Guides. San Francisco: Fog City Press.

Taylor, Leighton, ed., Timothy C. Tricas, Kevin Deason, Peter Last, John E. McCosker, Terrence I. Walker, and Leighton Taylor. 1997. *Sharks and Rays.* The Nature Company Guides. New York: Time Life Books.

Taylor, Valerie and Ron Taylor, ed., with Peter Goadby. 2000. *Great Shark Writings.* Woodstock and New York: The Overlook Press.

The Florida Museum of Natural History's International Shark Attack File:
www.flmnh.ufl.edu/fish/sharks/isaf/isaf.htm

The National Aquarium in Baltimore's jellyfish site:
www.aqua.org/animals/species/
jellies/facts.html

MAMMALS

Adler, Bill, Jr. 1992. *Outwitting Critters:
A Surefire Manual for Confronting Devi-
ous Animals and Winning.* New York:
The Lyons Press.

Brown, Gary. 1996. *Safe Travel in Bear
Country.* New York: Lyons & Burford.

Burt, William Henry. 1976. *A Field
Guide to the Mammals of North Ameri-
ca North of Mexico.* The Peterson Field
Guide Series. Boston: Houghton
Mifflin.

The California Center for Wildlife
with Diana Landau and Shelley
Stump. 1994. *Living with Wildlife:
How to Enjoy, Cope with, and Protect
North America's Wild Creatures Around
Your Home and Theirs.* San Francisco:
Sierra Club Books.

Herrero, Stephen. 1985. *Bear Attacks:
Their Causes and Avoidance.* Edmon-
ton: Hurtig Publishers.

Stokes, Donald and Lillian Stokes.
1986. *Stoke's Guide to Animal Tracking
and Behavior.* Boston: Little, Brown
and Company.

Van Tighem, Kevin. 1999. *Bears.*
The Canadian Rockies: Altitude
Publishing.

Whitaker, John O., Jr. 1998. *National
Audubon Society Field Guide to North
American Mammals.* New York: Alfred
A. Knopf.

Probably the web's best site on skunks
and opossums:
granicus.if.org/~firmiss/m-d/
md-main.html

Going batty? Get your bat facts
straight here:
www.batcon.org

An extensive tribute to ursine
wonders:
www.bears.org

Audio of wild pigs! (And you
thought this book was overpriced?):
www.catalinaconservancy.org/
animals/mammals/pigs.htm

Home base for moose lovers:
www.cutemoose.com/moosefac.htm

Tips, tricks, and training for you and
your pup:
www.familydogonline.com

The Mickey Moose Club, where
you can have fun and buy a Celtic
moose tattoo:
www.halcyon.com/moose/
welcome.html

Skunk natural history and chemistry
data:
www.humboldt.edu/~wfw2/
livingwskunks.html

Point your antlers to this moose
"browser":
www.mooseworld.com/
moosebrowse.htm

Quotes and more about all kinds of
bears:
www.nature-net.com/bears/
bearquot.html

Sweet-smelling skunk information,
plus some charming photos:
www.projectwildlife.org/
living-skunks.htm

The U.S. Fish and Wildlife Service's
black bear page:
species.fws.gov/bio_bear.html

GENERAL INFORMATION

Alden, Peter, Richard B. Cech, Richard Keen, Amy Leventer, Gil Nelson, and Wendy B. Zomlefer. 1998. *National Audubon Society Field Guide to Florida.* New York: Alfred A. Knopf.

Alden, Peter, Brian Cassie, Jonathan D.W. Kahl, Gil Nelson, Eric A. Oches, Harry Zirlin, and Wendy B. Zomlefer. 1999. *National Audubon Society Field Guide to the Southeastern States.* New York: Alfred A. Knopf.

Foster, Steven, and Roger Carras. 1994. *A Field Guide to Venomous Animals and Poisonous Plants: North America North of Mexico,* The Peterson Field Guide Series. Boston: Houghton Mifflin.

Grice, Gordon. 1998. *The Red Hourglass: Lives of the Predators.* New York: Delacourte Press

Media Projects Incorporated, ed. 1998. *Reader's Digest North American Wildlife: Mammals, Reptiles, and Amphibians.* Pleasantville: The Reader's Digest Association, Inc.

Zoological profiles from the University of Michigan: animaldiversity.ummz.umich.edu

Venomous creatures bibliography: www.calacademy.org/research/library/biodiv/biblio/venombib.html

The Smithsonian magazine, dating back to 1995: www.smithsonianmag.si.edu/smithsonian/search/atomzsearch.html

WILDLIFE REHABILITATION

The Humane Society of the United States: www.hsus.org

The Wildlife Rehabilitation Directory: www.tc.umn.edu/~devo0028

FEDERAL & SOUTHEASTERN STATE AGENCIES

Center for Biological Informatics of the U.S. Geological Survey www.nbii.gov/search/sitemap.html

Centers for Disease Control and Prevention: www.cdc.gov

Food and Drug Administration www.fda.gov

U.S. Fish and Wildlife Service endangered.fws.gov/wildlife.html

Alabama   alaweb.asc.edu

Arkansas   www.agfc.com

Florida   www.state.fl.us/fwc

Georgia   www.ganet.org/dnr

Kentucky www.state.ky.us/agencies/fw

Louisiana   www.wlf.state.la.us

Mississippi   www.mdwfp.com

North Carolina www.enr.state.nc.us

South Carolina water.dnr.state.sc.us

Tennessee   www.state.tn.us/twra

FIRST AID

Arnold, Robert E., M.D. 1973. *What to Do About the Bites and Stings of Venomous Animals.* New York: Collier Books, A Division of Macmillan Publishing Co., Inc.

Levy, Charles Kingsley, Ph.D. 1983. *A Field Guide to Dangerous Animals of North America including Central America.* Brattleboro: The Stephen Greene Press.

National Safety Council and Alton L. Thygerson. 1995. *First Aid Handbook.* Boston: Jones and Bartlett Publishers.

Thomas, Craig, M.D., and Susan Scott. 1997. *All Stings Considered: First Aid and Medical Treatment for Hawaii's Marine Injuries.* Honolulu: University of Hawaii Press.

Turkington, Carol. 1999. *The Poisons and Antidotes Sourcebook,* 2d ed. New York: Checkmark Books.

Emergency medical information in physician's terms: www.emedicine.com/emerg

The Mayo Clinic's "Sharing our tradition of trusted answers" slogan says it all: www.mayoclinic.com/home

Poisonous plants, pet-related information, and venomous creatures: www.pharmacy.arizona.edu/centers/poisoncenter/apdicindex.html

WebMD on stinging insects, with links to various topics for doctors and lay people: my.webmd.com/content/article/3215.104

AMERICAN ASSOCIATION OF POISON CONTROL CENTERS

February 2001

(Certified centers appear in boldface. See last entry for Animal Poison Center.**)**

ALABAMA

Alabama Poison Center
2503 Phoenix Drive
Tuscaloosa, AL 35405
Emergency Phone: (800) 462-0800 (AL only);
(205) 345-0600

Regional Poison Control Center
Children's Hospital
1600 7th Avenue South
Birmingham, AL 35233
Emergency Phone: (800) 292-6678 (AL only);
(205) 933-4050

ALASKA

Anchorage Poison Control Center
3200 Providence Drive
P.O. Box 196604
Anchorage, AK 99519-6604
Emergency Phone: (800) 478-3193;
(907) 261-3193

ARIZONA

Arizona Poison & Drug Info Center
Arizona Health Sciences Center
Room 1156
1501 North Campbell Avenue
Tucson, AZ 85724
Emergency Phone: (800) 362-0101 (AZ only);
(520) 626-6016

Samaritan Regional Poison Center
Good Samaritan Regional Medical Center
1111 E. McDowell--Ancillary 1
Phoenix, AZ 85006

Emergency Phone: (800) 362-0101
(AZ only);
(602) 253-3334

ARKANSAS

Arkansas Poison & Drug Information Center
University of AK for Med Sciences,
College of Pharmacy
4301 W. Markham, Mail Slot 522
Little Rock, AR 72205
Emergency Phone: (800) 376-4766
TDD/TTY: (800) 641-3805

CALIFORNIA

California Poison Control System

California Poison Control System - Fresno/Madera Division
Valley Children's Hospital
9300 Valley Children's Place
Madera, CA 93638-8762
Emergency Phone: (800) 876-4766
(CA only)
TDD/TTY: (800) 972-3323

California Poison Control System-Sacramento Division
UC Davis Medical Center
2315 Stockton Boulevard
Sacramento, CA 95817
Emergency Phone: (800) 876-4766
(CA only)
TDD/TTY: (800) 972-3323

California Poison Control System-San Diego Division
University of CA, San Diego, Medical Center
200 West Arbor Drive
San Diego, CA 92103-8925
Emergency Phone: (800) 876-4766
(CA only)
TDD/TTY: (800) 972-3323

California Poison Control System-San Francisco Division
San Francisco General Hospital
1001 Potrero Avenue, Room 1E86
San Francisco, CA 94110
Emergency Phone: (800) 876-4766
(CA only)
TDD/TTY: (800) 876-4766

COLORADO

Rocky Mountain Poison & Drug Center
1010 Yosemite Circle
Building 752
Denver, CO 80230-6800
Emergency Phone: (800) 332-3073
(CO only/outside metro area); (303) 739-1123 (Denver metro)

CONNECTICUT

Connecticut Poison Control Center
University of Connecticut Health Center
263 Farmington Avenue
Farmington, CT 06030-5365
Emergency Phone: (800) 343-2722
(CT only);
(860) 679-3456
TDD/TTY: (860) 679-4346

DELAWARE

The Poison Control Center
3535 Market Street, Suite 985
Philadelphia, PA 19104-3309
Emergency Phone: (800) 722-7112;
(215) 386-2100; (215) 590-2100

DISTRICT OF COLUMBIA

National Capital Poison Center
3201 New Mexico Avenue, NW,
Suite 310
Washington, DC 20016
Emergency Phone: (202) 625-3333
TDD/TTY: (202) 362-8563 (TTY)

FLORIDA

Florida Poison Information Center-Jacksonville
655 West Eighth Street
Jacksonville, FL 32209
Emergency Phone: (800) 282-3171
(FL only);
(904) 244-4480
TDD/TTY: (800) 282-3171 (FL only)

Florida Poison Information Center–Miami
University of Miami, Dept. of Pediatrics
Jackson Memorial Medical Center
P.O. Box 016960 (R-131)
Miami, FL 33101
Emergency Phone: (800) 282-3171 (FL only);
(305) 585-5253

Florida Poison Information Center–Tampa
Tampa General Hospital
P.O. Box 1289
Tampa, FL 33601
Emergency Phone: (800) 282-3171 (FL only);
(813) 253-4444

GEORGIA

Georgia Poison Center
Hughes Spalding Children's Hospital
Grady Health System
80 Butler Street, SE
P.O. Box 26066
Atlanta, GA 30335-3801
Emergency Phone: (800) 282-5846;
(404) 616-9000
TDD/TTY: (404) 616-9287 (TDD)

HAWAII

Hawaii Poison Center
1319 Punahou Street
Honolulu, HI 96826
Emergency Phone: (808) 941-4411;
(800) 362-3585
(outer islands toll free Kauai, Maui, Molokai, and Hawaii)

IDAHO

Rocky Mountain Poison & Drug Center
1010 Yosemite Circle
Building 752
Denver, CO 80230-6800
Emergency Phone: (800) 860-0620 (ID only)

ILLINOIS

Illinois Poison Center
222 S. Riverside Plaza, Suite 1900
Chicago, IL 60606
Emergency Phone: (800) 942-5969 (IL only)
TDD/TTY: (312) 906-6185

INDIANA

Indiana Poison Center
Methodist Hospital
Clarian Health Partners
I-65 at 21st Street
Indianapolis, IN 46206-1367
Emergency Phone: (800) 382-9097 (IN only);
(317) 929-2323
TDD/TTY: (317) 929-2336 (TTY)

IOWA

Iowa Statewide Poison Control Center
St. Luke's Regional Medical Center
2720 Stone Park Boulevard
Sioux City, IA 51104
Emergency Phone: (800) 352-2222;
(712) 277-2222

KANSAS

Mid-America Poison Control Center
University of Kansas Medical Center
3901 Rainbow Blvd., Room B-400
Kansas City, KS 66160-7231
Emergency Phone: (800) 332-6633 (KS only);
(913) 588-6633
TDD/TTY: (913) 588-6639 (TDD)

KENTUCKY

Kentucky Regional Poison Center
Medical Towers South, Suite 572
234 East Gray Street
Louisville, KY 40202
Emergency Phone: (800) 722-5725;
(502) 589-8222

LOUISIANA

Louisiana Drug and Poison Information Center
University of Louisiana at Monroe
College of Pharmacy, Sugar Hall
Monroe, LA 71209-6430
Emergency Phone: (800) 256-9822
(LA only)

MAINE

Maine Poison Control Center
Maine Medical Center
22 Bramhall Street
Portland, ME 04102
Emergency Phone: (800) 442-6305
(ME only);
(207) 871-2950
TDD/TTY: (877) 299-4447 (ME only);(207) 871-2879

MARYLAND

Maryland Poison Center
University of MD at Baltimore
School of Pharmacy
20 North Pine Street, PH 772
Baltimore, MD 21201
Emergency Phone: (800) 492-2414
(MD only);
(410) 706-7701
TDD/TTY: (410) 706-1858 (TDD)

National Capital Poison Center
3201 New Mexico Avenue, NW
Suite 310
Washington, DC 20016
Emergency Phone: (202) 625-3333
TDD/TTY: (202) 362-8563 (TTY)

MASSACHUSETTS

Regional Center for Poison Control and Prevention
Serving Massachusetts and Rhode Island
300 Longwood Avenue
Boston, MA 02115
Emergency Phone: (800) 682-9211
(MA & RI only);
(617) 232-2120
TDD/TTY: (888) 244-5313

MICHIGAN

Children's Hospital of Michigan
Regional Poison Control Center
4160 John R Harper Professional
Office Bldg., Suite 616
Detroit, MI 48201
Emergency Phone: (800) 764-7661
(MI only);
(313) 745-5711
TDD/TTY: (800) 356-3232 (TDD)

DeVos Children's Hospital
Regional Poison Center
1840 Wealthy SE
Grand Rapids, MI 49506-2968
Emergency Phone: (800) 764-7661
(MI only)
TDD/TTY: (800) 356-3232 (TTY)

MINNESOTA

Hennepin Regional Poison Center
Hennepin County Medical Center
701 Park Avenue
Minneapolis, MN 55415
Emergency Phone: (800) 222-1222
(MN);
(800) POISON1 (SD only)
TDD/TTY: (612) 904-4691 (TTY)

MISSISSIPPI

Mississippi Regional Poison Control Center
University of Mississippi Medical Center
2500 N. State Street
Jackson, MS 39216
Emergency Phone: (601) 354-7660

MISSOURI

Cardinal Glennon Children's Hospital
Regional Poison Center
1465 S. Grand Blvd.
St. Louis, MO 63104
Emergency Phone: (800) 366-8888;
(314) 772-5200

MONTANA

Rocky Mountain Poison & Drug Center
1010 Yosemite Circle
Building 752
Denver, CO 80230-6800
Emergency Phone: (800) 525-5042
(MT only)

NEBRASKA

The Poison Center
Children's Hospital
8200 Dodge Street
Omaha, NE 68114
Emergency Phone: (800) 955-9119
(NE & WY only);
(402) 955-5555

NEVADA

Oregon Poison Center
Oregon Health Sciences University
3181 SW Sam Jackson Park Road,
CB550
Portland, OR 97201
Emergency Phone: (503) 494-8968

Rocky Mountain Poison & Drug Center
1010 Yosemite Circle
Building 752
Denver, CO 80230-6800
Emergency Phone: (800) 446-6179
(NV only)

NEW HAMPSHIRE

New Hampshire Poison Information
Center
Dartmouth-Hitchcock Medical
Center
One Medical Center Drive
Lebanon, NH 03756
Emergency Phone: (800) 562-8236
(NH only);
(603) 650-8000

NEW JERSEY

New Jersey Poison Information and Education System
201 Lyons Avenue
Newark, NJ 07112
Emergency Phone: (800) POISON-1
(NJ only)
TDD/TTY: (973) 926-8008

NEW MEXICO

New Mexico Poison & Drug Information Center
Health Science Center Library
Room 130
University of New Mexico
Albuquerque, NM 87131-1076
Emergency Phone: (800) 432-6866
(NM only);
(505) 272-2222

NEW YORK

Central New York Poison Center
750 East Adams Street
Syracuse, NY 13210
Emergency Phone: (800) 252-5655
(NY only);
(315) 476-4766

Finger Lakes Regional Poison & Drug Info Center
University of Rochester Medical
Center
601 Elmwood Avenue
P.O. Box 321
Rochester, NY 14642
Emergency Phone: (800) 333-0542
(NY only);
(716) 275-3232
TDD/TTY: (716) 273-3854 (TTY)

Hudson Valley Regional Poison Center
Phelps Memorial Hospital Center
701 North Broadway
Sleepy Hollow, NY 10591
Emergency Phone: (800) 336-6997
(NY only);
(914) 366-3030

Long Island Regional Poison and Drug Information Center
Winthrop University Hospital
259 First Street
Mineola, NY 11501
Emergency Phone: (516) 542-2323;
(516) 663-2650
TDD/TTY: (516) 924-8811 (TDD
Suffolk);
(516) 747-3323 (TDD Nassau)

New York City Poison Control Center
NYC Department of Health
455 First Avenue
Room 123, Box 81
New York, NY 10016
Emergency Phone: (800) 210-3985;
(212) 340-4494;
(212) POI-SONS;(212) VEN-ENOS
TDD/TTY: (212) 689-9014 (TDD)

Western New York Regional Poison Control Center
Children's Hospital of Buffalo
219 Bryant Street
Buffalo, NY 14222
Emergency Phone: (800) 888-7655;
(716) 878-7654

NORTH CAROLINA

Carolinas Poison Center
Carolinas Medical Center
5000 Airport Center Parkway, Suite B
Charlotte, NC 28208
Emergency Phone: (800) 848-6946;
(704) 355-4000

NORTH DAKOTA

North Dakota Poison Information Center
Meritcare Medical Center
720 4th Street North
Fargo, ND 58122
Emergency Phone: (800) 732-2200
(ND, MN, SD only);
(701) 234-5575

OHIO

Central Ohio Poison Center
700 Children's Drive, Room L032
Columbus, OH 43205
Emergency Phone: (800) 682-7625
(OH only);
(800) 762-0727 (Dayton, OH only)
TDD/TTY: (614) 228-2272 (TTY)

Cincinnati Drug & Poison Information Center
Regional Poison Control System
3333 Burnet Avenue
Vernon Place - 3rd Floor

Cincinnati, OH 45229
Emergency Phone: (800) 872-5111
(OH only);
(513) 558-5111

Greater Cleveland Poison Control Center
11100 Euclid Avenue
Cleveland, OH 44106-6010
Emergency Phone: (888) 231-4455
(OH only);
(216) 231-4455

OKLAHOMA

Oklahoma Poison Control Center
Children's Hospital of Oklahoma
Room 3512
940 NE 13th Street
Oklahoma City, OK 73104
Emergency Phone: (800) 764-7661
(OK only);
(405) 271-5454
TDD/TTY: (405) 271-1122

OREGON

Oregon Poison Center
Oregon Health Sciences University
3181 SW Sam Jackson Park Road,
CB550
Portland, OR 97201
Emergency Phone: (800) 452-7165
(OR only);
(503) 494-8968

PENNSYLVANIA

Central Pennsylvania Poison Center
Pennsylvania State University
The Milton S. Hershey Medical Center
500 University Drive
MC H043, PO Box 850
Hershey, PA 17033-0850
Emergency Phone: (800) 521-6110;
(717) 531-6111
TDD/TTY: (717) 531-8335 (TTY)

Pittsburgh Poison Center
Children's Hospital of Pittsburgh
3705 Fifth Avenue
Pittsburgh, PA 15213
Emergency Phone: (412) 681-6669

The Poison Control Center
3535 Market Street, Suite 985
Philadelphia, PA 19104-3309
Emergency Phone: (800) 722-7112;
(215) 386-2100;
(215) 590-2100

RHODE ISLAND

Regional Center for Poison Control and Prevention
Serving Massachusetts and Rhode Island
300 Longwood Avenue
Boston, MA 02115
Emergency Phone: (617) 232-2120
TDD/TTY: (888) 244-5313

SOUTH CAROLINA

Palmetto Poison Center
College of Pharmacy
University of South Carolina
Columbia, SC 29208
Emergency Phone: (800) 922-1117
(SC only);
(803) 777-1117

SOUTH DAKOTA

Hennepin Regional Poison Center
Hennepin County Medical Center
701 Park Avenue
Minneapolis, MN 55415
Emergency Phone: (800) POISON1
(SD only);
(800) POISON1 (SD only)
TDD/TTY: (612) 904-4691 (TTY)

TENNESSEE

Middle Tennessee Poison Center
501 Oxford House
1161 21st Avenue South
Nashville, TN 37232-4632
Emergency Phone: (800) 288-9999
(TN only);
(615) 936-2034 (Greater Nashville)
TDD/TTY: (615) 936-2047 (TDD)

Southern Poison Center
875 Monroe Avenue
Suite 104
Memphis, TN 38163

Emergency Phone: (800) 288-9999
(TN only);
(901) 528-6048

TEXAS

Central Texas Poison Center
Scott and White Memorial Hospital
2401 South 31st Street
Temple, TX 76508
Emergency Phone: (800) POISON-1(TX only);
(254) 724-7401

North Texas Poison Center
Texas Poison Center Network
Parkland Health & Hospital System
5201 Harry Hines Blvd.
P.O. Box 35926
Dallas, TX 75235
Emergency Phone: (800) 764-7661(TX only)

South Texas Poison Center
The University of Texas Health Science Center - San Antonio
Department of Surgery
Mail Code 7849
7703 Floyd Curl Drive
San Antonio, TX 78229-3900
Emergency Phone: (800) 764-7661 (TX only)
TDD/TTY: (800) 764-7661 (TX only)

Southeast Texas Poison Center
The University of Texas Medical Branch
3.112 Trauma Building
Galveston, TX 77555-1175
Emergency Phone: (800) 764-7661 (TX only);
(409) 765-1420

Texas Panhandle Poison Center
1501 S. Coulter
Amarillo, TX 79106
Emergency Phone: (800) 764-7661 (TX only)

West Texas Regional Poison Center
Thomason Hospital
4815 Alameda Avenue
El Paso, TX 79905
Emergency Phone: (800) 764-7661
(TX only)

UTAH

Utah Poison Control Center
410 Chipeta Way, Suite 230
Salt Lake City, UT 84108
Emergency Phone: (800) 456-7707
(UT only);
(801) 581-2151

VERMONT

Vermont Poison Center
Fletcher Allen Health Care
111 Colchester Avenue
Burlington, VT 05401
Emergency Phone: (877) 658-3456
(toll free);
(802) 658-3456

VIRGINIA

Blue Ridge Poison Center
University of Virginia Health System
PO Box 800774
Charlottesville, VA 22908-0774
Emergency Phone: (800) 451-1428
(VA only);
(804) 924-5543

National Capital Poison Center
3201 New Mexico Avenue, NW
Suite 310
Washington, DC 20016
Emergency Phone: (202) 625-3333
TDD/TTY: (202) 362-8563 (TTY)

Virginia Poison Center
Medical College of Virginia Hospitals
Virginia Commonwealth University
P.O. Box 980522
Richmond, VA 23298-0522
Emergency Phone: (800) 552-6337;
(804) 828-9123

WASHINGTON

Washington Poison Center
155 NE 100th Street, Suite 400
Seattle, WA 98125-8012
Emergency Phone: (800) 732-6985
(WA only);
(206) 526-2121
TDD/TTY: (206) 517-2394 (TDD);
(800) 572-0638 (TDD WA only)

WEST VIRGINIA

West Virginia Poison Center
3110 MacCorkle Ave, S.E.
Charleston, WV 25304
Emergency Phone: (800) 642-3625
(WV only)

WISCONSIN

Children's Hospital of Wisconsin
Poison Center
9000 W Wisconsin Ave, MS 677A
Milwaukee, WI 53226
Emergency Phone: (800) 815-8855
(WI only);
(414) 266-2222

University of Wisconsin Hospital &
Clinics
Poison Control Center
600 Highland Avenue, F6/133
Madison, WI 53792
Emergency Phone: (800) 815-8855
(WI only);
(608) 262-3702

WYOMING

The Poison Center
Children's Hospital
8200 Dodge Street
Omaha, NE 68114
Emergency Phone: (800) 955-9119
(NE & WY only);
(402) 955-5555

ANIMAL POISON CENTER

ASPCA

National Animal Poison Control
Center
1717 South Philo Road, Suite 36
Urbana, IL 61802
Emergency Phone: (888) 426-4435;
(900) 680-0000

Index

ABOUT THE AUTHOR

F. Lynne Bachleda has been a freelance researcher and writer for twenty years. Born in Savannah, she calls Middle Tennessee home after earning her M. S. from Florida State University. She has written many articles for regional and national publications and currently writes about religion, especially Buddhism, for *Publisher's Weekly*. Her first book, *Blue Mountain: A Spiritual Anthology Celebrating the Earth* (Menasha Ridge Press), was named one of Amazon.com's Top 10 Spiritual and Inspirational Books for 2000. *Blue Mountain* was also nominated for a Networking Alternatives for Publishers, Retailers, and Artists (NAPRA) Nautilus Award. Her second book and the first in the Dangerous Wildlife series, *Dangerous Wildlife in the Southeast,* was published in October 2001.

In the interests of research, Bachleda has had numerous dangerous wildlife experiences of her own. To name a few, she's been bitten by a brown recluse, a cat, and a dog; she's been stung by yellow jackets, wasps, bees, and jellyfish; she's been cut by barnacles; and she's had two bouts of systemic poison ivy rash. Her dog was bitten on the head by a copperhead snake and also sprayed by a skunk at such close range that the dog's white fur turned yellow. Her childhood dog saved her from a diamondback rattlesnake, and more recently around the home, she's encountered a timber rattler, a pygmy rattler, opossums, and a bat (the latter actually in the house). While driving, she's hit a deer and a raccoon--even adopting the questionable tactic of bundling the injured raccoon into the back of her station wagon. She's passed within yards of a black bear while riding her bicycle, and she once raided a mother alligator's nest for eggs while filming a documentary.

Since 1988, Bachleda has taught visual art aesthetic education for the Tennessee Performing Arts Center's education department. She lives next to 600 acres of woods in a small town outside Nashville, along with her animals and old oak trees.